REDISCOVERING OSCAR WILDE

Princess Grace Irish Library: 8

THE PRINCESS GRACE IRISH LIBRARY LECTURES
(ISSN 0950-5121)

General Editor: C. George Sandulescu

THE PRINCESS GRACE IRISH LIBRARY SERIES
(ISSN 0269-2619)

General Editor: C. George Sandulescu

REDISCOVERING OSCAR WILDE

edited by

C. George Sandulescu

PRINCESS GRACE IRISH LIBRARY: 8

COLIN SMYTHE
Gerrards Cross, 1994

First published in 1994 by Colin Smythe Limited
Gerrards Cross, Buckinghamshire

British Library Cataloguing in Publication Data
Rediscovering Oscar Wilde — (Princess Grace Irish Library Series,
ISSN 0269-2619)
1. Wilde, Oscar
I. Sandulescu, C. George   II. Series
ISBN 0-86140-376-2

Produced in Great Britain
Typeset by Caroline Kopper
Printed and bound by T. J. Press (Padstow) Ltd, Cornwall

CONTENTS

v

Contents   vii

ACKNOWLEDGMENTS

The publication of this volume as well as the holding in Monaco of the May 1993 International Conference bearing the same title was made possible thanks to the generous support of the Jefferson Smurfit Foundation of Monaco, and of Dr Michael Smurfit, Honorary Consul of the Republic of Ireland, personally.

I also wish to extend warm thanks to my fellow-trustees for their strenuous work, enthusiasm and patience during the long months of preparation of this First Oscar Wilde Congress, and then of this very first volume of Conference Proceedings in the whole, most complex history of one solid century of Oscar Wilde Studies.

Oscar Wilde's grandson Merlin Holland has given his kind, enthusiastic and most competent support to us in the preparation of the Conference and of this volume of Proceedings emerging from it: for this relief much thanks!

Thanks are also extended to *la Fondation Princesse Grace de Monaco*, *le Gouvernement de la Principauté de Monaco*, *la Direction du Tourisme et des Congrès de Monaco*, *l'Office des Emissions de Timbres-Poste de Monaco*, and finally, to *la Société des Bains de Mer* of Monaco.

In conclusion, we all wish to express our most sincere gratitude to Caroline Kopper for having impeccably typeset this complex and difficult manuscript on the electronic facilities of the Princess Grace Irish Library of Monaco.

The Editor

OPENING ADDRESS BY
H. S. H. HEREDITARY PRINCE ALBERT
OF MONACO

This Fifth International Conference of the Princess Grace Irish Library is entirely devoted to the Irish poet, novelist, and playwright Oscar Wilde. It is something very special not only because the poet's grandson Merlin Holland is with us here today, but also because his father went to school at a stone's throw from here, in Place de la Visitation.

To celebrate this great writer, I am very glad to welcome among us Mr John Campbell, Ambassador of the Republic of Ireland to France, and also to thank Monsieur Jean-Michel Dasque, Consul Général of France to Monaco, for inviting the delegates to a welcoming party this evening.

I greet the outstanding scholars from so many countries who are taking part in this International Conference. The Princess Grace Irish Library has now become a very mature institute of scholarship, which enjoys the recognition, support and backing of many similar institutes the world over.

I wish full success to your discussions, and I am very much looking forward to the published Proceedings, emerging from your debates.

In order to mark the very special nature of our Conference, I now unveil the bust of Oscar Wilde, donated to this Institute of Culture in the Principality by the sculptor Kees Verkade.

I hereby declare this Conference open.

ADDRESS BY H. E. JOHN H. F. CAMPBELL IRELAND'S AMBASSADOR TO PARIS

I am very happy to be present for the opening of this Conference. It is a particular pleasure for an Irish Ambassador to be with you today, recalling the close friendship and special associations between Ireland and the Principality, symbolised in the active role of the Princess Grace Irish Library in Monaco.

The Library is a treasure house for scholars and students. With its nucleus in the personal collection of Irish books and music of Her Serene Highness Princess Grace, it stands as a testament to her interest in her Irish heritage. It is a unique asset. The Irish Government deeply values the part which it has played and continues to play, under the active direction of Professor Sandulescu, in fostering scholarship and promoting interest in Irish studies generally.

I would like to renew our warm appreciation to all those, and notably of course to His Serene Highness Prince Rainier III and his family, who have so generously supported and encouraged the work of the Library in the years since its foundation in 1984.

The Library's International Conference series has been a highlight of its cultural programme. I have no doubt that this year's Conference will be as lively and stimulating as any. With Oscar Wilde as the theme one would expect nothing less: and the distinguished panel of speakers matches the occasion.

A few months ago I stood by the grave of Oscar Wilde at Père Lachaise. The striking Epstein monument in Portland stone has recently been renovated. The assiduous attentions of Wilde's admirers had alas over the years taken their toll of the elegant monument in the form of unsightly graffiti. To help deal with this problem, the Irish Government was happy to take the initiative in contributing to this renovation work. Let us hope that it will be spared further despoliation from thoughtless, if well-intentioned, visitors.

On the day I was there, a quiet spring morning, many visitors paused in passing tribute. Of course *De Profundis* came to mind: 'For me the world is shrivelled to a handbreadth, and everywhere I turn my name is written on the rocks in lead.' But I have to say that more dominant in my own thoughts was the recollection of delight at my first acquaintance with Oscar Wilde's work — the exuberance of language and wit that could not fail to go to the head of any reader in Stendhal's ideal category of 'un jeune homme de vingt-cinq ans ayant senti les passions'. I may in fact have been nearer fifteen than twenty-five and the mixture was all the headier. But even today, with the putative wisdom of age, the freshness and exhilaration of Wilde's writing remains.

It is not surprising that interest and pleasure in Wilde's work remains lively. Though he left his native Dublin at an early age, Wilde remains a part of the city's literary heritage. He is commemorated in the newly established Dublin Writers' Museum and his plays are very often performed. Indeed, the splendid and widely acclaimed Gate Theatre production of *Salome* is being revived again in Dublin next week. In London, no less than two of the author's masterpieces are now being produced; *An Ideal Husband* and *Earnest*, whose importance is never lost on us, is enjoying success with Maggie Smith as the latest in a line of superb actresses to take up Lady Bracknell's mantle and handbag.

I like to reflect how some of the early influences on Wilde — his feeling for natural beauty and his first familiarity with the Greek world — occurred in an Irish setting, be it the physical landscape of Ireland or the Trinity years with Mahaffy. Having read myself for the first time in a Trinity College lecture-room the great ode in Sophocles' *Antigone* on the infinite variety of man, the self-indulgence is pardonable. At any rate, this Irish observer will follow with particular interest the rediscovery of Oscar Wilde over the next few days. I leave the floor now, with anticipation, to those better qualified to lead this renewed exploration. And I wish the Conference every success.

THE SUPREME QUARTET

C. George Sandulescu

It is a commonplace in Shakespeare Studies to use the phrase 'The Supreme Quartet' as a picturesque value-judgment to denote the quintessence of Shakespeare's dramatic art: four titles — *Hamlet*, *Othello*, *Lear*, and *Macbeth* (all men!) tower far above the other 33 plays in point of artistry.

If one were to turn now to Irish Studies in search of an analogous Quartet of stars of maximal magnitude and brilliancy towering far above the other 33 — or 99, to quote an Anthony Burgess title — I would begin by advancing three names, all obvious Nobel Prize Candidates (though the Swedish Establishment would more than frown upon the phrase...). They are Yeats, Joyce, and Beckett, in that order. And the Princess Grace Irish Library has already organised massive international Conferences devoted to each of them.

Today I wish to advance the challenging statement that it is Oscar Wilde the one who completes — or rather 'initiates' — the Supreme Quartet of Irish letters. But paradoxically, though we are today celebrating a solid century since the absolute peak of his success, this Conference rallying us here now is the first ever large-size representative Conference entirely devoted to Oscar. This perhaps leads us to another paradox: though he is by far the widest known and most generally popular and accessible of the gang of four, there is no standard edition of definitive texts — except a more than mediocre Collins... in spite of the obvious fact that the Oscar devotees are sure to have provided quite a sizable market for it as early half a century ago. Just compare this with the literally hundreds of scholarly get-togethers devoted to Joyce, and the dozens — even Summer Schools or Festivals — devoted to Yeats and Beckett... And this in spite of the fact that large chunks of the wide public bitterly complain, 'in public', that fully and exactly to understand what this gang of three did write poses problems. The paradox at this stage of the argument is the greater the public the fewer the critics, and their respective output, and conversely, the narrower the public, the greater the plethora of critics and criticism!

Now that Oscar is in the focus of attention, the question of reliable texts is far more urgent than appointed Editors and Publishers consider it to be. I'll give you one example: the Princess Grace Irish Library is starting NOW a permanent Research Project, provisionally called 'Theoretikos' (after one of Oscar's poems), and involving the participation of several scholars. But the obstacles seem insurmountable by comparison with Joyce, Yeats, or Beckett research, where the necessary tools are to be found in plenty. Not only that the Oscar Wilde texts are in the process of being destabilised — remember Francis Bacon's paradox 'The most corrected text is commonly the most corrupt'! — but there is no Concordance, there are no 'error-free' Computer Disks, and there is, of course, no Facsimile Edition of the Manuscripts (just think of the mammoth 60-volume Facsimile Garland Edition of Joyce!). By the side of the Beckett Journals and Centres, or the Joyce and Yeats Annuals and Newsletters, the work of Wilde, certainly the best known to the public, is the one most inadequately charted by the scholars. This, consequently, hampers the furthering of research.

We are here to try and remedy the situation. And the fact that the present Conference takes in *forty* papers, whereas all the previous Library Conferences were limited to *twenty* papers — see already Published Proceedings! — is circumstantial proof that the imbalance described above can indeed be remedied. The overcrowding is such, that, to be on the safe side, 'you'd better fasten your seat belts, for you may be in for a bumpy weekend!'. From now on, YOU take over! Thank you.

THE MIRROR OF NARCISSUS IN *THE PICTURE OF DORIAN GRAY*

Antonio Ballesteros González

Oscar Wilde's life and works show an always haunting obsession for the figure of Narcissus, for no other character in classical mythology has represented better the eternal conflicts between beauty and illusion, youth and death, all of them so dear to the brilliant writer. This presence of Narcissus in Wilde's mind is emphasized by Richard Ellmann, who, in his magnificent biography, recollects the fact that the Irish author possessed a bronze sculpture of the unhappy ephebus in his house in Tite Street, Chelsea. Significantly enough, the figure was complemented by a portrait of Wilde painted by Harper Pennington.[1]

Strange symbol for the newlyweds Mr and Mrs Wilde: Narcissus is the epitome of solipsism, of self love, a love which cannot be completely shared with the other. Narcissus is only able to love his own reflection, the fugacity of a shadow. The fascination for the beautiful youth impregnates many pages of Oscar Wilde's works. Allusions both to the solipsistic character and to the flower in which he was transformed after his cruel death can be found in poems like 'The Garden of Eros', 'The Burden of Itys', 'Athanasia', 'Charmides', 'Panthea' and 'Désespoir', where Narcissus — or the corresponding flower — is always identified with the abstract notion of beauty in relation with a concrete being.

The mythological figure also appears, with more complexity, in Wilde's tales, as in 'The Star Child' — where, differently from the poems, narcissism, or the bad use of beauty from a moral point of view, is considered a punishable sin — or in 'The Fisherman and His Soul', where the motif of the shadow, representing the outer soul since ancient anthropological beliefs, is related to several aspects of the

Narcissus myth as it is told by Ovid. Platonic readings and
interpretations of the myth — not very far from the description
of the Androgyne by Aristophanes in the *Symposium* — are
suggested in Wilde's critical writings collected in the volume
entitled *Intentions*,[2] and in several letters, especially those
addressing Lord Alfred Douglas, who is compared with the
beauty of the flower.[3]

There is a wonderful treatment of the Narcissus myth
in a parable Wilde told to André Gide, who had just published
a book about the wretched youth. The title of the story is 'The
Disciple':

> When Narcissus died, the flowers of the field were desolate and
> asked the river for some drops of water to weep for him.
> - 'Oh!' answered the river, 'if all my drops of water
> were tears, I should not have enough to weep for Narcissus
> myself. I love him.'
> - 'Oh!' replied the flowers of the field, 'how could you
> not have loved Narcissus? He was beautiful.'
> - 'Was he beautiful?' said the river.
> - 'And who should know better than you? Each day,
> leaning over your bank, he beheld his beauty in your waters.'
> - 'If I loved him', replied the river, 'it was because,
> when he leaned over my waters, I saw the reflection of my
> waters in his eyes.'[4]

But it is *The Picture of Dorian Gray* that better illustrates
Wilde's fascination with the complexities implied in the
Narcissus myth. As a matter of fact, much of this strange
narrative, written in 1891, deals with the different
possibilities of analysis that Ovid's fable in the Third Book of
the *Metamorphoses* entails. *The Picture* thus pertains to an
evolutive chain which is connected with many popular fictions
of the Victorian period taking duality as the main structural
and thematic factor. That chain would — for pragmatic
purposes — begin with the third edition of Mary Shelley's
Frankenstein (1831) and would include some significant works of
fantasy as Stevenson's *Dr Jekyll and Mr Hyde* (1886), leading
later to examples like Bram Stoker's *Dracula* or H. G. Wells's
The Invisible Man (both of them published in 1897). All these
narratives — the list is obviously abridged — participate of
the Gothic and Victorian parallel obsession for duality,
constituting thus a contrast with respect to the 'great' bourgeois

tradition of realistic fiction — no matter how oxymoronic a relation the last two words could establish.

The Victorian Age, mostly the last part of it, is a divided era, a fragmented crucible where the power and control of the Colonial Empire is defied by the darker side of a society, the inheritors of a dehumanizing Industrial Revolution which has created a sense of detachment in the individual, an irreparable feeling of invisibility, which is only one of the literary metaphors for the loss of identity.

Narcissus, as an aesthetic symbol, epitomizes from an anthropological and mythological perspective the search for identity, the impossible wish to integrate oneself with his own reflection. The individual is no longer projecting his fears to the outside: the 'enemy' is in his own mind, perhaps in his own body. 'This too was myself': Jekyll's sentence after accepting his moral duplicity represents the restrictions to which the human being is submitted in a hypocritical environment, and in this way it is linked with Dorian's 'It is part of myself' when referring to the picture. In the end, the process of going from an outer to an inner menace culminates with the development of psychoanalytical theories at the beginning of the twentieth century.

The Picture of Dorian Gray constitutes one of the most climactic steps in the Victorian study of duality. The picture is an image of what Theodore Ziolkowski calls 'the portrait as an anima', meaning an object faithfully representing the outer soul of a character.[5] In Dorian's case, as it is the general rule, there is an intrinsic knot between the individual and the object. Moreover, the picture is a projection of Dorian's soul, and the man's fate is compulsorily related to the destiny suffered by the portrait. In this respect, Wilde mixes the myth of Narcissus with another classical myth: that of Meleager, prototype of the outer soul motif. There are many reminiscences of these elements in popular folklore. Wilde's success consists in putting together so many classical, literary and folkloric themes (Faust or Don Juan should also be included) in a measured and coherent balance.

Ovid's story of Narcissus is always latent in *The Picture*. Much of the conflict in the narrative is propitiated by the problem of knowledge: every character possessing access to any knowledge of 'life' is doomed to die. This is a possible reminder of the soothsayer Tiresias when he is asked about Narcissus' fate after the child has been born, the watery product of his mother, the nymph Liriope,[6] being raped by the river Cephissus. *Si se non noverit*: 'If he does not know himself'. This reversal of the Delphic oracle 'Know thyself' is a capital idea in the structural development of the plot of the novel. As soon as a character knows 'too much', he or she will be punished.

Very early in the narrative, Dorian is identified with Narcissus by Lord Henry, who responds to Basil Hallward, the painter of the picture, about the point of 'having put too much of himself into his work':

> I really can't see any resemblance between you, with your rugged strong face and your coal-black hair, and this young Adonis, who looks as if he was made out of ivory and rose-leaves. Why, my dear Basil, he is a Narcissus [...].[7]

Narcissus, the same as Adonis — he is also compared later to Antinoüs or to 'a young Greek martyr' (p. 33), being most of these symbols of homosexual imagery — is a paradigm of pure beauty, the culmination of the Hellenic ideal Wilde was so fond of, strongly influenced in this respect by his Oxonian masters, Walter Pater and John Ruskin. The prophetic role of Tiresias, enigmatically determining Narcissus' fate, is fulfilled in *The Picture* by the two creators or father figures: Basil Hallward, the artist of painting, and Lord Henry Wotton, the artist of life or the dandy, in a sort of dual roles of the morality play — roughly speaking and respectively, the good and the bad angels fighting for Dorian's soul. But no matter how attractive and understandable this dichotomy could be, there is no doubt that — as in *Frankenstein* — both creators and masters in Dorian's learning process turn out to be a complete failure, as the boy's accusations throughout the story seem to emphasize. It is from the very moment when Dorian contemplates his portrait that we are aware of his similarity with Narcissus reflecting himself on the mirror-like surface of the pond:

> When he saw it [the picture] he drew back, and his cheeks
> flushed for a moment with pleasure. A look of joy came into his
> eyes, as if he had recognized himself for the first time [...]. The
> sense of his own beauty came on him like a revelation. He had
> never felt it before. (p. 45)

Before that, Dorian did not know himself. From that point on,
he will know too much and in a very short time, and both his
masters are responsible for his new ways of aprehending
reality. For there is a main difference between Dorian and
Narcissus: the latter is unconscious about the fact that the
reflection he sees is himself until it is too late, but the former
knows — he has witnesses proving that what he sees is true —
that he is contemplating his own self.

Hallward's reactions are pathologically narcissistic
from the very beginning: 'Every portrait that is painted with
feeling is a portrait of the artist, not of the sitter. The sitter is
merely the accident, the occasion' (p. 15). The artist maintains
with his work a father-progeny relation. But there is no way
back for his 'hideous progeny' once the latter has acquired the
secret knowledge of self identity. Dorian's accusation is all but
unfair: 'You like your art better than your friends. I am no more
to you than a green bronze figure. Hardly as much, I dare say.'
Ironically enough, Wilde is inserting here the
autobiographical presence of his green bronze Narcissus
sculpture.

On the other hand, Lord Henry is the *carpe diem*
supporter, suggesting a new Hedonism now that youth is
ephemeral. His corrupting influence can be seen both in the
pattern of his decadent dandyism and the intertextual lendings
of 'pernicious' books.[8] However, both mentors remain, for the
greatest part of the narrative, completely alienated from their
progeny's secret: the chiastic process by which his sins are
reflected in the mirror surface of the picture. Dorian-Narcissus
has been metamorphosed not into a flower, but into a monster,
the progeny produced by a divided self.

At the same time, Dorian's drama begins in the same
way as that of Narcissus, being loved and worshipped by men,
in an ambiguous context of homosexual connotations — a much
unusual feature in Greek mythology. These elements are
stressed by the aesthetic references to homosexual artists like

Buonarroti or the misogynist criticism of women and marriage. Once again, Wilde was obviously introducing here autobiographical projections. In short, Dorian will soon be loved by everyone, and this is the time for the presence of Echo, the other integral character in the tragedy of Narcissus as it is told by Ovid (not in other classical sources).

In the Roman elegiac poet's source, Echo is the epitome of entire otherness, not even possessing a known origin. Conversely, Sibyl Vane[9] — the clearest representative of the wretched nymph in *The Picture* — has a family, whereas Dorian is an orphan — a feature which is repeated in many Victorian narratives.[10] Dorian's identification with the mother, as seen from a psychoanalytical perspective, could be a reminder of Narcissus' search for his identity in the waters of the pond, the setting of his mother's rape by the promiscuous father. Forcing a biographical conclusion, Wilde is projecting into the text some curious fantasies about his childhood and family life, haunted by the powerful figure of 'Speranza' (Lady Wilde) and the absence of the Donjuanesque William Wilde, as Richard Ellmann points out.[11]

Sibyl Vane also suffers the consequences of having a possessive mother and the absence of a father, for Mrs Vane had been abandoned by her husband. Surprisingly enough, Mrs Vane's obsession coincides with that of Dorian in his given ideal identity of 'Prince Charming', his social disguise afterwards. Both mother and beloved share the monstruous feeling that Sibyl is nothing without her art, and then Sibyl is a parallel figure of Echo, whose only prerogative is her fragmented, but beautiful voice.[12] Dorian, like Narcissus, rejects the love of the female once he sees that she is real, that she is not only art and illusion. Both male characters can only love themselves, for, as Lord Henry lets Dorian know in his sententious style, 'You will always be in love with love' (p. 81).

Sibyl is equally doomed by Tiresias' *si se non noverit*. When she knows what she is — or what she is told she is, as she is reflected in others from a Lacanian point of view — the girl commits suicide. Like Echo, Sibyl has no clear identity: she is every night a different Shakespearian character. Her voice is given, she does not speak for herself. Mrs Vane has played the role of Juno, metaphorically punishing her daughter with a speech limitation, and partly for the same reason as the goddess: to quench her bitter resentment against the promiscuity of the male world. Obviously, Mrs Vane's purpose is to 'defend' her child trying to prevent her from making the same mistakes she made.

It is then ironical that Wilde uses the symbol of the flower to describe Sibyl. The narrator of *The Picture* says about the girl's brother, James Vane — the first representative in the novel of an unknown side of Victorian society for Dorian: 'He was like a common gardener walking with a rose' (p. 105). Irony is even more explicit and emphatic in another passage, where Sibyl trembles and shakes 'like a white narcissus' (p. 121), and her body 'swayed while she danced, as a plant sways in the water' (p. 132). Significantly, Wilde has formerly shown us a vision of Lord Henry playing with and destroying a flower. However, Sibyl is like a flower, a trampled one later (p. 140), only from the aesthetic perspective and as a would-be reflection of Dorian-Narcissus. When she is rejected, like her mother, she disappears into the domain of shadows,[13] her voice alone — like Echo's in the Ovidian fable — remaining in the other characters' memories.[14] Echo's *coeamus* (both 'let us meet' and 'let us make love' in Latin) turns desire into disappointment when Narcissus sees that she is not the being that could make him 'complete', in the sense given to the notion in Plato's narration of the myth of the Androgyne.[15]

The process of acquiring knowledge for Sibyl — and now that he has learned from Lord Henry, Dorian is Tiresias — is punished with death, being thus the first victim of the vampire 'Prince Charming'. Many more will come later, adding ugliness and sin to the portrait, Dorian's former mirror of beauty. Nevertheless, Dorian-Narcissus will suffer the gods' *nemesis* in the end.

It is precisely Sibyl's suicide what gives rise to the first changes in the picture, stressing Dorian's malignity. The portrait will be his evil side, the same as Hyde is the monster within Jekyll. Dorian's metamorphosis is produced in his reflection, causing the character paulatine horror and pain as far as the plot is developed. The picture is linked to another symbolic and haunted object: a mirror, 'one of Lord Henry's many presents to him' (p. 144). There is an ironic relation between the aristocrat's role as Tiresias and the present role, for the looking-glass is a reminder of the 'know thyself' notion. From that moment of consciousness on, both picture and mirror will be integrally disposed in a chiastic relation. Superficial thoughts of repentance bring about the symbolic act of opening the window.

The intellection of the portrait as the pond where Narcissus contemplates his reflection — his soul, in many Platonic and later Christian allegorical interpretations[16] — is clearly seen in the following passage:

> Once, in a boyish mockery of Narcissus, he had kissed, or feigned to kiss, those painted lips that now smiled so cruelly at him. Morning after morning he had sat before the portrait wondering at its beauty, almost enamoured of it, as it seemed to him at times. (p. 167)

Now Dorian has the intuition that he can only love himself, and this self love has been increased by the supposedly 'bad angel', Lord Henry Wotton, but Basil Hallward's role is not that of the 'good angel' either. His idealizing Dorian has also contributed to the latter's self knowledge, and from a Lacanian point of view the boy has also inferred from Basil his 'Narcissus-like tendency', as it can be deduced from these words:

> You had leaned over the still pool of some Greek woodland and seen in the water's silent silver the marvel of your own face. And it had all been what art should be — unconscious, ideal and remote. (p. 181)

The painter only conceives the sitter as an artistic object. Hallward loves the theme of Narcissus just for the character's ideal beauty, and this is what he is searching for in Dorian. This is why he is also punished after having faced his creatures, both the picture and Dorian, because he has 'known himself' too. It is extremely interesting that Wilde saw the three characters as refractions of his own image, as Richard Ellmann collects:

> Basil Hallward is what I think I am: Lord Henry what the world thinks me: Dorian is what I would like to be in other ages, perhaps.[17]

Thus, Wilde seems to establish an identification with the artist, whose creation is a mirror or a portrait of himself. The author is narcissistically reflected in his writing.

On the other hand, the fact that Dorian hides the picture in the schoolroom is coherent with his desire of acquiring self-knowledge, being the place a reminder of childhood, related to a process of 'remembrance of things past'. For Narcissus, going to the pond fulfils the same function from a metaphorical perspective, now that water is a reminder of his conception and an image of the father. However, the problem is the future, where the tacit Faustian pact will be claimed by an inexorable fate, no matter how unconscious Dorian seems to be about this fact.[18]

The inherent link between Dorian and the picture, the fact that they are necessarily related to each other, is proved by the character's reluctance to be separated from the object representing his 'outer soul'.[19] Dorian is more and more tied up to his reflection, the same process undergone by Frankenstein in relation with his monster or Jekyll with respect to Hyde. The intrinsic duality — or complexity — of human beings is emphasized by Gray himself:

> He used to wonder at the shallow psychology of those who conceive the ego in man as a thing simple, permanent, reliable, and of one essence. To him, man was a being with myriad lives and myriad sensations, a complex multiform creature that bore within itself strange legacies of thought and passion, and whose very flesh was tainted with the monstrous maladies of the dead. (p. 224)

The ramblings of 'Prince Charming' across the slums of London — the 'other' side of the Imperial splendours — the impiety of Dorian's vampiric blood-thirst in his desire to transgress forbidden limits, make him a parallel figure with that representation of evil and fragmentation, Mr Hyde. The reflected image of beautiful Narcissus turns itself into an amoral and corrupting monster who — like the Boeotian ephebus — is wooed both by men and women.[20] As Dorian tells Basil before he kills the painter, 'Each of us has heaven and hell in him' (p. 247).

However, the pleasure of a double life is paulatinely more and more terrible as far as the climactic moment of knowing oneself approaches. This is the reason why Dorian delights in oblivion by means of opium, for, in Faustian despair, 'he wanted to be where no one would know who he was. He wanted to escape from himself' (p. 294).

On the other hand, Dorian's desire of loving is impossible: his 'I wish I could love' (p. 319) expresses a kind of conceptual *contradictio in terminis*. Like Narcissus, he can only love himself, and the unveiling of this fact in Dorian's mind brings about his accomplishing his destiny after Hetty's hypocritical affair and Alan Campbell's suicide. Gray's awareness of breaking the condition imposed by Tiresias — *si se non noverit* — makes him attempt to get rid of all the evidences of his dual nature and fragmented self. First, he crushes the mirror that Lord Henry had given to him:

> Then he loathed his own beauty, and flinging the mirror on the floor, crushed it into silver splinters beneath his heel. It was his beauty that had ruined him, his beauty and the youth that he had prayed for. (p. 344)

However, there is still another mirror to destroy: the portrait ('For it was an unjust mirror, this mirror of his soul that he was looking at'), which, as Dorian says, had been conscience to him. By stabbing the magic canvas — an image of the painter and father, the same as the pond — Dorian kills himself. His transformation after death is a reversal of Narcissus' metamorphosis into a flower: the epitome of Victorian beauty is turned into a monster of evil and ugliness. It goes without saying that Dorian-Narcissus has reached the self-knowledge he was looking for.

NOTES

1   See R. Ellmann: *Oscar Wilde*. Penguin, Harmondsworth, 1988 (p. 242): 'On the mantelpiece was a small green bronze figure of Narcissus.'

2   In 'The Critic as Artist', one of the four essays in *Intentions*, Wilde establishes a relation between his biography and his literary works in sentences like 'The pallid figures on the tapestry are smiling at us, and the heavy eyelids of my bronze Narcissus are folded in sleep'. We have already alluded to the

green bronze figure of Narcissus in Wilde's house; the object will also be recurrent in *The Picture of Dorian Gray*.

3   See number 314: 'Douglas is [...] quite like a narcissus — so white and gold', and also number 398: 'O my love, you whom I cherish above all things, white narcissus in an unmown field.'

4   In R. Ellmann, op. cit., pp. 336-7.

5   See T. Ziolkowski: *Disenchanted Images. A Literary Iconology.* Princeton University Press, New Jersey, 1977.

6   Literally, 'the one with the form of a lily': the flower is a recurrent image once again. Narcissus, as Liriope's son, is transformed into a flower after his death. On the other hand, Cephissus is related to the pond where Narcissus contemplates his reflection in a curious parallel with his father's desire.

7   Oscar Wilde: *The Picture of Dorian Gray*. Minster, London, 1968 (p. 12). All the following references will be made to this edition.

8   Pater's *Studies in the Renaissance* and Huysmans's *A Rebours*.

9   Notice the irony of this name from a Wildean perspective, for 'Sibyl' — no matter how the author is playing with the metathesis regarding the two vowel sounds in the word — stands for 'prophetic connotations', as for instance in the well-known Sybil of Cumae, who plays a significant role in Virgil's *Aeneid* (The Descent into Hell episode). On the other hand, 'Vane' is homophonic with the word 'Vain', implicitly applicable to the whole Vane family.

10   Psychoanalytical interpretations would also trace here autobiographical implications. See J. Berman: *Narcissism and the Novel*. New York University Press, New York, 1990.

11   Cf. Ellmann, op. cit.

12   Dorian seems to be very sensitive to voices, for he says to Lord Henry: 'You know how a voice can stir one. Your voice and the voice of Sibyl Vane are two things that I shall never forget' (p. 84).

13   'I knew nothing but shadows', she will tell Dorian, taking Platonic concepts into account without probably knowing it (p. 137).

14   Indeed, the word *echo* is recurrent in many pages of the narrative, as in the significant 'A faint smile curving that sullen mouth was all the echo she could win' (referred to Sibyl's Brother; p. 110).

15   Plato: *Symposium*, 189D-193B.

16   See L. Vinge: *The Myth of Narcissus in Western European Literature Up to the Nineteenth Century*. Gleerups, Lund, 1967.

17   Ellmann, op. cit., p. 301.

18   'He never knew — never, indeed, had any cause to know — that somewhat grotesque dread of mirrors, and polished metal surfaces, and still water which came upon the young Parisian so early in his life, and was occasioned by the sudden decay of a beau that had once, apparently, been so remarkable' (p. 200).

19   'After a few years he could not endure to be long out of England, and gave up the villa that he had shared at Trouville with Lord Henry, as well as the little white walled-in house at Algiers where they had more than once spent the winter. He

hated to be separated from the picture that was such a part of his life, and was also afraid that during his absence some one might gain access to the room, in spite of the elaborate bars that he had caused to be placed upon the door' (p. 221).

20   A good example of Dorian's dual disintegration combined with the thirst for knowledge (caused by Lord Henry-Tiresias) is the following fragment: 'There were moments, indeed, at night, when, lying sleepless in his own delicately scented chamber, or in the sordid room of the little ill-famed tavern near the docks which, under an assumed name and in disguise, it was his habit to frequent, he would think of the ruin he had brought upon his soul with a pity that was all the more poignant because it was purely selfish. But moments such as these were rare. That curiosity about life which Lord Henry had first stirred in him [...] seemed to increase with gratification. The more he knew, the more he desired to know' (p. 202).

REFERENCES

Ballesteros Gonzáles, A., *Narciso: mito y dualidad conceptual en la literatura inglesa victoriana*. Ph. D. Thesis, Universidad Complutense, Madrid, 1993 (forthcoming).

Beckson, K. (ed.), *Oscar Wilde: The Critical Heritage*. Routledge, London,1970.

Berman, J., *Narcissism and the Novel*. New York University Press, New York, 1990.

Ellmann, R., *Oscar Wilde*. Penguin, Harmondsworth, 1988.

Ellmann, R. (ed.), *The Artist as Critic: Critical Writings of Oscar Wilde*. Random House, New York, 1969.

Green, B. A., 'The Effects of Distortions of the Self: A Study of *The Picture of Dorian Gray*', in *The Annual of Psychoanalysis*, 7 (1979): pp. 391-410.

Grinstein, A., 'On Oscar Wilde', in *The Annual of Psychoanalysis*, 1 (1973): pp. 345-62.

Kavka, J., 'Oscar Wilde's Narcissism', in *The Annual of Psycho-analysis*, 3 (1975): pp. 397-408.

Martínez, Victorio L., *Relaciones irónicas en la obra narrativa y dramática de Oscar Wilde*. Ph. D. Thesis, Universidad Complutense, Madrid, 1990.

Ovid, *Metamorphoses*. Bilingual text Latin-Spanish, trans. Antonio Ruiz de Elvira. C.S.I.C., Madrid, 1990.

Punter, D., *The Literature of Terror*. Longman, London, 1980.

Rank, O., *The Double*. Mansfield, London, 1989.

Shewan, R., *Oscar Wilde: Art and Egotism*. Macmillan, London, 1977.

Vinge, L., *The Myth of Narcissus in Western European Literature up to the Nineteenth Century*. Gleerups, Lund, 1967.

Wilde, Oscar, *The Picture of Dorian Gray*. Minster, London, 1968.

Wilde, Oscar, *The Complete Illustrated Stories, Plays and Poems of Oscar Wilde*. Chancellor Press, London, 1991.

Wilde, Oscar, *Intentions*. Methuen, London, 1913.

Ziolkowski, T., *Disenchanted Images. A Literary Iconology* Princeton University Press, New Jersey, 1977.

OSCAR WILDE AND THE SEMANTIC MECHANISMS OF HUMOUR: THE SATIRE OF SOCIAL HABITS

Mariano Baselga

When we talk about humour in literature, the name of Oscar Wilde often comes up. And this is true not only for any reader or spectator of his brilliant comedies but also for scholars and specialists in humour by itself, that is, those who try to explain what provokes laughing or smiling. A peculiar writer indeed, attracting the attention of both linguists and literary critics.

Actually, if a linguistic approach has been chosen, one is consequently supposed to be as 'neutral' as possible in the study of non-linguistic aspects of the texts. That is what we linguists are supposed to do whenever we dare invade the field of literary critics, adopting a deeply respectful attitude towards the texts and handling every single word very carefully. And there is every reason to be precautious with so thorny a question as humour, the trigger of human laughter, for in many respects the way it works in the mind is still a mystery. Having said this, there is still no obvious reason to exclude 'language-oriented' studies from literary criticism, since language, as a 'vehicle', exposes the results of its action but not the principles of its operation, which is what we are concerned with here. Therefore, even without bringing anything new under the sun, we could perhaps reach some interesting results if we make a number of remarks about some of Wilde's 'tricks' to get his audience to laugh or smile, taking as a starting point the study of *The Canterville Ghost* and *The Importance of Being Earnest*.

On the extra-linguistic dimension, it is not difficult to see that Oscar Wilde's comical scenes often take their source in social satire and non-conformism (sometimes even in scandal),

13

as we will try to show in some detail. Not so evident, however, are the linguistic mechanisms (the semantic ones especially) that provoke these comical effects, although we will try to point out the relationship between the author's social attitude and his linguistic performance. So, we believe that by studying a few semantic devices of Oscar Wilde's language it is possible to propose at least a partial explanation of his comical success in his own time. Unfortunately, in doing so we will take the risk David Crystal points out in his *Encyclopedia of Language*: 'Nothing more likely to kill a good joke than a linguistic analysis' (p. 62).

Although the present paper deals with humour, it is not our author's *irony* as such that we will study or discuss. On the one hand, its complexity falls out of the range of this paper. On the other — and above all — irony is not a semantic device, but rather a discursive one, frequently implying the use of much more than tangible linguistic elements alone. It is therefore to the field of semantics this paper will be restricted, keeping the focus on words, phrases and their meaning(s) — frequently more than one, as might be expected. The question is: how does Wilde work the meaning into humour and what has his social attitude to do with it?

As a first approach to Wilde's social rebelliousness, let us make a simple, intuitive and pretty obvious remark on a passage of *The Canterville Ghost*, where the mischiefs of the ghost over the centuries are depicted, immediately after his first meeting with the Otis's.

> Never, in a brilliant and uninterrupted career of three hundred years, had he been so grossly insulted. He thought of the Dowager Duchess, whom he had frightened into a fit as she stood before the glass in her lace and diamonds; of the four housemaids, who had gone off into hysterics when he merely grinned at them through the curtains of one of the spare bedrooms; of the rector of the parish, whose candle he had blown out as he was coming late one night from the Library, and who had been under the care of sir William Gull ever since, a perfect martyr to mental disorders; and of old Madame de Tremouillac, who, having wakened up one morning early and seen a skeleton in an arm-chair by the fire reading her diary had been confined to her bed for six weeks with an attack of brain fever, [...]. He remembered the terrible night when the wicked Lord Canterville was found chocking in his dressing-room, with the knave of diamonds half-way down his throat, and

> confessed, just before he died, that he had cheated Charles James Fox out of £50,000 at Crockford's by means of that very card, and swore that the ghost had made him swallow it. (p. 197)

As we can see, the main targets of the ghost's troublemaking are systematically the members of the upper class and/or the people, actions, common vices and symbols associated to them. The *Dowager* Duchess with all the vanity of her best lace-and-diamond attire, the fussy housemaids (whom we imagine frilly, shrill-voiced and pink-faced), a priest, the greedy card-sharper Lord Canterville are the helpless victims of a ghost who is apparently trying to emulate Robin Hood in his own way.

In passages like that — even more obvious sometimes — Oscar Wilde shows his contempt towards Victorian society, especially its most sacred icons. And the linguistic forms his social non-conformism can adopt are manifold, ranging from ridiculous descriptions like this to a wide variety of erudite allegories, such as the choice of the names — Otis is an epenthesis of the Greek pronoun 'hostis' which means 'anybody' — specific references like *Crockford's*, one of the famous gentlemen's clubs in London and a few others.

A few pages later, in a charming conversation with sweet Virginia 'who at times had a sweet Puritan gravity, caught from some old New England ancestor' (p. 206), the ghost cries out his exasperation at her moralizing attitude, saying:

> - Oh, I hate the cheap severity of abstract ethics! My wife was very plain, never had my ruffs properly starched, and knew nothing about cookery. Why, there was a buck I had shot in Hogley Woods, a magnificent pricket, and do you know how she had it sent up to table? However, it is no matter now, for it is all over, and I don't think it was very nice of her brothers to starve me to death, though I did kill her.
> - Starve you to death? Oh Mr Ghost, I mean Sir Simon, are you hungry? I have a sandwich in my case. Would you like it? (p. 206)

where we can see that, despite his utterly desperate existence, he radically refuses to accept conventional moral standards. In addition to that, Wilde 'helps' the ghost by presenting a completely ludicrous image of the supposedly well-to-do young girl who is scowling at the poor wretch. This procedure is a neat attack against conventions and transgresses the expectations of the 'right-doers' of that time.

So Wilde defines himself as a black sheep within Victorian England, as we can extensively see throughout his work. In *The Canterville Ghost* we can see varied examples of his ironical procedures, with a text clearly oriented towards social satire, though not exclusively. But it is in *The Importance of Being Earnest* that we can best see how his purely linguistic talent works and how it develops a parallel creativity in social satire. Or is it the other way round? Is it his creativity in social satire that develops a parallel linguistic talent?

Before getting down to the actual instances of the play, we would probably need to justify the idea that social and linguistic usages keep a relationship of some kind. The trouble is that *sociolinguistics*, the discipline which is supposed to deal with the relationship between society and language, has been imposing a sort of 'classificatory dissection' upon social classes and their respective varieties of linguistic performance rather than defining a bond or link between the actual activities and the 'environmental presuppositions' — linguistic and social in both cases.

It would appear that Modern Linguistics is still dragging the weight of the Sapir-Whorf hypothesis, the principles of *linguistic determinism* and *linguistic relativity*, which David Crystal (1987) describes as follows:

> We cut nature up, organize it into concepts, and ascribe significances as we do, largely because we are parties to an agreement to organize it in this way — an agreement that holds throughout our speech community and is codified in the patterns of our language. The agreement is, of course, an implicit and unstated one, *but its terms are absolutely obligatory*; we cannot talk at all except by subscribing to the organization and classification of data which the agreement decrees. (p. 15)

This implies that not only thought but also social behaviour would be entirely submitted to and dominated by language; an idea which is still theoretically acceptable, though contradicted in practice by a good deal of further research into different languages. However, another definition of the term *sociolinguistics* does not seem to make things much better. As the *Dictionnaire de Linguistique* by Jean Dubois et al. (1973, pp. 577-8) puts it, the scope of this term would range from the study of social and geographical varieties of language to the description of the speech acts by discourse analysis. Obviously, within this framework, the hypothesis of a link between linguistic and social performance would not be impossible, but certainly *non-linguistic*.

Fortunately, in the field of diachronic linguistics recent studies have given way to a less restrictive definition of language and have consequently renewed the scope of linguistics in general. Dick Leith (1983) and Jean Aitchison (1991) are two examples of this new tendency, chiefly aiming at the explanation of language change but with direct implications regarding the conception of language, for it is defined as a basically social phenomenon, which *undergoes* changes generated by the human society where it was born and bred, quite the opposite of Sapir and Whorf's postulate. The evidence Aitchison puts forward refers to the studies on pidgin languages, revealing a number of unexpected facts about the nature of human society and its means of communication:

> A new language may come into being when groups of people speaking different languages come into contact for the first time. When this happens, they sometimes bring into existence a restricted language system in order to cater for essential common needs. This restricted system is known as a **pidgin**. In certain circumstances, a pidgin can become elaborated, and grow into a language in its own right [...]. (p. 181)

We can therefore easily accept, considering some *pidgins* have already developed into *creoles* (i. e. mother languages of a whole community), the generalization that *social interaction is the basic and primary language generator* in any human community. We can then conclude there is a direct — though obviously not simple — relationship between linguistic and social usages.

As we have anticipated, *The Importance of Being Earnest* is extremely rich in that kind of correspondences, and in our view its success lies in the permanent play with linguistic and social presuppositions, a sort of tennis match in which Wilde 'beats back' any expected response. So there is a double parallel mechanism in his creation of humorous effects, though everything is dominated by the same principle: *the transgression of conventions*, which we can subdivide into linguistic and social, though we may obviously come across difficulties to tell them apart.

Victor Raskin (1985) distinguishes two communication modes to explain his semantic theory of humour: the *bona-fide* and the **non-*bona-fide*** ones, which arise by pairing one member from each of the following sets:

Set 1:   1a - The speaker makes the joke unintentionally
          1b - The speaker makes the joke intentionally
Set 2:   2a - The hearer does not expect a joke
          2b - The hearer expects a joke (p. 100)

According to this, Wilde would clearly stand within non-*bona-fide* communication because, on the one hand, his comical effects tend systematically to be of the 1b-2a type and on the other they always break the 'co-operative principle', according to which 'the speaker is committed to the truth and relevance of his text, the hearer is aware of his commitment and perceives the uttered text as true and relevant by virtue of the speaker's commitment to its truth and relevance' (p. 101). Naturally the situation in which the speaker does not expect comicality is funnier, particularly if the speaker is the only one to 'administer' the information. Moreover, humorousness increases greatly if the speaker is only committed to his own presuppositions that he gives out on a right-for-wrong basis, that is, completely the opposite way the hearer expects them to be.

The opening scene of *The Importance of Being Earnest* is a perfect example of the mentioned mechanism. Algernon and his manservant Lane hold a surprisingly rich dialogue where the disrespect towards social appropriateness is the master key to its comicity.

> ALGERNON. [...] Oh! [...] by the way, Lane, I see from your book that on Thursday night, when Lord Shoreman and Mr Worthing were dining with me, eight bottles of Champagne are entered as having been consumed.
> LANE. Yes, Sir; eight bottles and a pint.

> ALGERNON. Why is it that at a bachelor's establishment the servants invariably drink the Champagne? I ask merely for information.
> LANE. I attribute it to the superior quality of the wine, Sir. I have often observed that in married households the Champagne is rarely of a first-rate brand.
> ALGERNON. Good heavens! Is marriage so demoralising as that? (p. 321)

First, one of the most important rules of Victorian England regarding social stratification is implicitly broken, because neither the master nor the servant respect the established verticality. On the one hand, Lane has been caught sponging on his master's cellar, which he admits shamelessly, almost proudly; on the other, Algernon's reaction could not be more indulgent, taking it as the normal thing to do. Second, a highly sacred institution of Victorian England is lampooned here: Marriage, which is said to be demoralising and implicitly dull and the antithesis of enjoyment. So we can see again that the presuppositions in social matters are radically reversed, provoking thus hilarity from the very beginning of the play.

The battle against presuppositions goes on and on throughout the play, frequently without necessarily attempting to undermine social conventions, although it is somewhat arbitrary to draw a border line between 'socialhood' and 'languagehood' in that mechanism. For example, at the end of Act One, Algernon has a word with his servant and then with Jack Worthing:

> ALGERNON. I hope to-morrow will be a fine day, Lane.
> LANE. It never is, Sir.
> ALGERNON. Lane, you're a perfect pessimist.
> LANE. I do my best to give satisfaction, Sir.
> [...]
> JACK. If you don't take care, your friend Bunbury will get you into a serious scrape one day.
> ALGERNON. I love scrapes. They are the only things that are never serious.
> JACK. Oh, that's nonsense, Algy. You never talk anything but nonsense.
> ALGERNON. Nobody ever does. (p. 337)

In those lines that close the first act, we have one of the best examples of the double mechanism of Wilde's humour we can find in the play: first, Lane's words are both socially contrary to usage and semantically contradictory to what Algernon says; second, Algernon does the same with Jack's warning and scowling. Wilde, moreover, coins a new word that has belonged to the English vocabulary ever since: *Bunbury* — working both as a noun and as a verb — an extremely English euphemism that designates one of the most common social practices in England. In this case, then, both linguistic and social rules are broken by virtue of the same mechanism; the only difference lies in deciding what end of the string we are pulling.

The reason for Wilde's success is precisely that he caught his public both socially and linguistically unawares. That is, he mastered language so well that he realized rhetoric was the 'cleanest' and most invisible weapon against Victorian hypocritical and decadent habits. That is why we tend to identify Oscar Wilde with his famous sentences, such as '*It is only shallow people who do not judge by appearances*', and similar ones that yield the reverse result to what the hearer expects. And, if we have to decide whether social satire is the result or the cause of his semantic mechanisms for humour, we shall take the apparently most logical option: when he writes, he uses semantic mechanisms to *deconstruct* — using the Derridian term — social habits. The question is: did he do the same in his life, or rather the contrary?

REFERENCES

Aitchison, J. (1991), *Language Change: Progress or Decay?* Cambridge, Cambridge University Press.
Chastenet, J. (1961), *La vida cotidiana en Inglaterra al comienzo del reinado de Victoria*. Buenos Aires, Hachette.
Crystal, D. (1987), *The Cambridge Encyclopedia of Language*. Cambridge, Cambridge University Press.
Dubois, J. et al. (1973), *Dictionnaire de Linguistique*. Paris, Larousse.
Leith, D. (1983), *A Social History of English*. London, Routledge.
Raskin, V. (1985), *Semantic Mechanisms of Humour*. Dordrecht, etc, Reidel Publishing Co.
Sapir, E. (1921), *Language*. New York: Harcourt Brace.
Wilde, Oscar(1987), *The Complete Works of Oscar Wilde*. Leicester, Galley Press.

DORIAN GRAY'S ROOMS AND CYBERSPACE

Pia Brînzeu

Cyberspace refers to a computer-generated virtual reality. The persons interested in creating it put on a body-stocking and a data-glove which cover the sense organs and replace the sensory perceptions that normally come from physical objects with perceptions from simulated objects. The users are immersed in a computer-created three-dimensional reality in which the system picks up the voice commands, the gestures, and movements of the head or of the body, translating them to the virtual world. The computer can answer all possible actions because powerful software programs change the model in response to the user's behaviour. These changes can be simple rotations of the entire scene, with perspectives alternating appropriately or movements of the individual objects touched by the user. Everything is pretty crude so far, but future researches will certainly come to notable performances.[1]

It goes without saying that cyberspace offers a hitherto unimagined chance for the study of space representations in literature. Both the writer and the reader have a direct mental access to an artificial world which is more concrete than the simple mental frames of the imagination. It is also much more complex than a film representation because it allows direct interfering on the part of the consumer.

Although literary theoreticians have not yet dealt with cyberspace, they have defined and clarified the main problems of the theory of space in narrative. According to Ruth Ronen,[2] *space* in literature represents a *semantic construct* built with the help of linguistic structures which determine the actual or potential surroundings of the characters and objects. Space relations are perhaps one of the most clearly structured dimensions of meaning in a text, especially in novels in which the writers insistently describe the story-space, turning the main focus of their narrative to the cities, villages or houses that shelter the characters and incidents.

This is the case with Oscar Wilde's novel *The Picture of Dorian Gray* which offers numerous and elaborate descriptions of the rooms that locate the story-events.[3] Every chapter is situated within a different closed space, arranged in concentric circles around the very portrait of Dorian Gray. It is not by chance that the novel begins with a description of Basil Hallward's studio which has the picture in its middle. There is a divan 'of Persian saddle-bags' (p. 23) on which Lord Wotton is lying while chatting with the painter and long tussore-silk curtains stretched in front of the huge window facing the garden. Other pieces of furniture, such as the small Japanese tea-table, the piano with its stool, the platform for the model, the large wicker armchair, the sofa, and the painting-table with brushes and tubes are mentioned in Chapter Two.

Chapter Three takes us to the house of Lord Fermor on Albany Street and to Lady Agatha's on Berkeley Street, Chapter Four to Lord Wotton's library, Chapter Five to the shabby room inhabited by Sibyl Vane and Chapter Six to the little private room at the Bristol where Lord Henry, Basil and Dorian have dinner together.

These distinct spatial frames represent the outer realm of Dorian Gray's universe. It is the world of his social relations and of his extrovert existence, the place where he makes contacts and leads a life of pleasure. We are not given details about his personality (all we are told is that the youth is handsome, innocent and naive, that he loves the smell of roses and the sound of music), but we hear that he very often goes to the theatre and attends quite numerous dinner parties, and that he is very popular with the London aristocrats who are fascinated by his 'extraordinary personal beauty' (p. 23).

In Chapter Seven, the main topographic frame of the novel is moved to the house of Dorian Gray together with the portrait which has been placed in the Library. A new spatial circle opens around the portrait. It is the world which encloses Dorian's personality in order to unfold it to the eyes of the readers. Minute descriptions inform us about the dandy's hedonistic inclinations, about his love of beautiful objects and his refined taste for inner architecture. Dorian's house has an oak-panelled hall, with a beautiful Venetian lantern and a table on which the young man throws his hat and cape when he enters the door. The Library is a large octogonal chamber, decorated with some 'curious Renaissance tapestries' (p. 118), cream-coloured silk blinds, a clock on the mantelpiece, a table of dark perfumed wood thickly encrusted with nacre, a little marqueterie table, an open hearth, a large screen of gilt Spanish leather wrought with a florid Louis Quatorze pattern. There is also a purple satin coverlet, a late 17th century Venetian work heavily embroidered with gold, used by Dorian Gray to conceal the portrait.

Next to the Library are the bedroom with the olive-satin curtains, the onyx-paved bathroom, a conservatory (well-described in Chapter Seventeen) and a blue drawing-room.

The structure of the house unfolds horizontally and discloses a part of the building that is open to Dorian's friends and to the strangers that visit him occasionally. As long as the portrait is in the library, Dorian receives his guests there. After it has been moved upstairs, he leads his visitors to the conservatory (see Chapter Seventeen).

It is evident that this spatial area is frequented by a smaller circle of people than the one mentioned previously. It is closed and intimate, restricted to the hero's friends.

The interior settings inhabited by the main characters are from time to time enlarged with glimpses of the outside. The gardens of Basil Hallward, Lady Narborough or Dorian Gray represent extensions of the houses. Their flowers, trees, birds, fresh air, and impressive skies have positive connotations, transforming them into places of pleasure where the conversations started within the house can be agreeably continued.

Beyond the gardens are the London streets which appear to Dorian as a dangerous threat. Whether we hear the dim roar of London like 'the bourdon note of a distant organ' (p. 23) in Basil Hallward's studio or we perceive 'the rumble of the omnibuses and the clatter of the street cabs' (p. 97) in Sibyl Vane's room, we are aware that the streets have ominous effects. They are places of darkness and of unbearable monotony, 'like the black web of some sprawling spider' (p. 221). Their dimly lit pavements and evil-looking houses frighten Dorian in the crucial moments of his life: after he leaves Sibyl, when he kills the painter and when he is about to be killed by James Vane. Therefore, the time spent outside the house is reduced to the very short moments necessary for moving from one building to another.

In the second half of the novel — starting exactly with Chapter Ten — the stable geometry of Dorian's domesticity is overthrown. His decision to move the painting upstairs to the old school room moves the centre of the house to the attic and highlights the verticality of the house. From now on, Dorian will continuously ascend the stairs to the secret part of the building which encloses the enigma of his own personality. Vicious and immoral, corrupted and debased, he hides his real soul from the eyes of his friends. Whenever he leaves London, he is attracted to come back and to creep upstairs to have a secret look at himself. It seems as if he were constantly under the spell of the area circumscribed by the painting. In fact, Dorian's moral drama overlaps with his reclusion from the outer spaces to the core of his own house.

The relations with the exterior are stopped: doors are locked, windows closed and curtains drawn. Life in the Gray household becomes more and more artificial, in evident contrast with the life of the normal households of his friends. The psychological and spatial abyss which gets larger every day can no longer be bridged. Any attempt to do that finishes in death, as is the case with both Basil Hallward and Alan Campbell.

However, neither the coherent spatiality of the house nor its horizontality can be suspended for a too long period of time. The attic cannot remain its centre for ever. Dorian himself feels it when he destroys the painting: even if he perishes in the process, he brings the house back to normality, re-equilibrating its vertical and horizontal dimensions.

In the latter part of the novel, Dorian's universe is reduced to a very small spatial area. It becomes so narrow and self-contained that space seems completely annihilated. It falls within itself, in the same way in which Dorian lives henceforward only within his own soul. The freezing of space into immobility is simultaneous with the suspension of time. Dorian does not grow old, nothing changes around him, life pases without leaving any traces. The reader enters a world of unusual stasis, of a paralysis that affects the chronotopos. While initially the hero had a past (see the discussion in Chapter Three about Dorian's descent) and a future (in his prospects of marriage to Sibyl Vane), he now lives in a perpetual present only, outside any possibility of change. The only activity he repeatedly performs is that of opening and closing of doors.

It is interesting that all the chapters begin and finish with the characters' entering or leaving a room. The only exceptions are represented by the beginnings of Chapters Eleven and Nineteen. The other chapters alternate the following openings: the description of a room where the characters find themselves (Chapters One, Four, Five, Seventeen), a character — usually Dorian Gray — enters a room or a hall (Chapters Two, Six, Seven, Nine, Fifteen), comes back home (Chapters Twelve, Twenty), is in the room while the valet enters (Chapters Eight, Ten, Fourteen), gets out of a room (Chapter Thirteen), strolls in the streets to go to another house (Chapters Three, Sixteen), remains at home (Chapter Eighteen). The chapters finish with the leaving of a room or of a house (Chapters Two, Three, Five, Six, Eight, Nine, Fourteen, Fifteen, Sixteen, Nineteen), arriving at home or at another house (Chapters Four, Eighteen, Twenty), going from one room into the garden (Chapter Seven), from the garden into the house (Chapter One), moving from one room to another (Chapters Ten, Twelve, Fourteen, Seventeen), walking up and down the room (Chapter Thirteen).

The device gives rhythm and movement to an otherwise completely static novel, links rather disparate places, and refreshes the stifling atmosphere of the interiors with glimpses of street landscape. It also underlines the unusual travel of initiation undergone by Dorian Gray, who unlike a picaro, does not set out for a real journey, but moves only within his own house, travelling from one room to another.

It seems that a novel like *The Picture of Dorian Gray* that is totally devoid of action and deals with conversations and descriptions only, represents no interest for virtual transposition. Its static plot may discourage computer users from any attempts to interfere with the story. However, the 'virtual potentialities' inherent in the settings of such a novel are as rich as those to be found in a story crowded with incidents. Numerous operations can be performed starting from the spatial pattern of such a novel.

The most rewarding exercise for a cybernetic reader would be the operation of concretization. It implies the translation of linguistic structures into mental images, i.e. the transformation of words as verbal signs into images as iconic signs. This very complex semiotic operation is usually performed by stage or film directors who model the reality of the book and offer parallel variants to it. But while the spatial coordinates presented on the stage or in films are static, limited, and unequivocal, virtual reality appears as a flexible concept that may be constantly worked upon. It is evident that once a staging or a film is finished, neither the producers nor the public can interfere with the space established in it. The only thing they can do is to think of another performance. The possibilities offered by virtual reality to construct different types of topographical frames for the same story are unlimited. They can vary ad infinitum, depending only on the imaginative disposition of the user.

The process of concretization is interesting for each chapter of the book, but it might be most fertile in the case of spaces that have a *low degree of immediacy*. Certain vaguely described rooms (like those of Lady Agatha, Lord Fermor, and Sibyl Vane) can be given an interior shape. If the reader wants to respect the atmosphere, he needs a thorough knowledge of inner architecture, of historical details concerning the epoch, which might oblige him to consult other books as well. If not, he can make modern transpositions which also have a degree of unpredictability and may accordingly be of interest.

An ingenious reader might also fill Dorian Gray's house with mirrors. Except the Cupid-framed mirror which he has on one of the Library tables, there are no other mirrors mentioned in the novel. He does not need them because he uses the painting as 'the most magical of mirrors' (p. 136), but they would confer depth, and shadow reflections to the walls.

The reader could also increase or decrease the space between objects and/or places, turn the geometry of the house into a labyrinth or change the *topographical* level of the novel (i.e., the space as a static entity) into a *chronotopic* level (the structure imposed on space by the passage of time, events and/or people).[4] This would imply a more active participation of the reader in decoding the narrative level and the elements connected with description in this novel.

The *potential* settings, i.e., the ones which are not actualized in the book, can be turned into real settings as is the case with the west gallery of the house (where Dorian keeps his cedar chests storing the collection of ecclesiastical vestments) and with the latticed music room in which he 'used' to give concerts. One could also imagine the objects that form his collection of exotic musical instruments, pieces of jewelry, and embroideries described in Chapter Eleven, insist on vestimentary details (enlarging the rather scarce indications given by the author when he refers to the 'silk-embroidered cashmere dressing-gown' of Dorian Gray/p. 122/or the black silk dress of the housekeeper/p. 148) or actualize general asertions (such as the following, for instance: 'His mode of dressing, and the particular styles that from time to time he affected, had their marked influence on the young exquisites of the Mayfair balls and Pall Mall club windows who copied him in everything that he did, and tried to reproduce the accidental charm of his graceful, though to him only half-serious fopperies', p. 161). Not to say anything about the interesting olfactive experiments that may be tried when dealing with the references to smells and perfumes that abound in all chapters.

Other experiments would permit to move some characters (such as the trio Lord Henry, Basil Hallward, Dorian Gray) from one spatial frame (e.g., the painter's studio in Chapter Two) to different other rooms and analyse the differences. One could also reduce all the settings of the book to one single room. The choice might fall on the school-room, which would thus annihilate the symbolic core of the house and would make the three concentric circles of the novel overlap.

Other experiments might deal with the *principal frames* of the novel being turned into *secondary frames* and viceversa: after the crime, Dorian stands on the balcony of the school-room and looks down in the street where he sees a woman with a fluttering shawl that sings, until a policeman goes to silence her. Certainly it would be of no difficulty to descend and join them, or open what they call, in computer terminology, a window, embedding the story of the woman within that of Dorian.

There will no longer be *inaccessible* settings for the reader, i.e. settings which remain undescribed because they are not entered by the characters (as is, for example, the blue drawing-room). The computer user can open all doors and visit the most hidden corners of Selby Royal.

Virtual reality also offers the possibility of a change in the point of view. *The Picture of Dorian Gray* is a third person narration which offers an exterior and limited point of view as to the feelings and impressions of Dorian. Entering virtual reality, the reader might re-live the novel from a different angle, similar to that of a first person narration. Becoming Dorian Gray himself, he is allowed a more intense participation which opens tremendous possibilities to the experimentation with human psychology.

Last, but not least, although the story is poor in incidents, one might as well insist upon its plot. Different variants for the hero's life can be imagined (marriage, children, change of location, etc.), as well as several endings to the book.

Naturally, the above discussion is far from being exhaustive. It explores only a part of the potentialities for computer simulation inherent in novels such as Oscar Wilde's *Picture*. It cannot be denied, however, that the possibilities offered by a spatially centred narrative are as rewarding as those given by any other type of writing.

NOTES

1   E. Dyson, 1990, 'Virtual Reality: Spreadsheets for Industry', *Release 1.0*, 8 October, p. 4 (see also *PC Magazine*, November 1990, and *Electric Word*, February 1991).

2   R. Ronen, 1986, 'Space in Fiction', *Poetics Today*, volume 7, number 3, p. 421.
3   Oscar Wilde, *The Picture of Dorian Gray*, Penguin Books, 1985.
4   G. Zoran, 1984, 'Towards a Theory of space in Narrative', *Poetics Today*, volume 5, number 2, p. 315.

SALOME: WILDE'S RADICAL TRAGEDY

Edward Burns

Salome is a radical tragedy in its reworking of the basis of
theatrical form, the relation between spectacle word and
meaning. Wilde uses, and pits against each other, what he
perceived as a Hellenistic/pagan idea of representation, and a
Judaeo-Christian one. The first is in the domain of the look; it
is Salome's domain, and within it language must find structures
that subvert and annihilate the meanings that accrue to
narrative, measure, comparison. The second, the Judaeo-
Christian, is the domain of the word, of narrative, of cause and
consequence, and it is the domain created by Iokanaan, as
prophet and precursor, and inhabited unwillingly by the
paranoid Herod.

In the Gospel narrative Salome is the embodiment of a
sequence of transactions between the other characters.

> When the daughter of the said Herodias came in, and danced,
> and pleased Herod, and them that sat with him, the king said
> unto the damsel, 'Ask of me whatsoever thou wilt, and I will
> give it thee' [...]. And she went forth, and said unto her mother,
> 'What shall I ask?'. And she said, 'The head of John the
> Baptist'. And she same in straightway with haste unto the king,
> and asked, saying, 'I will that thou give me by and by in a
> charger the head of John the Baptist.'
>   And the king was exceedingly sorry; yet for his oath's
> sake and for their sakes which sat with him, he would not reject
> her. And immediately the king sent an executioner, and
> commanded his head to be brought: and he went and beheaded
> him in the prison. And brought his head in a charger, and gave it
> to the damsel: and the damsel gave it to her mother. (The Gospel
> according to St Mark 6.22-28)

This narrative implicates Salome in a complex of
sexual, familial and political relations, within which she is a
kind of go-between, transmitting and activating the desire of
others in ways that cause and resolve a crisis in the story and in

the social network it represents. She is not, in the biblical account, the agent of her own desire. But we know that Wilde takes his cue from visual representations of Salome, paintings of the Renaissance and of his own time. She is thus taken out of a narrative context, isolated and framed so that she can generate other narratives. The dominant source for this is perhaps to be found in the paintings of Gustave Moreau. In conversation Wilde spun apocryphal extensions and conclusions to the story, all focused on Salome's hallucinatory visual presence.[1]

In the play Salome is at the centre of an agon of 'the look'. This is more powerful, I feel, in the later English version than in Wilde's original French. Where the French uses two separate words for the act of looking and for 'having a look of', the English version has a single word, 'look', for the two ideas, and plays obsessively with the ambiguity that word acquires as it passes from one to the other of the usages the French keeps distinct.

> THE YOUNG SYRIAN. How beautiful is the Princess Salome tonight!
> THE PAGE OF HERODIAS. Look at the moon! How strange the moon seems! [...]
> THE YOUNG SYRIAN. She has a strange look.

compare to:

> LE PAGE D'HERODIAS. Regardez la lune. La lune a l'air très étrange.

And, a little later:

> THE YOUNG SYRIAN. How beautiful is the Princess Salome tonight!
> THE PAGE OF HERODIAS. You are always looking at her. You look at her too much. It is dangerous to look at people in such fashion. Something terrible may happen.
> THE YOUNG SYRIAN. She is very beautiful tonight.
> FIRST SOLDIER. The Tetrarch has a sombre look.
> SECOND SOLDIER. Yes: he has a sombre look.
> FIRST SOLDIER. He is looking at something.
> SECOND SOLDIER. He is looking at someone.
> FIRST SOLDIER. At whom is he looking?
> SECOND SOLDIER. I cannot tell.

Again:

> PREMIER SOLDAT. Le tétrarque a l'air sombre.
> SECOND SOLDAT. Oui, il a l'air sombre.
> PREMIER SOLDAT. Il regarde quelque chose.
> SECOND SOLDAT. Il regarde quelqu'un.

Salome's own dynamic in the play is predicated by the dangerous seeing, the desiring look that she reflects back from Herod and the Syrian onto Iokanaan. In this perhaps she is like the moon — as a reflector of other's light, receiving but giving back in a cold 'sterile' form. The moon, according to Wilde, is the most important character in the play. Aubrey Beardsley, in his illustrations to *Salome*, put Wilde's face, the face of the most observed of all observers, on the moon, as well as on Herod. We can imagine the moon is looking, but we create this by looking at it, it is a form of projection; the moon does not look. But Salome threatens attempts to place her by looking at her, by being herself the source of the desiring look, by reversing its source — by being less of a moon than the other characters want her to be.

    The first section of the play, leading up to the entrance of Salome, is a kind of prologue, in which the dominant ideas of the piece are dispersed in the dialogue of the minor characters. The religious disputes of the Jews allow Wilde to set his exploration of the relation of sight to word to belief in a theological context, and to activate the Judaeo-Christian/Hellenistic contrast I referred to at the start.

> FIRST SOLDIER. The Jews worship a god that you cannot see.
> THE CAPPADOCIAN. I cannot understand that.
> FIRST SOLDIER. In fact, they only believe in things you cannot see.
> THE CAPPADOCIAN. That seems to me altogether ridiculous.

Then the unseen Iokanaan is heard for the first time. But Salome makes Iokanaan visible, by ordering the soldiers to bring him out of the cistern. The structure of Salome's apostrophe to Iokanaan is that of a sequence of comparisons, itself implying a subversive reversal of the biblical word, *The Song of Songs*. *The Song* is constructed from comparisons:

> His head is as the most fine gold, his locks are bushy, and blacke as a raven. His eyes are as the eyes of doves by the rivers of water, washed with milk, and fitly set. [...] His legs are as pillars of marble, set upon sockets of fine gold; his countenance is as Lebanon, excellent as the Cedars.
> His mouth is moste sweete, yea he is altogether lovely.
> (The Song of Solomon 5.11-16)

In Christian tradition *The Song* is read allegorically, as a metaphor of Christ's relation to the church, thus diffusing its aesthetic/erotic content. Salome's use of it subverts not simply this devotional meaning, but the very process of comparison and analogy by which that interpretation is constructed. She uses comparison not to focus on her object, but to continually slip away from it; it is as if her desire is trapped and made to circulate within language itself. Iokanaan's language, in contrast is always purposive, either coming out of or pointing to an action. In that sense he is the most conventionally 'dramatic' character, the one constructed out of a more conventional relation of word to action. Wilde creates a tension between this, the power of the word, and the immobility of his stage situation, which empowers him when he is invisible, thus like the God of the Jews, to be believed in, but renders him vulnerable, when visible, to Salome's activation of the hazards of visual pleasure. In the beginning was the word, but not for Salome, who exists in the domain of the look, and whose narrative is plotted by the hazards of looking and being looked at. Salome works out her fate within the domain of the visual, rejecting, or unable to comprehend, anything of the Judaic notion of belief in the invisible of the primacy of word over vision.

The language of the play seem stiflingly otiose, and yet this very effect of decadent over-kill is haunted by the sense that the simile, so repetitively the vehicle of Herod, Salome and the young Syrian's imagination, is a dangerous instrument — double-edged, reversible, like mirror images or like, for Herod and perhaps for Wilde, the relation between masks and faces:

> Your beauty troubled me [...]. But I will look at you no more.
> Neither at things nor at people should one look. Only in mirrors
> should one look, for mirrors do but show us masks.

Simile here seems to create, in the space between the thing
compared and the comparison, the space of desire — the desire
to annihilate meaning. In *Salome* structures of simile negate the
process by which a comparison illuminates the nature of its
object, and so might help to construct a symbolic language
through which to decode and articulate its meanings, in favour
of pure aesthetic pleasure. Herod abandons the use of simile as
interpretation in the face of his prescience of disaster. He
retreats into aestheticism defensively — 'You must not find
symbols in everything you see. It makes life impossible. It were
better to say that stains of blood are as lovely as rose petals.'
For Herod here, the function of comparison is just to say 'as
lovely'. Herod accuses Herodias of sterility, but she turns this
back against him. For Herod Herodias's language is sterile in
its reductiveness, it is jarringly comonsensical, it produces no
further likeness, so cannot, within his terms, create: 'the moon
is like the moon, that is all.' For Herodias, Herod's language is
sterile, 'ridiculous' (ridiculous is a key-word in the play) in its
creation through similitude, mirroring, echoes. Salome's
comparisons alternate between expressions of aesthetic
pleasure and of loathing, both aspects of desire. The process of
comparison in itself implies the fear of an annihilation of
meaning, the deadness of the moon, a sterility of desire that
may yet be a sterility to celebrate in its freedom from
consequence, and its abandonment to instantaneous dissolution.

The third section of the play is initiated by Herod's
entrance, and returns us to the gospel narrative. This is because
Wilde's Herod is still, as his Salome is not, defined by that
narrative. Both in Matthew and in Mark the story is a kind of
parenthesis introduced to demonstrate the growing fame of
Jesus. In Matthew 14.1-2 (the two are remarkably similar):

> At that time Herod the Tetrarch heard of the fame of Jesus, and
> said unto his servants, 'This is John the Baptist; he is risen from
> the dead; and therefore mighty works do show forth themselves
> in him.'

In the Gospels, the idea of resurrection resurrects the story of John, and Herod's mistaken belief in that resurrection introduces the idea of the eventual resurrection of Christ; Herod's paranoid state of mind creates a typology within the story which is in itself an elegant inversion of the typology which for a Christian reader gives the story of the Baptist meaning, his meaning being that he is the 'pre-cursor', the forerunner, the 'type' of Christ. The two dominant ideas here — of resurrection from the dead, and of the spectacle of the miraculous — the 'showing forth' of which Herodias is cynically bored, but of which Herod is still afraid — are reworked by Wilde. Both are related, and exist for Herod on a kind of mental loop in which his prescience of events takes the place of the elegantly circular structure of the Gospel narrative. Herod, like the page, imposes a structure of foreboding on the apparently random action. This allows him to recognise, perhaps to some extent to admit to sharing, the page's love for the Syrian, but the main source of Herod's prescience is his closeness to, his ability to share in, to some extent to believe in, the purposive and forward-looking language of Iokanaan — the 'word' which, being in the beginning, is thus the source of action, not a passively descriptive or reactive account of it. 'Ridiculous' is a key term in the play in that the ridiculous lies in the perception of a disproportion of words to spectacle. It points to a crisis of belief, of conviction. Perhaps Wilde is acting out a crisis of belief within a drama of desire. Desire and belief must be distinguished — the notion of Salome as Christian convert which occurs in some sources and parallel texts is rejected by Wilde. Instead he overlaps two theatrical forms, the tragedy of thwarted desire, and the mystery play, the drama of realised belief. Theatre is in a way the domain of the ridiculous; or, rather, all theatrical spectacle is potentially ridiculous, in the risks it must take to convince us of the unlikely and the untrue. Few plays run those risks as daringly as *Salome*.

NOTES

* I would like to thank Matthew Pearson for his contributions to this piece.

* All references to the French text of *Salomé* are taken from the Methuen edition *Salomé, La Sainte Courtisane, A Florentine Tragedy*, London, 1909.

* All biblical quotations are from the *Authorised Version*.

1   Cf. R. Ellmann, pp. 322-5.

POWER STRUCTURING: THE PRESENTATION OF OUTSIDER FIGURES IN WILDE'S PLAYS

Richard Allen Cave

In *The Soul of Man Under Socialism* Wilde paid Henry Irving a tribute of a kind that it is rare for actors to receive: the terms were not those of vague eulogising; instead Wilde offered an incisive analysis of the actor's technical achievement as the grounds for his praise:

> [Irving's] object was to realise his own perfection as an artist, under certain conditions and in certain forms of Art. At first he appealed to the few: now he has educated the many. He has created in the public both taste and temperament. The public appreciate his artistic success immensely. I often wonder, however, whether the public understand that that success is entirely due to the fact that he did not accept their standard, but realised his own.[1]

Wilde saw Irving as creating the taste by which his art was to be understood and enjoyed, thereby enlarging the imaginative sympathies of his audience.

What is remarkable about Wilde's view is that it almost exactly corresponds in its central idea with an observation of Ellen Terry's about Irving. However, she — the experienced player — significantly changed the emphasis, seeing Irving's success as a triumph of will over adverse personal circumstances. In her *Memoirs* she repeatedly recalls the actor's problems (his dragging leg, his difficulties with enunciation, his unromantic features) as cause to marvel at his particular success. But here she was compelled to effect a careful discrimination between his individual achievement and what conventionally passes for success, namely popularity:

> After a lapse of years I began to wonder if Henry was ever
> really popular. It came naturally to most people to dislike his
> acting. [...] but he forced them, almost against their will and
> nature, out of dislike into admiration. They had to come up to
> him, for never would he go down to them. This is not
> popularity.[2]

Edward Gordon Craig, like his mother, saw Irving's success as
wholly a matter of power, the forceful projection of a stage
persona considerably at odds with the man's own physical
reality. What is perhaps even more remarkable in this context
is that Irving's most memorable impersonations were all
outsider figures (Mathias in *The Bells*, Shylock,
Mephistopheles, Cardinal Wolsey, Eugene Aram): criminals,
transgressors of the moral law and embodiments of values
totally opposed to the pieties enshrined in Victorian orthodox
conceptions of goodness and propriety. Irving was the first
actor-manager to lower the auditorium lights during a
performance. By a dynamic assertion of his will Irving
enthralled his audiences, compelling them to watch
mesmerized in the dark what they would dread to confront in
the light of day. He had seemingly the power to take
spectators out of their social selves, which may account for the
unease that is manifest in many accounts of his acting. But what
disturbed others was for Wilde, Craig and Terry a cause for
congratulation.

   Irving remained one of Wilde's special 'heroes'[3]
throughout his lifetime (despite Irving's refusal to protest
against the banning of *Salome*); even in Reading Gaol he was
writing to Ross asking for news of the actor's movements and
current productions. The publication of Wilde's letters and the
recent work of critics such as Kerry Powell and Katharine
Worth have shown us the extent to which some roles in Wilde's
plays were created with specific players in mind; no role was
devised expressly for Irving. Yet all Wilde's plays contain
outsider figures whose 'otherness' is designed to challenge and
disturb but who compel a degree of fascination. In their
respective dramas they grow to be figures of considerable
power. None of the likely impersonators of these roles could be
relied on (however charismatic as performers) to possess a
dynamism comparable to Irving's; Wilde had to find a way of

creating a correlative for that power extrinsic to (though supportive of) an actor's personal authority and command. I would argue that he succeeded in this by deploying actors within the stage space in what for the time was a highly innovatory manner. His stage directions, when interpreted *spatially*, show Wilde devising a number of subtle visual strategies to stimulate and control an audience's imaginative engagement with particular roles.

Wilde was not of course the first nineteenth-century dramatist to take advantage of the new possibilities for scenic realism, especially in the staging of interiors, to develop a sense of the playworld extending beyond the visible limits of the stage itself, or to exploit the stage space metaphorically as emblematic of a particular character's psychological space. Wilde knew his Ibsen and crucially *Hedda Gabler* where stage space is deployed in these ways; and he had seen and admired as a younger man the Bancrofts' staging of Robertson's social comedies where an offstage world is often powerfully evoked to create ironic or ominous tensions with the situation being played out on-stage. Consider, for example, Act III, scene iii of *Society*, where Sidney Daryl's electioneering speech at the hustings heard from offstage continually disrupts and offers an unwelcome commentary on his rival Chodd's attempts (on-stage) at courting the heroine Maud Hetherington. Daryl's words seem to voice all Maud's objections to the odious Chodd, which Victorian codes of propriety in women would not permit her to express aloud. Or there is the instance of the end of Act II of *Ours* where the sounds of a long procession of regiments marching with their bands must seem to approach and recede (the offstage situation to be imagined is the march-past of the troops before Queen Victoria prior to their embarkation for the Crimea); as each company of soldiers passes in review so the emotional desperation between the pairs of lovers on-stage builds inexorably towards the moment when they too must part. Though Robertson deployed stage space with increasing freedom and creative ingenuity, he never explored its potential to define varying types and degrees of personal power, as Wilde was to do, when he began to create characters with the force of will to transform a seemingly alien space into an environment that more readily flatters their particular identities.

We are fortunate in this context to possess two revealing sketches for stage designs for plays by Wilde, one of which (a ground-plan for the last act of *Lady Windermere's Fan*) is definitely in his own hand, the other (chiefly the work of Charles Ricketts) was made during a conversation with Wilde about a suitable setting for *Salome* and exactly matches Ricketts' published account of their deliberations.[4] What is immediately noticeable is how starkly simple the designs are: what nowadays we would term 'minimalist'. They readily support Katharine Worth's observation: 'Wilde's stage directions really call for a rather bare stage; it is defined in terms of "spaces" with a few focal points.'[5] The sketch for *Salome* shows simply the low wall surrounding the cistern in which Iokanaan is imprisoned to the audience's left, complemented by a steeply rising staircase off to the right towards the rear of the stage which is overhung with what Ricketts describes as 'the perpendicular fall of strips of gilt matting which should not touch the ground [...] [forming] a sort of aerial tent above the terrace'; behind this a large moon is partially visible in a sky of 'rich turquoise blue'.[6] When Ricketts realised this design later for a private staging of the play in 1906 he added the required throne for Herod to the extreme right and slightly downstage of the cistern, though the suggestion implied by its absence from the earlier design is that the throne was to be carried in later in the action when Herod and his entourage make their sudden, unexpected entrance from the banquet.

Compared with settings for historical dramas as staged in the Nineties by Irving or Tree and their contemporaries (or even Bernhardt, for whom the play was devised) this is remarkably clean in its aesthetic lines and wholly uncluttered with period detail. Isolated within the otherwise bare reaches of the stage, cistern, throne and moon, those focal points about which the whole tragedy will revolve, become immediately *significant*: a symbolist setting for a symbolist play. As in Robertson's *Society*, offstage space becomes immediately as important as what is to be seen: Iokanaan's voice from his prison below stage continually disrupts the flow of action and comments critically on the sounds of revelry coming from the banqueting hall which we imagine as beyond the staircase to our right. Quickly the space is defined by the dialogue as Herod's private terrace and we learn too that the cistern is guarded by his soldiers and cannot be opened except by his express command; the throne, when it appears, is an emblem of his authority as Tetrarch. This territory is wholly Herod's. Yet from the moment of her entrance, Salome, seemingly so slight, pale and dove-like a figure, will gradually take possession of that space and make it hers by right of conquest; and the process defines her implacable inner strengths of desire and will-power. She exploits the Syrian's infatuation for her to get the cistern opened and gain access to Jokanaan; she toys with Herod's lust for her to lure him into promising to fulfil her extreme wish; and, when she dances, she steadily marks that whole place with the brand of her unique sensuality. The reward she asks for and repeatedly insists on brings cistern and throne into a terrible conjunction that compromises Herod's authority at every level, moral and political, and triumphs over his attempt to mould her to his gross patriarchal will. Granted her wish, Salome leans over the rim of the cistern, listening for sounds of Iokanaan's execution, like a figure of Nemesis controlling the fate of the individuals even in that offstage world below. Though it ultimately costs her her life, she has secured herself a status in legend and art that eternally recreates her victory over masculinist tyranny. Wilde's suggestions for a possible setting, which Ricketts sketched under his instruction refine the stage-picture down to the basic functional elements required by the action; by so doing he devised a means of consistently drawing an audience's attention to the power relations between the characters that structures the whole action.

Wilde's own groundplan for *Lady Windermere's Fan* is for the final act and it refers merely to the placing of a sofa within the spatial organisation of the stage. The scenery required is the same as for Act One, but Wilde was anxious that the disposition of the furniture should not be such as to place Mrs Erlynne in the same position as that occupied by the Duchess of Berwick in the earlier act, since he wished no lingering memory of how the characters were arranged in the

first scene to colour an audience's response to the grouping of the
actors in the fourth one. No parallels were to be drawn: 'It
impoverishes the effect.'[7] The whole discussion with George
Alexander in this letter shows Wilde to be acutely responsive
to the spatial dimensions of drama in performance and the
ways that audiences are likely to read the stage images placed
before them. He had precise effects he wished to achieve and
nothing must stand in the way of their theatrical realisation.
The better to understand what those precise effects were, it is
necessary to see how his prescriptions for this last scene are
part of a carefully organised series of strategies throughout the
play involving the deployment of stage space.

　　After the small-scale scene in the Morning Room of the
Windermeres' home for Act One, the stage must needs be opened
up to its fullest dimensions for the complex setting required for
Act Two. We are in a brilliantly lit drawing room from which a
wide door to the side leads into a ballroom where a band is
playing and couples are seen to be dancing; more doors at the
rear of the stage open on to an illuminated terrace. The central
focus for the early part of the scene is, however, a further
doorway to stage left, where Lady Windermere stands to
receive her guests at what is her coming-of-age party. It is a
ritual of great formality as the guests' names are announced
aloud and they proceed courteously to greet their hostess before
passing into the drawing room in search of friends and
acquaintance with whom to talk. Because of the sheer dignity
and decorum that prevails, a real tension builds up for the
audience who are aware that Lady Windermere is anxiously
waiting for the arrival of Mrs Erlynne, whom she plans to
insult publicly by slapping her face with a fan. To do so would,
socially, be an act of profound indiscretion. It is precisely the
iron control imposed by the ritual over hosts and guests which
Mrs Erlynne is counting on in staging her entry: she has the
courage to risk provoking a scene, because she knows few women
would have the courage actually to stage a scene in public on
her arrival. When the moment arrives and Lady Windermere
falters, drops the fan and bows coldly to the woman she
supposes is a rival for her husband's affection, we are shown
how strong and constricting the pressures are within such
rituals to enforce a particular social tone.

The stage space as it is first revealed to us belongs properly to Lady Windermere: it is her house and her birthday reception. Within minutes of playing time, Mrs Erlynne takes over that space completely. Before she is announced, she is a subject only for scandalised gossip among the women and salacious witticisms amongst the men: 'the women', as Lord Augustus admits, 'are very down on her. I have been dining with Arabella this evening! [...] She didn't leave a rag on her. [...] (*Aside*) Berwick and I told her that didn't matter much, as the lady in question must have an extremely fine figure.'[8] After her arrival Mrs Erlynne circulates round the groups seated in the drawing room, cleverly manipulating the men, who cannot resist her, to introduce her to the women (of whom she admits she is afraid) with whom she establishes an instant rapport. For all her professed fears, she is an embodiment of relaxed charm and, having completed a circle of the stage, departs for the ballroom on Lord Windermere's arm leaving everyone utterly captivated and falling over themselves to offer her invitations to their homes. The one-time object of scandal is now a subject for total admiration. As we come to appreciate later, Mrs Erlynne is projecting here a meticulously calculated persona; she has assumed a mask with a studied objective in view. It is nothing less than a magnificent performance that not only upstages Lady Windermere completely but actually displaces her from the scene altogether.

It might be argued that the episode is merely sensationalist (what used to be termed 'strong' or 'good' theatre); but that is not to take proper account of its place within the psychological structuring of the play. It is necessary that this moment makes an impact since the episode gives a very precise organic impetus to the next act. When Mrs Erlynne seeks to persuade Lady Windermere not to be so rash as to try and elope with Lord Darlington out of injured vanity, she speaks with particular intensity about the likely consequences: 'You haven't got the kind of brains that enables a woman to get back. You have neither the wit nor the courage.'[9] Act Two has proved that Lady Windermere lacks Mrs Erlynne cool nerve, her dynamism and the nonchalance that comes only to someone with an assured self-control. The power invested in the character by virtue of Wilde's use of stage space is in time seen to be a succinct expression of her complex psychology. Later, in Act III, Mrs Erlynne saves Lady Windermere from a compromising situation by apparently compromising herself. The final stage-picture, after Lady Windermere has escaped unseen, isolates Mrs Erlynne in a doorway to stage right against an assemblage of men, who have just been indulging in protracted chauvinist banter at her expense. Far from being cowed by their superiority in number, she stands her ground, then calmly walks forward to take the incriminating fan out of Lord Windermere's hands. Again it is the sheer physical control of the woman that impresses.

To return to the final act and the letter commenting on the ideal disposition of the sofa within the scene is to see Wilde developing this calm that is the correlative of a deep inner fortitude yet further. The sofa is to be placed 'not parallel with the footlights' (a now rather dated way necessitating that the actors in large measure play out to the audience) but angled and situated slightly left of centre, so that if the actress playing Mrs Erlynne 'sits on the upper side', she should be in a position to 'hold the centre of the stage and be its central figure'. This idea was not the consequence of watching rehearsals; rather, he confesses, it was how he imagined the situation 'in my own rough draft of the stage-setting for this act, made when I was writing the piece'.[10] The insight that the letter shows into the significances which can be read into the spatial relations of a group of actors on stage Wilde was in possession of therefore throughout the composition of the play and he controlled those relations as a deliberate strategy. When Wilde took issue with Alexander about where precisely in the play to reveal to the audience that Mrs Erlynne was Lady Windermere's mother, he insisted that, whatever other change was agreed on, one detail of the structuring had to be maintained: that the audience's interest should not cease from being 'concentrated on Mrs Erlynne, to whom dramatically speaking belongs the last act'.[11] Alexander, of course, prevailed to some extent and the revelation of the mother-daughter relationship was brought forward to the close of Act Two. This served to heighten Mrs Erlynne's decision, after feeling suddenly the full pain of maternal love when she twice was called upon to save her daughter's reputation, to renounce that

love for good without ever revealing her actual identity to
Lady Windermere. Psychologically this would be a less notable
development of the character, were the precise relationship
between the women not known by the audience till the actual
moment of renunciation, which was Wilde's original plan. Too
much would happen in too short a period of playing-time for
the audience to give it all due weight of attention; and the
momentousness of the final decision, which deliberately
frustrates audience-expectation of a conventional scene of
reunion between long-lost mother and daughter, would be
robbed of much of its dramatic impact.

When Mrs Erlynne enters the final scene, her mind is
already virtually set on departure; scrupulously she tests Lord
and Lady Windermere in turn and sees that she has rightly
judged that, to save their marriage, she must make a further
renunciation. Wilde stresses in his letter to Alexander that,
having seated the actress playing Mrs Erlynne on the sofa, she
must remain there till her exit; she may rise and seat herself
again when the text permits this, but must on no account 'walk
about, or cross, or the like', since that would be 'melodramatic,
but not dramatic or artistic'.[12] While Windermere paces
anxiously to and fro, dreading what Mrs Erlynne's every word
might reveal, and Lady Windermere darts off-stage and back
in quest of a photograph of herself and her child, Mrs Erlynne
remains a still presence, perfectly composed, at the centre of all
the movement. For husband and wife she plays different roles
in turn; for each she acts the woman each supposes her to be —
for him, the heartless, immoral adventuress; for her, the kind,
emotional and sentimental friend — that way she keeps them
both contented. If there is any cost to her in what she does, she
keeps it securely hidden, a mystery that the audience, however
sensitive, can only guess at. She, whom the Windermeres
expected for different reasons to be utterly distraught (and an
audience too that was trained by precedent to look for a
conventionally impassioned conclusion to the story of a mother
with a past) is completely self-possessed. The inner power of
the woman is what enables her rightly to hold the centre of the
stage.

I began by quoting Ellen Terry's observation on Henry
Irving, how 'he forced [audiences], almost against their will

and nature, out of dislike into admiration' and how 'they had
to come up to him, for never would he go down to them'. The
same might be written of Mrs Erlynne to explain how Wilde
justifies his final description of her in the play as 'a good
woman'. After the discussions about her in Act One, the
audience are led to suppose they may read her particular
character according to known type, but by a consistently
inventive and original use of stage space which continually
invests the actress playing her with different manifestations of
power, Wilde demands that they revise their judgement. In Mrs
Erlynne he creates a woman who by virtue of being an outsider
has developed a shrewd but prodigious intelligence, having
the measure of all the other characters in the drama whom she
can consequently handle with great expertise. She is powerful
because she is a consummate actress, who only once risks
revealing an aspect of her true self when she pleads with Lady
Windermere not to follow her example. Acting is to her an
intellectual stimulus and a resource in preference for the shame
that the social world of the play (and of the auditorium)
might expect to be her burden. It was essential to Wilde's
strategies with the character that Alexander follow to the
letter his prescriptions for the placing and movement of the
actors about the stage: only then would the play in performance
bring the audience to new and subtle levels of moral sensitivity.

Space does not allow me to discuss in such detail the
handling of the outsider figures in Wilde's remaining plays, but
he continued to develop the technique evolved in *Salome* and
Lady Windermere's Fan. Mrs Arbuthnot in *A Woman of No
Importance* is visibly isolated in her black dress within the
warmly glowing colours of Lady Hunstanton's evening party
and her hovering on the edges of the action except when
deliberately summoned to speak with others suggests a
conscious sense of 'otherness' that sets her always apart. Once
the nature of her relationship with Lord Illingworth is
revealed, one sees in the marked contrast between her unease
and his buoyant placing of himself at the centre of the social
group a graphic illustration of the double standards that obtain
in this world. But the situation changes in the final act which
is set in Mrs Arbuthnot's home where Illingworth noticeably
intrudes by overriding her instructions to her maid, Alice, not to

admit him. He confidently forces his presence on that space and assumes on the basis of his title and his newly discovered paternity the right to *place* everyone within the space to his liking. Gerald's suggestion that his parents marry would, if followed through, give Illingworth that right absolutely; Mrs Arbuthnot's refusal on the grounds of morality is a bid to maintain her integrity and her independence to move within the space she has created as home as she chooses. Frustrated, Illingworth tries to place her psychologically by labelling her a whore, but she prevents the word being uttered by striking him in the face with his glove. The traditional, ritual gesture signifying a challenge is one to which he cannot reply: he is both silenced and dismissed from the space. The suave, poised aristocrat has been shown his inherent vulgarity which denies him a place in a home where conscience has developed in the owner a refined moral scruple. His trivial moral standards eventually deny him any authority. The deployment of actors within the stage space in *A Woman of No Importance* encourages an audience to view the hypocrisies within a system of double standards in respect of sex and gender from a sophisticated moral perspective. The visual dynamics of the play in performance focus an audience's attention on the power relations between the central characters such that the final reversals leave spectators questioning the grounds which determine why anyone may be classed as an outsider. What exactly constitutes 'importance'?

An Ideal Husband offers us two outsider figures: there is Mrs Cheveley, an adventuress, in whom power resides because she knows the secret of Chiltern's past and there is Sir Robert himself, the apparently model and moral husband and politician, who, as she claims, is the equal of herself by virtue of his past but who holds a secure place in the forefront of society, as long as that past is not publicly known. The hold Mrs Cheveley has over Chiltern allows her to insinuate her presence into his home and even tyrannise over his wife and she clearly enjoys displaying her power; notably she does not attempt to take over the space so much as render its possessors disturbed about their right to its possession. The whole play is concerned with ploys to expel Mrs Cheveley from the stage, to restore to Sir Robert right of ownership and its related authority: the stage space becomes, as the plot develops, a correlative for Chiltern's reputation. Having succeeded through Goring's aid in subverting Mrs Cheveley's power, Chiltern finds he may still have to vacate the space as a show of respect for his wife and proof of his repentance. Her continuing love may require that he become socially an outsider in circumstances that might to the public seem even more strangely compromising than an outright exposure. Throughout the play Chiltern writhes under a woman's power, the second — his wife's — is infinitely subtler and more pervasive than Mrs Cheveley's bargaining and blackmail. Even at the end Sir Robert is unsure whether he has a right to join the family luncheon-party until his wife kisses him and warmly encourages him to join them; his security will never again be absolute, but will always rest on her continuing generosity. She talks of a 'new life [that] is beginning',[13] but it is one in which power will in future be shared between them, which is no easy prospect for a man as power-hungry as Chiltern.

In *The Importance of Being Earnest* we never see Lady Bracknell in a space that might be described as her own, not that that prevents her from endeavouring majestically to commandeer any room she enters and impose on it her sense of order and value. It may seem odd to call Lady Bracknell an outsider; but, as she insists on projecting a persona of high earnestness and social propriety, she is decidedly at odds with antinomian tenor of Algie's flat where she intrudes on a discussion concerning the delights of bunburying and again with the morning room at Woolton where she disrupts two pairs of lovers embracing passionately. If she seems bizarrely out of place on both occasions, it is because she seems the one person not leading a double life or consciously playing a role. Taking the central position within each of these scenes and riding down opposition with her stentorian tones, she insists that she is the best judge of what is acceptable behaviour and that the young model themselves on her rigorous self-discipline. Yet she noticeably lacks that fine *sprezzatura*, that nonchalance that is the mark of the true aristocratic temper; her tone invariably suggests a deep-rooted anxiety about the appearances that she is trying so firmly to keep up. By a masterstroke of constructional tact Wilde withholds the vital piece of information that explains her nature, on which the actress must build her conception of the role, until nearly the end of the play. Why does she rudely talk down others, abuse the niceties of grammar and polite etiquette by refering continually to her husband and herself as 'I and Lord Bracknell', and appraise people entirely in terms of their material assets? Defending her view of Algernon as a decidedly eligible contender for the hand of a ward as prosperously endowed as Cecily Cardew, she suddenly admits:

> I do not approve of mercenary marriages. When I married Lord Bracknell I had no fortune of any kind. But I never dreamed for a moment of allowing that to stand in my way.[14]

She is not an aristocrat to the manner born; but, perpetually haunted by the prospect of being considered an upstart bourgeois, she projects an image of what she considers the ideal aristocrat to be. She too is a role-player, which is why she is afraid of any place that appears to encourage a lax atmosphere, lest inadvertently, as here, her mask should slip. (Maggie Smith is currently structuring her whole performance to lead to this moment of revelation. Surprisingly the director has not encouraged the rest of the cast to react to her words in any way: they leave merely a conventional pause for the expected burst of laughter, so do not support the social implications of Dame Maggie's reading to make it properly *telling*.) It is noticeable that for the rest of this scene, Lady Bracknell's tone is no longer domineering, except when interrogating Miss Prism, a member of the servant class, who anyway did not hear her account of her past. Once Lady Bracknell is shown on her own admission to be leading as complex a life of subterfuge as everyone else on stage, then she is no longer the outsider and is accepted more comfortably into the prevailing tone of the scene. Her need to assert her power loses its purpose and she can even accept correction from Jack that to embrace a lover in public is not a displaying of signs of triviality but a vital expression of earnestness. The feared Gorgon of Act One has been tamed. The tableau at the curtain-line of *The Importance of Being Earnest* is the one conclusion to a play by Wilde where all possible tensions that are a

50 *Rediscovering Oscar Wilde*

consequence of intricate power-relations between the characters within the stage-space are allayed. In no other play by Wilde has the outsider been so readily assimilated by the social group on stage, thereby bringing the drama to what is in every sense the *perfect* ending.

NOTES

1   Oscar Wilde, 'The Soul of Man Under Socialism', *The Fortnightly Review*, Vol. 55, February 1891, p. 311.
2   E. Craig and C. St John, *Ellen Terry's Memoirs*, (London, 1933), p. 173. Terry also recalls Irving confessing to her: 'I was thinking [...] how strange it is that I should have made the reputation I have as an actor, with nothing to help me — with no equipment. My legs, my voice — everything has been against me. For an actor who can't walk, can't talk, and has no face to speak of, I've done pretty well' (Ibid., p. 82).
3   See Wilde's letter of March 1882 to Mrs George Lewis in *The Letters of Oscar Wilde*, edited by R. Hart-Davis (London, 1962), p. 105.
4   The groundplan for *Lady Windermere's Fan* is reproduced in *More Letters of Oscar Wilde*, edited by R. Hart-Davis (London, 1985), p. 110, where it forms part of a long letter to George Alexander dated February 1892 during rehearsals for the first production of the play. The sketch of the stage design for *Salome* is to be found in the collection of the Witt Library of the Courtauld Institute in the University of London. The original is now lost but it was photographed by Gordon Bottomley and the positive painted over with watercolour by Bottomley's wife to match the sketch; a number of such photographs of Ricketts' early work were subsequently given to Sturge Moore, which is how they found their way into the University of London Library along with the rest of the Sturge Moore bequest. The design is reproduced in *Charles Ricketts' Stage Designs* by Richard Allen Cave (Theatre in Focus Series, Cambridge, 1987), and to accompany is article, 'Stage Design as a Form of Dramatic Criticism' in *Irish Literature and Culture*, edited by Michael Kenneally (Gerrards Cross, 1992), where it is reproduced opposite p. 86.
5   K. Worth, *Oscar Wilde*, Macmillan Modern Dramatists, London and Basingstoke, 1983, p. 91.
6   C. Ricketts, 'The Art of Stage Decoration', *Pages On Art*, London, 1913, pp. 243-4.
7   *More Letters of Oscar Wilde*, p. 110.
8   Oscar Wilde, *Lady Windermere's Fan*, edited by I. Small, The New Mermaids, London and Tonbridge, 1980, p. 32.
9   Ibid., p. 57.
10   *More Letters of Oscar Wilde*, pp. 110-111.
11   *The Letters of Oscar Wilde*, p. 308.
12   *More Letters of Oscar Wilde*, p. 111.

13   Oscar Wilde, *Two Society Comedies*, edited by I. Small and R. Jackson, New Mermaids, Tonbridge and New York, 1983, p. 270.

14   Oscar Wilde, *The Importance of Being Earnest*, edited by R. Jackson, New Mermaids, London & New York, p. 91.

THE NEGLECTED YEARS: WILDE IN DUBLIN

Davis Coakley

Oscar Wilde grew up in a unique medical and cultural milieu which was centred on Merrion Square in Dublin. The middle of the last century was a time when Dublin possessed a leading international school of medicine largely due to the efforts of a remarkable group of physicians and surgeons. Several of these men lived near each other in Merrion Square and they were renowned not only for their medical achievements but also for their interest in art and literature. They attracted the leaders of the cultural life of Dublin to their tables and at these dinners 'wit and anecdote circulated with the port'. 'What biographer' asked Oliver St John Gogarty 'has realised the influence of such an atmosphere on the development of Oscar Wilde.'

Oscar's father, William Wilde, was one of the most brilliant and diversified members of the Irish School of Medicine. In 1851 Wilde married Jane Francesca Elgee, a woman who had already won the hearts of the Irish people because of her involvement with the revolutionaries of 1848. She was cheered by the citizens whenever her carriage was recognised on the streets of Dublin. Before his marriage to Speranza, Wilde bought 21 Westland Row. This was a medium sized Georgian residence which, although it was situated on a busy street, had the advantage of overlooking the park of Trinity College. Number 21 now belongs to the university and it is intended to refurbish some of the rooms as a Wilde museum.

Oscar was born on 16th October, 1854 at 21 Westland Row and he was baptised at the neighbouring St Mark's Church. At Westland Row, the Wildes began to attract the leaders of the scientific, literary and artistic world to their home. These included the poet Samuel Ferguson, the sculptor John Hogan and the brilliant mathematician William Rowan

Hamilton. Speranza was also improving her relationship with
the establishment at Dublin Castle following her erstwhile
revolutionary activity. However, the Wildes needed a better
address if they were to make a significant impact on society.

Most of the leading doctors of the city lived a short
distance away on Merrion Square, the most imposing Georgian
Square in Dublin. In 1762, Lord Fitzwilliam of Merrion had
asked the architect, John Ensor, to design a square which would
be bounded on the west by the lawns of Leinster House, the
mansion of the Duke of Leinster. It was anticipated that these
fine houses with their elegant interiors would serve as town
houses for the country's aristocracy. However the Act of Union
between Great Britain and Ireland in 1801 reduced the demand
dramatically as the aristocracy began to gravitate to London.
The leaders of the liberal professions of law and medicine
filled the resultant social hiatus, and they moved into the
houses of the aristocracy on Merrion Square. In 1855 William
Wilde moved into No. 1 Merrion Square. It was a big house and
there was a staff of six servants to help run it. The children
had a German governess and a French bonne. The interest of the
Wildes in classical Greece and Rome was manifested by the
number of casts depicting subjects from antiquity on the walls of
the rooms. Speranza was an enthusiastic supporter of the
neoclassical revival which stimulated interest in the classical
world of Greece and Rome. Her own Greek learning is apparent
in her poetry.

William Wilde and Speranza read to their children at
bedtime. Speranza read the poetry of the Young Ireland poets
and Oscar said years later that he was trained by his mother
'to love and reverence them as a Catholic child is the saints of
the calendar'. Many years later when Oscar Wilde wished to
express his pain and anguish he reverted to the ballad form of
the Young Ireland era in *The Ballad of Reading Gaol*. The
metre which he adopted was used by the poet Denis Florence
MacCarthy to express Ireland's distress under English rule in a
short poem entitled *New Year's Song* which was written in 1844
and published in *The Nation*:

> There's not a man of all our land
> Our country now can spare,

> The strong man with his sinewy hand,
> The weak man with his prayer!
> No whining tone of mere regret,
> Young Irish bards, for you;
> But let your songs teach Ireland yet
> What Irishmen should do!
> [...]
> And wheresoe'er that duty lead,
> There, there your post should be;
> The coward slave is never freed,
> The brave alone are free!

When these lines are compared with the lines of one of the best known stanzas of *The Ballad of Reading Gaol*, the link between the two poems becomes apparent.

> And all men kill the thing they love,
> By all let this be heard,
> Some do it with a bitter look,
> Some with a flattering word,
> The coward does it with a kiss,
> The brave man with a sword.

A New Year's Song was included in the edition of *The Spirit of the Nation* which was published in 1845. This book had a major influence on Speranza and she would have used it when reading to her children.

Fifteen years after the Union between Great Britain and Ireland, the Duke of Leinster sold Leinster House to the Dublin (later Royal) Society and a large lecture theatre was built on the south side of the house. Leinster House was developed into the cultural nucleus of the city, and when Oscar was ten years old the National Gallery was opened on its grounds. The Gallery's collection was small during the early years but nevertheless some very fine paintings were acquired. Many of the themes of these paintings were biblical, and I think it was worth noting, in view of Oscar's subsequent interest in Salome, that two of the paintings which the gallery bought depicted St John the Baptist in the Wilderness and a third depicted the beheading of the saint. The Beheading of John the Baptist was acquired in 1864.

The physician William Stokes lived at No 5 Merrion Square, and his family made a major contribution to the Celtic revival. His son Whitley became a leading Celtic scholar, and his daughter Margaret wrote extensively on Irish archaeology. She was also a book illustrator, and it may have been in 5 Merrion Square that Oscar Wilde developed his love for beautiful books. William Stokes and William Wilde were lifelong friends, and they shared many interests.

The Library of Trinity College Dublin has in its possession a play entitled *The Sisters-in-Law* by J. H. Jellett, a Provost of the University. It is a comedy which is based on the intellectual eccentricities of the Stokes family. Stokes and many of his friends were members of a Shakespearean Society which was founded by the Reverend Robert Perceval Graves, grandfather of the poet Robert Graves. The society met in the houses of the members, and on these occasions excerpts from the plays were performed. We can see from all this that acting and writing plays formed an integral part of the social scene in Merrion Square.

John Pentland Mahaffy, Oscar Wilde's mentor at Trinity, was greatly influenced by William Stokes. The young Mahaffy was fascinated by Stokes' conversational powers. Stokes, according to Mahaffy, never sat at the head of the table during dinner, and he never carved any dish but he devoted himself wholly to conversation, supported by a very brilliant and witty family circle.

Mahaffy became one of the greatest and wittiest conversationalists of the last century, and his company was sought by the aristocracy of Europe. He wrote a book in 1887 entitled *The Principles of the Art of Conversation*. Even though written many years after Mahaffy's conversations with Stokes, the influence of the latter can still be seen in the work. For example, we find the following on page 78 of *The Principles of the Art of Conversation*:

> I have heard a witty talker pronounce it the golden rule of conversation *to know nothing accurately*. Far more important is it, in my mind, to demand no accuracy. There is no greater or more common blunder in society than to express disbelief or scepticism in a story told for the amusement of the company.

I have been able to establish that the witty talker whom Mahaffy quoted was William Stokes because in an obituary

sketch of Stokes which Mahaffy published in MacMillan's
magazine, he recalled the following:

> I remember sitting beside him at dinner, when a scientific man of
> this kind was boring us with his talk. He turned to me, and said
> with emphasis: 'There is one golden rule of conversation —
> *know nothing accurately.*'

Thus Stokes' sensible advice on conversation was elaborated by
Mahaffy in his book. It is fascinating to see how Oscar Wilde
in his essay 'The Decay of Lying' developed the theme with
even more enthusiasm in a parody of Mahaffy's work.

> Many a young man starts in life with a natural gift for
> exaggeration which, if nurtured in congenial and sympathetic
> surroundings, or by the imitation of the best models, might grow
> into something really great and wonderful. But, as a rule, he
> comes to nothing. He [...] falls into careless habits of accuracy,
> [...] begins to verify all statements made in his presence, [and]
> has no hesitation in contradicting people who are much younger
> than himself.

Mahaffy knew Oscar Wilde from childhood as he was a
frequent visitor to No 1, Merrion Square. At 1 Merrion Square,
the Wildes were in a much better position to entertain, and
they soon became celebrated for the number of dinner parties
which they gave, and the remarkable people who attended
them. Visiting celebrities from abroad made their way to the
house. Oscar and his brother were allowed to meet the
distinguished guests, and to sit quietly listening to the
conversation. At these receptions, Speranza developed her
conversational skills. 'Never be malicious, it is so vulgar', she
observed, 'epigram is always better than argument in
conversation, and paradox is the very essence of social wit and
brilliancy. The unexpected, the daring subversion of some
ancient platitude, are all keen social weapons.' They were
weapons which her son would learn to use with great skill.

The residents of Merrion Square had a key to the
private gardens that formed the centre of the square. This was
a beautiful park where the young Wildes could play, well
protected from the poor children of the lower classes, and the
harsh realities of post-famine Dublin. It was a wonderful place
for children, yet not far from this magnificent square, there

were some of the poorest slums in Europe. Oscar could empathise with the thoughts of the statue of his Happy Prince, and I quote:

> Round the garden ran a very lofty wall, but I never cared to ask what lay beyond it, everything about me was so beautiful. My courtiers called me the Happy Prince, and happy indeed I was, if pleasure be happiness. So I lived, and so I died. And now that I am dead they have set me up here so high that I can see all the ugliness and all the misery of my city, and though my heart is made of lead yet I cannot choose but weep.

It is interesting that the theme of one of his other very fine children's stories 'The Selfish Giant' centres around a beautiful garden from which the village children are excluded.

The Wilde children spent a number of summers at Glencree in the Wicklow mountains in a farmhouse near the newly opened Glencree reformatory for Catholic boys. The chaplin of the institute, the Reverend Prideaux Fox became friendly with Speranza, and she attended mass at the reformatory with her children. Forty years later, Father Fox who was a man of great personal integrity wrote about these encounters with Speranza.

> I enjoyed many a pleasant hour with this excellent Lady [...] it was not long before she asked me to instruct two of her children, one of them being that future erratic genius, Oscar Wilde. After a few weeks I baptised these two children, Lady Wilde herself being present on the occasion.

The baptisms did not change the childrens' religious practice but years later Oscar would remark to friends that he had a recollection of having been baptised a Catholic as a child. He used the theme of a second baptism to great effect in *The Importance of Being Earnest*.

When Oscar was ten years old, his father built a villa overlooking Lough Corrib in County Mayo. He called it Moytura, and it was situated on an estate of 170 acres which Sir William Wilde had acquired when the property of his mother's family, the Fynnes, was sold. It was an area rich in archaeological treasures, and William Wilde recorded his researches around Cong in his book *Lough Corrib and Lough Mask*. From an early age, his children accompanied their

father on his archaeological expeditions, and they mixed with
the local people. In his book William Wilde described his
discovery of a curious structure, an unmortared building with
two crypts on the west face, when he was on an expedition with
'his son Oscar' in 1866. During his holidays in the West of
Ireland Oscar became familiar with the stories and
superstitions of the area, and these would influence both his
life and writing in later years. William Wilde told Oscar a
story which he had heard when he was young about an
absentee English landlord:

> My father used to have a story about an English landlord who
> wrote from the Carlton to his Irish agent, and said: 'Don't let
> the tenants imagine that by shooting you, they will at all
> intimidate me.'

Oscar would later use this story in his lecture *Impressions of
America* which he first gave in London in 1883.

Oscar and his brother William were sent to Portora
Royal School to prepare for University. In a number of
biographies of Wilde, it is suggested that the ethos at Portora
was very illiberal. This was not the case and the headmaster
of the school, the Reverend William Steele, was remarkably
liberal for his time. His first act as headmaster was to open the
school to the sons of Catholic parents. He was disappointed
that so few came but some did, and one of them became a
professor at St Macartan's Seminary in Monaghan. In my view
the influence which Portora had on shaping Oscar Wilde has
been underestimated. Louis Claude Purser, a classmate of Oscar,
who subsequently became Professor of Latin at Trinity College
Dublin said that at Portora there was —

> a far greater width of culture and diffusion of ideas than in any
> other school with which I have been acquainted; it was in that
> respect more like a college of a university than a middle-class
> school.

On 10th October, 1871, just six days from his
seventeenth birthday, Oscar matriculated at Trinity College.
Trinity with its great reputation for Classical Studies was an
ideal environment for him. The classical school of the
university was very famous at the time with teachers such as

John Pentland Mahaffy, Arthur Palmer, and Robert Yelverton
Tyrell.

Mahaffy and Tyrell influenced and inspired Wilde
greatly, and he would write later, 'I got my love of the Greek
ideal and my knowledge of the language at Trinity from
Mahaffy and Tyrell.' Mahaffy was famous for his wit and
conversational ability, and according to his friend the Oxford
scholar A. H. Sayce

> No one enjoyed more than he did visiting the country houses of
> Great Britain, where he found ancient traditions, good manners,
> interesting personages, excellent cuisine and, not unfrequently,
> splendid libraries.

In 1874, Wilde helped Mahaffy with his book *Social
Life in Greece*, and three years later both men travelled
together to explore the antiquities of Greece. Mahaffy was also
a gifted sportsman as well as being a brilliant intellectual. He
was not, however, unaware of his talents, and he once
remarked:

> Take me all round. I am the best man in Trinity College.

As an undergraduate, Wilde did not disappoint his
tutors or his parents, and he crowned his academic career at
Trinity by winning the Blue Ribbon of Classical Scholarship,
the Berkeley Gold Medal. During these undergraduate years at
Trinity, Wilde also began to develop his interest in aesthetics
which at that time had a powerful advocate in John Ruskin.
Ruskin was a lifelong friend of Henry Acland, Regius Professor
of Medicine, in Oxford. Acland was a very cultured man, and a
friend of both William Wilde and William Stokes. He wrote a
biography of William Stokes. When Oscar entered Trinity, the
university had a course on aesthetics, and the architecture of
one of the buildings was inspired by John Ruskin's teaching.
This was the museum building which was built in 1854, the
year of Oscar's birth. It was designed by the Irish architect
Benjamin Woodward, who was a friend and admirer of Ruskin.
Ruskin visited the college to see the building in 1861, and he
described it as:

quite the noblest thing ever done from my teaching.

In 1874, Oscar left Trinity for Oxford. Oscar was a mature student with three years of university behind him when he arrived at Oxford. He had been educated by some of the best classical scholars of the period, and John Pentland Mahaffy, master of the art of conversation, had taken a special interest in him. In his book *Son of Oscar Wilde*, Vyvyan Holland emphasised the influence which Mahaffy had on his father's development:

> It has frequently been said that Ruskin moulded my father's character at Oxford, but it would be more accurate to say that Ruskin watered the seeds that had been sown by Mahaffy.

INTELLECTUAL WORDPLAY
IN WILDE'S CHARACTERIZATION
OF HENRY WOTTON

Jean M. Ellis D'Alessandro

There are several instances in *The Picture of Dorian Gray*[1] that resemble the points debated by Herbert Francis Bradley,[2] and I want to look firstly at some of these so as to show Wilde's employment of them in Wotton's characterization, and, then, in order to better define the figure of the protagonist as a dialectician, as he works to persuade Dorian, at Wilde's use of rhetoric, that instrument of deceit,[3] in Wotton's conversation. It should be understood, however, that Wilde is not so interested in the context of the theories he uses, as in giving Wotton's discourse and reflections a philosophical and intellectual veneer, and this study is, therefore, not aimed at the context of the philosophical theories implicated, but at their employment.[4]

    The story is closely involved with the question of appearance and reality, a problem examined at length by Bradley, and brought into focus by Lord Henry himself. Wotton, in fact, responds to Hallward's bewildered question, commenting that Dorian's change has nothing to do with him, that Dorian is simply showing himself as he really is ('It is the real Dorian Gray — that is all', p. 92), and in so doing he introduces the concept of appearance and reality, as he does later when asking rhetorically, 'before which Dorian? The one who is pouring out tea for us, or the one in the picture?' (p. 94). This concept is then fully centred when Hallward says, 'I shall stay with the real Dorian, [...] at least you are like it in appearance' (p. 94). As a matter of fact, Dorian is stunned by Lord Henry's conversation and his elaboration of ideas, and he is estranged from his environment as he stands in front of the finished portrait. The feeling is so appalling that it causes a sense of sickness and desperation in him, and the change that this brings about modifies his outlook on life. His reaction, showing a 'self' susceptible to change and to feelings of self-estrangement, classifies this as 'self' as appearance, if Bradley's theory is taken into consideration (Bradley, *op. cit.*, p. 80). As Bradley explains, it is difficult to fix limits to man's mutability, but there is a point where man is no longer the same person, and he queries with regard:

> This creature lost in illusions, bereft of memory, transformed in mood, with diseased feelings enthroned in the very heart of his being — is this still one self with what we knew? (*op. cit.*, p. 81)

He continues, 'a thing may look identical or different, accordingly as you look at it. Hence in personal identity the main point is to fix the meaning of a person' (Bradley, *op. cit.*, p. 81). Both Hallward and Wotton do this; each in his own way tries to establish Dorian's personal identity.

The concept of appearance and reality concerns Lord Henry Wotton's characterisation, too. There is the self as appearance, a mere pose that Basil Hallward is aware of, and dislikes, and this regards the metaphysician, the Wotton who is superficially facetious, ironic, and full of witticisms, and who is always changing (p. 80). Then, there is the self as reality that comes to the fore when talking of his wife who has fled with another, and this concerns the Wotton man of habits:

> The house is rather lonely without her. Of course, married life is merely a habit, a bad habit. But then one regrets the loss even of one's worst habits. Perhaps one regrets them the most. They are such an essential part of one's personality. (p. 244)

Bradley, when speaking of the 'self' as reality, comments with regard to the man of habits:

> This is the self of the individual. The self will contain his environment, now only the usual or average; his habits and the laws of his character — as he usually behaves and to which he behaves. Hence, it is his habitual disposition and contents, and not his hour to hour changes. (*op. cit.*, pp. 77-8)

For both Lord Henry and Bradley, ideas belong to the reign of appearance, and as Wotton tells Hallward they offer no clue to the sincerity of the person expressing them (p. 78). In fact, Lord Henry's ideas as expounded to Dorian are purely intellectual cogitations, aired for the sake of experiment, and not with regard to sincerity, after all 'it was no matter how it ended, or was destined to end' (p. 118). As Basil Hallward remarks, Lord Henry is indifferent to everyone (p. 77). He is not interested in other people's ideas but in their emotions: 'how delightful other people's emotions were! — much more delightful than their ideas, it seemed to him' (p. 81).[5] All is simply a game, a game to experiment with the power of words to bring to the surface passions that, through mental speculation, could be a source of delight for him, and Dorian, with his hidden passions and inexperience, is the perfect subject, a *tabula rasa*, for his analysis. He is not in any way concerned to prove the rightness or wrongness of philosophical doctrines.

A further *trait-d'union* between Wotton and Bradley can be seen when Bradley, talking of subjective sensation, 'under which we may include dream and delusion of all kinds', notes that the facts —

> go to show that, as we can have the sensation without the object, and the object without the sensation, the one cannot possibly be a quality of the other. The secondary qualities, therefore, are appearance, coming from the reality, which itself has no quality but extension. (*op. cit.*, p. 13)

Wotton enjoys sensations and as he sits 'dreaming on these things' (p. 119), he reflects —

> that as one watched life in its curious crucible of pain and pleasure, one could not [...] keep the sulphurous fumes from troubling the brain, and making the imagination turbid with monstrous fancies and misshapen dreams. (p. 117)

Or, further, when talking to Dorian, Lord Henry tells him that their lives depend on memories:

> a chance tone of colour in a room [...], a line from a forgotten poem [...], a cadence from a piece of music [...] — I tell you,

Dorian, that it is on these things that our lives depend. [...] our
own senses will imagine them for us. (p. 248)

When Lord Henry opens his discourse with Dorian, he
is led into it by Dorian's question on influence, and, after
settling Dorian with an enigmatic answer, he broaches the
subject of self-development[6] — to realize one's nature perfectly
— that is what each one of us is here for. People are afraid of
themselves, nowadays. They have forgotten the highest of all
duties, the duty that one owes to oneself (p. 84).

His line of thought is close to Bradley's, although the
contexts are far different. Bradley writes, in fact:

> The man whose nature is such that by one path alone his chief
> desire will reach consummation, will try to find it on that path,
> whatever it may be, and whatever the world thinks of it; and, if
> he does not, he is contemptible. Self-sacrifice is too often the
> 'great sacrifice' of the trade, the giving cheap what is worth
> nothing. To know what one wants, and to scruple at no means
> that will get it, may be harder than self-surrender. (*op. cit.*, p. 6)

Wotton develops the question by attacking traditional beliefs,
and presents belief in society and religion as fanaticism
producing terror (p. 84), as against the joy coming from self-
development. Fanaticism forces people to forget that their
highest duty is to themselves, and it governs their choices.
Wotton points out that 'the mutilation of the savage has its
tragic survival in the self-denial that mars our lives' (p. 85),
where 'mutilation' reflects obliquely Bradley's use of the word
and Wotton's attitude towards society and religion finds
support in Bradley's theorising:

> Our orthodox theology on the one side, and our common-place
> materialism on the other side [...] vanish like ghosts before the
> daylight of free sceptical enquiry. I do not mean, of course, to
> condemn wholly either of these beliefs; but I am sure that either,
> when taken seriously, is the mutilation of our nature. Neither,
> as experience has amply shown, can now survive in the mind
> which has thought sincerely on first principles; and it seems
> desirable that there should be such a refuge for the man who
> burns to think consistently, and yet is too good to become a
> slave, either to stupid fanaticism or dishonest sophistry. (*op.
> cit.*, p. 5)

At the same time, Dorian's own words attest Wotton's success, for he reflects as he looks at the picture, 'the life that was to make his soul would mar his body' (p. 91), where 'mar' is echoed from Wotton's discourse. Dorian thus acknowledges implicitly that he accepts Lord Henry's view that were he to follow a life of social morality and religious thought, and thereby save his soul, this very kind of life would mar his body through the suppression of his desires.

He, Wotton, metaphysician, one of the elect, who poses everything as a question of intellect, has found someone to whom he can reveal the mysteries of life, and, at the same time, he can experience the results of its effects. He is already half-satisfied, for:

> He was conscious [...] that it was through certain words of his, musical words said with musical utterance that Dorian Gray's soul had turned to this white girl and bowed in worship before her. (p. 117)[7]

Music is consistently associated with Dorian and his friends, and 'music' is one of the first words to evince Wotton's growing influence over Dorian. When Lord Henry tells Dorian that 'all influence is immoral [...] from a scientific point of view' (p. 84), he enlarges on the subject pointing out that a person who is influenced becomes 'an echo of some one else's music' (p. 83), and as he talks, Dorian is aware that his words seem to acquire a will of their own and a wilfulness that acts on the senses. He notes that 'music had stirred him like that' (p. 85), 'but music was not articulate' (p. 85), and the word continues to reverberate, captivatingly, in his mind as he stands in the garden of Basil's studio. Wotton's reference to his own 'musical words' having 'musical utterance' finds a correspondence in Dorian's thoughts as he reflects, bewildered, on Lord Henry's conversation, for, much in line with what Wotton wants, he realizes, that it is words, not art, not music, that have creative power, and that it is, in particular, those words that 'seemed [...] to have a music in their own':

> Words! Mere words! How terrible they were! How clear, and vivid, and cruel! One could not escape them. And yet what a subtle magic there was in them! They seemed to be able to give a

plastic form to formless things, and to have a music of their own
[...] Mere words! Was there anything so real as words? (p. 85)

By the time he finishes talking, Wotton has chipped
away all that has upheld Dorian's views on life up to that
moment. However, since his words are directed towards
eliciting response, he cannot afford to stop here. He has moved
from the bondage of influence to the freedom of self-
development, and this must be further advanced before he can
move on to the question of youth and beauty where he will put
his knowledge of rhetoric to the test.

As his first long discourse with Dorian draws to its
conclusion, Wotton makes greater use of rhetorical figures, and
in so doing he takes his leave of Bradley, materialism and
religion, to delve for a moment into his philosophy of life. He
opens his discourse with the *propositio*, setting out the topic of
his conversation, and developing his idea of the benefits of
living life to the full. He states what he considers the best for
mankind; however, as he develops his argument, Wotton
detracts something from each clause with respect to the
previous, and the eclipsis (*detractio*) tightens and intensifies
the woof of the sentence:

> I believe that if man were to live out his life fully and
> completely, were to give form to every feeling, expression to
> every thought, reality to every dream — I believe that the world
> gain [...]. (p. 85)

The anaphora ('I believe that [...] I believe that') unites the
two parts of the sentence, and leads him to predict the results
(*praesumptio*) if his theory were followed, 'we would forget all
[...] and return to the Hellenic wish — to something finer,
richer, than the Hellenic ideal, it may be' (p. 85), and with the
ploce he underlines what is seemingly his ideal. However, the
comparison 'return [...] to something finer [...] than', gives the
lie to his words that simply imply that he is wanting this, and
offers a false reality through suggestion, a reality that is
further undermined by the dubitative nature of the closing
words, 'it may be', where the 'it' is pleonastic but in a masterly
fashion it enhances his theory giving it an air of
thoughtfulness.

Wotton carefully singles out his terms of expression as he speaks, such as can be seen in 'form to every feeling, expression to every thought, reality to every dream', where the asyndetic structure, which is important when wanting to offer a strong expressive load, is reinforced by the parison, and together they evidence what it means to live to the full. Yet, on analysis of the parison, the first and last words of each phrase set up a dichotomy, for Wotton has made subtle use of a *contrapositum*, where two different things are closely conjoined. In fact, as 'form' becomes 'expression', and this, in turn, becomes 'reality', so 'feeling', moving in a contrary sense, becomes 'thought' and this, in turn, becomes 'dream'. On the one hand, there is a movement towards reality and, on the other, a movement towards dream, or appearance. It is a fine example of *ordo artificialis*, where thoughts and words catch the attention, and between semantic increase and quantitative reduction, a contrary is looked for. The mixture of reality and appearance works together to create an illusion of something concrete and worthwhile, but the emphasis on the tangible is belied by the subtle play on the intangible, and it is no more than the creation of subjective sensation already noticed elsewhere. The hyperbolic nature (*dementiens*) of the phrase that sees dream as reality, colours the expression that lends itself to signifying more than in reality exists. Language is infected and thus appears to be what it is not, and as Bradley says, 'anything the meaning of which is inconsistent and unintelligible is appearance, and not reality' (Bradley, *op. cit.*, p. 75), but Dorian under the hypnotic effect of words perceives them giving plastic form to the chaotic formlessness of his emotions.

Wotton presses his message home still further, using *admonitio* and *ominatio*, asserting that when we refuse to satisfy our desires we are punished. He reveals the dangers and dehorts (*admonitio*) his listener against refusal, 'every impulse that we strive to strangle broods in the mind, and poisons us'; we are potential murderers of ourselves if we resist, and the alliteration in 'strive to strangle' evidences the concept. If we are influenced by nothing but our own impulses we act and make our dreams reality, and after this we have memory, 'the recollection of a pleasure, or the luxury of a regret. The only way to get rid of a temptation is to yield to it' (p. 85). The *ominatio* foretells the probable effects of resisting self-development, 'your soul grows sick with longing, with desire for what monstrous laws have made monstrous and unlawful' (p. 85). The antithesis (*comparatio*), present in his words, shows a comparison of things in themselves contrary, such as the 'luxury of a regret', the idea of yielding to 'temptation', and of desiring what laws 'have made monstrous', and evidences his manipulation of language so as to confound Dorian and keep his attention. Dorian is aware that Lord Henry's words contain 'wilful paradox', but they touch 'some secret chord' (p. 85), and the youth never tries to understand what the paradox concerns. At the same time, the ploce places the stress on 'monstrous', and this together with the polyptoton, linking 'laws' and 'unlawful', evidences the part played by society in the question: society has passed outrageous laws to show desire animalesque and wrong. Wotton, then, simulates an exclamation (*exclamatio*) so as to display greater emotion, for 'it is in the brain, and in the brain only, that the great sins of the world take place' (p. 85), the ploce, once again, evincing where the stress is to fall, all is pure thought, mental speculation, and subjective sensation.

As he talks, Wotton plays on the difference between 'youth' and 'boyhood', qualifying them metaphorically, in 'your rose-red youth' and 'rose-white boyhood', an image that he later takes up, warning Dorian that 'time is jealous of you, and wars against your lilies and roses' (p. 88). It is a further example of joining two contrary things together as though they were similar (*contrapositum*). Through historical association the images become redolent of the wars of the roses ending with the white-rose of York marrying the red-rose of Lancaster and establishing the House of Tudor of great and glorious reign. Hence, through the imagery, Dorian is suggested as being androgynous, uniting the characters of both sexes, red with passion, and white with innocence, and Henry's task is to bring the two parts to a fruitful union through experience. In fact, Wotton is implicitly pointing out that if Dorian manages harmoniously to unite the two parts of his personality, his life too could be a long and glorious one.

Wotton then turns to Dorian describing the youth's inner conflicts, conflicts that Dorian thought known to himself alone, 'passions that have made you afraid, thoughts that have filled you with terror, day-dreams and sleeping dreams whose mere memory might stain your cheek with shame', where isocolon, ploce, and alliteration, have a role in singling out the important elements. Once again, Wotton elaborates a binary line, for, if, on the one hand, he extrapolates the passions that Dorian has known, and internalizes them, turning them away from realization, so that they become thoughts and then dreams, on the other hand, he offers an explanation for this interiorization. It is due to the influence of society and religion, that they produce fear, terror, and shame, on account of their being considered taboo, and here he links abstrusely back to the close of the first part of his discourse, where he pointed out that man is governed by his 'terror' of society and religion. Therefore, Dorian is strangling his impulses, not living them out, he is killing his potential instead of realizing himself, and all this is due to the pressure put on by society. Wotton is a master of language and controls his words carefully, so as to elicit response. He links the chain of his argument subtly, through complicated patterns, and as he does so, he raises his voice implicitly in opposition to that of society.

Some hours later, Wotton continues his act of persuasion and, returning to the main theme, (*reditus ad propositum*), he opens with the topic 'youth' (p. 80). He then, in open contrast, places before Dorian the ugliness of ageing, and he dwells on the point, *commoratio*, so that Dorian is brought to regard it as very important:

> Some day, when you are old and wrinkled and ugly, when thought has seared your forehead with its lines, and passion branded your lips with its hideous fires, you will feel it, you will feel it terribly. Now, wherever you go, you charm the world. Will it always be so? (p. 88)

Having made his point on the ugliness of ageing, Wotton moves to its opposite and introduces the topic of beauty developing his idea till admiration gets the better of him (*admiratio*), 'to me, Beauty is the wonder of wonders' (p. 88). It is something that stupefies, that involves the mind in emotions so intense that it becomes the prince of divine right, sovereign over all, and needs nothing to explain it because it is.

Wotton moves from youth and beauty viewed individually, to youth and beauty seen as being conjoined: 'when your youth goes, your beauty will go with it' (p. 88), and he builds a picture of mortal decay to show what will happen to Dorian with the passing of time. Here he uses the voice of universal experience (*experientia*), and *ominatio* returns to add a warning note, for there will be no triumphs left and memory will make those of the past bitterer than defeats. He dwells on the point once again (*commoratio*), 'you will become sallow, and hollow-cheeked, and dull-eyed. [...] You will suffer horribly' (p. 88), and he allows his voice to die away once more without finishing the sentence. The polysyndeton slows down the pace and allows full emphasis to fall on the words that Wotton wants to evidence, while the anaphora strengthens through repetition the image of horror and anguish awaiting Dorian in the future. Wotton's discourse is mirrored in Dorian's thoughts as he stands before the picture. They offer a clear demonstration that Wotton's wordgame is having the right effect and that Dorian is coming under his influence. The images Dorian uses, in fact, find a correspondence in Wotton's, even the polysyndeton creates the same effect of underlining the physical ruin awaiting him in the future:

> Yes, there would be a day when his face would be wrinkled and wizen, his eyes dim and colourless, the grace of his figure broken and deformed. [...] He would become dreadful, hideous, and uncouth. [...] I shall grow old, and horrible, and dreadful. (p. 91)

Wotton's next move is to place two ways of life before Dorian, and both are presented as a group of imperatives reinforced by the pounding presence of the asyndeton. The pure beauty of Dorian's days of youthful splendour is placed in contrast with those who would want to influence him, make him charitable, generous-natured, and loving, as according to tradition and social convention. Wotton, however, exhorts him (*adhortatio*), to do differently and places the matter in a diverse light by putting it in unusual terms, 'realize your youth [...] don't squander the gold of your days.' He proceeds then to detract from the values of traditional conventions offering a form of criticism, (*extenuatio*), 'listening to the tedious, trying to improve the hopeless failure, or giving away your life to the ignorant, the common, and the vulgar. These are the sickly aims, the false ideals, of our age.' In so doing, Wotton makes it seem as though Dorian's youth is worth all the gold in the world; it is precious and of the purest metal, and by being charitable he would be squandering it, throwing it away, casting his pearls before the swine. These things are 'the sickly aims, the false ideals, of our age', and while the asyndeton gives the sentence something dry and real, the imagery instead with the qualifying negative attributes, 'sickly', and 'false', shows contamination. Wotton has infected conventional morality with a vague unhealthiness that is aimed at demolishing Dorian's reserves, and it calls for response, being counter to what is generally considered valid and worthwhile.

Wotton then stresses, with a further series of imperatives, in an asyndetic construction, what Dorian should do. The epizeuxis (*subjunctio*) and the polyptoton, are on hand to give added vigour to his words:

> Live! Live the wonderful life that is in you! Let nothing be lost upon you. Be always searching for new sensations. Be afraid of nothing. (p. 88)

In this exhortation, the epistrophe unites the two central sentences, while the *exclamatio* allows him to display simulated and artfully designed emotions. Dorian is to realise his life to the full, and Wotton gives him four new commandments to help him do so, before bringing his discourse to its culminating point:

> A new Hedonism — that is what our century wants. You might be its visible symbol. With your personality there is nothing you could not do. The world belongs to you for a season. (p. 88)

In a climactic moment, Dorian is elevated to the position of a new Jesus, not the mystic symbol of an invisible presence, but the visible symbol of a new philosophy. Dorian would be able to do all he wished — for a season. Wotton is aware that all passes

— even a new order, religion, or philosophy, and Bradley also notes:

> Existing philosophies cannot answer the purpose. For whether there is progress or not, at all events there is change; and the changed minds of each generation will require a difference in what has to satisfy their intellect. (*op. cit.*, p. 6)

Wotton then enters his conclusion, for he knew the right psychological moment to calm down and let his words take effect. He, furthermore, softens his speech and with delicacy mentions how flowers return perfect each year, but that youth can never return. Wotton ends his speech with an image of degenerate senility, putting the key features before the eyes of his hearer and illuminating each detail (*commoratio*):

> The pulse of joy that beats in us at twenty, becomes sluggish. Our limbs fail, our senses rot. We degenerate into hideous puppets, haunted by the memory of the passions of which we were too much afraid, and the exquisite temptations that we had not the courage to yield to. (p. 89)

The unifying scheme offered by the merismus (*distributio*), allows Wotton to resume the initial proposition (old age as against youth and beauty), and to examine the parts of his discussion, while alliteration, parison, eclipsis, and asnydeton, offer rhetorical colouring and movement. The epizeuxis adds vehemence to the conclusion, and looks back rhetorically to 'Live! Live the wonderful life that is in you', so much so that the expressions become synonymous one of the other, and the whole conversation is rounded off with an epanalepsis, as Wotton returns to the point from where he had started, 'Youth! Youth! There is absolutely nothing in the world but youth' (p. 89).

Wilde's characterisation of Wotton required the traits of a metaphysician and a dialectician to complete it; for the former, Bradley was on hand and, for the latter, he had his own classical scholarship and skill with words, and Lord Henry takes over the role of the sophist who plays out an intellectual wordgame with Dorian and exploits the concept of appearance to give his discourse an intellectual bias. Under the influence of Lord Henry's wordplay, Dorian's innocence becomes experience, his kindness cruelty, his godliness devilishness. Wotton shows that the power of words to persuade (*ars bene dicendi*) and move the passions is superior to other arts: Hallward's art is ineffective on its own to bring Dorian to self-realization, for words are needed to illustrate its potential; a book, no matter how 'poisonous', cannot influence because all art is sterile, and without Wotton's teaching the written word would have no meaning outside of itself; and music leads simply to a chaos of sensations unless it is associated with words. Wotton, in fact, makes use of all three to gain Dorian for himself, showing that words can create a composition as finely coloured as a picture, as tempting as a book, and as pleasing as a piece of music.[8] They can deceive through appearing to be what they are not, and create a tangible reality that is nothing but the stuff dreams are made of.

Through the power of words to teach, delight, and move, Wotton creates a world of fiction, or of dream, and he creates a protagonist for it, Dorian, but Dorian can live in this world only so long as he obeys the rules, only while he accepts, without questioning it, to play Wotton's game Wotton's way. Dorian proves thus to be yet another of the many monsters that fill literature, the product of a novel Frankenstein, a creature unable to live without his creator. Once he decides to go his own way, Wotton's words lose their hold over him, the spell breaks, and he finds himself in a world of reality. In this world, evil is his custom and he sees himself, finally, as he really is. Dorian cannot accept the horror of reality and tries to draw back into his world of illusion, but he is unable to do so for Wotton has gone, and with him the magic of his intellectual wordplay. The game is over.

NOTES

1   All quotations are from *The Picture of Dorian Gray*, in *Plays Prose Writings and Poems*, Dent, London, 1980.

2   All quotations are from H.F. Bradley, *Appearance andReality, A Metaphysical Essay*, Swan Sonnenschein, London, New York, Macmillan, 1893. Bradley reached Merton College, Oxford, some four years before Oscar Wilde's arrival at Magdalen College. In 1876 Bradley published *Ethical Studies*, followed in 1883 by *The Principles of Logic*, where he denounced the deficient psychology of the Empiricists. *Appearance and Reality*

was Bradley's most ambitious work, and Wilde seems to have had a fair knowledge of his ideas already prior to the publication of the new volume. This is highly probable both on account of Wilde's interest in philosophy, documented from his Oxford days, and because Bradley's ideas were well-known, and had brought him many followers. In the Preface to the volume Bradley states that he wrote the first two-fifths in 1887-8, and it is this part which is of greater interest to this examination of the figure of Henry Wotton, and the remainder over the following three years. They are years when Wilde was trying to become famous, to make money editing *Woman's World*, and busily planning his novel, the first version of which appeared in 1890 in *Lippincott's Magazine*. In associating Wotton with Bradley, I am in no way diminishing the overall importance of Pater whose influence is not under discussion here, not even when theories seem to overlap, as in the case of habit.

3   See 'La scienza della persuasione', by L. R. Santini, in H. Lausberg, *Elementi di Retorica*, Il Mulino, Bologna, 1969, vii-xxix, pp. vii-ix. 'De Retorica' in *The Work of Aristotle*, Vol. II, Encyclopaedia Britannica, London, 1952, pp. 593-675. 'De Oratore' in *Le Opere di Marco Tullio Cicerone*, U.T.E.T., Turin.

4   Cf. J. Culler, *On Deconstruction. Theory and Criticism after Structuralism*, Cornell University Press, Ithaca, New York, 1982. Culler writes, 'to identify a passage or sequence as figurative is to recommend transformation of a literal difficulty [...] into a paraphrase that fits the meaning assumed to govern the message as a whole', p. 243. See also, W. Nash, *Rhetoric. The Wit of Persuasion*, Blackwell, Oxford, 1989; D. Leith and G. Myerson, *The Power of Address. Explorations in Rhetoric*, Routledge, London, 1989.

5   John Stuart Mill, *On Liberty*, 1859. In this, as a point of interest, Wilde has taken his distance from John Stuart Mill's theories. Mill in his essay *On Liberty* asserts that to think about a subject means to consider other views, not merely to develop one's own. Wilde, instead, places Wotton in opposition to this, for Wotton airs and develops only his own views. He recognizes that there are opposing positions but discards them as negative and not worthy of further consideration. However, his refusal to compare his views with those of others could indicate that, as Mill says, he did not know, in any proper sense of the word, the doctrine he professed. It is a further point in favour of the theory that Wotton is promoting appearance, both in himself and in his philosophy. See also, *The Letters of Oscar Wilde*, ed. R. Hart-Davis, London, 1962, p. 237, where Wilde writes to W. L. Courtney, speaking of John Stuart Mill, 'I have gained nothing from him' (1889).

6   N. Kohl, *Oscar Wilde. The Words of a Conformist Rebel*, Cambridge University Press, 1989, first published at Heidelberg in 1980. Kohl comments on the similarity between Wotton's idea of self-development and Bradley's philosophy of self-realization (pp. 158 ff).

7   R. Ellmann, *Oscar Wilde*, Hamish Hamilton, London, 1987,
     p. 289. Ellmann writes that Wilde would himself lounge for
     hours and hours in order to find the right cadence.

8   In 'The School of Giorgione', (*Theories of the Renaissance*,
     1873), Pater states that the arts cannot supply the place of each
     other, but reciprocally lend each other force, and that in music
     is to be found the time measure of perfected art. Ellmann, *op. cit.*,
     p. 289, writes that Wilde attributed the same interest in speech
     to the Greeks, and quotes from him, 'their test was always the
     spoken word in its musical and metrical relations. The voice
     was the medium, and the ear the critic'(*The Function and Value
     of Criticism; With Some Remarks on the Importance of Doing
     Nothing: A Dialogue*).

OSCAR WILDE IN NAPLES

Masolino D'Amico

Early in September 1897 Oscar Wilde left Berneval for Naples where he had decided he would live with Lord Alfred Douglas. The trip was apparently made possible by some money the aesthete had been given by Vincent O'Sullivan, a young Irish-American writer he had befriended in Paris. Recollecting the episode many years later, O'Sullivan wrote, handsomely: 'it is one of the few things I look back on with satisfaction. It is not every day that one has the chance of relieving the anxiety of a genius and a hero.' In Naples Wilde and Alfred Douglas checked into the *Hôtel Royal des Etrangers* in the via Chiatamone (not exactly on the via Partenope, facing the Castello dell'Ovo, as Richard Ellmann has it, but not far; Wilde's latest and best biographer must have had today's Royal Hotel in mind). It was an expensive establishment, and as Douglas relates in his autobiography they ran up a bill for £68 in a fortnight. Still, the manager did not fret — an English Lord had prestige on the Continent in those days — and the account was eventually settled months later, when Douglas left Naples for good. The two friends were still in the hotel on 25 September, 1897, but soon after they moved into a private address in Posillipo, then a fashionable part of the town. The villa they rented is still visible at what is now 37, via Posillipo. At the time it was called Villa del Giudice (or 'Villa Giudice, Posilippo', as Wilde styled it in his correspondence) after the name of its owners. Later and until recently it was called Villa Douglas, and it was inhabited by families of British stock; indeed descendants of the del Giudice family told a reporter of the Neapolitan daily, *Il Mattino* (12 August 1979) — 'in a sultry August afternoon' — that their ancestor had lost the villa to Alfred Douglas during a game of cards played in Sorrento, a five of diamonds being the instrument of Fate. This, however, seems fanciful. Neither Douglas nor his main biographer, H. Montgomery Hyde, make any mention of the fact; while on the contrary we have every reason to believe that the two lessees found it increasingly difficult to pay the rent. We also know that soon after the definitive split with Douglas in February 1898, Wilde moved to a cheaper address.

In Naples Wilde cut a rather conspicuous figure, for reasons connected with the international uproar made by his trial and conviction. His literary excellence was a matter of hearsay, as none of his works was available to an Italian audience. In a letter of 21 October 1897 the aesthete says that he has entrusted a young and no doubt goodlooking native friend, Rocco, whom he describes as a poet and his private Italian teacher, with the task of translating *Salome*. Nothing seems to have come out of that, but later, in December, Wilde asks Smithers to send him a copy of *Dorian Gray*. 'There is a Neapolitan poet, and good English scholar', he writes, 'who wants to translate it, and I want the Italians to realise that there has been more in my life than a love for Narcissus, or a passion for Sporus: fascinating though both may be.'

What the Italians were able to realise was at any rate sufficient to alert the local newspapers. *Il Mattino*, which was and still is the leading Neapolitan daily, felt obliged to comment on Wilde's rumoured presence in town through its own founder and coeditor, the well-known writer Matilde Serao. Her article came out on 7 October, 1897. It was signed 'gibus' with a small g — one of her journalistic pseudonyms — and on the whole it seems a small masterpiece of professional sloth. Not having bothered to check on the piece of news, the writer fills her space asking herself (or rather himself, as she speaks in the masculine gender) questions which remain unanswered, keeping her — or his — tongue firmly in her (his) cheek.

> Someone has announced that Oscar Wilde, the English *decadent* [...] is in Naples. This announcement has put several people including the humble undersigned in a certain anxiety bordering with panic. What? Oscar Wilde in Naples? But it would be a calamity, the British aesthete among us, even if — as it is understood — he is hiding under an assumed name! We should have at hand the most unsufferable kind of bore that contemporary chronicles have inflicted upon the patient public!

She goes on to remind the readers of how inescapable Wilde's notorious trial had been at the time, and of how much ink had gone to comment the severity of Her Majesty's penalty on offenders of his kind. Then, mercifully, silence had settled in. But now that silence may be over, *gibus* warns: 'Wildean chronicles' threaten to break out again like a new plague! Is it really necessary, she wonders? And first of all, is the 'unhappy one' really lurching in our midst?

> I do not think so. He must still be in a cruel English gaol [...]. But the misunderstanding may be explained. A most scrupulous enquiry done by my informers has discovered that Wilde's accomplice has been here in Naples, in Posillipo's alluring quietness, in a secluded villa where he seems to be attending to his literary pursuits. He is that young Lord Douglas who adds so little honour to the name of one of the greatest historical families of Great Britain. And may the Lord have pity on the beardless roué, so enamoured with aesthetics, and leave him alone in the company of his graceful phantoms!

Two days later Matilde Serao's sloppy reporting was countered by a piece which came out in a rival periodical, *Il Pungolo parlamentare* (9-10 October 1897). The article is unsigned and is believed to have been written by Eugenio Zaniboni. It stated with absoluted certainty that Wilde was in Naples after all, and moreover, it boasted a small sort of interview with him. Admittedly, the reporter did not get much out of the harassed aesthete; yet his candid account of his own efforts does add a few brushstrokes to the portraits we have of Wilde in his Italian exile.

'Oscar Wilde is at the villa del Giudice at Posillipo', Zaniboni writes, 'where there are splendid furnished apartments.' He goes on describing how the janitor at the villa, a woman, tried to discourage the unannounced visitor, saying in her Neapolitan dialect that 'Milord' did not want to see anyone. Undeterred, the narrator asked to see 'Milord's' servant. He was made to wait —

> in front of a door with opaque blue and white glass, at the ground floor: that was Oscar Wilde's apartment [...]. The place was very beautiful. All around, flower beds kept with the utmost care; farther on, shadowy alleys, and beyond the trees,

the vastity of the calm sea, of a livid hue that stretched to the horizon. A deep silence.

The servant comes. 'Lord Douglas' is out; 'il signor Wilde' is in, but will not see anyone. Zaniboni insists, and at the end the servant reenters to speak to his master. Five minutes later, Zaniboni is admitted. We shall now let him speak without interruptions.

I entered and sat on a chair.

Gods in heaven! Whom on earth had been announced by that dog, the servant? Coming in my direction, I saw a white bulk exhaling tenderness, and that greeting which promised to be too hearty — I swear to you, O my readers — did not please me at all.

But of a sudden all the warmth of the first moment vanished utterly. The man Wilde came closer, but with a slow pace and an ice-cold, questioning stare.

- Signor Wilde — I began, just to gain time — I apologize: maybe your servant has mispronounced my name.

- That's right... I thought...

- At any rate, since the fact you are in Naples is known, will you be so kind as to tell me for how long you have been here?

- My friend and I came to Naples about one month ago. We checked into the *Hôtel Royal des Etrangers*; last Thursday we moved here.

- And will you be staying long?

- Well... We do not know. The place is delightful, maybe we shall stay a little longer, at least...

- And you, Signor Wilde, will you concern yourself with art; maybe you have — have you not? — preferred this sweet solitude in order to achieve a spiritual calm such as a writer needs so badly?

- Well... At the moment... No, not really. I haven't as yet decided what I am going to do. It depends on how long I am going to stay here.

- And you have left England for a long time.

- I do not understand.

I repeated my question, but to no avail. England must have had a strange effect on the superman's nervous system: he widened his eyes as if I had asked him to square the circle, and stood there dumbly, motionless, as if he were pursuing faraway memories long since dormant.

I realised my faux pas. So I said goodbye to him and I went. He nodded to me lightly and retired.

This is, or so it seems, all that can be gathered from Neapolitan newpapers in the way of firsthand impressions on

Oscar Wilde; and it is not much. In retrospect, it may be a pity
that Matilde Serao, unlike the clumsy Zaniboni, failed to meet
the 'Milord inglese'. Serao had a quick wit and an eloquent pen,
and her portrait would have been memorable. Moreover, Serao
was a lifelong friend of Eleonora Duse, the Italian diva whom
Wilde would unsuccessfully try to get interested in *Salome*
shortly after. In Naples Wilde handed a copy of the play to
Cesare Rossi, the well-known actor-manager, who according to
the aesthete was 'astounded' with it, but said he had no actress
who could possibly touch the part. This happened in
November; earlier on, in a letter of 21 October, Wilde had seen
it coming. 'Unfortunately most of the tragic actresses of Italy –
with the exception of Duse', he had written, 'are stout ladies,
and I don't think I could bear a stout Salome.' Later, on 10
December (the date is uncertain) he wrote Smithers: 'Eleanora
[sic] Duse is now reading *Salome*. There is a chance of her
playing it. She is a fascinating artist, though nothing to
Sarah.' (For a reversal of this opinion, read G. B. Shaw classic
1895 piece comparing the two primadonnas.) Wilde could have
seen Duse's acting in Naples, where she was in December, at
the Teatro Mercadante, appearing in *Magda* — this was the
Italian title of *Heimat* by Hermann Sudermann — and in *La
seconda moglie*, viz. the Italian adaptation of *The second Mrs
Tanqueray* by Pinero. Duse had not been in Naples for a few
years, and in the words of her biographer William Weaver,
'the papers were full of warm, welcoming articles, including
some by her old friend Matilde Serao.' Had Serao been
conquered by the charm of the author of *Salome*, she might
have recommended the play to Duse. But even in that case it
seems probable that Wilde's bad luck would have held. Duse
was a strong actress of a new, realistic school, and would
hardly find *Salome*'s fancy jewellery to her taste. Moreover,
she was now deeply involved with another poet, Gabriele
d'Annunzio, who was working very hard at persuading her to
appear in *his* verbose costume melodramas. Fresh in her
repertory was a verse playlet entitled *Sogno d'un mattino di
primavera*: in it a young girl has gone mad after her lover was
stabbed in her bed. When Duse acted it in Rome shortly after
her stay in Naples the audience hated it, and only restrained
its hostility as the Queen was in the theatre. *Sogno* was

presented as a curtain raiser; when Duse reappeared in the
centre piece — Goldoni's *La locandiera* — there were polemical
cries of 'Viva la Duse!' and 'Viva Goldoni!'. At the time Italy's
great tragedienne had just too many controversial items on her
hands to be expected to wage another war on behalf of a
foreigner with Wilde's scandalous reputation to boot.

'EACH MAN KILLS THE THING HE LOVES': THE IMPERMANENCE OF PERSONALITY IN OSCAR WILDE

Lawrence Danson

When the painter Basil Hallward first meets the eye of Dorian Gray across a room crowded with 'huge overdressed dowagers and tedious Academicians', 'a curious sensation of terror', he tells Lord Henry Wotton, 'came over me. I knew that I had come face to face with someone whose mere personality was so fascinating that, if I allowed it to do so, it would absorb my whole nature, my whole soul, my very art itself.' Hallward's hostess — 'a peacock in everything but beauty', Lord Henry calls her — intercepts Hallward as he struggles toward the door to escape; she introduces him 'to Royalties and people with stars and garters and eldery ladies with gigantic tiaras and parrot noses', until 'Suddenly I found myself face to face with the young man whose personality had so strangely stirred me. We were quite close, almost touching. Our eyes met again. It was reckless of me, but I asked Lady Brandon to introduce me to him.'[1]

Only a glance, yet in it Basil finds not just a pretty face but a 'personality'. The word has become so naturalized in our vocabulary of television personalities, of girls and guys with great personalities, that Wilde's use of it here in *Dorian Gray* may seem less odd than it should. So I want to ask what Basil designates by the word: how does one recognize a personality, what would it mean to be absorbed by or to escape one, why would anyone be so 'strangely stirred' or even 'terrified' of it as Basil is? And I want to ask that question partly because 'personality' is a Wildean keyword from the time of his earliest reviews and lectures through his writing of *De Profundis*; and also because Wilde's use of the word suggests

82

that one of the defining problems of early twentieth-century literary modernism is already present in Wilde's *fin de siècle* aestheticism. By way of epigraphic shorthand, I adduce three quotations. First, from T.S. Eliot:

> The progress of an artist is a continual self-sacrifice, a continual extinction of personality. [...] Poetry is not a turning loose of emotion, but an escape from emotion; it is not the expression of personality, but an escape from personality. But, of course, only those who have personality and emotions know what it means to want to escape those things.[2]

Then from Ezra Pound:

> In the 'search for oneself', in the search for 'sincere self-expression', one gropes, one finds some seeming verity. One says 'I am' this, that, or the other, and with words scarcely uttered one ceases to be that thing.[3]

And then Wilde himself:

> Was there no permanence in personality? Did things come and go through the brain, silently, swiftly, and without footprints, like shadows through mirrors? Were we at the mercy of such impressions as Art or Life chose to give us?[4]

For Eliot in 'Tradition and the Individual Talent', personality is something too much with us, a confining embarrassment of singularity from which we need to escape into the impersonality (whatever *that* is) of art — although the second part of Eliot's proposition ('only those who have personality [...] know what it means to want to escape [it]') suggests that to be personality-laden is also a privilege reserved for the poetically elect. Simultaneously and at whatever cost to logic, this burden of selfhood is for Ezra Pound the always-evanescing sign of our involvement in a universal flux which makes even the godlike 'I am' merely a fiction among other fictions, the shortest of imagist texts.

This contradictory notion of a personality that is at once imprisoning and insubstantial is so far from being a new problem with the artists Virginia Woolf called Georgians that we can return even beyond the Edwardians into deepest Victorian days to find it already present in Wilde's precursor,

Walter Pater.[5] In The Conclusion to *The Renaissance* — 'that book', Wilde called it in *De Profundis*, 'which has had such a strange influence over my life'[6] — Pater had erected personality into a 'thick wall [...] through which no real voice has ever pierced on its way to us, or from us to that which we can only conjecture to be without'.[7] But in the very passage where Pater constructs the potentially solipsistic wall of personality, he also submits the individual to a scientific-seeming process of 'continual vanishing away, that strange, perpetual, weaving and unweaving of ourselves'.[8]

Under the pressure of Pater's analysis, individuality becomes the always-vanishing, unsayable thing it is for Pound. The sentence I quoted by Pound appears in the course of his attempt to distinguish Imagism from Impressionism: to define his terms, Pound says he must speak autobiographically or, as he puts it, 'from the inside'; ironically, his demurrer — 'one says "I am" this, that, or the other, and with words scarcely uttered one ceases to be that thing' — recalls Pater's impressionistic statement in The Conclusion to *The Renaissance*: 'all that is actual in [experience is] a single moment, gone while we try to apprehend it, of which it may ever be more truly said that it has ceased to be than that it is' (Hill 188). In its original form, as an essay in the *Westminster Review* of 1868, Pater took this deconstruction a melancholy step further:

> Such thoughts seem desolate at first; at times all the bitterness of life seems concentrated in them. They bring the image of one washed out beyond the bar in a sea at ebb, losing even his personality, as the elements of which he is composed pass into new combinations. Struggling, as he must, to save himself, it is himself that he loses at every moment. (Hill 273)

Replying to the Arnoldian quest for the 'object as in itself it really is', Pater had asked, 'what is this song or picture, this engaging personality presented in life or in a book, to *me*?' (Hill xix-xx). Pater thereby installs personality both as the receptor of those impressions that are all we know of life, and as the impression above all others that it is our privilege to receive. Yet with a contradictoriness similar to the one we find in the later modernists, the personality which designates both the perceiver of impressions and the impression to be received is that which at every moment unweaves, dissolves, loses itself in the very struggle to save itself.

At times in Wilde's career, too — and *The Picture of Dorian Gray* is one such time — the word 'personality' bears the weight of unresolvable contradictions. But in the early 1880s, lecturing in America and reviewing in London, Wilde often used the word in counterpoint to the word 'perfection' in a way to make personality a virtually quantifiable quality, simply half of the equation which equals 'art'.[9] Thus Henry Irving is 'a great actor because he brings to the interpretation of a work of art the two qualities which we in this century so much desire, the qualities of personality and perfection'.[10] The former quality, belonging to the artist, brings the stamp of individuality; the latter, belonging to the medium, turns what would otherwise be mere idiosyncracy into the universality — or what Eliot would call impersonality — of art: 'the manner of an artist is essentially individual, the method of an artist is absolutely universal. The first is personality, which no one should copy; the second is perfection, which all should aim at (*Reviews* 46: 20 February 1886). A tumultuous decade later, when his own personality was literally imprisoned in Reading Gaol, he described himself to Alfred Douglas as 'an artist [...] the quality of whose work depends on the intensification of personality' (*Letters* 425). And reviving the old pair, personality and perfection, he managed to associate himself with another artist who combined those qualities: 'nor is it merely that we can discern in Christ that close union of personality with perfection [...] but the very basis of his nature was the same as that of the nature of the artist, an intense and flamelike imagination' (*Letters* 476). Christ, Wilde wrote in words which will bring me back to *The Picture of Dorian Gray*, 'Christ, like all fascinating personalities, had the power, not merely of saying beautiful things himself, but of making other people say beautiful things to him' (*Letters* 484).

It is the power exercised also by Lord Henry Wotton, that otherwise dubiously Christ-like personality, who both fascinates and makes fascinating those who hear his epigrams. And — more pertinently for my purposes — it is the power the still-voiceless Dorian Gray initially exerts over Basil Hallward. In pursuit of the Wildean notion of personality, I want to inquire further about Dorian's first appearance in the novel, when Basil, explaining to Lord Henry why he refuses to exhibit the portrait of the exquisite young man which is also (Basil claims) 'a portrait of the artist [...] the secret of my own soul' (52), describes his meeting with the personality which so strangely stirred and terrified him.

And I begin by noting the wide semantic range the word makes available. At one extreme of stability and presence — and, as we've seen in Pater, already under pressure from another extreme — is what Maude Ellmann calls 'the unified transcendent consciousness that the nineteenth century had understood as "personality"'.[11] For the psychologist Dr Henry Maudsley, in *The Pathology of Mind* (1879), personality is the 'physiological unit of organic functions'.[12] Noting that in sleep and dream 'our conscious functions are in the greatest distraction', Maudsley nonetheless believes that 'the organism preserves its identity' by virtue of 'something deeper than consciousness [which] constitutes our fundamental personality'. Presumably, then, a quality of any or all people, this is the transcendent, essential personality which the OED defines as 'the quality, character, or fact of being a person as distinct from a thing; that quality or principle which makes a being personal'. But the word's entrance into Maudsley's clinical vocabulary suggests another, less transcendent or essential, possibility: the personality which is 'something deeper than consciousness' can be made available for measurement, be found to deviate from a norm, and be susceptible to clinical intervention, cure, and change. Personality must be malleable if the clinician is to be a therapist rather than merely a taxonomist.

Every personality is distinct from every other and, when healthy, continuous with itself: therefore all personalities are equal — except that some personalities are more equal than others. The slippage from 'personality' designating mere personhood to 'personality' designating a special person with qualities different in kind or degree from those who, while demonstrably persons, are not quite personalities, has clearly happened by the time of *Dorian Gray*. And it has happened not only in the culture of science but of the commodity. Thus we find in the *Pall Mall Gazette* of

1891 descriptions of Mr Bradlaugh as 'one of the most unique personalities' (30 January 1891, p. 3) and of Rossetti 'as a grand man; head and shoulders above his associates, with a magnetic personality charged with greatness' (16 January 1891, p. 1). Bradlaugh and Rossetti share a distinction with Sir Robert Chiltern in Wilde's *An Ideal Husband*, described in a stage direction as 'a personality of mark. Not popular — few personalities are. But intensely admired by the few, and deeply respected by the many'.[13] Bradlaugh, Rossetti, and Robert Chiltern are personalities of the sort designated by the OED Supplement's definition 3.b: 'a person who stands out from others either by virtue of strong or unusual character or because his position makes him a focus for some form of public interest.'

This is the commodified personality whose portrait sold copies of *Vanity Fair* in the late nineteenth century as it still does in the late twentieth. It is the media personality who is more intensely organized, more distinctively itself than other less personified persons are, yet who — and here again we find a contradiction in the modern notion of personality — depends for its existence upon the perceptions of the less personified consuming others. This personality is supposed to be outstanding by virtue of some 'strong or unusual character' it personally possesses, yet its existence as personality depends on its being the 'focus [...] of public interest'. The strength or distinctiveness of the public personality is the product of the public interest it produces; simultaneously, this commodified personality is for those whose interest confers that status the sign that personality is an appropriable real thing that can give substance to their own more tenuous personalities.

It is only a step from the commodified realm of the public personality to the aesthetic realm inhabited by the 'engaging personality presented in life or in a book' which Pater celebrates in the Preface to *The Renaissance* (Hill xx).[14] The fifteenth century in Italy, according to Pater, was a time especially 'productive in personalities, many-sided, centralised, complete' (Hill xxiv). Therefore fifteenth-century Italy 'can hardly be studied too much': eliding again the space between the 'personality presented in life *or* in a book', Pater specifies among the quattrocento's curricular claims 'its concrete works of art, its special and prominent personalities, with their profound aesthetic charm' (Hill xxiii). The 'aesthetic charm' that in a book takes the form of literary character or authorial style exists equally in the personalities outside of books — equally in the 'work of the artist's hands, or the face of one's friend' ('Conclusion', Hill 189). When Pater suppressed The Conclusion from the second edition to protect 'those young men into whose hands it might fall' (Hill 186) he had in mind the implications of his conflation of life and book for the collector or connoisseur. The aesthete becomes a consumer of personalities and, like other consumers, the aesthete (though with more passionate taste) seeks out those fair personalities 'in life or in a book' which can give 'the highest quality to your moments as they pass' (Hill 190). Imprisoned within the wall of personality yet feeling at every moment the self weaving and unweaving itself, Pater's aesthete seeks, and in the process creates, those answering personalities who give the most 'pleasurable sensations' to the *condamné* in his passionate isolation.

All these senses — the scientific, the commodified, and the aesthetic — are at work when Basil is overcome by Dorian's amazingly projective personality. And so too is another sense not hinted at by the OED but related to all the others: the fine or responsive personality is sexually *sympathique*, shares (as Basil's glance reveals) a sexual secret. We may not want to apply the hermeneutic sledgehammer wielded by the Marquess of Queensberry at the first of Wilde's trials: according to the Marquis and his lawyers, *The Picture of Dorian Gray* 'was designed and intended by the said Oscar Fingal O'Flaherty Wills Wilde and was understood by the readers thereof to describe the relations and intimacies of certain persons of sodomitical and unnatural habits tastes and practices'.[15] But even readers more sympathetic than Queensberry may think they understand that what passes between Basil Hallward and Dorian Gray is a glance of homosexual recognition, its revelatory power certified by Basil's ability to see right through the screen of dowagers and dullards who rather than separating them only confirm their tremulous bond within the secret world of men who desire one another.

The only trouble with this interpretation is that it puts the reader in the position of knowing more than Dorian knows. The answering homosexual personality that Basil supposedly recognizes in Dorian is at this point in the novel in advance of the facts. Dorian's initial charm is the invitation of the blank page; what Basil calls Dorian's personality will be almost literally dictated to him in the form of Lord Henry's epigrams, read into him by Lord Henry's 'poisonous' yellow book, painted for him by Basil. Dorian's coming-out is simultaneously a reading-in: his homosexual personality, like the commodified personality, exists first in the eyes of others. What Basil recognizes in Dorian at that first meeting, Dorian himself only recognizes later, when, for instance, Lord Henry gives him such useful information as that 'the only way to get rid of a temptation is to yield to it' (62), and Dorian, thus enlightened, becomes 'dimly conscious that entirely fresh influences were at work within him'. Lord Henry's words 'had touched some secret chord that had never been touched before, but that he now felt was vibrating and throbbing to curious pulses': 'Why', Dorian wonders, 'had it been left for a stranger to reveal him to himself?' (64).

How, then, does Basil recognize Dorian's personality before that young man has recognized it in himself? What Wilde constructs here in the opening chapters of *The Picture of Dorian Gray* is a circular system of recognitions. Basil's 'terror' when he first finds himself 'face to face with the young man whose personality had so strangely stirred' him registers the homosexual panic of his *self*-discovery; yet that discovery can only occur through Basil's recognition of Dorian's personality — a personality which cannot exist in Dorian until Basil has first read it into Dorian by projection from the personality he discovers in himself by reading Dorian.

Wilde provides a partial explication of this reading process in The Preface to *Dorian Gray*: 'it is the spectator and not life that art really mirrors.' Or again, in his answer to the novel's first critics: 'each man sees his own sin in Dorian Gray. What Dorian's sins are no one knows. He who finds them has brought them.'[16] In our current *fin de siècle* Wilde's paradoxes about the subjectivity of reading are in danger of sounding like academic truisms. So I turn to another Wilde story about

another infinitely readable personality and about another
painting, 'The Portrait of Mr. W. H.', published almost exactly
a year before the first version of *Dorian Gray*. In that story
about a circle of young men who seek the identity of 'the onlie
begetter' of Shakespeare's Sonnets, Wilde's narrator at one
point begins an unexceptionable testimony to the affective
power of Shakespeare's drama: 'we become lovers when we see
Romeo and Juliet, and Hamlet makes us students' — and so on.
What immediately follows, however, complicates the
situation:

> Art, even the art of fullest scope and widest vision, can never
> really show us the external world. All that it shows us is our
> own soul, the one world of which we have any real cognizance.
> And the soul itself, the soul of each one of us, is to each one of us
> a mystery. It hides in the dark and broods, and consciousness
> cannot tell us of its workings. Consciousness, indeed, is quite
> inadequate to explain the contents of personality. It is Art, and
> Art only, that reveals us to ourselves. (77)

Here, reproduced as a problem in the reception of art, is the
problem of Basil Hallward's first meeting with Dorian Gray.
The 'contents of personality' derive from the work of art which
makes us what we are; yet 'all that [art] shows us is our own
soul' — presumably ours (since there is something to show) from
before we read it in the work of art.

'Personality', then, is simultaneously the proof of a
remarkable individuality which sets its possessor apart from
the world of persons who are not necessarily personalities, and
also a foundationless fiction that can make a pose more real
than the supposed stability of Victorian earnestness. Hence in
'The Portrait of Mr. W. H.' the narrator's fearful puzzlement
when he loses the conviction he had previously held about the
identity of 'the onlie begetter': '[...] was there no permanence in
personality? Did things come and go through the brain,
silently, swiftly, and without footprints, like shadows through
mirrors? Were we at the mercy of such impressions as Art of
Life chose to give us?' (81). Faced with the discovery that the
individuating personality weaves and unweaves itself, the
Wildean aesthete submits himself to the destructive element
and finds there two related recourses. One of these is art:
Basil's way; the other is crime: Dorian's way. And the copula

that links these two is the sexuality Basil Hallward discovers in himself at the moment he creates the personality of Dorian Gray.

In pursuit, then, of the personality that Basil Hallward recognizes with terror and fascination, fearful that it will absorb his whole nature yet strangely stirred by it, we come to the focal point which, so often in Wilde, joins art to crime to homosexuality. Like the poisoner and aesthete Thomas Griffiths Wainewright ('Pen, Pencil and Poison'), whose 'disguises intensified his personality' and who created 'an intense personality [...] out of sin', Dorian Gray is of the opinion that 'insincerity [...] is merely a method by which we can multiply our personalities':

> He used to wonder at the shallow psychology of those who conceive the Ego in man as a thing simple, permanent, reliable, and of one essence. To him, man was a being of myriad lives and myriad sensations, a complex multiform creature that bore within itself strange legacies of thought and passion, and whose very flesh was tainted with the monstrous maladies of the dead. (154)

The 'strange legacies of thought and passion' and 'the monstrous maladies' that congregate in the 'complex multiform creature' Dorian discovers himself to be gesture toward the sexual secret the novel dares to speak mainly by absence and silence. The language of 'taint' and 'malady' licenses the homophobic Queensberry's condemnatory reading of *The Picture of Dorian Gray* as a 'sodomitical' novel. That language is the tribute Wilde paid to the society which would sentence him to hard labour for, in effect, underwriting the criminalization of his sexual personality. Unlike the personality of Victorian heterosexual earnestness — the personality defined by shallow psychology as 'simple, permanent, reliable, and of one essence' — the personality Dorian discovers is complex, impermanent, unreliable, non-essential.[17] In it we may think we recognize Oscar Wilde's own desperately unearnest personality and, partly because of him, we may think we recognize ourselves.

Wilde never produced a unified field theory of personality to reconcile the contradictions which animate the word — contradictions still present when later modernists

propound an *impersonal* theory of art to save themselves from
the terror and fascination which overcome Basil Hallward. In
The Picture of Dorian Gray, personality is the necessary subject-
matter of art: as Basil tells Lord Henry, 'there are only two
eras of any importance in the world's history. The first is the
appearance of a new medium for art, and the second is the
appearance of a new personality for art also. What the
invention of oil-painting was to the Venetians, the face of
Antinous was to late Greek sculpture, and the face of Dorian
Gray will some day be to me' (55). Antinous designates the
subject-matter of an art which presents the male self to itself in
ideal form as an object for its own adoration; so the subject of
this art is the artist himself. Basil discovers that the pursuit
of this ego- and art-ideal threatens what he had hoped to
preserve. He tells Dorian that 'from the moment I met you, your
personality had the most extraordinary influence over me. I
was dominated, soul, brain, and power by you' (132). Dorian's
influence reveals Basil to himself, but the revelation brings
with it not only the terror of domination but the threat of
dispersal, figured as a destructive exposure to the realm of
publicity: 'whether it was the Realism of the method, or the
mere wonder of your own personality, thus directly presented to
me without mist or veil, I cannot tell. But I know that as I
worked at [the portrait], every flake and film of colour seemed
to me to reveal my secret. I grew afraid that others would know
of my idolatry' (133).

  Hearing Basil's confession, Dorian 'wondered if he
himself would ever be so dominated by the personality of a
friend. [...] Would there ever be some one who would fill him
with a strange idolatry?' (134). In Wilde's fable, the circle is
closed when Dorian in turn finds himself dominated by a
personality and filled with a strange idolatry. That
dominating personality is his own, the one created in him by
the idolatrous artist who must be killed by the thing he loves,
by the personality which kills itself.

NOTES

1   *Oscar Wilde* (The Oxford Authors), ed. I. Murray (Oxford, Oxford University Press, 1989), 53.
2   T.S. Eliot, 'Tradition and the Individual Talent' (1917), in *Selected Essays* (London, Faber and Faber, 1932), pp. 17, 21.
3   E. Pound, *Gaudier-Brzeska: A Memoir* (London, John Lane, 1916), 98.
4   *The Portrait of Mr. W. H.*, ed. V. Holland (London, Methuen, 1958), 81.
5   Cf. M. H. Daruwala, 'The Discerning Flame: Of Pater and *The Renaissance*', *Victorians Institute Journal* 16 (1988): 85-127: '[...] underlying not only Pater's major preoccupations, but also all those areas where he is most influential in his relationship with Wilde and Yeats, is the theme of personality in all its varied expressions' (p. 85).
6   *The Letters of Oscar Wilde*, ed. R. Hart-Davis (New York, Harcourt, Brace and World), 471.
7   W. Pater, *The Renaissance: Studies in Art and Poetry*, ed. D. L. Hill (Berkeley, University of California Press, 1980), 187.
8   For the contradictions in Pater's idea of personality, see P. Meisel, *The Absent Father: Virginia Woolf and Walter Pater* (New Haven, Yale University Press, 1980); 111-114.
9   For the pair 'personality/perfection', see R. Shewan, *Oscar Wilde: Art and Egotism* (London, Macmillan, 1977), 20-22.
10   *Reviews*, ed. R. Ross (The First Collected Edition of the Works of Oscar Wilde) (London, Methuen, 1908, rpt. London, Dawsons of Pall Mall, 1969), 17: 9 May 1885. Cf. the review of 'Mr Pater's Last Volume' (22 March 1890): 'in Mr Pater, as in Cardinal Newman, we find the union of personality and perfection' (*Reviews* 545).
11   M. Ellmann, *The Poetics of Impersonality* (Brighton, Harvester, 1987), 16.
12   H. Maudsley, M. D., *The Pathology of Mind* ('Being the Third Edition of the Second Part of *The Physiology and Pathology of Mind*, Recast, Enlarged, and Rewritten') (New York, Appleton, 1896), 12. To add to the bibliographical confusion, this is a version of the edition originally published in 1879.
13   *Two Society Comedies*, ed. I. Small and R. Jackson (New Mermaid edition) (London, Ernest Benn, 1983), 139.
14   On aestheticism and commodity culture, see R. Gagnier, *Idylls of the Marketplace* (Stanford, Stanford University Press, 1986); R. Bowlby, 'Promoting Dorian Gray', *Oxford Literary Review* 9 (1987): 147-63; J. Freedman, *Professions of Taste* (Stanford, Stanford University Press, 1990).
15   This was part of the so-called 'Plea of Justification' filed by Queensberry, rpt. in *The Trials of Oscar Wilde*, ed. H. Montgomery Hyde (London, William Hodge, 1948), 344.
16   S. Mason, *Art and Morality* (London, Palmer, 1912), p. 81.
17   On Wilde's anti-essentialism, see J. Dollimore, *Sexual Dissidence* (Oxford, Clarendon Press, 1991), pp. 3-18.

THE OXFORD OF PATER, HOPKINS, AND WILDE

Denis Donoghue

I propose to begin with biographical comments, simple indeed, on the relations between Pater and Hopkins and, later, between Pater and Wilde. I'll then try to be a little speculative and to describe the spiritual fellowship between them and other writers. Near the end, I'll have occasion to use the word 'feminine' as it is used by Yeats and by another writer who for the moment may remain nameless. And this word will enable me to end with a notion about the rhetoric of modern literature and criticism, so far as it bears — it seems to me — on the recognition of Pater, Hopkins, and Wilde.

*   *   *

In October 1858 Walter Pater went up to Queen's College, Oxford, on a scholarship of £60 a year for three years from the King's School, Canterbury. He spent his undergraduate years discarding his Anglican faith, showing off his newly acquired agnosticism, and learning enough German to read Hegel. He was not an assiduous scholar, but he kept up with the matters that interested him: Greek philosophy, mythology, aesthetics, English poetry, French fiction. He had not yet looked at enough paintings to make him think of writing, as he later did, a series of studies in the aesthetic history of the Renaissance. Nor did he manage to correlate his enthusiasms with the basic requirements of examinations. His degree was a poor Second, not even a gentleman's Third. Hopkins and Wilde were far more accomplished students in their undergraduate years.

Late in 1862 Pater joined the Old Mortality, a discussion-group of undergraduates and junior fellows most of whom were agnostic. In January 1863 he had the audacity to seek a clerical fellowship at Brasenose. In the summer, another clerical fellowship turned up at Trinity College. Pater won neither of them. But on 5 February 1864, he was elected to a probationary fellowship in Classics at Brasenose, a non-clerical one, fortunately. His academic qualifications were pretty poor, but he was known to be widely read, to be familiar with German philosophy and scholarship, and to have an air of distinction. These qualities were enough for Brasenose, intellectually a nondescript college, its students distinguished only on the playing fields. They toiled at games and played at books, as Humphry Ward said. Pater's main duty was to coach them for their examinations in Greek and Latin, a task he performed well enough. On 20 February 1864 he read to the Old Mortals a paper on 'Fichte's Ideal Student', in which he advocated 'self-culture' and declared that he did not believe in the immortality of the soul. S. R. Brooke, a devout Anglican, wrote in his diary that Pater's talk was 'one of the most thoroughly infidel productions' it had ever been his pain to hear.[1] Brooke conveyed his sense of outrage to Gerard Manley Hopkins, an undergraduate at Balliol. Hopkins then suggested to his mentor Henry P. Liddon that they should start a rival essay-club to oppose the agnosticism of Old Mortality. The result was the Hexameron Essay Society, established 'to promote discussion upon subjects of interest so far as may be consistent with adherence to the doctrines of the Catholic Faith'.[2] Edward Caird's note on Pater for the *Dictionary of National Biography* describes his first essay as 'a hymn of praise to the Absolute'. This probably refers to Pater's first performance at the Old Mortality, or to an extended version of it called 'Diaphaneitè' that he wrote a few months later. These performances shocked a few of the members and caused local scandal. Pater liked to show off his irreligious character as a token of his modernity and to exemplify an *avant-garde* by uttering this version of it. He enjoyed breathing the thin air of speculation.

On 5 February 1865, Pater's fellowship was confirmed. The fact that he hadn't earned it wasn't allowed to count. He was evidently the sort of Fellow his college wanted. So the problem of a career was solved. Under the Commissioner's Statutes of 1854 a fellowship was a benefice for life, provided the holder accepted the conditions attached to it. These were not arduous. So Pater was secure, a bachelor don, a middle-class Fellow of moderate but never endangered means, as Edward Thomas described him. For the rest of his life he moved between Oxford and London; Oxford for teaching, reading, writing, and the company of good-looking young men; London for the flourish of being, if only for a few years, a man of the world as well as a man of letters.

* * *

In the Trinity term of 1866 Benjamin Jowett sent Hopkins to Pater for tutoring. Hopkins had come up to Balliol on a scholarship in April 1863. He was now fairly well established as an undergraduate and he was respected by colleagues who shared his concern for ritual and Anglican doctrine. His personal life in other respects was often a torment. Mainly but not exclusively attracted to young men, he worried over his susceptibility to beauty in any form; it distracted him from his true spiritual life. In a period of ten months, according to one of his diaries, he found himself guilty of 1,564 sins, an average of five a day: 238 of these were sexual. He was much troubled by nocturnal emissions, and given to masturbation. Fasting and other forms of penance were his response to these sins of the flesh.

On 2 May 1866 Hopkins made a note in his journal:

> Coaching with W. H. Pater this term. Walked with him on Monday evening last, April 30. Fine evening bitterly cold. 'Bleak-faced Neology in cap and gown'. No cap and gown but very bleak.[3]

'Bleak-faced Neology in cap and gown' is a line from Rev. Charles Turner's sonnet 'A Dream'. Neologists were theologians who tried to subdue the doctrines of Christianity to a rationalist interpretation. Turner thought he could thwart such men by firing twenty sonnets across their bows. For 31 May Hopkins's journal reads:

> A little rain and at evening and night hard rain. — Pater talking
> two hours against Xianity.[4]

Presumably the sentiments Hopkins had to listen to were the ones Pater delivered to Old Mortality. The text, like the soul in Pater's account of it, has not survived, but 'Diaphaneitè' probably gives the gist of it. A barely disguised love-letter to his friend Charles Shadwell, it dreams of a beautiful form of life that only a few figures from literature and history could even adumbrate.

But Hopkins was immune to Pater's two hours of agnosticism. No church was high enough for him. The particular issue that impelled him to become a Roman Catholic was his doubt about the historical legitimacy of the Church of England in administering the Eucharist. Belief in the Real Presence required a ground in Infallibility, and he thought the only such ground was papal infallibility. On 17 July 1866 Hopkins decided that he could no longer receive Communion in the Church of England. Three months later, on 21 October Newman received him into the Roman Catholic Church. On 7 November 1866 he wrote to Liddon, denying that he had let himself be dazzled into Catholicism. On the contrary, he told him, he became a Catholic on the same conviction that makes two and two four.

Meanwhile he wrote essays for Pater, including 'The Origin of Our Moral Ideas', an attack on Utilitarianism. Pater underlined a few notable phrases in it but otherwise did not annotate it. Hopkins's papers during that term were mostly on Plato, morality and aesthetics, and the discrimination of pagan and Christian virtues. Hopkins's conversion suspended for a few months the relation between him and Pater. An invitation to join Pater on a reading party, much appreciated in advance, did not materialize. But the relation was soon mended. Pater was capable of resentments, but not inclined to maintain them for long. Hopkins was moving resolutely toward the priesthood and eventually committed himself to the Society of Jesus. He entered the Jesuit novitiate at Roehampton on 7 September 1868 and was ordained priest on 23 September 1877. Pater couldn't have diverted him from the path to Rome.

But Hopkins still kept doubtful company. On 29 May 1868 he saw Swinburne and was introduced to the artist Simeon Solomon, known to the few as a homosexual. On 17 June he lunched with Pater and they went to Solomon's studio and the Academy. Hopkins and Pater were divided on religious belief, but their interest in art, aesthetics, and homoerotic sentiment kept at least a mild friendship going. Even when Hopkins became a priest, he continued to visit Pater. In February 1879, assigned to St Aloysius's Church at Oxford, he dined with him and his sisters.

As a writer, Hopkins was much closer to Ruskin's spirit than to Pater's. Like Ruskin, he paid attention to the glowing sundry of the world. He looked at things. 'What you look hard at seems to look hard at you', he noted, and enjoyed the double hardness. Pater was already a relativist, a modernist of drift, he looked at objects only in the hope of provoking himself to a tone or a sensation somewhat aside from them. Phenomena did not interest him for any other reason. As his pupil for a term, Hopkins learned how to conduct an argument in philosophic terms that would at least be understood if not accepted by an opponent. On the question of belief, Pater should have minded his own business. But Hopkins's faith was not at risk on that cold evening.

So they were at Oxford, but each had his own sense of the place. It was fashionable during those years to display one's sensibility in an expressed and defined relation to Oxford. Cambridge was already moving toward science and worldly versions of philosophy, but Oxford was still to be found between Plato, Aristotle and Hegel, its terms of allusion were linguistic, ethical, and aesthetic. Its typical achievement, and one of its supreme accomplishments, was the Oxford English Dictionary, begun in 1884 and, till supplements became necessary, completed in 1928. Pater liked Oxford, but he did not share the sense of historical radiance it incited in Newman, Arnold, and Hopkins. In Easter 1865 Hopkins wrote a poem 'To Oxford' —

> [...] for nothing here
> Nor elsewhere can thy sweetness unendear.
> This is my park, my pleasaunce.[5]

In 'Duns Scotus's Oxford' he writes of 'Towery city and branchy between towers'. Duns Scotus, who is thought to have lectured at Oxford about 1301, gave Hopkins cause to imagine that the true spirit of the university proceeded from medieval Christianity through the honorable error of the Oxford Movement to Dr Newman. Hopkins's Oxford was not, therefore, the sum of Newman, Jowett, Max Müller, Ruskin, Arnold, Pater, and the Oxford Hegelians; it was Catholic Oxford, baptised by Hopkins's desire.

Pater did not think of Oxford in this numinous style. The choice between Oxford and London was always available, but nothing much depended upon making it or sticking by it. Domestic convenience, rather than his spirituality, was the issue. Sometimes, he thought that the chief merit of Oxford was that it was not London; at other times, that that merit was not especially felicitous. But he never doubted that the Oxford of Newman, Arnold, and Jowett was a significant force in cultural life. In the poem 'Oxford' Edward Dorn expresses feelings about the place that Pater would not have understood:

> Oxford was never intended for defeat
> as I understand it it was born
> as a dirty necked attempt
> to keep clear of the establishment [...]

and later in the same poem:

> Can't
> you tell yourselves it is time
> Oxford stopped having a place
> in English life as sanctuary [...][6]

It was as sanctuary that Pater and Hopkins, in their different tones, valued Oxford; even when it became the scene of distress for each of them.

In May 1869, as if to divert attention from his notoriously plain features, Pater started dressing as a dandy: top hat, black tailcoat, silk tie of apple-green, dark striped trousers, yellow gloves, patent leather boots. On vacation, he travelled mainly in France, Germany, and Italy, either with his sisters or, as in the summer of 1865, with Shadwell.

Sometimes, as in the Long Vacation of 1867, he contented himself with the pleasures of a reading party at Sidmouth.

The circle of Pater's friendships in Oxford and later in London was not large. Shadwell, Gosse, Bussell, Mark Pattison and his wife, Mr and Mrs Humphry Ward, Bywater, and Mandell Creighton occupied most of it, and there were some additions from time to time, such as Vernon Lee and William Sharp. There were also a few with whom Pater formed literary affiliations, notably Swinburne, George Moore, Lionel Johnson, and Arthur Symons. These relations were agreable, but Pater also required them to be serviceable. Ethereal as he generally appeared, he was not above nudging his friends to review his books or otherwise to write in his favour. He found adverse criticism extremely painful, even when it came from insignificant people, so he went out of the way of decorum to arrange for cordial reviews. Oscar Wilde and D. S. MacColl responded congenially to his requests that they might review his books. Pater was not a relentless impresario in such matters, but he was worldly enough, if it could be quietly managed, to do himself a good turn. It is surprising, then, that he was not more careful in his choice of associates. He became prudent, but only when scandal obtruded.

*   *   *

In his essay on Botticelli, published in August 1870, Pater remarked of him that 'in an age when the lives of artists were full of adventure, his life is almost colourless'. There was not even a legend to dissipate. 'Only two things happened to him', Pater said, 'two things which he shared with other artists: — he was invited to Rome to paint in the Sistine Chapel, and he fell in later life under the influence of Savonarola, passing apparently almost out of men's sight in a sort of religious melancholy, which lasted till his death in 1515, according to the received date.'[7] It is typical of Pater to speak of colourlessness and then to add without comment the colour of a luridly ascetic name. Savonarola was not as vivid to Pater as to Hopkins, who took Origen and Savonarola as his masters in discipline and burned his poems, it may be, in imitation of Savonarola's more famous bonfire of vanities. Pater was drawn to people to whom, apparently, little or nothing had happened. But he often qualified his appreciation of them by mentioning in their vicinity someone to whom much had indeed happened.

Pater's own life was virtually colourless; whatever colour it had, he added from the impulsions of his desire to an almost blank canvas. Two things happened to him. He conceived the frivolity of becoming a minister of the Anglican Church, and was thwarted in the conceit. Then in the years between 1873 and 1877 he became something of a scandal. Specifically, between the publication of *Studies in the History of the Renaissance* (1873) and that of W. H. Mallock's *The New Republic*, which appeared in *Belgravia* from June to December 1876 and as a book in March 1877, he got himself into endless trouble.

The scandal might have started in January 1867 when Pater published in the *Westminster Review* a review-essay on Winckelmann's *History of Ancient Arts among the Greeks*. The essay is in all essentials an account of Winckelmann's life and work, relying mainly on Joseph Eiselein and Otto Jahn for the biography, and on Hegel for the theory of Greek sculpture. It is also a revision, indeed a correction, as David J. Delaura has shown in *Hebrew and Hellene in Victorian England* (1969), of Arnold's essay, 'Pagan and Medieval Religious Sentiment'. If Pater had not published it anonymously, he would have caused offence by several paragraphs on Winckelmann, including this one:

> That his affinity with Hellenism was not merely intellectual, that the subtler threads of temperament were interwoven in it, is proved by his romantic, fervid friendships with young men. He has known, he says, many young men more beautiful than Guido's archangel. These friendships, bringing him in contact with the pride of human form, and staining his thoughts with its bloom, perfected his reconciliation with the spirit of Greek sculpture.[8]

'Perfected' is a bold claim. Long after Pater's death, Ingram Bywater said of the essay, in a letter to Hermann Diels:

You will notice, I think, a certain sympathy with a certain aspect of Greek life; I must tell you that that was not confined to him.[9]

Pater's essay on Winckelmann, if it had been widely recognised as his, would have shocked his clerical colleagues at Brasenose by its claim that 'the broad characteristic of all religions as they exist for the greatest number, is a universal pagan sentiment, a paganism which existed before the Greek religion, and has lingered far onward into the Christian world, ineradicable, like some persistent vegetable growth, because its seed is an element of the very soil out of which it springs'.[10]

Not content with that affront, Pater published in October 1868 a review-essay — anonymously, again — on William Morris's poems, in which he warmed to a pagan sense of life:

> One characteristic of the pagan spirit these new poems have which is on their surface — the continual suggestion, pensive or passionate, of the shortness of life; this is contrasted with the bloom of the world and gives new seduction to it; the sense of death and the desire of beauty; the desire of beauty quickened by the sense of death.[11]

Up to that point, Pater's article was just a review, though an exotic one, especially when he permitted himself to say of 'that whole religion of the middle age' that it was 'but a beautiful disease or disorder of the senses', and that such a religion 'must always be subject to illusions'.[12] But he would not let well enough alone — or even reasonably well. He ended the review with seven paragraphs for which Morris's poems provided little warrant. These paragraphs, when they appeared in somewhat changed form as the Conclusion to *Studies in the History of the Renaissance*, impelled readers to associate Pater with hedonism, high-toned corruption.

*   *   *

In his first term at Magdalen College, Oxford, Wilde read *Studies in the History of the Renaissance*, 'that book', as he later remarked, 'which has had such a strange influence over my life'.[13] It is possible that Pater's book, rather than

Huysmans's *A Rebours* or another claimant, is the 'yellow book' Wilde's Lord Henry sends to Dorian Gray, who imitates it in his progress to immorality. The chapters on Leonardo and Winckelmann are suggestive enough for that purpose. Wilde's statement that the yellow book was 'partly suggested' by *A Rebours* leaves space enough for Pater's book. *Studies in the History of the Renaissance* became, Wilde said, 'the golden book of spirit and sense, the holy writ of beauty', taking the occasion to quote those phrases from Swinburne's sonnet on Gautier's *Mademoiselle de Maupin* and to make significant fellowship between four morally questioned writers. Wilde never changed his opinion, that Pater's prose in the book on the Renaissance was far superior to Carlyle's and to Ruskin's. He kept extolling it to every qualified reader he met.

Wilde's career at Oxford began in October 1874 when he went up to Magdalen on a scholarship. Ruskin was then Slade Professor of Art, and Wilde attended his lectures. He even allowed Ruskin to persuade him to put their ostensibly shared socialism into practice. At Ruskin's request he joined a gang of undergraduate road-diggers to mend a road in Ferry Hinksey; an episode that Joyce recalled, in his essay on Wilde, by remarking that in Wilde's Oxford years a pompous professor named Ruskin was leading a crowd of Anglo-Saxon adolescents to the promised land of the future society — behind a wheelbarrow.[14] For a time, Ruskin became Wilde's prophet, priest, and poet. After graduation, they kept in communication for a while. On 28 November 1879 they went together to the Lyceum to see Henry Irving as Shylock and afterwards to a ball given by Millais and his wife to celebrate their daughter's marriage. In later years, Wilde recalled his years at Oxford mainly in association with Ruskin's lectures and the personality they displayed. But Ruskin's moral bearing was too much for Wilde in the long run. He gradually turned to Pater, having succumbed to his style.

Wilde did not meet Pater till his third year at Oxford. In July 1877 he published an article on the Grosvenor Gallery in the *Dublin University Magazine* and sent a copy of it to Pater. A few references to Greek islands, handsome boys, and Correggio's paintings of adolescent beauty alerted Pater to the writer's disposition. He thanked Wilde for the article, praised the cultivated tastes it displayed, and invited him to make 'an early call upon your return to Oxford'.[15] They met in late October. By November Pater was writing to 'My Dear Wilde' and lending him Flaubert's new book, *Trois Contes*, a gathering of 'Un Coeur simple', 'La Légende de Saint Julien l'Hospitalier', and 'Hérodias' — the last of which greatly influenced Wilde's *Salome*. Wilde sent Pater a few of his poems, and Pater urged him to change to prose: 'prose is so much more difficult', he told Wilde as he told everyone. It is probable that Pater came to regard Wilde as one of the young men upon whom a reading of the Conclusion to *Studies in the History of the Renaissance* might have a regrettable effect. If so, his misgiving was belated. By 1877, when Pater suppressed the dangerous pages, Wilde had already read them and accepted the way of life they implied.

The friendship flourished, but Pater never really liked Wilde, he thought his charm somewhat vulgar. In turn, Wilde thought Pater timid for not living up to the daring of his prose. They saw each other from time to time. Wilde introduced Pater to selected friends — Douglas Ainslie, and much later Lord Alfred Douglas — during the years in which Pater was becoming more conservative. But Pater and Wilde did not write about each other's work till June 1887 when Wilde published an anonymous review of *Imaginary Portraits* in the *Pall Mall Gazette*. The review didn't amount to much, but it extolled Pater's mastery of prose and gave prominence to a sentence in 'A Prince of Court Painters' — the study of Watteau — which became nearly as famous as Pater's great aria on the Lady Lisa. Wilde writes:

> The account of Watteau is perhaps a little too fanciful, and the description of him as one who was 'always a seeker after something in the world that is there in no satisfying measure, or not at all', seems to us more applicable to him who saw Mona Lisa sitting among the rocks than to the gay and debonair *peintre des fêtes galantes*.[16]

The sentence enabled Wilde to complain that Pater's prose was somewhat laborious:

Here and there one is tempted to say of Mr Pater that he is 'a seeker after something in language that is there in no satisfying measure, or not at all'.[17]

But in the end Pater's artistry wins Wilde over: 'when all is said, what wonderful prose it is...'

On the strength of the review, Pater felt himself justified, when *Appreciations* came out on 15 November 1889, in asking Wilde to review it. 'If I am intrusive in saying this', he wrote to him, 'I am sure you will forgive me...' Wilde reviewed it under his own name in the *Speaker* on 22 March 1890, and drew attention to the essay on Wordsworth as the best thing in the book. But the most striking part of the review was its comparison of Pater with Newman: in each, we find 'the union of personality with perfection'. That Wilde doesn't make much of the comparison is of little account: his making anything of it is what matters.

Wilde was even then working on 'The Critic as Artist', a dialogue he published in the July and September 1890 issues of the *Nineteenth Century* and again in *Intentions* (1891). Here Pater's practice as a critic is the main justification for Wilde's theory of criticism as creation: the critic takes the work of art as starting-point for a new creation. Who cares whether Ruskin's views on Turner are sound or not, Wilde's Gilbert says to Ernest?:

Who, again, cares whether Mr Pater has put into the portrait of Mona Lisa something that Lionardo never dreamed of? The painter may have been merely the slave of an archaic smile, as some have fancied, but whenever I pass into the cool galleries of the Palace of the Louvre, and stand before that strange figure 'set in its marble chair in that cirque of fantastic rocks, as in some faint light under sea', I murmur to myself, 'She is older than the rocks among which she sits; like the vampire, she has been dead many times, and learned the secrets of the grave; and has been a diver in deep seas, and keeps their fallen day about her; and trafficked for strange webs with Eastern merchants; and, as Leda, was the mother of Helen of Troy, and, as St Anne, the mother of Mary, and all this has been to her but as the sound of lyres and flutes, and lives only in the delicacy with which it has moulded the changing lineaments, and tinged the eyelids and the hands.' And I say to my friend, 'The presence that thus so strangely rose beside the waters is expressive of what in the ways of a thousand years man had come to desire'; and he

answers me, 'Hers is the head upon which all "the ends of the
world are come", and the eyelids are a little weary.'[18]

Gilbert's further reflections, on beauty, form, music, and
subjectivity, are applied Pater: illogical, indeed, since Pater's
paragraph about Mona Lisa testifies to his own impression and
should merely be the starting-point for anyone else's. Wilde's
impression should be yet another act of creativity, not a mere
recitation of Pater's. But the passage has its propriety as one in
which two people, Gilbert and his friend, make love by
murmuring quotations to each other.

The friendship between Pater and Wilde virtually
came to an end in the winter of 1891. While *The Picture of
Dorian Gray* was still in manuscript and before he started
serial publication of it in July 1890 in *Lippincott's Monthly
Magazine* Wilde showed it to Pater. The following March, he
published the Preface to it in the *Fortnightly Review*: it is pure
Pater, a celebration of music and the uselessness of art. It is not
clear what part of the book Pater took exception to. If Wilde
told the truth under Edward Carson's cross-examination in the
first trial on 3 April 1895, he didn't delete any part of *The
Picture of Dorian Gray* but he made an addition to it. 'In one
case it was pointed out to me', Wilde said, 'not in a newspaper
or anything of that sort, but by the only critic of the century
whose opinion I set high, Mr Walter Pater — that a certain
passage was liable to misconstruction, and I made an
addition.'[19] It is probable, as Donald Lawler has argued, that
the passage in question is the one in which Basil Hallward
refers to several young men whose lives have been ruined,
allegedly, by their association with Dorian Gray. Wilde
added a few sentences in which Dorian disclaims responsibility
for introducing any of these men to vice or folly.[20]

A few weeks later, Wilde introduced Lord Alfred
Douglas to Pater. The meeting didn't lead to a friendship:

> Wilde had an immense opinion of Pater and spoke of him
> always with reverence as the greatest living writer of prose. I
> tried to appreciate Pater and he personally was kind to me, but
> quite apart from the fact that he had practically no
> conversation and would sit for hours without saying more than
> an occasional word, I never could bring myself to have more
> than a very limited admiration for his far-famed prose, which

has always seemed to me artificial, finicking and over-
elaborated to an exasperating degree. I have altogether livelier
recollections of Mr, now the Reverend Dr Bussell, Pater's most
intimate friend at Brasenose College, for he was a fine musician
and had a devotion to Handel and Bach.[21]

It is clear that Pater's sense of the relation between Lord Alfred
and Wilde, added to common rumour about Wilde's sexual life,
made him decide that minor textual changes in *Dorian Gray*
were not quite enough. With intrepidity unusual for him, he
arranged to review the book and to take the occasion to
repudiate not only Lord Henry but his creator.

The review began with predictable gestures of praise
for Wilde's cleverness, but Pater soon indicated where he
diverged from Wilde:

> A wholesome dislike of the commonplace, rightly or wrongly
> identified by him with the *bourgeois*, with our middle-class —
> its habits and tastes — leads him to protest emphatically
> against so-called 'realism' in art.[22]

It is strange to find Pater holding out the possibility that 'the
commonplace' might not be justly identified with the habits
and tastes of the *bourgeoisie*. More than Arnold, Ruskin, or
Newman, it was Pater who made this identification
mandatory. Now that it has been appropriated by Wilde, he
must dissociate himself from it. Pater assumes that Wilde's
novel is designed to recommend 'a dainty Epicurean theory' for
the middle class. But it fails, according to the author of *Marius
the Epicurean*:

> A true Epicureanism aims at a complete though harmonious
> development of man's entire organism. To lose the moral sense
> therefore, for instance, the sense of sin and righteousness, as Mr
> Wilde's hero — his heroes are bent on doing as speedily, as
> completely as they can, is to lose, or lower, organisation, to
> become less complex, to pass from a higher to a lower degree of
> development. [...] Lord Henry, and even more the, from the first,
> suicidal hero, loses too much in life to be a true Epicurean —
> loses so much in the way of impressions, of pleasant memories,
> and subsequent hopes, which Hallward, by a really Epicurean
> economy, manages to secure.[23]

Once he has disowned Lord Henry, whom Wilde evidently intended to be recognisably Paterian, Pater can afford to be generous. Lord Henry is 'the spoiler of the fair young man', but Dorian — though an unsuccessful experiment in Epicureanism — is 'a beautiful creation'. The moral of the story is that 'vice and crime make people coarse and ugly'. Ordinary readers should take the novel as if it were a story by Poe about *doppelgänger*, not of two persons but of a man and his portrait. A few more words of praise, and the review ends.

No quarrel ensued, but the friendship lapsed. Even before the review appeared, Wilde was speaking harshly of Pater to Richard le Gallienne. And then or later, Vincent O'Sullivan heard Pater say 'something very severe about "Mr Wilde", as he called him, which I prefer to leave in darkness'.[24] But in February 1893 Wilde sent Pater a copy of *Salome*, presumably to remind him that in happier times Pater had given him Flaubert's stories and the idea for the play. No reply from Pater has survived.

When Wilde heard of Pater's death, he asked, according to Max Beerbohm, 'Was he ever alive?'.[25] But in July 1895 Wilde arranged that a batch of fifteen books sent to him in prison would include Pater's *The Renaissance*. Two months later, a further batch had *Greek Studies*, *Appreciations*, and *Imaginary Portraits*. Robert Ross, visiting Wilde in prison in May 1896, undertook to send him *Gaston de Latour* when it came out on 6 October. Another list of requested books, submitted to the prison authorities on 3 December 1896, included Pater's posthumous *Miscellaneous Studies* (1895). In the long letter to Lord Alfred, written from Reading Gaol at intervals between January and March 1897, Wilde had Pater in mind on several occasions. Recalling the passage in *Studies in the History of the Renaissance* where Pater says that our failure consists in our forming habits, Wilde found himself guilty: his habit of giving in to Lord Alfred 'had stereotyped my temperament to one permanent and fatal mood'. Thinking of the distinction between contemplating the spectacle of life and engaging in life, Wilde quoted — inaccurately, and placing it in *Marius the Epicurean* rather than in the essay on Wordsworth — Pater's remark that 'to witness this spectacle with appropriate emotions is the aim of all culture'. In the same letter, Wilde said of Christ that 'his morality is all sympathy' — which is what Pater said of Botticelli. And Wilde recalled the passage in the book on the Renaissance in which Pater refers to Michelangelo as 'one of those who incur the judgment of Dante, as having "wilfully lived in sadness"'. Wilde tells Lord Alfred:

> I remember during my first term at Oxford reading in Pater's *Renaissance* — that book which has had such a strange influence over my life — how Dante places low in the Inferno those who wilfully live in sadness, and going to the College Library and turning to the passage in the *Divine Comedy* where beneath the dreary marsh lie those who were 'sullen in the sweet air', saying for ever through their sighs:
>
> > Tristi fummo
> > nell' aer dolce che dal sol s'allegra.
>
> I knew the Church condemned *accidia*, but the whole idea seemed to me quite fantastic, just the sort of sin, I fancied, a priest who knew nothing about real life would invent. Nor could I understand how Dante, who says that 'sorrow remarries us to God', could have been so harsh to those who were enamoured of melancholy, if any such there really were. I had no idea that some day this would become to me one of the greatest temptations of my life.[26]

Finally, in a letter of 16 April 1900 to Robert Ross, Wilde described a recent trip to Rome, where on Easter Sunday he attended Vespers at the Lateran:

> Music quite lovely: at the close a Bishop in red, and with red gloves — such as Pater talks of in *Gaston de Latour* — came out on the balcony and showed us the relics.[27]

Inaccurate again, as Rupert Hart-Davis has noted. Wilde is thinking of the bishop in 'Denys L'Auxerrois' who, 'in vestments of deep red in honour of the relics, blessed the new shrine. [...] At last from a little narrow chest, into which the remains had been almost crushed together, the bishop's red-gloved hands drew the dwindled body.'

The relation between Pater and Wilde was genuine, but there were limits to it. Whitman once wrote: 'He most honours my style who learns under it to destroy the teacher.' Neither Hopkins nor Wilde honoured Pater's style in that degree.

Hopkins was not in any lasting sense Pater's pupil; schooled as he already was in the academies of Keats, Newman, and Ruskin. Wilde learned whatever he needed from Pater, but unlike Pater he was a man of the theatre and he delighted in greasepaint and first nights. Pater gave him metaphors and allusions, and he used them provocatively, but Wilde did not need to get rid of Pater to clear a space for himself. The essay on Winckelmann makes a case in point. Wilde transcribed whole sentences from it at Oxford, and used it to develop his own thinking. He noted especially the suggestive passage in which Pater contrasts Greek sensuousness with Christian asceticism; the one is shameless and childlike, it does not fever the conscience; the other discredits the slightest touch of sense. The word 'touch' stirs Pater's mind to further intimations of sensuous pleasure, and he immediately quotes without comment the passage from 1 Samuel 14 in which Jonathan says: 'I did but taste a little honey with the end of the rod that was in my hand, and lo! I must die.' I remind you that Jonathan's father, Saul, has ordained that none of his people will eat food till the Philistines are defeated; and Jonathan, who has not heard of the edict, innocently dips his staff into a comb of honey and puts it to his mouth. When Saul learns of this, he determines that his son must be put to death. But the people protest, and Jonathan is pardoned. 'My father has troubled the earth', Jonathan says. It is pertinent to mention that Jonathan has defied his father and persisted in his great friendship with David, a relation many readers have deemed to be homosexual. So the taste of honey has often been taken as figurative and erotic. Pater's context, his essay on the notorious homosexual Winckelmann, makes these intimations emphatic. An association of imagery brings together Greek sensuousness, the artistic life, homosexual friendship, and transgression. Pater has to show Winckelmann released from the intoxication of that honey by being pagan. 'From this intoxication', he says, 'Winckelmann is free: he fingers those pagan marbles with unsinged hands, with no sense of shame or loss.'[28] 'Fingers', not 'looks at'.

In the poem 'Hélas!' Wilde recalls Pater's quotation of the passage from Samuel:

> To drift with every passion till my soul
> Is a stringed lute upon which all winds can play,
> Is it for this that I have given away
> Mine ancient wisdom and austere control?
> Methinks my life is a twice-written scroll
> Scrawled over on some boyish holiday
> With idle songs for pipe and virelay
> Which do but mar the secret of the whole.
> Surely there was a time I might have trod
> The sunlit heights, and from life's dissonance
> Struck one clear chord to reach the ears of God:
> Is that time dead? lo! with a little rod
> I did but touch the honey of romance —
> And must I lose a soul's inheritance?[29]

It is a poem of second thought in which Wilde alludes not only to Pater's 'Winckelmann' and the drifting Conclusion to *Studies in the History of the Renaissance* but to the Coleridge of 'The Eolian Harp'. In romantic literature the sounds of the wind through the lyre are generally received as inspiration, the true voice of feeling as if it were verified by nature. But Wilde's poem emphasises the dark side of drifting, yielding to every passion. It is ironic that what is lost is 'austere control', since that phrase, too, is Paterian in his later emphasis on *ascesis*, the self-discipline required for the achievement of a style. The move from 'scroll' to 'scrawled over' mimes the twice-written character of the life; the first, inscribed by God; the second, a boyish scrawl. In the last lines Wilde makes the association with Jonathan explicit, as if to say: 'I didn't know that what I did was forbidden, and maybe the people who love my plays will demand that I be pardoned'. To make way for the last line, the rhetorical question, Wilde changes the structure of Jonathan's sentence. In Samuel the sentence makes a strong ethical discrepancy between the minor quality of the act and its appalling consequence; the transition is effected by the exclamation 'lo!'. 'I did but taste a little honey with the end of the rod that was in mine hand, and lo! I must die.' In Wilde's poem the 'lo!' is brought forward to anticipate the discrepancy it isn't called upon to enact, the littleness is given to the rod rather than to the amount of honey, and Jonathan's 'I must die' is changed to refer to spiritual death, 'And must I lose a soul's inheritance?'. The poem uses the motifs that Pater has assembled — sensuousness, pleasure, art, homosexual

friendship, pagan blitheness, the touch and taste of honey —
but it recalls, to rebuke these, the Christian asceticism that
Pater mentioned only to relegate. The teacher is not destroyed,
but a lesson is recited different from his.

The Oxford of Pater, Hopkins, and Wilde was a
homosocial sanctuary. Pater might spend an evening denouncing
Christianity, but it was more significant that he spent it with
Hopkins, a young man like himself of homoerotic disposition.
But homoerotic inclination was merely one aspect of an
antinomian character Pater, Hopkins, and Wilde shared.
'Antinomian' is Pater's word: in *Studies in the History of the
Renaissance* he uses it to mean not opposition to orthodoxy but a
quiet declaration of independence, a determination to stand
apart from official values. Antinomian is not synonymous with
antithetical. Antithetical means engaging in a conflict with
official values; antinomian writers choose to sequester
themselves rather than accept those values or even challenge
them.

The antinomian stance was also adopted by
heterosexual writers. Yeats is antinomian when, in his essays
on symbolism, he advocates reverie rather than argument or
ratiocination. As a mode of consciousness, reverie is not
concerned with administrative zeal, getting on in the world,
celebrating a common sense of reality by describing its features.
It is a purely internal act of vision, meditation, in which the
mind delights in its heuristic power and goes its own way.
Yeats is also antinomian in the poem 'In Memory of Major
Robert Gregory' when as a good subjectivist for the moment he
speaks of the secret discipline by which the gazing heart
doubles her might; as the mind looks at an object, refuses to
capitulate to it, and returns empowered to itself. I think he had
an antinomian disposition in view again when he said that
Pater's ideal of culture could only create feminine souls. 'The
soul becomes a mirror not a brazier.'[30] I think, but cannot prove,
that Yeats associated homosexuality with feminine souls in
men; the passive role. I recall in this context, too, the passage
in 'The Tragic Generation' in which Yeats wonders about
Marius the Epicurean — 'the only great prose in modern
English' — whether it hadn't 'caused the disaster of my
friends'. It taught us, he said, 'to walk upon a rope tightly

stretched through serene air, and we were left to keep our feet upon a swaying rope in a storm'.[31] Pater had made us learned, Yeats says. He cannot have meant it literally since he himself was not learned. He meant, I think, a certain tone that goes with the other adjectives in Pater's vicinity, 'ceremonious and polite, and distant in our relations to one another'. Yeats had in mind mainly Lionel Johnson, Arthur Symons, and later in the Dublin of the Abbey Theatre he meant Synge, more distant than any of them. The storm for which a swaying rope is useless is, I think, the world according to nineteenth century science, positivism, realism, the naturalism that leaves a mind helpless before its contents. Yeats is holding Pater responsible for much trouble, but an antinomian writer — Pater, Symons, Johnson, Yeats — would not have it otherwise or lose the honey of it. These writers, homosexual or not, are Paterian in temper; as distinct from Yeats's masculine heroes, princes of the Italian Renaissance, adepts of Blake and Nietzsche.

Hopkins's Catholicism was his version of the antinomian impulse. After the exertions of the Oxford Movement, Catholicism didn't challenge Anglicanism, it merely went its own way and yearned, as Hopkins did, for spiritual continuity with Duns Scotus and an Oxford innocent of the Reformation; innocent, too, of the traffic of the English language, in its Elizabethan phase, with imports from France and Italy. In 1900, according to Yeats's introduction to the *Oxford Book of Modern Verse*, everybody got down off their stilts, stopped taking absinthe, and gave up converting to Catholicism, but in Pater's Oxford the path to Rome was taken by people of antinomian intention, Hopkins being one such.

But it was not necessary to go to Rome. Wilde went to Confucius. To the extent to which official culture, diversely represented in Oxford by Arnold, Jowett, and Ruskin, was predicated upon commonsense, realism, and the definition of reality in civic and social terms, Wilde dissented from it and from the politics of will that it enforced. In his review-essay on Confucius he said of the perfect man, in Confucius's vision of him, that 'he does not try "to bring about his own good deeds"'.[32] Such a man waits upon deliverances from above, for which he is not responsible. Confucian virtues are not those that make empires.

Studies in the History of the Renaissance and *Marius the Epicurean* were golden books not only to Wilde but to the Oxford of Hopkins and Wilde; mainly for the chapter on Winckelmann that Wilde and many of his generation annotated; and for the theme of passionate friendship, nuanced by religious questing, that Pater developed again in *Marius*. These books played in Pater's Oxford the part played more widely a few years later by Whitman's Calamus poems; copies of the books were given as presents from one Uranian to another and became passwords, tokens, signs of recognition between men who came together on the authority of their difference.

But I want now, finally, to come back to our writers in relation to the rhetoric of modern literature and criticism. In an early issue of *Scrutiny* Q. D. Leavis reviewed Santayana's *The Last Puritan* under the title 'The Last Epicurean'. The review is respectful to the point of taking Santayana seriously as a novelist, not merely as a philosopher. The gist of Leavis's argument, however, is that while Santayana is convincing in the work of diagnosis, he is naive in the value he offers as positive... 'He seems to affirm that the polish of Eton and Oxford, provided it has a European setting to preclude insularity, displays the very perfection of human grace.' Although Santayana has ridiculed the genteel tradition in philosophy, he appears to foster it in himself:

> Professor Santayana is probably the last very distinguished mind to cherish that tradition, which is the reason that this review is headed 'The Last Epicurean'. Not 'Epicurean' with reference to the original Epicurus of course; the adjective is intended delicately to suggest a relationship with the Oxford branch of the family. Pater, though his literary art was at the opposite extreme from Professor Santayana's, was also a victim of the feminine charm of Oxford. It is rumoured moreover that Professor Santayana voluntarily resided for some years on Boar's Hill, the very sanctuary, it would appear from what one reads and hears, of the English genteel tradition.[33]

The question to ask is: what is going on in Q. D. Leavis's review, especially in her association of Pater with the genteel tradition in English academic life — a tradition 'on its last legs' — and his capitulation to the feminine charm of Oxford?

One way of dismissing a writer is by claiming that the wisdom of time has already disposed of him. Another way is by claiming that he never managed to enter securely upon the history of a society, a culture, or a language. Henry James begins his essay on D'Annunzio by asking why the figure of the aesthete, a figure that made such a stir in the world only a few years before, has now receded, and he explains the disappearance by saying that the figure, in its English form, was never exemplified by a really powerful personality. He evidently has in view Beardsley, Symons's obituary essay on Beardsley, besides Pater and Wilde, and he wonders whether the figure of the aesthete would not have 'taken' if it had been embodied not in these but in D'Annunzio. He implies that history has, in any case, made its decision to exclude aesthetes from any story worth telling.

It is my understanding that Q. D. Leavis's rhetoric serves much the same purpose. Her association of Pater with the genteel tradition and subjection to the feminine charm of Oxford implies that his work cannot have any serious part in the production of a new literature. I remind you that *Scrutiny* was a journal devoted to the naming and elucidation of a new literature in which the creative figures were deemed to be as Eliot and Pound. F. R. Leavis appropriated Hopkins, in *New Bearings in English Poetry*, as the creative force in the early manifestations of modern poetry, mainly because he could be shown to have a poetic relation to Dryden and to count as a working alternative to Tennyson and Swinburne. A poetry whose chief exemplars were Hopkins, Eliot, and Pound, with Yeats a little in the background, could be claimed as new. In that claim the work of Pater, Wilde, Symons, Lionel Johnson, and the early Yeats could be represented as running into the sands of Rupert Brooke.

That *Scrutiny* was a Cambridge enterprise is much to the point because Leavis, in encouraging the work of I. A. Richards, William Empson, L. C. Knights and other young critics, points to Pater's impressionism as yet another version of the genteel tradition, designated feminine because of its implied passivity before experience. The Richards of *Practical Criticism* and *Principles of Literary Criticism*, like the F. R. Leavis of *Revaluation* and the Q. D. Leavis of *Fiction and the*

Reading Public, points to a sense of language and literature that offers itself, by contrast with Oxonian feminity, as sturdy, intelligent, dynamic: I hesitate to say 'masculine'.

The last question is one I can only formulate. To what extent should Leavis's version of modern literature as the work of Eliot, Pound, and D. H. Lawrence in the main, be accepted; since it results in the exclusion of Pater, Wilde, and Yeats's entire 'Tragic Generation' and denies to them any creative part in the direction of modern literature?

It is my conviction that there cannot be 'one story and one story only' in the historical presentation of modern literature. There is no merit, no grace, in answering one totalization with another. There must be several stories. Of these, one begins (I would argue) with Pater and Wilde. Pater's *Studies in the History of the Renaissance* leads to Arthur Symons's *The Symbolist Movement in Literature* and eventually to Edmund Wilson's *Axel's Castle*. Wilde's *Intentions*, emphasising one aspect of Pater, propounds the role of fictiveness in modern literature and leads eventually to *The Necessary Angel* of Wallace Stevens. I simplify, of necessity, in such a sketch as this.

NOTES

1   Quoted in G. Monsman: 'Pater, Hopkins, and Fichte's Ideal Student': *South Atlantic Quarterly*, 70 (1971) p. 366.
2   Ibid., p. 369.
3   *The Journals and Papers of Gerard Manley Hopkins*, edited by H. House and G. Storey (Oxford, Oxford University Press, 1959) p. 133.
4   Ibid., p. 138.
5   *The Poems of Gerard Manley Hopkins*, edited by W. H. Gardner and N. H. MacKenzie (Oxford, Oxford University Press, 1970) p. 21.
6   E. Dorn, *The Collected Poems 1956-1974* (Bloinas, California, Four Seasons Foundation, 1975) pp. 209-210.
7   W. Pater: *The Renaissance: Studies in Art and Poetry: The 1893 Text*, edited by D. L. Hill (Berkeley, The University of California Press, 1980) pp. 39-40.
8   Ibid., p. 152.
9   Quoted in W. W. Jackson, *Ingram Bywater* (Oxford, Clarendon Press, 1917) p. 79.
10   *The Renaissance*, p. 160.
11   'Poems by William Morris': *Westminster Review*, October 1868, p. 309.

12   Ibid., p. 302.
13   *Selected Letters of Oscar Wilde*, edited by R. Hart-Davis (Oxford, Oxford University Press, 1979) p. 199.
14   *Critical Writings of James Joyce* edited by E. Mason and R. Ellmann (New York, Viking Press, 1959) p. 202.
15   W. Pater, *Letters*, edited by L. Evans (Oxford, Clarendon Press, 1970) p. 24.
16   Quoted in *Walter Pater: Critical Heritage*, edited by R. M. Seiler (London, Routledge and Kegan Paul, 1980) p. 163.
17   Ibid., p. 165.
18   Oscar Wilde, *The Artist as Critic: Critical Writings of Oscar Wilde* edited by R. Ellmann (Chicago, University of Chicago Press, 1969) pp. 366-367.
19   H. Montgomery Hyde (editor), *The Trials of Oscar Wilde*, p. 124: quoted in D. Lawler, *An Inquiry into Oscar Wilde's Revisions of The Picture of Dorian Gray* (New York, Garland Publishing Inc., 1988) p. 55.
20   Lawler, *supra*, pp. 55-56.
21   Quoted in R. M. Seiler (editor) *Walter Pater: A Life Remembered* (Calgary, University of Calgary Press, 1987) p. 157.
22   W. Pater, *Uncollected Essays* (Portland, Maine, Mosher, 1903) p. 126.
23   Ibid., pp. 128-129.
24   V. O'Sullivan, *Aspects of Wilde* (London, Constable, 1936) p. 12.
25   Quoted in R. Ellmann, *Oscar Wilde* (New York, Knopf, revised edition, 1988) p. 52.
26   Oscar Wilde, *Selected Letters*, p. 199.
27   Ibid., p. 357.
28   *The Renaissance*, p. 177.
29   *Complete Works of Oscar Wilde*, with an introduction by V. Holland (New York, Harper and Row, 1989) p. 709.
30   Yeats, *Autobiographies* (London, Macmillan, 1955) p. 477.
31   Ibid., pp. 302-303.
32   *The Artist as Critic: Critical Writings of Oscar Wilde*, p. 226.
33   Q. D. Leavis: 'The Last Epicurean': *Scrutiny*, Vol. IV, No 3, December 1935, p. 328.

WILDE AND THE IDEA OF A THEATRE

Joseph Donohue

As the centenaries of Oscar Wilde's major writings for the stage occur during the present decade, the need for a new point of view on the playwright and his plays in the broad and various contexts of the theatre of his age has become clear. At the outset it is obvious that the subject for reassessment extends well beyond the drama itself, taken as a literary artifact, to the professional stage of West End and Broadway houses and of the actor-managers George Alexander, Herbert Beerbohm Tree, Lewis Waller, and Charles Frohman, who produced a remarkable series of Wilde's plays in London and New York in the brief period 1892-95. In the context of Continental avant-garde drama, however, the subject also encompasses the theatre of Ibsen, Strindberg, and Maeterlinck, for whose plays Wilde asked while in prison — an alternative stage, a kind of anti-theatre with respect to the commercial, featuring plays mostly unstageable in England (as the uproar over Ibsen's *Ghosts* and the failure of Wilde's own *Salome* to pass the English censor suggest), though much in evidence on the Continent.

Connected with these two spheres of activity, yet distinct in crucial ways, was a private, radical notion of the theatre conceived by Wilde himself. This highly unorthodox idea of a theatre emerges even in his earliest dramatic efforts, *Vera, or The Nihilist* and *The Duchess of Padua*; is articulated in an intensely symbolic way in the later *Salome*; and informs the full range of his critical writings and even his poetry (as in the sonnets to Sarah Bernhardt and Ellen Terry). Deriving certain features from Maeterlinck's 'static' theatre and the symbolist tradition exemplified by Baudelaire and Mallarmé, Wilde's idea of a theatre is nonetheless authentically his own: a theatre that conjures images of idealized emotional states

118

and crises, an interior theatre of the heart and soul, of suffering and loss. Wilde's professional reputation grew rapidly, beginning in 1892, as the flamboyant author of the main-stream comedy-dramas *Lady Windermere's Fan, A Woman of No Importance,* and *An Ideal Husband* and of the 'trivial' comedy *The Importance of Being Earnest.* And yet the celebrity who, wearing a green carnation in his lapel and smoking a cigarette, sauntered onto the stage of the St James's Theatre on the opening night of *Lady Windermere's Fan* and congratulated his audience on their success was also, and simultaneously, writing for a private yet more comprehensive ideal theatre, a theatre whose idea was obscured by the scintillating wit and engaging characters of these four West End successes but was nonetheless present. As late as 1894, during the initial stages of composition of *The Importance of Being Earnest,* a scenario on a guilty love affair and an abandoned marriage sent by Wilde to George Alexander identifies that idea in its abiding concern for authentic personal feeling: *'I want the sheer passion of love to dominate everything.* No morbid self-sacrifice. No renunciation. A sheer flame of love between a man and a woman. That is what the play is to rise to.'

The clarity and singularity of Wilde's idea are typical of his approach to dramatic creation. He was comparably clear about the governing idea of *The Duchess of Padua,* whose 'two great speculations and problems', he wrote to Mary Anderson in 1883, are 'the relations of Sin and Love'. Ten years later he confided to a correspondent who had praised the New York production of *Lady Windermere's Fan* that its idea was essentially psychological:

> A woman who has had a child, but never known the passion of maternity [...] suddenly sees the child she has abandoned falling over a precipice. There wakes in her the maternal feeling — the most terrible of all emotions. [...] She rushes to rescue, sacrifices herself, does follies — and the next day she feels, 'This passion is too terrible. It wrecks my life. I don't want to know it again. It makes me suffer too much. Let me go away. I don't want to be a mother any more.' And so the fourth act is to me the psychological act, the act that is newest, most true.

These are examples of a consistent, if quite complex, idea about the theatre that unifies Wilde's approach to writing for the stage and endows the great range of that writing in style and subject with a coherence and a moment that, for the most part, would seem to have gone unobserved in criticism up to the present time.

The reassessment I propose consequently looks to a wide range of topics, including the history of Wilde's involvement and sustained labor in the professional London theatre, his aspirations as a poetic dramatist, his practice as a critic and theorist of the drama, his determined bid for success in the public arenas of the theatre, literature, and journalism, and the implications of that success for his personal life. Moreover, it entails scrutiny of such major topics as Wilde's views of the nature and purpose of the theatre, the social occasions of the performed play, and the dramatist's relationship to audience and society.

At the same time, it is essential to consider the ways in which Wilde's own life and personality make their way into the broader subject, characterizing it definitely. An understanding of Wilde's personal predicament here is of crucial importance: it is fundamental to see Wilde's plays as adopting an attitude broadly reflective of Wilde's own, complex character. As Wilde himself and Wilde's dramatic characters frequently remind us, modern literature and modern life itself in this period were busily at work defining the age of the individual — an age when the artist's life was perceived to be intimately and deeply implicated in his art. Ibsen told us we could read the record of his life, hidden though it was, in his plays. Picasso said to his friend John Richardson, 'My work is like a diary. To understand it, you have to see how it mirrors my life.' Wilde's dandiacal figures, like Lord Goring in *An Ideal Husband* and Lord Illingworth in *A Woman of No Importance*, are especially well-endowed spokesmen: 'To love oneself', says Goring, 'is the beginning of a lifelong romance'; 'People nowadays are so absolutely superficial', Illingworth comments, 'that they don't understand the philosophy of the superficial.' Goring and Illingworth are conspicuous instances of authorial surrogates, but the more covert signs of Wilde's intervention in his own works lie almost everywhere. 'I took the drama, the most objective form known to art', he explained to Lord Alfred Douglas in the long confessional letter written from Reading Prison, now known as *De Profundis*, 'and made it as personal a mode of expression as the lyric or the sonnet.' As Wilde's spokesman Gilbert puts it in 'The Critic as Artist', 'Man is least himself when he talks in his own person. Give him a mask, and he will tell you the truth.' Reading Richard Ellmann's biography *Oscar Wilde* on its appearance in 1988 underscored my conviction that analysis of Wilde's personal predicament was a crucial part of the Wildean critical enterprise. Wilde's plays should be seen as adopting an attitude deeply reflective of his own personality and of the necessarily covert relationship, as he sensed it, between objective form and subjective content.

For Wilde that relationship remained a necessary but difficult one, given his need to cultivate his keen desire for self-fulfillment in private life and his conflicting need to succeed by accepting the exigencies of professional life as a working dramatist in the public theatre — as he did in capitulating to George Alexander's insistence that the revelation of the identity of Mrs Erlynne as the mother of Lady Windermere must occur no later than the end of the second act. In her 1986 study *Idylls of the Marketplace* Regenia Gagnier characterizes Wilde's entire literary output as conditioned by the formative pressures and glittering spectacle of the capitalistic bourgeois marketplace. Gagnier's rejection, for purposes of her argument, of any notion of Wilde's autonomous personal life is directly countered, in effect, by Ellmann's blithe assumption of a coherent, autonymous psychological makeup fueling intense intellectual and emotional drives. Ellmann and Gagnier have thus, to a considerable extent, effectively set the terms of further discussion.

And yet neither Gagnier nor Ellmann appears to take any substantial interest in the theatre of Wilde's time, let alone in Wilde's own manifest fascination with the stage. Indeed, Ellmann's dismissive attitude toward the contemporary theatre of his subject — both the West End theatre of Pinero, Jones, Grundy, and their fellow playwrights, and the avant-garde Continental theatre of Maeterlinck, Ibsen, Strindberg, and their iconoclastic and symbolist brothers — leads him to what I believe is a biased and superficial reading of Wilde's career as a dramatist. The essential conclusion that

Ellmann reaches is that, after a false start in the poetic drama, Wilde abandoned it and, with measured cynicism, began writing charming and witty but ultra-conventional plays for a philistine upper-middle-class audience. To be sure, George Alexander's offer to the struggling dramatist of £50 against royalties to write a modern comedy did not fall on deaf ears, and the resultant series of successful comedy-dramas between 1892 and 1895, culminating in the brilliant farce of *The Importance of Being Earnest*, might in itself indicate that Wilde had abandoned the manner of those early, seemingly false starts. But the reputation as a comic dramatist that those four sumptuously produced plays established for Wilde has served to obscure the more fundamental fact that in writing them he changed only his artistic *métier*, not his sense of the way he conceived of human nature and how to represent it in dramatic art; changed his stylistic strategies and their verbal manifestations, but not his conviction of the necessity for representing human passions, needs, and desires on the stage in ways that remained faithful to genuine experience as he saw it and felt it in his own, private ways.

The problem that consequently lies still unresolved in Wilde criticism remains one of reconciling Wilde's successful 'realistic' plays (to give them that simplistic and often misused term) — that series of stunning successes beginning with *Lady Windermere's Fan* in 1892 and ending (all too abruptly, at the point of his trial and conviction for homosexual offences) with *The Importance of Being Earnest* in 1895 — reconciling the generic features, including familiar plot elements, and the general stylistic qualities of those four plays with his evident continuing interest in writing other kinds of dramatic fare altogether. Some examples: at about the time *The Importance of Being Earnest* opened in February 1895, he wrote to George Alexander offering to read him 'the vital parts of my Florentine play', a play in blank verse that he later called '*Love and Death — Florentine Tragedy*'. This play and *La Sainte Courtisane*, a blank-verse tragedy whose typescript Wilde, while held in Holloway Prison in April 1895, directed Robert Ross to retrieve from his Tite Street house, were 'plays of a completely different type', he told Lord Alfred Douglas in his long letter from Reading Prison. Even as the clouds were gathering over *The Importance of Being Earnest* in April 1895, Wilde roughed out the scenario for the poetic tragedy *The Cardinal of Avignon*.

Moreover, the familiar critical explanation, repeated essentially without variation by Ellmann, to the effect that Wilde finally abandoned the 'poetic' approach to dramaturgy in favor of a more commercial product because he couldn't live off the proceeds of poetry, ignores the persistent presence of certain pointed ethical qualities and experiential features lying implicit within the ostensible conventionalities of the four later plays. Those qualities and features were well obscured, it would seem, by Wilde's calculated and sometimes brilliant exploitation, as Kerry Powell's recent *Oscar Wilde and the Theatre of the 1890s* (1990) demonstrates, of the contemporary genres of comedy-drama and farcical comedy. And, of course, such preoccupation with West End success entirely passes over the key work, *Salome* — as does Patricia Flanagan Behrendt, unaccountably, in her otherwise interesting and useful study of sexuality in Wilde's works, *Oscar Wilde: Eros and Aesthetics* (1991).

Overall, then, criticism has neglected to set Wilde's dramaturgical efforts in contexts at once more perspicuous and more personal, and so has yet to come to terms with what remains, ostensibly, the puzzlingly ambiguous profile of the author of *Salome* and *Lady Windermere's Fan* (to identify one pair of seemingly antithetical or unconnected works) in order to clarify the vital substance it frames.

At the same time, any critical approach that aspires to the kind of reconciliation of apparent inconsistency that I have been advocating here must be wary of too great a preoccupation with the biographical and the theatrical; rather, it must be broadly enough based to address the concerns of intellectual, social, and cultural history along with those of the theatre itself. As they relate to the central presence (I take it to be central) of Wilde's own personality as it informs his writings for the theatre, these concerns lead us to scrutinize an illusionistic stage world filled out by Wilde's expansive genius and passionate dedication to art — a world enlivened also by literary and pictorial art, criticism, critical theory, and journalism; and a world that also includes Wilde's personal relationships with contemporaries such as Whistler and Shaw, his conversations, and his letters (a truly valuable resource) every bit as much as it encompasses the more private — and yet ever less so as time went on — realm of his homosexuality and his relationships with men, and boys.

What finally emerges at the centre of interest is, then, the complex identity of Wilde as a man of the theatre. The most readily accessible aspect of this issue is, as I have suggested, the public stage, the commercial theatre. There, the role adopted by the professional dramatist normally conforms in broad measure to the needs and demands of star actors, actor-managers, and paying audiences. In this arena of activity Kerry Powell's book on Wilde and his contemporary professional theatre identifies with welcome precision and full example the dramatic genres and sometimes specific plays under whose influential presence Wilde was apparently quite consciously working. Powell's sturdy, well-argued scholarship can be built upon to good effect, and it is bound to have a salutary influence on studies of this aspect of Wilde's dramaturgical activities.

Wilde's original and independent intellect, however, led him to resist and partly to subvert the role of the professional dramatist — one of the masks he so ostentatiously wore — in the interests of his own private values and ends. Ultimately, Wilde's position with respect to the theatre of his time was as ambivalent as it was complex, and in certain ways unique, even though in other ways it remained completely representative of the character of the contemporary professional dramatist. Faced with this complexity, criticism must understand that coming to terms with the agenda and goals of the contemporary French symbolist theatre is of equal importance to assessing the apparent formative influence upon Wilde's writing for the theatre of the practices of the late Victorian commercial stage. Nor does this describe the practical limits of the reassessment here proposed. An additional area of influence hardly touched upon in criticism to date is the example of the post-Elizabethan poetic drama — early on, that of Webster, but most notably the Romantic drama of Shelley. The text of *The Cenci*, whose subject involves a terrible crime and its terrible revenge, lurks like a cloak-and-dagger assassin behind the often lurid and derivative verse of

Wilde's *The Duchess of Padua*, but its more important influence on Wilde's play, in the example of Shelley's unorthodox central character of Beatrice Cenci and his radical ideas of human innocence, lies deeper than mere words.

The orientation of a study of the kind I propose, then, must finally point toward a more integral and holistic understanding. There are some bountiful rewards in store, I believe, for critical perseverence toward that end. For, in the process of coming to terms with the full range, style, and character of Wilde's writing for the theatre, a study of this sort may also clarify and perhaps even alter to some extent our sense of the nature of *fin de siècle* theatre, art, literature, and culture. In any case, a study of Wilde and the theatre inevitably entails a study of the late nineteenth-century theatre as a whole, as well as antecedents ancient and otherwise. The reassessment I propose thus carries the additional purpose of describing Wilde's ideal theatre both in itself and in respect to the heterodox values of *fin de siècle* artistic and cultural life. For, notwithstanding the personal, even private character of his artistic values, the impact of Wilde's writing on the theatre of his age was so striking, and his own absorption of its chief features so thorough, that any fresh scrutiny of Wilde's idea of a theatre must inevitably broaden into an inquiry into the nature of the theatre of his age and the cultural life it illuminated and itself conditioned.

And so, as we approach the one hundredth anniversary of Oscar Wilde's death in Paris, it is appropriate to reconsider the true character of the plays to which he devoted himself, early and late in his career. Undoubtedly, there will be many a centenary production of *The Importance of Being Earnest*, in both three- and four-act versions, just as there has already been, in advance of its centenary, a sparkling and very satisfying London revival of *An Ideal Husband* directed by Peter Hall that captures much of the true seriousness lying just beyond the glittering wit and bold character outlines of that still eminently playable play. It may be too much to ask for revivals of *Vera* and *The Duchess of Padua*, dramaturgically inexpert as they are; but *Salome*, I would think, will richly repay the attentions of a director who has the wit and insight to take the play in its full dimensions of lush but ironic eroticism and simultaneous parody of a gaudy symbolist tradition. We can hope that the combined effect of persistent intelligent attention to the scripts of these plays as dramatic vehicles, and to the significance of the looming profile of the author himself that has always lain behind them, will go far toward some necessary clarifications. 'I live in fear of not being misunderstood', Wilde once said. A century later, it may be safe, and even more entertaining, to attempt a greater understanding.

OSCAR WILDE AND DRAMATIC STRATEGIES

Irène Eynat-Confino

In his letter of 2 June 1897 to Lord Alfred Douglas, Oscar Wilde wrote:

> If I were asked of myself as a dramatist, I would say that my unique position was that I had taken the Drama, the most objective form known to art, and made it as personal a mode of expression, as the Lyric or the Sonnet, while enriching the characterisation of the stage, and enlarging — at any rate in the case of *Salomé* — its artistic horizon.[1]

In this paper, I would like to bring under attention the expression of Wilde's personal drama by two rhetorical and dramatic strategies: encoding and displacement. Wilde used these strategies to display his views on homosexuality and to give voice to his feelings and misgivings about Lord Alfred Douglas whom he had met not long before he wrote *Salomé*.

It was in 1891, probably in June, that Oscar Wilde met the young Lord Alfred Douglas.[2] Several months later, Wilde left for Paris, where he remained from October to December. There he met with Symbolist poets and writers and became a *habitué* of Mallarmé's *Mardis*. It was in Paris that Wilde wrote *Salomé*. He wrote it in French, which he knew well. The play underwent light editing in the hands of his friends Stuart Merrill, Adolphe Retté, Marcel Schwob and Pierre Loüys, then he offered the play to Sarah Bernhardt.[3] Captivated by the role of Salomé, Sarah Bernhardt and her acting company started rehearsals in view of the production of *Salomé* in French, in London. The play was presented in London to the Examiner of Plays for the Lord Chamberlain, the Censor, in June 1892, but the license was refused. The reason was simple enough: the law did not permit any theatrical performance

127

presenting Biblical characters before a large audience. Sarah
Bernhardt's production of *Salomé* was cancelled.

The play was published in French in Paris and in
London in 1893. The English translation appeared on 9 February
1894. Several of Wilde's scholars suggest that Wilde not only
corrected Lord Douglas's version but translated anew the whole
play.[4] Aubrey Beardsley's illustrations to the English text
offered a visual, graphic equivalent to the performance that
did not take place. *Salomé* has since attracted many artists in
theatre, opera, dance and cinema, and has even been published
in London in 1986 as a comic strip, illustrated by David
Shenton.

ENCODING

Salomé was written in 1891, the heyday of the Symbolist
movement in Paris. The Théâtre d'Art, founded a year before by
the poet Paul Fort and a group of young painters, the Nabis,
was luring more and more Symbolist poets to the stage.
Symbolist theories of drama and theatre proliferated. New
aesthetic tenets were variously formulated by Mallarmé,
Charles Morice, Paul-Napoléon Roinard, François Coulon, Paul
Adam, Pierre Quillard, Saint-Pol Roux, Camille Mauclair,
Gustave Kahn and Albert Mockel, to name but a few. Drawing
from Schopenhauer, Swedenborg and Wagner, they agreed on
several basic issues, like the multilevel narrative and the
mandatory use of encoding strategies and devices. As Gustave
Kahn wrote, the play should be 'une oeuvre à plusieurs degrés',
bearing a multiplicity of meanings. The fabula had to be
accessible to the larger audience while the philosophical
import might be comprehended by the happy few.[5] As for
encoding strategies, Mallarmé wrote in 1891:

> To name an object is to disminish by three quarters the
> enjoyment of the poem prompted by the delight of guessing little
> by little; to suggest, that would be the real dream. It is the perfect
> usage of this mystery that constitutes the symbol: evoking an
> object little by little, through a series of decodings, to show a
> state of mind.[6]

Wilde learned quickly. In his Preface to *The Picture of
Dorian Gray*, published that same year, he wrote:

All art is at once surface and symbol. Those who go beneath the surface do so at their peril. Those who read the symbol do so at their peril.

Salomé written in French, was Wilde's swift response to the Symbolist theories of drama. What Wilde designated as 'surface' is the dramatization of the Biblical tale of John the Baptist and his death. The fabula keeps the chief ingredients of the Biblical plot: Iokanaan the prophet is Herod's prisoner; Salomé dances before Herod and demands Iokanaan's head; Herod complies with her wish. The fabula keeps the mythical heroes too: Iokanaan, Herod, Herodias, and Salomé. The intertextuality entailed by the use of the mythical story and its heroes, turns the play's discourse into an encoded one.

Wilde's Iokanaan is a composite character of John the Baptist and John the Evangelist, his speeches follow the spirit of the Biblical tale. He preaches an ethical code of behaviour that, as Wilde shows, is no longer valid in a pleasure-seeking society. The dramatic situation is doubly ironic, first because the physically powerless Iokanaan is invested with spiritual power, affecting the lives of all those who hear him; second, because Iokanaan's ideal of purity and his own virtuous behaviour lead to death and destruction. Wilde's portrayal of Iokanaan as young and passionate is due, as J. E. Chamberlin has found, to the influence of Ernest Renan's *La Vie de Jésus*.[7]

Salomé, Wilde's protagonist, draws on the many representations of the Salomé in literature and in visual arts. Wilde's contemporaries did not fail to recognize his many artistic and literary sources, like Heinrich Heine, Flaubert, Mallarmé, Maeterlinck, Anatole France, Marcel Schwob, Théophile Gautier or Gustave Moreau. After all, Salomé was, in Carl Schorske's words, 'the fin-de-siècle's favorite phallic female'.[8] Nina Auerbach counts her 'among the female demons who possess so much nineteenth century art'.[9] But Wilde departed from the mythical figure and, as Richard Ellmann has shown, he innovated by endowing Salomé with a motivation of her own. She does not demand Iokanaan's head on her mother's bequest, as in the Biblical tale, but does so because she has tried to seduce him and was rejected. William

Archer, in his review of the play in 1893, considered Salomé 'an oriental Hedda Gabler'.[10] As Norbert Kohl explains, Wilde subverted the Victorian image of the submissive woman.[11] Feminist critics like Gail Finney and Jane Marcus have seen in Salomé the image of the New Woman, the modern woman rejected by the Victorian society.[12] Elaine Showalter, prompted by Beardsley's illustrations, detects in *Salomé* a gay subtext and interprets the use of the female heroine as a masking strategy.[13] Thus, the image of Wilde's *Salomé* perceived — both by his contemporaries and by the scholars today — is an aggregate, a product of intertextuality.

The text is rich in oral and visual imagery and easily lends itself to interpretation, whether from a feminist, a gay studies, or an anthropological point of view. It is by decoding — Mallarmé's 'déchiffrement' — and by trying to 'read the symbol' — that we can apprehend what lies, in Wilde's words, 'beneath the surface'. I will not go over the lunar, solar, and Dionysian imagery of the play, which has been explored by many of Wilde's scholars. Instead, I would like to dwell shortly on the scene that offers the most powerful visual images of the play: the scene of the dance and the kiss of the severed head. This scene is set apart not only because of the subversive nature of the actions performed, but because these actions are the kinetic signs of the underlying pagan rite which identifies Iokanaan with Orpheus and indirectly presents the case of the homosexual poet.

This rite evolves in three stages. The first is marked by the dance, the kinetic equivalent of the prayer; the second — by Herod's incantation. The third is the sacrificial stage. During these three stages, Salomé displays a fundamental change, going from self-exposure to self-assertion and annihilation. Or, on a mythical level, from the dancing supplicant she turns into the tetrarch's superior, to whom Herod's incantation of offerings is addressed. The incantation, punctuated by Salomé's repeated request, gradually reveals her metamorphosis into a god-like figure who demands its due: a human life. But this figure still partakes of human nature. A hybrid Salomé will be sacrificed, a slaughtered victim.

The text does not describe the dance and the reader is aware only of its effect within the dramatic fiction. For the reader, the dance is invisible, the more powerful because of its invisibility. Was it not Mallarmé who contended that the most beautiful theatre is the imagined one? Borrowing a Symbolist technique, Wilde provided his reader with allusions only.

A stage direction indicates that Salomé takes off her sandals, an allusion to the nudity beneath the seven veils. By baring her feet, Salomé displays humility before Herod — an act of surrender, since she has the rank of a Princess and is also his wife's daughter. The bare foot is a Christian symbol of humility and poverty. Although Salomé's baring of her feet is a gesture of public exposure, it is a momentary gesture, fleeting as the dance, similar to her brief kneeling in front of Herod before she raises to claim her due, Iokanaan's head. For Salomé the Princess, baring her feet is a short-lived concession to Herod. She transcends her status as a Princess.

But by baring her feet and displaying her nudity, Salomé severs her link with purity and virginity, as the sandals are the attributes of the Moon, the Goddess of Chastity. The foot is also a Freudian phallic symbol. 'Dove-like feet', this is the simile (used by Herod) for Salomé's feet. Still, the dove, emblem of innocence, virginity, peace and hope, was also the favorite bird of Venus. Throughout the play, the image of Salomé has been associated with the moon; now it is enriched with the attributes of Venus.

Salomé dances in a pool of blood. To wash one's feet is a rite of purification, but Wilde reverses the traditional symbolism. Polluted with blood, Salomé is, perversely, still a virgin, like Diana the huntress, Goddess of the moon. Connections — the Symbolist *correspondances* — are established between her dancing in a pool of blood and the moon, which has become 'red as blood', as Herod says. Another allusion at Salomé's rising above and beyond human condition.

Salomé's feet are bathed in the blood of the Young Syrian who has committed suicide because of her. Her dance, a baptism of blood, excludes her from the company of men and women. Godlike or insane, she is frenzied like the Thracian Maenads bent upon tearing Orpheus in pieces because he avoided all women after he had lost Eurydice. The gestural and oral allusion to the Orpheus myth is reinforced by the figure of Iokanaan. Like Orpheus, so Iokanaan's power is in his voice, in his words. So was Wilde's power; and he, too, shunned the company of women.

Salomé's dance is an act that lays bare not only her body. According to Paul Diel, the foot is an ancient symbol of the soul.[14] Thus, Salomé's barefoot dance is a visualized unveiling of the self, an act of self-acknowledgement. But the act of unveiling, of unmasking, brings about the negation of life, death — as if the veil is a prerequisite for living. On the copy of the play he offered to Bearsdley, Wilde wrote: 'for the only artist who, besides myself, knows what the dance of the seven veils is, and can see that invisible dance.'

The ritualistic mood of the whole scene of the dance and its retribution is reinforced by the musicality of Herod's incantation and by the almost identical repetition — seven times — of Salomé's request for the head of Iokanaan.

After the dance, Salomé demands Iokanaan's head 'on a silver charger'. The overtones are those of pagan rites, not of cannibalism, as Ewa Kuryluk claims.[15] Salomé has godlike passions, fierce, excessive, shameless. Deprived of the object of her desire, she severs all ties with living human beings, rising above the human condition, a monster and a goddess at the same time. She is the Goddess for whom the Young Syrian has sacrificed himself. Like the Gods, she demands the immolation of human beings. Like the Gods, she is above human laws, obeying a law of her own.

By displaying Salomé's kiss to the severed head of Iokanaan, Wilde defied the Symbolist tenets. This breach of aesthetic and social conventions comes as a self-revelation, a self-exhibition, and as an insult to the audience. But Wilde breaches not only the Symbolist aesthetic code, he also defies the Aristotelian. His play, originally referred to in the French title as 'un drame', was defined in its English translation as 'a tragedy'. It is beyond the scope of this paper to examine whether the play complies with the Aristotelian aesthetics, but I would like to call attention to Wilde's fusion of genres in this play. Salomé's kiss of the severed head introduces into the scene an unmistakable element of horror, typical of the *Grand Guignol*. Unmistakable too is Wilde's brilliant handling of the final scene. Treading on blood in her frenzy for her victim Iokanaan, Salomé isolates herself from society. In this scene, by a masterly stroke, Wilde achieved the seemingly impossible: the blurring of the boundaries between sin and innocence, between the human and the inhuman. For when the god-like monster is led to slaughter it undergoes a subtle transformation: powerless, already smeared with blood, a mad maiden between overpowering soldiers, she becomes a victim. Salomé becomes what René Girard calls the functional victim, whose death will restore peace and order — but a victim nevertheless. She who has dared to infringe a taboo and perform the unspeakable is now powerless and soon to be killed. She who has killed poetry in its budding and possessed it only as a dead metaphor, has doomed herself to death.

But if Salomé is offered to the gaze as a victim, she is not an innocent one. Neither is Iokanaan, portrayed as a fanatical young man. The only characters who embody the melodramatic exemplar of the innocent victim are the Young Syrian, seduced, exploited, and driven to suicide by Salomé, and the Page, who loses the Young Syrian, his beloved.

DISPLACEMENT

The act of looking, the gaze, is one of the main motives of the play, as critics like Peter Raby and Gail Finney have shown.[16] In fact, Wilde uses the gaze as a displacement strategy. The act of looking, the gaze, acknowledges the sensuous bond between the various characters: between Salomé and the Young Syrian in love with her, Salomé and Iokanaan, Herod and Salomé, and between all the characters and the moon. The oral warning against the act of looking, the enjoinment not to look at the object of one's desire, is repeated throughout the play but does not prevent the gaze. On the contrary, the warning intensifies and magnifies the object of desire (the only one who obeys the warning is Iokanaan). In other words, the negative enjoinment is intended to create the apparently opposite effect: that of looking at the forbidden object. This dramatic strategy is not unrelated to what Jonathan Dollimore defines as Wilde's 'transgressive aesthetic' and his 'subversion of the depth model'.[17] This strategy endorses the decentred look instead of the direct gaze, the marginal instead of the central, and the invented dramatis personae instead of the mythical.

Thus, the rich symbolic imagery, the mythical allusions, the startling statements, the appalling acts and the musical incantations of the play, function similarly to the verbal warning. They are intended to divert the reader's or the spectator's look from what seems only a narrative digression, the love of the Page and the Young Syrian. Their relations are portrayed as a counterpoint to the relations between Salomé and Iokanaan, Herod and Salomé, or Herod and Herodias. While it is lust that binds Salomé to Iokanaan, Herod to Salomé and Herodias to Herod, the bond between the Page and the Young Syrian is a bond of love. Until the moment the Young Syrian's gaze fell upon Salomé, their relations were based on the Page's worship of and devotion to the Young Syrian and on the latter's tender compliance. This was a one-sided but nevertheless fulfilling love for both, until the Syrian was seduced by Salomé. The Page's love for the Young Syrian is moving, and so is his suffering when his beloved dies. His poignant lament serves both as a tragic comment and as a counterpoint to Salomé's frenzied kissing of the Iokanaan's severed head.

It is this 'veiled' plot, the love between the two men and its tragic end, that turns *Salomé* into Wilde's 'personal mode of expression'. Aubrey Beardsley was well aware of the centrality of this argument to the Wildean discourse. His illustration 'The Woman in the Moon', the frontispiece to the English translation, shows Wilde's features as the Woman in the moon looking compassionately at the one pair of lovers in the play, the Young Syrian and the Page. A second illustration, 'A Platonic Lament', shows again Wilde's features in the sky, looking gravely at the Page, who covers the Young Syrian's dead face with caresses.[18]

It is not homosexual lust that is at the centre of the play's thematics but love between two men, love, that deep feeling that attached Wilde to Alfred Douglas, whom he had met shortly before he wrote the play *Salomé*. There is in Wilde's delicate representation of the emotional bond between the Page and the Young Syrian an element of apprehension, if not of premonition. Or was it a warning? Wilde's own emotional bond to Alfred Douglas would be one-sided and disastrous for Wilde.

*   *   *

At his trial in 1895, Wilde did not use the techniques of subterfuge. Like Salomé, who took off her seven veils in a sterile act of self-exposure that brought her to her death, so did Wilde's rejection of the strategies of encoding and displacement in personal life bring·him nearer to death. After this self-exposure, there remained for Wilde nothing but the elegy of *De Profundis* and *The Ballad of Reading Gaol*.

Wilde left prison in 1897, left England, and died in Paris three years later at the age of forty-six, his creative powers long gone. Was veiling the condition for his art?

NOTES

1   Oscar Wilde, *The Letters of Oscar Wilde*, ed. R. Hart-Davis (New York, Harcourt, Brace & World, 1962), p. 589.
2   R. Ellmann, *Oscar Wilde* (London, Hamish Hamilton, 1987), p. 306.
3   Ellmann, p. 353.
4   C. S. Nassaar, *Into the Demon Universe: A Literary Exploration of Oscar Wilde* (New Haven and London: Yale University Press, 1974), p. 80-81; P. Raby, *Oscar Wilde* (Cambridge, Cambridge University Press, 1988), p. 102.
5   G. Kahn, 'Un théâtre de l'avenir, profession de foi d'un moderniste', in *La Revue d'art dramatique* , 15 septembre 1889.
6   '*Nommer* un objet, c'est supprimer les trois-quarts de la jouissance du poème qui est faite du bonheur de deviner peu à peu; le *suggérer*, voilà le rêve. C'est le parfait usage de ce mystère qui constitue le symbole: évoquer petit à petit un objet pour montrer un état d'âme, par une série de déchiffrements.' (*My translation*) in J. Huret, *Enquête sur l'évolution littéraire*, (Paris, Charpentier, 1891), p. 60.
7   J. E. Chamberlin, *Ripe Was the Drowsy Hour: The Age of Oscar Wilde* (New York, Seabury Press, 1977), p. 176.
8   C. E. Schorske, *Fin-de-Siècle Vienna: Politics and Culture* (New York, Vintage Books, 1981), p. 224.
9   N. Auerbach, *Woman and the Demon: The Life of a Victorian Myth* (Cambridge, Mass., Harvard University Press, 1982), p. 75.
10   W. Archer, 'Mr Oscar Wilde's New Play', in *Black and White* (11 May 1893), v. p. 290. Rpt. in *Oscar Wilde: The Critical Heritage*, ed. K. Beckson (London, Routledge & Kegan Paul, 1970), p. 142.
11   N. Kohl, *Oscar Wilde: The Works of a Conformist Rebel* (Cambridge, Cambridge University Press, 1989), p. 192.

12   G. Finney, *Women in Modern Drama: Freud, Feminism, and European Theater at the Turn of the Century* (Ithaca, Cornell University Press, 1989), pp. 55-78; J. Marcus, 'Salome: The Jewish Princess Was a New Woman', *Bulletin of the New York Public Library* (1974), pp. 95-106.

13   E. Showalter, *Sexual Anarchy: Gender and Culture at the Fin de Siècle* (London, Bloomsbury, 1991), pp. 144-168.

14   P. Diel, *Le Symbolisme dans la mythologie grecque* (Paris, Payot, 1966), p. 87.

15   E. Kuryluk, *Salomé and Judas in the Cave of Sex* (Evanston, Ill., Northwestern University Press, 1897), pp. 218-20.

16   Cf. Finney, p. 59; Raby, p. 114.

17   Cf. J. Dollimore, *Sexual Dissidence: Augustine to Wilde, Freud to Foucault* (Oxford, Clarendon Press, 1991), pp. 39-100.

18   Wilde's features appear as those of Herod in a third illustration. 'Enter Herodias'.

ETHICS AND AESTHETICS IN
THE PICTURE OF DORIAN GRAY

Michael Patrick Gillespie

Socrates' pronouncement that 'the unexamined life is not worth living' can serve as a valuable preliminary assumption for anyone undertaking an interpretation of Oscar Wilde's *The Picture of Dorian Gray*. In a broad structural sense, this epigraph captures the rhetorical and intellectual design of the process that propels that novel's narrative discourse: it moves forward through a dialogic that turns on questions of how Dorian, his friends, and the readers themselves respond to the events constituting the life of the title character. From a more focused thematic perspective, Socrates' words direct attention to the importance that Wilde's novel assigns to analysing the relation between an individual's spiritual disposition and the pattern of behaviour that he chooses to follow. Thus, this ludic insight subtly illuminates Wilde's alignment of the integral association of art and morality, and it offers a sound interpretive premise for responding not simply to Dorian but to the whole work.

Nonetheless, despite the suitability of Socrates' admonition as an interpretive guide, one must resolve a number of ontological and epistemological questions before any evaluation of Wilde's writing based upon its valorization of self-reflexivity can proceed. Specifically, a commitment to an interpretive analysis of the moral postures of various individuals in the novel implicitly accepts the need for a clearly understood system of ethics to serve as the foundation for all such assessments. This acknowledgment does not dictate the endorsement a particular set of principles. It does, however, require that any such approach will delineate very precisely a stable and consistently applied system of values and that this method will suppress any contingent conjecture regarding events

137

of the novel. Furthermore, the need to ensure an even-handed implementation of such a procedure dictates that it avoid precipitating exclusionary interpretations that impose constricted readings on the work. (The role of ethics in literary criticism remains, for some, a problematic issue with its relation to aesthetic response still open to debate. Examples of how a recent critic has sought to clarify the issues appear in J. Hillis Miller's *The Ethics of Reading*.[1])

The limitations inherent in such reductive analyses become apparent when one looks at the adverse effects of prescriptive applications of ethical standards in a number of the early responses that contemporary reviewers made to Wilde's novel. Such readings have predicated their views on single-minded assumptions about the nature of *The Picture of Dorian Gray*, and these efforts present cautionary examples of the ease with which one can slip into moralistic (as opposed to moral) interpretations. The approach that I advocate effectively counteracts such tendencies without losing the insights afforded a literary analysis that foregrounds the conjunction of ethical and aesthetic standards. It achieves this equilibrium by seeking the midpoint between intellectual anarchy and mechanical responses, not simply touching the range of opinions that a cross-section of readers might hold but also remaining attentive to the diverse attitudes that shaped Wilde's views throughout the process of composition.

To clarify the aesthetic/ethical relationship and to highlight the explicative options open to the reader who acknowledges it, I would like to explore the conclusions that one might derive from two complementary principles that shape the narrative strategy of Wilde's writing: while his novel eschews the deterministic application of conventional morality, it does not fall into the reductive mode of dismissing all value systems. In fact, the narrative discourse of *The Picture of Dorian Gray* actively enables a range of possible interpretations, each specifically dependent upon a clear ethical disposition as its point of departure.

On the surface, these statements may seem tame to the point of banality, but such a view misses the imaginative implications of this both/and approach. The ethical structure of Wilde's narrative discourse represents itself as the delineation of multiplicity without anarchy: an artistic experience that privileges the post-Modern gesture of subjectivity while denying the plausibility of endless variation. This controlled pluralism offers important interpretive protocols, heretofore given little attention in interpretations of *The Picture of Dorian Gray*.

To exploit the options suggested by these perspectives, my rhetorical strategy will follow a dual track. Extra-textually, I will elaborate upon the concept — already alluded to in my reference to J. Hillis Miller — that any epistemological position depends upon inherent ethical assumptions to lend support to its conclusions. Further, I will explore the ways that individuals derive their personal moral and artistic supposition from a tradition of linked ethical and aesthetic concerns that has evolved over centuries of intellectual inquiry. (Wilde, of course, studied this tradition as a Classics scholar at Oxford. Wilde's tutor, Walter Pater, ably summarized these views in *The Renaissance*, a work that had such a profoundly affective impact upon Wilde's process of creation.) Intra-textually, I will examine the ethical system — specifically indentified as the New Hedonism propounded by the character Lord Henry Wotton — that brings so much attention to bear upon the behaviour of Dorian and all of the other characters in the novel and that raises moral issues that a reader must of necessity resolve — consciously or not — to form a lucid interpretation of the work. In this manner, without privileging a specific analytical method, I will seek to lay out the hermeneutic alternatives that immediately become apparent when one accepts the concept that *The Picture of Dorian Gray* gains aesthetic force from the possibility of diverse interpretations offered by narrative's responsiveness to a range of alternative ethical systems.[2]

Before proceeding, however, I should acknowledge the paradox upon which the methodology that I advocate rests: I believe that ethical choices inform all human action, and so our interpretations of fictional characters cannot avoid considerations based upon some set of values. At the same time, I have asserted that one can exercise ethical judgement from a number of possible points of view. From this one might argue that when personal values condition intellectual responses the danger of a purely idiosyncratic interpretation arises.

I do not believe, however, that my premise warrants such a simplistic conclusion, for, while one may find within any group of readers support for a number of different ethical positions, reference to the broad outlines of Western philosophical thought (the cognitive and cultural system that informs the milieu in which Wilde's art functions) sustains the concept that they all derive their views from a common ethical heritage, and this in itself provides the common referentiality necessary to prevent individual views from degenerating into solipsistic reverie. Nonetheless, the course of intellectual disputation often obscures traditional points of convergence. With this in mind, before exploring alternative readings of *The Picture of Dorian Gray*, I feel the need to identify the salient elements that define the parameters of an aesthetic/ethical inquiry by tracing the development of moral philosophy through Western thought by showing how convergent and divergent moral values have combined to inform modern views on aesthetics.[3]

The dialectics of Socrates underscore the fact that our society has long affirmed the ideal of right conduct. They further show how we have sought to discover and articulate the moral tenets configuring our conduct in a fashion appropriate to our beliefs. Plato extended these considerations beyond the Socratic concern for immediate material gain to the examination of a system — designated as ethics — that functions as a means to goodness and that sees goodness as a means to happiness.

In subsequent discourse, however, it became apparent that this approach did not fully delimit the parameters of philosophical inquiry. Aristotle, in fact, saw ethics as the science of right conduct, but he did not see goodness as a means to happiness. (For him happiness is activity, specifically activity in accordance with virtue.) Aristotle sought to clarify these views through the methodical study of values, chiefly in his *Nicomachean Ethics*, through a rigorous analysis of attributes considered virtuous, and through his articulation of the Golden Mean, the middle ground between extremes of behaviour. (The debate over whether goodness led to happiness arguably remained a central philosophical question until the eighteenth century when Kant began to assert the importance of doing right simply for its own cause and apart from self-interested motivations.)

From the Stoics on through the writings of St Augustine, to the Scholastics (especially St Thomas Aquinas), and then in the works of the Humanists, discussions related to ethics centered upon how and why goodness produced happiness. During the Renaissance, however — in writers as diverse as Machiavelli, Luther, and Hobbes — a series of pragmatic alternatives arose to challenge the implicit idealism of debates about ethical conduct. (One might argue that the underlying cynicism of such writers as Machiavelli grew out of a predictable reaction to views of some Christian philosophers that linked ethical behaviour as much with the avoidance of guilt as with the pursuit of happiness.) With David Hume a growing sense of the subjectivity of ethical endeavours became an explicit part of the discourse. In the nineteenth century Jeremy Bentham and other Utilitarians articulated, even more emphatically than did Hume, concepts of a normative ethics that seemed to preclude reliance upon objective standards to guide behaviour. Nonetheless, despite this fluctuation from age to age of the position and the methaphysical justification of ethics in the social matrix, no one mounted a sustained and convincing argument against its ineluctable presence.[4]

This evolving view of ethics as a personal standard for behaviour provided an important transitional concept for what would ultimately become Wilde's view of the relation of art and morality. The emerging sense of a subjective ethics served an enabling function in the development of mid-nineteenth-century aesthetic attitudes like those of the Pre-Raphaelite Brotherhood. Assertions of the efficacy of diverse moral systems provided the basis for a strong analogous argument for the validity of a range of aesthetic views: if at its heart our moral system admitted a relativistic bias (no matter how apparently small), then attempts to restrict value judgements of lesser significance, like those relating to aesthetics, would be ludicrous.

Buoyed by this critical latitude, the Pre-Raphaelites rejected all artistic conventions designed to heighten the effect of a work through artifice and emphasized truthfulness and simplicity, often reflected in a devotion to Nature. Furthermore, they took a utilitarian position that gave value to art works as ends in themselves rather than as means to separate goals. The Pre-Raphaelites laid the groundwork for the view of art as aesthetically and ethically self-contained, summed up in the single phrase — art for art's sake — that impelled the Aesthetic Movement.

Introduced and championed in France by Théophile Gautier, Charles Baudelaire, Gustave Flaubert, and Stéphane Mallarmé, the Aesthetic Movement found an able English spokesman in Walter Pater. All of these men subscribed to the doctrine that art represents the supreme value because it stands as self-sufficient and has no aim beyond its own perfection. To this end, they asserted that the function of a work of art lies simply in its existence and in its ability to exude beauty, indifferent to current social values.

This proposition advances a critical redefinition of the relationship of art and morality, and it provides an important perspective on Wilde's novel. At first glance, art for art's sake may seem a direct rejection of morality in favour of pleasure, but the Aesthetic Movement in fact took a far more complex view of the relationship between the two. Rather than denying a place for ethics within an aesthetic experience (the either/or choice), it instead denied primacy to conventional value systems and bluntly asserted the validity of alternative moralities (the both/and alternative).

While England was still absorbing this new interpretation, in France artistic attitudes continued to evolve. The Aesthetic Movement gave way to the Decadents who held that Art occupied a position totally opposed to Nature — both in the sense of nature as a physical force of biological change and in the sense of nature as a metaphysical condition presenting standards of morality. In place of the heightened sensitivity of the Pre-Raphaelites, artists like Rimbaud advocated 'the systematic derangement of all senses'. With a self-conscious and restless curiosity, the Decadents placed art as supreme to Nature, and they attacked accepted standards through over-refined sensibilities and an aggressive perversion of convention. It was against this backdrop that Wilde offered his rendering of the relationship between art and morality in *The Picture of Dorian Gray.*

One needs, however, to avoid the too easy correlation with Wilde's work and contemporaneous Continental aesthetic/ethical attitudes. The 1895 trials that eventually led to Wilde's incarceration at hard labour for two years may have associated him in the popular imagination with Decadence and the Decadent Movement. Nonetheless, the artistic concerns of his writing in fact took up less sensational yet far more sophisticated issues. Specifically, the Aesthetic Movement, and in particular the views of Walter Pater as he articulated them in *The Renaissance,* provided Wilde with rigorous yet unconventional creative standards. These criteria permitted a multiplicity that went beyond narrow moral lines without succumbing to the extravagant nihilism of the Decadents.[5]

Moreover, Pater grounded his version of the Aesthetic Movement upon an acknowledged — if somewhat idiosyncratic — system of values in a fashion that clearly appealed to Wilde's imagination. As Wilde himself surely knew, despite the aura of iniquity that the concept suggests to some, Pater's advocacy of the idea of art for art's sake does not abandon ethics. Even his notion of autonomous art, seemingly aloof from the influence of moral judgement, rests upon clear, though admittedly unconventional, ethical standards. As the famous conclusion to *The Renaissance* demonstrates, Pater's views offer a new approach to ethical/aesthetic thinking.

> *Philosophiren,* says Novalis, *ist dephlegmatisiren, vivificiren* (to philosophize is to cast off inertia, to vitalize). The service of philosophy, of speculative culture, towards the human spirit, is to rouse, to startle it to a life of constant and eager observation. Every moment some form grows perfect in hand or face; some tone on the hills or the sea is choicer than the rest; some mood of passion or insight or intellectual excitement is irresistibly real and attractive to us, — for that moment only. Not the fruit of experience, but experience itself, is the end. A counted number of pulses only is given to us of a variegated dramatic life. How may we see in them all that is to be seen in them by the finest senses? How shall we pass most swiftly from point to point, and be present always at the focus where the greater number of vital forces unite in their purest energy?
>   To burn always with this hard, gemlike flame, to maintain this ecstasy, is success in life. In a sense it might even

be said that our failure is to form habits: for, after all, habit is
relative to a stereotyped world, and meantime it is only the
roughness of the eye that makes any two persons, things,
situations, seem alike. While all melts under our feet, we may
well grasp at any exquisite passion, or any contribution to
knowledge that seems by a lifted horizon to set the spirit free
for a moment, or any stirring of the senses, strange dyes, strange
colours, and curious odours, or work of the artist's hands, or
the face of one's friend. Not to discriminate in every moment
some passionate attitude in those about us, and in the very
brilliancy of their gifts some tragic dividing of forces on their
ways, is, on this short day of frost and sun, to sleep before
evening. With this sense of the splendour of our experience and
of its awful brevity, gathering all we are into a desperate effort
to see and touch, we shall hardly have time to make theories
about the things we see and touch. What we have to do is to be
for ever curiously testing new opinions and courting new
impressions, never acquiescing in a facile orthodoxy of Comte,
or of Hegel, or of our own.[6]

Neither virulently iconoclastic like the Decadents nor
prescriptively conventional like the mainstream Victorian
critics, Pater's views embrace the need for clearly articulated
standards yet reject the analogous proposition that those
standards of necessity impose a rigid, narrow range of
interpretive options. Nonetheless, despite Pater's wide-
ranging and unconventional opinions on the way that one might
approach aesthetic sensation, he acknowledges the hierarchy
of values and sustains the systematic cohesion that one expects
in ethically influenced views of art. In fact, his self-conscious
efforts to foreground the role of philosophy through the
quotation from Novalis signals, to my mind, Pater's own
unwavering sense of the inexorable conjunction of some set of
moral principles and the highest forms of aesthetic pleasure.

Despite this innovative theoretical approach, Pater's
best known effort to put these views into practice, his novel
Marius the Epicurean, leaves one still unsure of the artistic
potential of his epistemology. *Marius the Epicurean* affirms
Pater's belief in the unification of art and morality by
attempting to provide an imaginative context for these views.
Unfortunately, its philosophical ambitiousness cannot
compensate for its creative weaknesses. The depictions not only
of Marius but of all the other major characters seem shallow
and formalistic, there only to elucidate some theme.

Additionally, the discourse of the novel follows a pattern of pedantic exposition rather than one of imaginative narration. *Marius the Epicurean* does, however, introduce intellectual issues that prepare one for Wilde's more accessible and balanced discourse on the topic of the relation of moral values and art.

In fact, the narrative of *The Picture of Dorian Gray* privileges the affiliation of ethics and aesthetics in a manner that parallels *Marius the Epicurean*, and, by a radical articulation of this association, it challenges readers to assess their own concept of this relationship. The novel does not prescribe a single mode of answering the questions implicit in its discourse, but it does foreground an internal ethical programme — New Hedonism. This system makes a direct claim for the shaping effect of art upon one's character, and it asserts the primacy of a doctrine of pleasure that absolves individuals from the ordinary responsibilities for their actions. Readers measure its effect by contrasting it with the conventional Victorian morality in the work and with whatever ethical systems, conventional or otherwise that they bring to the text.

The singular difference between these two works emerges from the divergent impact of their representations. Pater's discourse remains firmly under the control of his philosophical concerns, and so it often takes the form of a heuristic. Wilde's narrative, on the other hand, while implicitly acknowledging the impact of his aesthetics upon thematic and stylistic concerns, keeps its author's creative powers in the forefront of the reader's imagination.

The most sustained representation of the way that this artistic temperament configures one's moral position appears early on, when Lord Henry introduces the concept of New Hedonism into the narrative during his first conversation with Dorian.

> Nothing can cure the soul but the senses, just as nothing can cure the senses but the soul. (p. 20)

> Ah! realise your youth while you have it. Don't squander the gold of your days, listening to the tedious, trying to improve the hopeless failure, or giving away your life to the ignorant, the

common, and the vulgar. These are the sickly aims, the false
ideals, of our age. Live! Live the wonderful life that is in you!
Let nothing be lost upon you. Be always searching for new
sensations. Be afraid of nothing [...] A new Hedonism — that is
what our century wants. You might be its visible symbol. With
your personality there is nothing you could not do. The world
belongs to you for a season. (Wilde's ellipsis) (p. 22)

Lord Henry's appeal to Dorian, in language far blunter and yet
far more imaginative than Pater's narrative, unambiguously
rejects the call of Duty that resonates throughout so much
Victorian literature.

Nonetheless, despite his extravagant, solipsistic
speech, in two important gestures he underscores a commitment
to his own kind of moral perspective. In his reference to the soul
in the first quotation, Lord Henry acknowledges a
metaphysical dynamics operating within the human condition
while stopping short of suggesting a set of values that could
govern behaviour. A few pages later, in propounding his New
Hedonism, he presents not a nullification of values but a
hierarchy of standards that contrasts sharply with the
world's. Lord Henry's introduction, however, stands as a bare
outline of this system. As the narrative unfolds, both he and
Dorian provide a far clearer sense of what the ethics of New
Hedonism entail.

Despite his role as the novel's most vocal exponent of
New Hedonism, a great irony nonetheless informs Lord Henry's
character, for no matter how extravagant his language, he
seems to do relatively little. In this case, however, action does
not stand out as the only measure of one's commitment, for in a
running commentary on Dorian's life that encompasses the
length of the novel, Harry manages to offer a clear sense of
what he believes and of his own manner of involvement. Early
on, he makes clear the privileged position that he assigns to
any new experience — whether direct or voyeuristic — when he
shares with Basil Hallward his reaction to the news of
Dorian's engagement to Sibyl Vane.

If a personality fascinates me, whatever mode of expression that
personality selects is absolutely delightful to me. Dorian Gray
falls in love with a beautiful girl who acts Juliet, and proposes
to marry her. Why not? If he wedded Messalina he would be
none the less interesting. You know I am not a champion of

> marriage. [...] I hope that Dorian Gray will make this girl his
> wife, passionately adore her for six months, and then suddenly
> become fascinated by someone else. He would be a wonderful
> study. (pp. 73-74)

Basil protests against such an outspoken articulation of
New Hedonism by refusing to believe that Harry holds views
as cynical as his statements suggest. Lord Henry, however,
rebuffs this meliorative gesture and counters with an unblinking
assessment of human nature. 'The reason we all like to think so
well of others is that we are all afraid for ourselves. [...] We
praise the banker that we may overdraw our account, and find
good qualities in the highwayman in the hope that he may
spare our pockets' (p. 74).

Harry's ethical positions, however, go beyond the
simple negation of popular pieties. In fact, despite his self-
avowed fascination with artificiality, he bases his mode of
conduct upon a Rousseau-like naturalism that attests to his
affinity with the Pre-Raphaelites:

> Pleasure is the only thing worth having a theory about. [...] But I
> am afraid that I cannot claim my theory as my own. It belongs to
> Nature, not to me. Pleasure is Nature's test, her sign of
> approval. When we are happy we are always good, but when
> we are good we are not always happy. (p. 77)

Lord Henry's love of paradoxes causes him to introduce some
potential imprecision into his statement — with the meaning
that he assigns to the term good arguably shifting in midsentence. Nonetheless, the association of goodness and pleasure
introduces a metaphysical benefit into some forms of action:
going back to the Greek philosophers, Harry conjoins goodness
and happiness, thus injecting ethical considerations into his
world. Of course, Lord Henry's ethics evolve from a subjective
consciousness and remain fixed in a marginal position, spurning
the conventional markers for right behavior. He tells Dorian as
much when he comforts the young man over the death of Sibyl
Vane:

> Good resolutions are useless attempts to interfere with
> scientific laws. Their origin is pure vanity. Their result is
> absolutely *nil*. They give us, now and then, some of those
> luxurious sterile emotions that have a certain charm for the

weak. That is all that can be said for them. They are simply
cheques that men draw on a bank where they have no account.
(p. 100)

Dorian, like Lord Henry, also subscribes to New
Hedonism, but one can derive useful insights from differences in
the way the two men adhere to their views. Dorian's
acceptance of this ethical system develops over the course of
the novel, and his active development of its implications — as
opposed to Harry's voyeuristic approach — provides ample
illustration of the facets of New Hedonism. He says as much to
Lord Henry when explaining his infatuation with Sibyl Vane.
'[I]t never would have happened if I had not met you. You
filled me with a wild desire to know everything about life'
(pp. 47-48).

The need to immerse oneself in unfamiliar sensations
stands as the informing element of this love that he feels for
Sibyl, and as the motivating force guiding Dorian's behaviour.

> Why should I not love her? [...] Night after night I go to see her
> play. [...] I have seen her in every age and in every costume.
> Ordinary women never appeal to one's imagination. They are
> limited to their century. [...] But an actress! How different an
> actress is. (pp. 50-51)

As Dorian becomes more involved in New Hedonism, its tenets
become more obvious. Gratification emerges as a positive good,
and innovation stands out as the key to satisfaction.

> When he thought of her, it would be as a wonderful tragic figure
> sent on to the world's stage to show the supreme reality of love.
> A wonderful tragic figure? Tears came to his eyes as he
> remembered her childlike look and winsome fanciful ways and
> shy tremulous grace. He brushed them away hastily, and looked
> again at the picture.
>   He felt that the time had really come for making his
> choice. Or had his choice already been made? Yes, life had
> decided that for him — life, and his own infinite curiosity about
> life. Eternal youth, infinite passion, pleasures subtle and secret,
> wild joys and wilder sins — he was to have all these things.
> The portrait was to bear the burden of his shame: that was all.
> (p. 105)

This passage marks a crucial point in the narrative. It
captures Dorian in a moment of irresolution before he has

accepted the fact that his private ethics run counter to the public morals of Victorian society. It shows, on one hand, how the transmutation of his sorrow over Sibyl's death into a source of satisfaction becomes a positive act coinciding with his new ethical sense. At the same time, the passage reflects how Dorian still feels the need to displace the burden of shame generated by a lingering sense of obligation derived from his old moral values.

Within a short time, however, this ambivalence resolves itself into a more clearly defined ethical attitude. When Basil Hallward calls upon Dorian shortly after Sibyl's death, Dorian's unconventional view of grief shows the effect that New Hedonism is beginning to have:

> It is only shallow people who require years to get rid of an emotion. A man who is master of himself can end a sorrow as easily as he can invent a pleasure. I don't want to be at the mercy of my emotions. I want to use them, to enjoy them, and to dominate them. (p. 108)

With the indoctrination of Lord Henry taking effect, Dorian comes to read Sibyl's death from a purely New Hedonistic perspective.

> As a rule, people who act lead the most commonplace lives. They are good husbands, or faithful wives, or something tedious. You know what I mean — middle-class virtue, and all that kind of thing. How different Sibyl was! She lived her finest tragedy. (p. 109)

One should note the ethical position inherent in this gesture. Like any moralist, Dorian judges Sibyl's behaviour according to a pre-determined set of standards. The radical nature of such values shocks the conventional Basil Hallward, but they remain ethical standards nonetheless.

After the death of Sibyl Vane, Dorian seems to become increasingly inured to the liberating views of this alternative ethical system. In a passage that appears early in chapter eleven, the narrative summarizes Dorian's evolving feelings.

> Yes: there was to be, as Lord Henry had prophesied, a New Hedonism that was to recreate life, and to save it from the harsh, uncomely puritanism that is having, in our own day, its

> curious revival. It was to have its service of the intellect,
> certainly; yet, it was never to accept any theory or system that
> would involve the sacrifice of any mode of passionate
> experience. Its aim, indeed, was to be experience itself, and not
> the fruits of experience, sweet or bitter as they might be. Of the
> asceticism that deadens the senses, as of the vulgar profligacy
> that dulls them, it was to know nothing. But it was to teach man
> to concentrate himself upon the moments of a life that is itself
> but a moment. (pp. 130-131)

In this stark articulation of the aims of New Hedonism one sees
a far different moral view than anything expressed in
conventional approaches. Nonetheless, it stands as a viable
alternative to traditional ethical programmes. As one would
expect in the outline of any moral system, Lord Henry
delineates New Hedonism by laying out its goals, providing
guidance on how to achieve those goals, and establishing a
means for judging behaviour in relation to those goals.

This detailed description of New Hedonism, however,
does not in itself legitimize it, and so its function within the
discourse stands open to debate. Specifically, the question
remains as to whether the assumptions governing this system's
structure possess sufficient depth to provide the necessary
ethical support to govern the way Dorian lives. The discourse
of the last two chapters offers at best an ambiguous answer.

Chapter nineteen opens with the articulation of
apparently divergent moral positions by the two heretofore
leading proponents of New Hedonism. Dorian, during a
discussion with Lord Henry, declares his intention to follow the
conventional path towards reformation. 'I have done too many
dreadful things in my life. I am not going to do any more'
(p. 209). Harry, in contrast, remains ostensively aloof from
pangs of conscience produced by Victorian morality. 'Death and
vulgarity are the only two facts in the nineteenth century that
one cannot explain away' (p. 213).

Nonetheless, the disparities stand as less distinct than
they initially appear, for even Lord Henry seems to retain, if
not certain traditional scruples, an obvious squeamishness with
regard to the details of some of Dorian's more extravagant
experiments in seeking out new experience. When, for example,
Dorian hints at a personal involvement in a truly violent act —
the killing of Basil Hallward — Harry offers an equivocal

response, and thus avoids confronting the limits of new experience.

> 'What would you say, Harry, if I told you that I had murdered Basil?' said the younger man. He watched him intently after he had spoken.
> 'I would say, my dear fellow, that you were posing for a character that doesn't suit you. All crime is vulgar, just as all vulgarity is crime. It is not in you, Dorian, to commit a murder. I am sorry if I hurt your vanity by saying so, but I assure you it is true. Crime belongs exclusively to the lower orders. I don't blame them in the smallest degree. I should fancy that crime was to them what art is to us, simply a method of procuring extraordinary sensations.' (p. 213)

As the conversation continues, however, Dorian refuses to allow Lord Henry the easy dismissal of consideration of the moral consequences of one's behaviour. Instead, he turns the discourse to a reflection on the metaphysical implications of all human action. 'The soul is a terrible reality. It can be bought, and sold, and bartered away. It can be poisoned, or made perfect. There is a soul in each one of us. I know it' (p. 215).

Harry's response blithely sidesteps the issues of consequence and responsibility by denying the existence of the soul as the metaphysical force that would validate such concerns: 'the things one feels absolutely certain about are never true.' In this unwillingness to confront Dorian's more extreme vision of New Hedonism — one that encompasses murder as a new experience — Harry shows an imperfect acceptance of the system that he had articulated earlier in the novel. Nonetheless, he retains a basic fidelity to New Hedonism, dismissing his friend's inchoate efforts to embrace conventional morality through reformation as nothing more than an attempt to acquire a previously unknown experience. 'I should think the novelty of the emotion must have given you a thrill of real pleasure' (p. 210).

Lord Henry in fact gives no real credence to the idea of Dorian's returning to the acceptance of a conventional Victorian morality. Harry goes beyond simply rationalizing Dorian's apparent minor deviations from the values of New Hedonism.

He lauds his friend's life as an ideal representation of this alternative ethical system.

> I wish I could change places with you, Dorian. The world has cried out against us both, but it has always worshipped you. It always will worship you. You are a type of what the age is searching for, and what it is afraid it has found. I am so glad that you have never done anything, never carved a statue, or painted a picture, or produced anything outside of yourself! Life has been your art. You have set yourself to music. Your days are your sonnets. (p. 217)

Dorian's unwillingness to take comfort in such encomiums, however, attests to his growing ambivalence regarding the efficacy of New Hedonism, and it confronts readers with the question of how to assess most effectively the ethical implications of his behaviour. The final chapter of the novel underscores this conflict by its parallels with the close of chapter seven after Dorian's fight with Sibyl Vane but before he has learned of her death. In the earlier episode, Dorian discovers the first slight change that has insinuated itself into his picture, and he resolves to reform his life. In the closing pages of chapter twenty, Dorian returns to the picture to assess the results of resisting the temptation to seduce Hetty Merton. 'A cry of pain and indignation broke from him. He could see no change, save that in the eyes there was a look of cunning, and in the mouth the curved wrinkle of the hypocrite' (p. 221). Within moments of this discovery, Dorian seizes the knife that he had used to murder Basil Hallward with and stabs the picture, thus killing himself.

Despite the obvious closure that this gesture imposes upon the action, it does little to dispel the ambiguity that has conditioned the discourse. Did New Hedonism fail Dorian, or did he fail to make a sufficient commitment to its tenets? The act itself resolves Dorian's fate, but it raises issues reflective of how our judgement of the ethical principles condition broad interpretations of action in the novel.

I do not believe that one can arrive at a definitive answer to this question by recourse to the narrative, for too many variables intervene and make valid a range of diverse interpretations. These circumstances have not, however, dissuaded any number of readers from offering, in a definitive fashion, very different interpretations based upon a variety of ethical positions ranging from harsh condemnations to unqualified approval of Dorian's behaviour.[7] Each reading contributes illuminating perspectives on the nature of Dorian and on the disposition of the narrative discourse. At the same time, each in itself can offer no more than a partial resolution of the issues raised by the novel.

This condition enforces the necessity for the both/and approach to interpretation: the scope of valid explications of the discourse suggests the need to articulate an interpretive strategy that draws directly upon the ethical perspective of the individual reader while acknowledging the need for awareness of the range of alternative views that contribute to a full sense of the ethical/aesthetic meaning of the work.[8]

In fact, the oscillation of the narrative discourse provides a functional illustration of the interpretive model that I have already suggested. The solipsism of New Hedonism frankly appeals to the ego of every reader, and, at the same time, the obvious pressure to conform to social mores that recurs throughout the narrative also evokes conditions familiar to us all. As we confront the ambiguities of the ethics of New Hedonism, we face, more directly than in most acts of interpretation, the impact exerted upon our aesthetic sense by our ethical views. Thus, assessing *The Picture of Dorian Gray* gives us the self-reflexive opportunity to increase our awareness of the standards that shape our interpretive assumptions.

The propositions of the novel, however, go beyond a simple philosophical exercise, for they enable us to indulge a range of alternative ethical responses without incurring the consequences that such actual behaviour would provoke. Thus *The Picture of Dorian Gray* — like *Oedipus Rex*, *King Lear*, or *Paradise Lost* — certainly builds upon our sense of our own ethical values. More to the point, however, it illuminates these values and those of alternative ethical systems within the security of an artistic milieu, without a sense of guilt or responsibility for what has occurred.

In consequence, *The Picture of Dorian Gray* does not and should not bring us to a new ethical position or reinforce our old one. Rather, through the actions of its characters its discourse establishes within us a sense of the wide-ranging aesthetic force that ethics exerts upon a work of art. Furthermore, Wilde's novel gives us the opportunity to enhance the mix of our aesthetic and ethical views by extending our sense of the possibilities for interpretation beyond those delineated by our immediate hermeneutic system.

NOTES

1. *The Ethics of Reading.* New York, Columbia University Press, 1987; see also his *Versions of Pygmalion*. Cambridge, Harvard University Press, 1990. Miller's assessment of how ethics shapes aesthetic views stands as far more prescriptive than my own, but I still see value in his articulation of the issue.

2. Not every critic would support the view that ethics and aesthetics function interdependently in *The Picture of Dorian Gray*. For an elaboration of view that the novel 'examines frankly the consequences of substituting an aesthetic for an ethical conscience', see D. Manganiello's 'Ethics and Aesthetics in *The Picture of Dorian Gray*'. *The Canadian Journal of Irish Studies 9* (December 1983), 25-33.

3. For a more detailed look at the relationship of ethical views to literary interpretation, see R. Hoopes' *Right Reason in the English Renaissance*. Cambridge, Harvard University Press, 1962. Although Hoopes wrote this study over thirty years ago, it remains a useful scholarly survey of the topic.

4. One can, of course, find sporadic articulations of such a view throughout history. It is not, however, until the rise of Existentialism in the middle of the 20th century that this perspective gained legitimacy as an alternative school of thought.

5. R. Ellmann has pointed to this connection between Wilde and Pater, and has also noted the influence of Ruskin, in his essay 'Overtures to *Salome*'. In *Oscar Wilde: A Collection of Critical Essays*. Ed. R. Ellmann. Englewood Cliffs, Prentice-Hall, 1969. In my view, Ellmann takes a reductive approach in this view that '[i]n *Dorian Gray* the Pater side of Wilde's thought is routed, though not deprived of fascination'. Nonetheless, he rightly draws attention to the informing impact of both men upon Wilde's aesthetics.

6. I. Murray reprints the 1888 conclusion of Pater's *The Renaissance* in her edition of *The Picture of Dorian Gray*, pp. 225-229. This quotation appears on pp. 227-228. All quotations from Wilde's novel are taken from this edition.

7. Such views are reflected in the contemporary newspaper reviews of the novel already mentioned. One also finds a very precise ethical position articulated in several recent critical works. Traditional moral readings of *The Picture of Dorian Gray* appear in C. S. Nassaar's *Into the Demon Universe: A Literary Exploration of Oscar Wilde*. New Haven, Yale

University Press, 1974. P. K. Cohen takes a similar approach in his *The Moral Vision of Oscar Wilde.* Rutherford, N.J., Fairleigh Dickinson University Press, 1978. Examples of the same sort of ethical reading from a very different perspective, the social hermeneutics of gay criticism, appear in the following essays: ed. Cohen's 'Writing Gone Wilde: Homoerotic Desire in the Closet of Repression'. *PMLA* 102 (1987), 801-813; and J. Dollimore's 'Different Desires: Subjectivity and Transgression in Wilde and Gide'. *Genders 2* (Summer 1988), 24-41.

8   This process calls to mind the writerly text, as described by R. Barthes, that demands the active engagement of the reader to complete its meaning. For a full discussion of this concept see Barthes' *S/Z.* Trans. R. Miller. New York, Hill and Wang, 1974.

WILDE'S 'PLAYS OF MODERN LIFE' ON THE CONTEMPORARY BRITISH STAGE

Robert Gordon

While not revived with anything like the frequency of *The Importance of Being Earnest*, *Lady Windermere's Fan* and *An Ideal Husband* have been presented by British theatre producers fairly regularly since the Second World War. By contrast, it appears that *A Woman of No Importance* received no major production in Britain in this period until the Glasgow Citizens' Theatre presented it in 1984.

Peter Hall's revisionist production of the original four-act version of *The Importance of Being Earnest* (1982) may be seen to have initiated a new kind of interest in the performance of Wilde's plays in the contemporary British theatre. Hall dispensed with the exquisitely poised aristocratic acting and stylised visual effects of the Gielgud productions which had been so influential from the time of his famous 1939 revival. At the National Theatre in 1982, Judi Dench was a decidedly middle class and quite naturalistically characterised Lady Bracknell in a sepia-toned setting whose first act called to mind nothing so much as an 1890s production by George Alexander. The realism of the production style was a timely reminder of the connection between that play and the three society dramas which preceded it between 1892 and 1894. The period accuracy of the decor for Acts I and IV, and the low-key acting style reminded an audience that no matter how witty and artificial the conception and plot of *The Importance of Being Earnest* is, the play does refer pointedly if playfully to the upper class milieu of late Victorian London.

Steven Berkoff's innovative *Salome* at the National Theatre in 1988 uncompromisingly set the action in the context of an upper class 1920s country house weekend party, startling the audience into a recognition of the literal truth about the hedonistic milieu so often obscured under more than just seven veils of decadent pseudo-Biblical Cecil B. de Millinery. In so doing, he liberated the grotesque humour which more conventionally operatic or poetic productions have suppressed, revealing the savage and sophisticated domestic comedy contained within Wilde's Symbolist Gesamtkunstwerk.

These theatrical attempts to express the complex relationships between the fictional world and social reality in plays which quite clearly demand a certain degree of stylisation in performance, taken together with the production of the three society plays by Philip Prowse at the Glasgow Citizens' Theatre during the mid-1980s, represent a clear break with the old conventions of staging Wilde's plays, preparing the way for Philip Prowse's magnificent production of *A Woman of No Importance* which ran for a year from 1991 and Peter Hall's subtle and exquisitely acted revival of *An Ideal Husband* which opened in November 1992 and is still running in the West End of London. Viewed in conjunction with Maggie Smith's 1993 critical and commercial triumph in Nicholas Hytner's production of *The Importance of Being Earnest*, the British theatre of the 1990s can be said to be rediscovering Oscar Wilde with almost as much excitement as it first discovered him in the 1890s.

Reading the reviews of the production of *A Woman of No Importance* one is struck by way in which literal-minded and unintentionally philistine theatre journalists echo the confusion and distaste of early reviewers and later commentators on this most difficult of Wilde's commercial successes. Wilde himself had anticipated contemporary reception theory by almost a century in his curtain speech after the triumphant first night of *Lady Windermere's Fan*:

> Ladies and gentlemen: I have enjoyed this evening immensely. The actors have given us a charming rendering of a delightful play, and your appreciation has been most intelligent. I congratulate you on the great success of your performance, which persuades me that you think almost as highly of the play as I do myself.

Post-structuralists remind us of the extent to which literary works read their readers, and the typically simplistic and patronising responses to *A Woman of No Importance* form a revealing profile of the average London theatre reviewer as an earnest hedonist without the imagination to conceive that the play's late Victorian theatre conventions are merely the vehicle through which Wilde so shrewdly captures the interest of his contemporary middle class audience in order to express a series of complex and engagingly modern arguments about English society's double standard with respect to class and gender. (This is a bit like accusing *Hamlet* of being a potboiler because it is based on a tradition of revenge melodrama, or, for that matter of writing off *The Importance of Being Earnest* for being a silly 19th Century farce!)

Jack Tinker, writing in *The Daily Mail*, (10 October 1991) typifies the vulgar criticism of the play's alleged inadequacies at its most banal.

> This is probably the least important of Oscar Wilde's best-known successes. Indeed, whenever I have the rare occasion to renew acquaintance with it I am forced to conclude that his entire reputation must be sustained by that other subject of importance — Ernest. However if there is one man to distract us from its impossibly awkward melodramatic moralising, it is Philip Prowse. As designer, he can ravish the eye with sets and costumes whenever, as director, he most needs to distract our ears from Wilde's crude gear-changes, with the scintillating anagrams [sic] juddering into sickly social conscience. [...]. Sadly to quote, Wilde as so often, chooses to hang 'full panoplies of his brilliance on a worn-out clothes-horse of a plot'. Worse, to my mind, he hands out all the brilliance to the bad-mouthers. To the good and dogooders, he bequeaths the clothes-horse [...]. One is left with the depressing conclusion that, having his heart in the right place regarding embryo women's lib, Wilde could not make his pen follow suit [...] [Mrs Arbuthnot] is and remains a self-righteous bore.

Tinker's attack on the play is so muddled, that he almost succeeds by accident in making most of the important points one might wish to raise in its defence. I have always felt that the play's ingenuity lies in the way Wilde deliberately establishes a dialectical tension between the epigrammatic worldliness of his dandy philosophers and the tragicomic naivety of the honest Puritans, undermining the complacency of the very same audience which might a year before they saw *A Woman of No Importance*, have been just a little affronted by the moral rehabilitation of the witty and worldly Mrs Erlynne, the woman with a past of *Lady Windermere's Fan*.

By seeming to begin where the earlier play had left off, Wilde initially tricks his audience into a ready acceptance of the dandy's code of worldliness which he knew he could not presume upon when writing *Lady Windermere's Fan*. The more the audience enjoys the paradoxical immoralism of the sophisticated dandies, Lord Illingworth and Mrs Allonby, the greater will be the shock when it discovers how vicious and corrupt Illingworth actually is. If Illingworth is as dangerously attractive a personality in the first two acts of *A Woman of No Importance* as Wilde reputedly was in his dazzling society appearances, he is in no way a replica of the naughty but warm-hearted Lord Darlington of the earlier play. In all of Wilde's society plays it is the naively moral characters who grow and acquire the wisdom to understand the erring nature of the passionate individual. But in *A Woman of No Importance* it is the mechanics of the melodrama plot that engineers the gradual development of Christ-like wisdom, not the persuasive wit or machinations of the dandies. To have made the Wildean aesthete Lord Illingworth the embodiment of the paternalistic and imperialistic values of late Victorian capitalism is in many respects Wilde's stroke of genius.

In conversation with Herbert Beerbohm Tree who was about to essay the role of Illingworth, Wilde himself was as ever narcissistically conscious of the potency of this new stage creation:

> This witty aristocrat [...] in my play is unlike anyone who has been seen on the stage before. He is like no one who has existed before [...]. He is certainly not natural. He is a figure of art. Indeed, if you can bear the truth, he is MYSELF.

Equally, however, it could be claimed that Wilde was the fallen woman, Mrs Arbuthnot, which accounts for the force of the second major ironic reversal of audience expectations. The implication that on the philosophical plane (given that they are able to learn from their mistakes and their suffering) the tragic Christian world view achieved by the Puritan characters is the only serious basis for human relationships provides a theatre audience with the unsettling experience of having to re-think its earlier accommodation of Wilde's witty arguments in favour of unrestrained hedonism. A final shock is conveyed by the ending: the necessity for Hester, Gerald and Mrs Arbuthnot to live in America clearly demonstrates the impossibility of living a genuinely moral life within the hypocritical and moralistic society of late Victorian England. Small wonder that, as Shaw observed in his review of *An Ideal Husband*,

> They laugh angrily at his epigrams like a child who is coaxed into being amused in the very act of setting up a yell of rage and agony.

Wilde's love affair with Lord Alfred Douglas was at the height of its intensity while he was writing *A Woman of No Importance* and it is surely not fanciful to hear in the pseudo-Biblical prose of Mrs Arbuthnot's speeches to Gerald in Act IV Wilde's expression of his own shame about the guilty secret he was hiding from his wife Constance:

> I am a tainted thing. But my wrongs are my own, and I will bear them alone [...] marriage is a sacrament for those who love each other. It is not for such as him, or such as me. Gerald, to save you from the world's sneers and taunts I have lied to the world. I could not tell the world the truth. Who can, ever?

Equally, it is impossible not to read Hester's sweeping condemnation of men and women who have sinned and Mrs Arbuthnot's bitter expressions of hatred for the aristocrat who wronged her as projections of the feelings Wilde imagined Constance might experience when she discovered the true nature of his friendship with Lord Alfred.

Wilde's passionate identification with the situation and suffering of each major character in turn seems to me to give the play its peculiar intensity. Far from being a simplistic mismatch of self-conscious *bon mots* and mawkish melodrama it employs the full range of Wilde's characteristic prose styles, including the language of Biblical parable from the stories, the bejewelled idiom of the nineteenth century Hellenist, the paradoxical immoralism of the Paterian aesthete as elaborated in the essays and dialogues and the virtuoso epigrammatic juggling of Wilde's own social performances. In my opinion, those very qualities which make it so easy to ridicule and so difficult to perform, distinguish it from its sources in French boulevard drama and the English well-made play as a disturbing masterpiece in the mannerist style which explores as a psychological phenomenon the doubleness which characterises late Victorian sexual morality, social values and political ideas.

The opening of Philip Prowse's production established the terms of the drama's complex interplay of styles as a key to its dialectic of counterpoised meanings. While members of the audience were still finding their seats, they witnessed an extended pantomime in which a barefoot young aristocrat (later identified as Lord Alfred) played a mock game of croquet. This opening focussed the audience's attention on an ornately gilded autumnal setting with a lily pond and ornamental urns, backed by a vast gilt picture frame exhibiting a landscape painting after Claude, before which Sir John and Lady Caroline Pontefract langorously strolled with Hester Worsley. The opening exchange about English country houses and the joke about America having no country made immediate sense of the visual image. Wilde's English country is completely landscaped, nature utterly transformed into art. The spontaneity of the young American woman (played by a black actress, Julie Saunders, as if to accentuate the character's position as outsider) is shown in direct contrast to the elaborate artifice of the English women's magnificent peacock attire, heavy with jewellery and causing the men to pale into insignificance, at least until the carefully prepared entrance of Lord Illingworth.

The full significance of the visual imagery became apparent at the opening of Act II when the audience applauded the rococo drawing room with its gigantic round seat (placed just where the lily pond had been) upholstered in a series of the most artfully clashing striped, checked and spotted fabrics, and adorned with a multitude of oversized cushions of similarly clashing designs, whose deliberately chosen melange of brown, red, gold, yellow, orange and black were a visual analogue of Lady Hunstanton's cultivated mental disorder. It was a kind of cornucopia of bric-a-brac, transformed into an interior 'landscape' by the gilt picture frame, which this time

162

contained nothing but a voluminous gold curtain obviously made
of wood and therefore not real. Having observed how nature
had been preserved as a dead thing in the first act, the
audience is at this point faced with a distorted mirror image of
the first scene re-assembled so that inanimate articles of
furniture alarmingly threatened to come to life. The women
again moved in and out of the clusters of overdecorated
artefacts, sometimes blending into the array of objects, at other
moments garishly clashing with them. The unifying element in
this surrealist masterpiece was gold, the image of Mammon
from which all the artefacts might be derived and seemingly
the substance into which all would be melted down.

An interval was placed between the first and second
acts, the second and third acts being played almost continuously
in the same room with only a very short pause after Act II when
the lights dimmed, and we saw Mrs Arbuthnot in silhouette for
a few moments before she made a slow exit. After a mere thirty
second pause in half-light to signify the passage of time, Lord
Illingworth and Gerald entered to begin Act III. This had the
advantage of maintaining audience interest in the
psychological sub-text of the drama rather than serving up the
play in compact segments of intense action. The decor for the
final scene was effected by flying in a flat backdrop of window-
frames and curtains in front of which were placed some isolated
items of furniture, the whole of this dressed mutedly in black
with very deep blue curtains. Behind the windows could be
glimpsed the first act landscape, as though one could see the
Hunstanton country house from Mrs Arbuthnot's windows.
(Society grandeur from the distant perspective of the outsider.)

What Prowse had done as a designer was to establish a
level of stylisation for the performance akin to the semi-
abstract terms of Symbolist painting, flat yet nonetheless
realistic figures exaggeratedly posed in landscapes imbued
with their own life. The acting, in particular that of Barbara
Leigh-Hunt as a calculatedly vague Lady Hunstanton, John
Carlisle as a thin and saturnine Lord Illingworth (no attempt to
suggest the figure of Wilde) and Cherry Morris playing Lady
Caroline as a Lady Bracknell in waiting, maintained the
measured gravitas of the most sophisticated comedy of
manners, allowing the quiet intensity of the melodrama

(especially in the tactful performance of Carol Royle as Mrs Arbuthnot) to achieve a decorum which brought to mind the rhetoric of the King James Bible. At only a few moments did the younger actors' mistaken attempts at conversational realism made the idiom appear stilted.

The symmetrical groupings of characters within the baroque picture frame allowed the audience to notice the different habits of thinking reflected in the peculiar language Wilde has invented for each character. Employing the minimum of external movement, every actor developed a distinctive speech style to characterise each of the would-be sophisticates. Such refinement of playing brought the emotional sub-text of the drama to life in a completely new way, the pauses and the shifts of mood and rhythm evoking a sense of intellectual and passionate activity submerged beneath the necessary constrictions of an elaborate and rigid social code.

Far from revealing characters as mere mouthpieces for the author — a conventional reason for deriding Wilde's drama — this production enabled one to identify the fashionable upper middle class dialect as the emblem of *fin-de-siècle* London sophistication. Having grasped the significance of the play's verbal style, one was better able to discern the subtle differences between one intellect and another, and observe the way each individual intelligence struggles with the drive towards power and the force of passion in the construction of an unique personality.

The restrained yet measured handling of Mrs Arbuthnot's Biblical rhetoric by Carol Royle, emphasised the un-Christian vengefulness of her puritan code. Rather than appearing as a helpless melodramatic victim, she came across as proud, bitter and self-punishing, her understandable hatred for Illingworth equalled by her hatred for herself. One noticed how carefully Wilde has expressed the ironic distance between every character's psychological motive and their professed moral position. Because one never felt inclined to laugh at this Mrs Arbuthnot, one felt it was proper to laugh (at first) at the naivety of Hester, and more especially at the youthful inconsistency of Gerald's views, alternating from moment to moment between Old and New Testament morality in fatuous attempts to rationalise his instinctual selfishness under changing sets of circumstances.

Philip Prowse's interpretation of a highly experimental drama was conveyed by means of an un-English theatricalist *mise-en-scène*, which quite clearly had the critics divided over the relative merits of play and performance. Peter Hall's delightful production of *An Ideal Husband*, on the other hand, received almost unanimous acclaim when it opened on 11 November, little over a year after *A Woman of No Importance*. Perhaps the reviewers recent re-acquaintance with another of Wilde's society plays had prepared them for *An Ideal Husband*. Perhaps they were temperamentally more in tune with the English classicism of Hall's approach. Possibly *An Ideal Husband* is a less problematic text. Certainly its subject matter of personal corruption and public scandal, with its pointed references to the hypocritical moralism of the popular press ensured that it would again become extremely topical.

Whatever the case, Hall's production succeded largely through his intelligent casting which enabled him to use the special qualities of his actors to achieve a perfect balance between the melodrama plot and the comedy of manners characterisation. The careful balance of political context and domestic setting revealed a comic pattern of Christian fall and redemption with an underlying allegorical structure comparable with that of a late Tudor Interlude or an early comedy of Shakespeare.

The style of performance borrowed the theatrical glamour of the pre-*Look Back in Anger* West End star system (even to the extent of casting Michael Denison and Dulcie Gray as Lord Caversham and Lady Markby) to serve a new purpose. Mrs Cheveley's ravishing heliotrope and emerald-green gowns would not have been disdained by Margaret Leighton or Coral Browne, though it would be misleading to imply that the production was sumptuous. The use of spectacle was minimal, the cubic volume of an average-sized West End stage being transformed into a gold box encapsulating the play's three locations which were quite abstractly delineated by furniture and window frames and doorways.

Anna Carteret was cynically self-assured as Mrs Cheveley maintaining a witty playfulness which never degenerated into melodramatic villainy; David Yelland as Sir Robert Chiltern was the perfect public school prefect, subtly suggesting the inability of his class to confront the effects of years of emotional repression. As Lady Chiltern and Lord Goring, Hannah Gordon and Martin Shaw illuminated unexpected possibilities within the text. She captured every nuance of the puritan psyche in distress, starting with smug and selfish idealisation of her husband, which suddenly gave way to violent and un-Christian hatred of his erring humanity; in Act IV, she subtly portrayed the hesitant comic progress toward genuine moral awareness. Martin Shaw was padded to resemble a middle-aged Oscar Wilde, creating a charmingly decadent figure who was outgrowing the wicked attractions of worldliness and moving towards the image of Christ as artist which Wilde was to conceive in tragic form in *De Profundis*. Shaw's performance suggested an Oscar who having met Alfred Douglas in his youth, had tired himself of homosexual passion before meeting Constance in his early forties.

The expert playing of Gordon, Shaw and Yelland who were able to produce mercurial changes of mood from pathos to farce, produced an almost Brechtian effect distancing the audience from whole-hearted empathy with the characters, in order to allow them to appreciate the ironies produced by Wilde's deliberate manipulations of the plot. It was exciting to hear a West End audience laugh spontaneously at the hypocritical posturing of the Chilterns in Act IV as well as at the wit of Lord Goring and the trivial conventionalities of Lord Caversham and Lady Markby. As in Prowse's production, one was struck by how deliberately Wilde has pointed up the contradictions between what the characters feel and what they think and believe, demonstrating the psychological complexity inherent in roles which on a cursory reading appear to be merely stock types.

It was an interesting feature of the production that the quartet of actors playing the major characters appeared to be in their early forties. This lent force to the argument of dandyism against puritanism. An audience was not witnessing the corruption of the innocents, but a battle to the finish of self-righteous moralism and cynical worldly wisdom, in which although the worldy-wise arguments win, the dandy himself is forced to compromise his freedom because he realises how much he also desires the conventional pleasures of marriage. Without much overt directorial manipulation of the *mise-en-scène* — the giant gold coin with its head of Queen Victoria was the only obvious visual statement — Hall managed to rivet the audience's attention by animating the arguments concerning the relationship between the personal and the political, arguments which are as pertinent to the culture of the 1990s as Wilde's trials unfortunately showed them to be in the 1890s.

While waiting impatiently for Jack to return with Miss Prism's handbag in the final scene of *The Importance of Being Earnest*, Gwendolen utters the famous line, 'The suspense is killing. I hope it will last', which draws the attention of the audience to the brilliant manner in which Wilde has in that play integrated the erotic experience of a dramatic plot unfolding in theatrical performance with a philosophical discourse on pleasure.

Philip Prowse and Peter Hall have found different methods of releasing in the theatre the complex subtext which in each of the two society dramas measures the love of pleasure against the pleasure of love. Notwithstanding the strictures of generations of critics, these dialectical plays of wit and feeling demonstrate their power to delight large audiences whenever they are given competent performances.

'THE CRUCIFIXION OF THE OUTCASTS': YEATS AND WILDE IN THE NINETIES

Warwick Gould

TABLEAUX VIVANTS

'The Nineties began in 1889 and ended in 1895. At least the Wilde Nineties did so, and without Wilde the decade could not have found its character.'[1]

Had W. B. Yeats, not Richard Ellmann, written these sentences, only the dates would have had to be changed. Yeats's tragic Nineties begin in 1894 and end with Wilde's death. Where Ellmann offers us from the outset a 'Wilde refulgent, majestic, ready to fall' (p. xiii), Yeats's hero is a 'comedian [...] in the hands of those dramatists who understand nothing but tragedy' (*Au* 287).[2]

Yeats's prevailing myth of the Nineties is 'The Tragic Generation', Act IV of *The Trembling of the Veil* (1922). It might have been named 'London and Paris after Wilde' as Act II is named 'Ireland after Parnell'. Wilde identified consciously with Parnell,[3] but Yeats saw his fall upon a world stage, thus endorsing Wilde's own view that he stood 'in symbolical relation to the art and culture of my age' (*Letters* 466). Part of Yeats's tragedy is the exhaustion of tragedy. The book closes with the realisation that 'comedy, objectivity, has displayed its growing power once more' (*Au* 348). Comedy has its day in *Dramatis Personae 1896-1902*, the much later, separate, but overlapping account of the Irish movement of the same years. Appropriately, that book is dominated by George Moore, 'more mob than man' (*Au* 431). Antithetical patterns of comedy and tragedy, developed for *A Vision*, are strung within and between the two accounts (*Au* 333, 348-9).

The Moore Nineties and the Wilde Nineties closed for Yeats in antithesis in November-December 1900. The comic closure was provided by Moore's trying to force 'delicious singing [...] breasts' upon the play they were writing, *Diarmuid and Grania*.[4] Yeats later was to blame all incoherence in his own plays upon collaboration with this 'artless', fluid man (*Au* 436, *VP* 792). The tragic closure was provided by Wilde's death. Its impact, especially upon (in Yeats's immediate circle) Althea Gyles, made and destroyed by that counter-culture Wilde's fall had engendered, was profound. Gyles, the Irish designer of those book covers whereby Yeats took the 'total book' from decoration to magical talisman, had a good deal to weep about. She had been seduced and abandoned by the now-bankrupt Leonard Smithers, but was to illustrate *The Harlot's House* for Smithers' Maturin Press in 1904. Her determination to dedicate a volume of her poems to Wilde's 'beautiful memory' eventually led to an American publisher's rejection.[5] Her *pietà* for the dead Wilde — for 'nobody ever lived who was so kind' — was a tragic chorus which roused Yeats to a memory of Homer's women weeping over Patroclus, 'yet each weeping for her own sorrow'.[6]

Some might be surprised to hear a claim for *Wilde* as the pre-eminent tragic presence of Yeats's myth. Yeats was less preoccupied by Wilde's homosexuality than by his courage as an Irish hero in the dock — 'a Provincial like myself' (*P & I* 150).[7] Puzzled by the curious unreality of the Rhymers' Club before 1895 (*Au* 303), Yeats now found a symbol in Wilde at the pre-tragic moment — he had been 'meant for a man of action'.[8] This judgment had been formulated by 1897 as Yeats sought to distinguish for himself between Wilde's deployment of genius and that of talent.[9] When Vincent O'Sullivan reported Yeats's judgment to Wilde himself in Naples, in late 1897 or early 1898, Wilde heavily commented: 'It is always interesting to hear Yeats' opinion about one.'[10] He had anticipated the judgement himself.[11]

More enduring than Le Gallienne's 'Romantic Nineties',[12] or Beerbohm's 'Beardsley Period', Yeats's myth seeks 'a full explanation of th[e] tragedy'[13] of an entire generation — Beardsley, Mathers, Davidson, Dowson, Johnson, Symons, Gyles and others. Their fates are central to Yeats's youthful 'myth' in 'reply' to the myth of 'progress'. 'I took satisfaction in certain public disasters, felt a sort of ecstasy at the contemplation of ruin.' The fantastic romances of 1896 anticipate an imminent dispensation born from 'all that our age had rejected' (*VP1* 932).

In 1896 Arthur Symons wrote of Dowson in *The Savoy* 'with some of that frankness which we usually reserve for the dead',[14] and did so with Dowson's wry consent.[15] By February 1898, Yeats was already constructing his myth of Lionel Johnson, who did not die until 1902, and in as public an organ as *The Bookman*.[16] Yeats developed his vignette on Johnson in the Dublin *Daily Express*, 27 August 1898, with the added remark,

> As Axel chose to die, so he has chosen to live among his books and between two memories — religious tradition of the Church of Rome and the political tradition of Ireland — and from these he gazes upon the future.

An 'ecstasy of combat' was added to soften the portrait of Johnson as the laureate of those who 'renounced the joy of the world without accepting the joy of God' (*UP2* 89-92, 117-8).[17] This Johnson was Yeats's to create and martyr[18] while the real Johnson, who made no moan, even when Yeats reused the piece — epitaph or headnote — in the Brooke & Rolleston *A Treasury of Irish Poetry in the English Tongue* in 1900, might well have echoed Michael Robartes's response:

> He wrote of me in that extravagant style
> He had learnt from Pater, and to round his tale
> Said I was dead; and dead I choose to be. (*VP* 373)[19]

At the same time, Symons wrote his essay 'Aubrey Beardsley'[20] for the *Fortnightly Review* (May, 1898), with the artist dead not two months, and Yeats, who recognised his own conversations in it, drew in turn upon the essay himself (*Mem* 98).[21] These early acts of judgment, on Wilde, Johnson, Beardsley, Dowson show matter being shaped for the *tableau vivant* which is *The Trembling of the Veil*.[22]

False memory exaggerated the real difference in age and writerly status between Wilde and the members of the Rhymers' Club: Wilde did, after all, come to the Cheshire Cheese.[23] In Yeats's limelight, Wilde becomes the focus of their tragedies. Lionel Johnson, who, like Wilde (Yeats suspected), had access to 'psychological depths [Yeats] could never enter' was to tell Yeats of Wilde's 'beggars and blackmailers' — in effect his 'feasting with panthers'. Contemplation of the tale and its teller yielded to Yeats the 'Vision of Evil' (*Au* 306),[24] which he used to shape his portraits of Beardsley and others (*Au* 310).

Yeats did not see Wilde again after the spring of 1894. He failed to confront him in May 1895 at Oakley Street and again at the Courts when he brought messages of sympathy from Irish writers.[25] Yeats began to construct the myth of 'The Tragic Generation' while living through the trials — catalyst or catastrophe — and aftermath. In gaol, in exile, dead, Wilde defined the tragic curve of the period.

In 1908, Yeats brought Johnson and other biographical *tableaux* out of scrapbooks for the last volume of his *Collected Works in Verse and Prose*, and Wilde into his Journal, an icon of

> [a]ctive virtue as distinguished from the passive acceptance of a
> current code [...] theatrical, consciously dramatic [...] wearing a
> mask. (*Mem* 151)

Wilde's influence on Yeats's mask theory goes back to Christmas 1888 and that reading of the proofs of 'The Decay of Lying'.[26] Wilde as auto-icon of self-possession was developed in a review of *A Woman of No Importance* in 1895. Yeats didn't much care for the play, but it taught him that even minor characters,

> witty or grotesque persons [...] all, in fact, who can be
> characterised by a sentence or a paragraph, are real men and
> women; and the most immoral among them have enough of the
> morality of self-control and self-possession to be pleasant and
> inspiriting memories. There is always something of heroism in
> being always master enough of oneself to be witty.[27]

Mask theory was developed in the 1910 lectures on personality which contain much of the actual writing that went into 'The Tragic Generation', five years before the 'First Draft' of Yeats's autobiography. The cursed writers of Yeats's generation were martyrs to the adage 'the noblest art is always a forlorn hope, a dangerous attempt' (*YT* 65). Over their tragedy and Yeats's doctrine of experimental living —'The Grey Rock', one might say, in prose draft — hangs the spectre of Wilde, omnipresent, never mentioned.[28]

The 1915 draft autobiography expressed much personal and political material, later suppressed or reshaped for *The Trembling of the Veil* and *Dramatis Personae*. Wilde is deployed in two main contexts: as the author of 'The Decay of Lying' whose self-possession embarrasses the clumsy Yeats on Christmas Day in Tite Street, 1888, his copy of Pater's *The Renaissance* heralding the last trump against dullness. Later, after memories of the Smithers circle, and Beardsley's 'icy passion for reality', news arrives of the released Wilde once more in Dieppe, with Dowson and a cheering crowd, developing 'wholesome tastes' at a 'house of ill fame', with 'cold mutton'.[29] Anecdote and hearsay, Yeats's vignettes are a halfway house to myth, via sometimes proleptic obituary.

A Vision (1925, 1937), developed in 1917-22, discovers in autopsy Wilde's line of life rather than his tragic flaw. An 'Assertive Man' whose Body of Fate is 'enforced failure of action', Wilde shares Phase 19 with another actor, Mrs Patrick Campbell. The diagnosis criticizes Wilde's nature — by turns 'pretty, feminine, insincere [...] violent, arbitrary and insolent' — but forgives his way of life — '[a] weakness of the antithetical, "the soul [...] intoxicated by its discovery of human nature" which says "I would be possessed by" or [...] possess that which is Human' (*AV A* 84, *B*, 150). Wilde 'understood his weakness, true personality was impossible, for that is born in solitude, and at his moon one is not solitary' (*Au* 294). The author of *De Profundis* would have agreed.[30]

INEXORABLE CURTAIN

The multiple time shifts of *The Trembling of the Veil* itself assume an overall shape of disaster, exhaustion, slight recovery. The double deployment of Wilde taken over from the draft *Autobiography* is central to this shape. In Act I, 'Four Years', Wilde defeats Henley in a battle of wit, and Christmas Day in Tite Street, 1888 reveals Wilde 'triumphant' and 'at the happiest moment of his life' (*Au* 131, 136). Foredooming of Wilde vies with admiration, anachronistic gratitude for Wilde's kind notice of *The Wanderings of Oisin and Other Poems*,[31] and a captious recognition of the 'half-civilized [...]

man of action', his writing spoiled by 'vague impressiveness', who 'could not endure the sedentary toil of creative art' (*Au* 135, 138), the *parvenu* glimpsed by the fellow provincial.

Wilde re-enters *The Trembling of the Veil* in Act IV, 'The Tragic Generation'. It begins with an article of faith — 'Art is Art because it is not Nature' — which is then tested to destruction. The opening confrontation at Florence Farr's Avenue Theatre in 1894 finds John Todhunter, Bernard Shaw and Yeats facing 'outraged convention'. The melancholy Todhunter and his *Comedy of Sighs* are destroyed.[32] Shaw, in the rearguard, can 'confound his enemies' with *Arms and the Man*.[33] *The Land of Heart's Desire* was the curtain raiser to these plays. The productions become an interior play within 'The Tragic Generation'. The main narrative jumps forward a whole year to Wilde's action against the Marquess of Queensberry before cutting back to Wilde's entrance at the Theatre, too late for Yeats's play but in time to praise as 'Sublime, wonderful, wonderful' Yeats's story 'A Crucifixion',[34] later collected as 'The Crucifixion of the Outcast'.

Based upon the *Vision of MacConglinne*, this parable, amenable to Wilde,[35] tells of the crucifixion of an Irish gleeman of the 11th century, at the hands of inhospitable monks, to whose abbot he sings a bard's curse, and his final rejection by birds and wolves, fellow outcasts which begin to devour him before he dies on the Cross. Recently returned from Paris where he had seen Villiers de l'Isle-Adam's *Axel*, Yeats himself was perhaps a little doom-eager, but projects the mood onto Wilde and relates Wilde's admiration to 'the turn his thoughts had taken' (*Au* 287). The theories of *Intentions* — that 'literature always anticipates life' (*AC* 308), had made a doom-eager Wilde a biographical commonplace even by 1894,[36] and he asked for *The Secret Rose*, in which 'The Crucifixion of the Outcast' had been collected, in prison (*Letters* 523).

As early as 1904 Yeats recasts Wilde at the Avenue Theatre into *theatrum mundi*,[37] as 'an unfinished sketch of a great man' who 'showed great courage and manhood amid the collapse of his fortunes' (*Wade* 32). Wilde is an unconscious mummer, acting while discovering his intention to act, fulfilling a role of which nobody quite knows the script. 'We begin to live when we have conceived life as tragedy', says

Yeats towards the end of 'Four Years' (*Au* 189). The realisation
is in the end inseparable from the better accounts of the period.
Vincent O'Sullivan, in a tale that might have been scripted in
the same mood, recalls Wilde driven from a Naples restaurant
by a rubber-necking post-theatre crowd, giving money to a
'tragic beggar' and —

> murmur[ing] in English: 'You wretched man, why do you beg
> when pity is dead?'. From that hour I felt that the inexorable
> curtain had begun to fall and that Oscar Wilde had lived.[38]

To Yeats, Wilde's decision to face trial and imprisonment was
the securing of Wilde's 'renown' (*Mem* 79; *Au* 289). If we find
something unworthy in Yeats's hope that 'tragedy might give
[Wilde's] art a greater depth', it was evidently in part a
response to the change of public mood that came with his
impending conviction. Bringing it upon himself, and publicly
recognizing that fact, Wilde had made 'of infamy a new
Thermopylae' (*Au* 290).

The Trembling of the Veil is better read as a Balzacian
apocalypse, one revealing not the unachieved future, but the
present, envisioned retrospectively.[39] It required a tragic hero
out of phase,[40] who refused the 'exile' and silence of the
Rhymers (*Au* 294). As he wrote it, Yeats *became* one of those
'dramatists who understand nothing but tragedy', Wilde — his
insolent actor who created a brief antinomian interval. Yeats's
daring moralist of 'contemptuous wit' (*Au* 294) is the satirizing
Irish bard. His crucifixion, however, allows other outcasts to
discover their vocation, to live as poets.

REALITY ON THE TIGHT-ROPE

When the harlots dance upon the pavement at Wilde's
conviction, Yeats's Rhymers 'break up in tragedy, though we
did not know that till the play was finished' (*Au* 300). His
decadents are stylised from fact into myth in a sequence of
tales. Good examples are the cold mutton tale: 'But tell it in
England, for it will entirely restore my character.' We must
trust the tale if not the teller. Dowson's protest against
Symons's 'too vivid' *Savoy* account of him is overtaken by
events: 'Arrested, sell watch and send proceeds' is the telegram

from Dieppe, but it is the baker who comes off worse in the court, not the 'illustrious' English poet, the drunken Dowson (*Au* 327-8). 'Yeats's stories, so wonderful as to seem like fiction, have a solid basis in truth', observes Kelsey Thornton. True decadents are 'fundamentally involved in creating the image' of themselves 'that the mythologizers have been blamed for'. Dowson made 'for himself a biography to fit his view of art'.[41]

Yeats's stylised biographies are — as Thornton remarks — 'vicarious potential autobiographies'.[42] Their contours hold up well against Beardsley's, Dowson's, Wilde's letters, and Yeats's own. The strange stillness Yeats freezes over these tragedies reflects his own impotences, painfully chronicled in the draft autobiography, which concludes 'I am too exhausted; I can do no more' (*Mem* 134). His publishing triumphs of 1899, long deferred, had a hollowness. *The Countess Cathleen* in production was undercut by exhausting battles. For both Yeats and Wilde the bills of mortality had been long: Beardsley, Lady Wilde, Constance Wilde, Susan Yeats, Dowson, Wilde himself. Bullen and E. J. Oldmeadow, whose *The Dome* was the only successor to *The Savoy*, teetered on the edge of disaster or went over it.

But Yeats took circumstance and hearsay one stage further into myth, and Wilde, of course, was the avatar. Yeats's tales are parables, none more so when their hero is Wilde himself. Yeats had characterised Wilde for the readers of the *Boston Pilot* in 1889 as 'the most finished talker of our time'.[43] Reviewing *Lord Arthur Savile's Crime* for *United Ireland* in 1891 Yeats had been delighted by the subversiveness and beguiled by the harmlessness of its 'shower of paradox'. He recalled *Intentions* with its 'extravagant Celtic crusade against Anglo-Saxon stupidity'. *Intentions* 'hides within its immense paradox some of the most subtle literary criticism we are likely to see for many a long day' (*UP1* 203-4).[44]

'What the paradox was to me in the sphere of thought, perversity became to me in the sphere of passion' (*Letters* 466). When Wilde went to jail, '[r]eality' was indeed 'on the tight-rope' (*CW* 43). Mr Erskine's 'Verities' became acrobats in earnest in *The Savoy* period, indeed, Yeats, who traces the 'philosophy' of the period back to Walter Pater, adopts Wilde's metaphor in 'The Tragic Generation', wondering if the 'attitude of mind of which [*Marius the Epicurean*] was the noblest expression' had not —

> caused the disaster of my friends. It taught us to walk upon a rope tightly stretched through serene air, and we were left to keep our feet upon a swaying rope in a storm. (*Au* 302-3)

Wilde, of course, had time to reflect upon such energies and enervations. 'Morality does not help me. I am a born antinomian. I am one of those who are made for exceptions, not for laws.'[45] These are gaoled sentences from the frustrated father whose 'Confraternity of the Fatherless' projected a ritual for agnosticism: '[o]nly that is spiritual which makes its own form' (*Letters* 468). Wilde, as surely as Huysmans, sought religion in its antiself, and his attempt focuses that subversive and paradoxical art which Wilde had mobilised outside.

That counter-culture was the 'dangerous attempt', an exception which flourished for a limited lease, its foreclosure proving some rather remorseless rules. Those who were associated with Wilde perforce shared Wilde's antinomianism. What else could they do? Declaring 'warfare on the British public at a time when we had all against us [...]. Outlaws, whether they have offended through their virtues or their vices, soon discover that if they do not support one another no one else will' (*Mem* 90-91).[46] Their weapons were those 'dangerous things', the paradoxes of Wilde's dialogues (*AC* 307). These they explored to desperate ends, as Wilde reflected upon his own paradoxes in *De Profundis*. Yeats's Owen Aherne, for instance, destroys himself by enacting in the disaster of his life —

> the curious paradox, half borrowed from some fanatical monk, half invented by himself; that the beautiful arts were sent into the world to overthrow nations, and finally life herself, by sowing everywhere unlimited desires, like torches thrown into a burning city. This idea was not at the time, I believe, more than a paradox, a plume of the pride of youth.[47]

Antinomianism in the period had many sources, but one ringing statement of its character is surely Pater's reverie upon the 'spirit of rebellion and revolt against the moral and religious ideas' of the early middle ages.

In their search after the pleasures of the senses and the
imagination, in their care for beauty, in their worship of the
body, people were impelled beyond the bounds of the Christian
ideal; and their love became sometimes a strange idolatry, a
strange rival religion. It was the return of that ancient Venus,
not dead, but only hidden for a time in the caves of the
Venusberg, of those old pagan gods still going to and fro on the
earth, under all sorts of disguises. And [...] this rebellious and
antinomian element, the recognition of which has made the
delineation of the middle age by the writers of the Romantic
school in France [...] so suggestive and exciting [...] is found alike
in the history of Abelard and the legend of Tannhäuser. More
and more as we come to mark changes and distinctions of temper
in what is often in one all-embracing confusion called the
middle age, that rebellion, that sinister claim for liberty of heart
and thought, comes to the surface. The Albigensian movement,
connected so strangely with the history of Provençal poetry, is
deeply tinged with it. A touch of it makes the Franciscan order,
with its poetry, its mysticism, its 'illumination', from the point
of view of religious authority, justly suspect. It influences the
thoughts of those obscure prophetical dreamers, like Joachim of
Flora, strange dreamers in a world of flowery rhetoric of that
third and final dispensation of a 'spirit of freedom' in which
law shall have passed away.[48]

When we extrapolate from Pater's *The Renaissance* to those
upon whom it was a profound influence, we note at once that
among the elect of late Victorian England the ideas of
renovatio mundi and final perfectibility flourish
undifferentiatedly during that *fin de siècle* crisis. Prophecy is
the background against which such energies flower.
Antinomian practitioners are prepared to bide their time only
as their await their hour: 'the future is what artists are' (*AC*
263, 284). When Marjorie Reeves and I tried to explore the
Joachimist 'Myth of the Eternal Evangel' in a number of 19th
and 20th century figures, Yeats and Wilde among them, we
found *The Savoy* crucial to any consideration of antinomianism
in the period. That journal descries the emotional curve of a
crisis: catastrophe, defiant camaraderie beyond the pale,
decline — dating from W. H. Smith's refusal to handle the
journal, as they had refused to handle *The Picture of Dorian
Gray* (*OW* 305). Claiming that Blake's 'Antaeus setting Virgil
and Dante upon the Verge of Cocytus' which accompanied
Yeats' essay on Blake's Dante illustrations was by Beardsley,
that retailer put *The Savoy* out of business, and *The Morning*

Chronicle would not even print Yeats's protest letter because it included Beardsley's name.[49] By mid-October the journal was doomed.[50] Month by month, the contents of *The Savoy*[51] provide a barometer of cultural crisis, a time after a time, a time before a time. Its terse witness of Beardsley's illness — 'The Death of Pierrot', 'Ave atque Vale' — the abandonment of *Under the Hill*, Yeats's 'The Tables of the Law', and poems such as Johnson's 'Münster: A. D. 1554', or Dowson's 'Venite Descendamus' and 'Let us go hence' mark Titanic defeat. The hostile cultural climate did not end with the magazine's closure, nor even with the exhaustion of Wilde's sentence,[52] and even as courageous a publisher as A. H. Bullen 'made' Yeats leave 'The Tables of the Law' and 'The Adoration of the Magi' out of *The Secret Rose* (1897), issuing them privately some months later (*VSR* 269-70).

Intentions was, and remained the formative text for Yeats. The 'antinomian' Gilbert, the 'artistic critic' as 'mystic', is the Paterian heretic who would usher in the Age of the Holy Spirit, believing that '[ae]sthetics are higher than ethics' and 'belong to a more spiritual sphere'. That third status beyond the dispensation of 'middle class respectability' is the 'true culture' of self-fulfillment where men will not do but be, that of 'perfection of which the saints have dreamed', where 'sin is impossible', a culture inherently as 'dangerous' as 'all ideas, as I told you, are so' (*AC* 406-7).[53] The notion of intellectual danger' mystic and artistic, is taken up in all of Yeats's *Savoy* stories, but most notably in his Joachimist 'The Tables of the Law' (*VSR* 159-60), about a spoiled priest and spiritual outlaw.

In 1898 Symons had detected in Beardsley's work —

> an art in which evil purifies itself by its own intensity, and by the beauty which transfigures it [...] evil itself, carried to the point of a perverse ecstasy, becomes a kind of good, by means of that energy which, otherwise directed, is virtue. The devil is nearer to God, by the whole height from which he fell, than the average man who has not recognised his own need to rejoice or repent. And so a profound spiritual corruption, instead of being [...] 'immoral' [...] is more nearly, in the final and abstract sense, moral, for it is the triumph of the spirit over the flesh, [...] [i]t is a form of divine possession. (p. 25)

This thinking[54] comes from conversations with Yeats, who supplied Plotinus *On the Nature of Good and Evil* from which Symons quotes the view that good and evil are interdependent: 'such is the supervening power of good, that whenever a glimpse of perfect evil is obtained we are immediately recalled to the memory of good by the image of the beautiful with which evil is invested.'[55] That beauty, 'so difficult' (*Au* 333), was the art of an antinomian culture.

The *Trembling of the Veil* follows the same curve as 'The Tables of the Law', the Joachimist crisis narrative which parallels Wilde's 'L'inutile résurrection' as a failed dream of human perfectibility. Pre-apocalyptic fervour for the Age of the Spirit yields to a new age which arrives anyway, in a different shape, and exhausts antinomian energy. *The Savoy's* outcasts had tried to usher in the age of Wilde's 'Critic as Artist' but 'the tide sank' (*Au* 315).

ANTINOMIAN REALITIES: SMITHERS'S MORTAL LEASE

Ian Small has recently addressed the long-overdue issue of Wilde the 'Professional Writer', and in adversarial mood. For Small, Richard Ellmann's life is the latest in a long line of hagiographies. The myth of 'the infamy of Wilde's homosexuality and the tragedy of his early death', according to Small, begins with Wilde's self-presentation. 'Wilde troped his own life', creating, as Regenia Gagnier has argued, a 'media personality'.[56] The overlooked evidences of his hard work as a writer and editor, his manuscripts and business correspondence show 'a side of his personality which Wilde's own troping of his life had attempted to conceal' (p. 34). To flaunt his genius, Wilde concealed the work of his talent. 'A great artist invents a type' (*AC* 307): Wilde invented a Wilde who was, in Small's small phrase, 'extremely good copy' (p. 35).

There are problems with this line of argument. Replaced in context, Small's evidence — largely concerning Wilde's early career — confirms the myths it is advanced to qualify. Wilde was a dangerous exception, a presence of whom publishers were wary, even before he had been able to construct himself.[57] Alexander Macmillan's letter, hastily and furtively rejecting *The Picture of Dorian Gray* — 'We have done very little in the way of such strong situations [...] something [...]

rather repelling [...] I am sure it is not for us, and I do not like to keep it any longer'[58] — if read in context of the Macmillan Archive of Readers' Reports, shows that Wilde was a scandal to orthodox publishing even before the newspaper controversy over the *Lippincott*'s publication of the work (20 June 1890).

A studied prejudice against new Irish writing which differed from Irish stereotypes prevailed at Macmillan.[59] Against that background (which included the rejection of the *Fairy Tales*[60] in 1888), Wilde's fate stands out as exceptional. The rejection of *Intentions* at the end of 1890 showed the firm triumphantly nasty, vindicated by the press controversy over *Dorian Gray*, and by W. H. Smith's rejection of that 'filthy' book. Wilde had acquired 'the sort of reputation that would [not] help a volume of miscellanies from his pen'.[61]

Revisionist accounts of Wilde's self-troping ignore the contemporary evidence (long available in Hart-Davis and Stuart Mason) of the growing *public* ostracism of Wilde and his movement, and the precarious recourse to fringe publishing via Leonard Smithers. Wilde liked the centre of the stage, but to ignore the cascade which his tragedy prefigured is to capitulate to a diminished version of the Wilde myth, to write it down, rather than off. Yeats's tragedy was that of a generation; Wilde had a nodal role within it. It is, in the end, 'its own evidence', like Wilde's 'fine lie' (*AC* 292). But then Yeats did not have to 'shamelessly read [...] up his subject' in the British Museum, he lived it.

Macmillan's reports for 1900 show W. B. Yeats being elaborately and carefully rejected. On the face of it the rejections of Yeats and Wilde have little in common. One seems ethical, the other is political. Wilde's book had a homosexual subtext. Yeats's beloved Maud Gonne had cost Macmillan's Reader, John Morley, his seat in Parliament. Worse, by organising the Irish voters in Newcastle to vote tactically for a Socialist candidate in that 1895 election on the issue of amnesty for Irish treason felony prisoners, she had cost him his Chief Secretaryship for Ireland, a post from which he had a unique opportunity to study police reports on the doings of members of the IRB such as Yeats and Gonne. No doubt he took a continuing interest in Irish revolutionary affairs during the '98 Centenary celebrations where Yeats and Gonne were prominent. Yeats remained outspoken against the Boer War and against the visit of Queen Victoria to Dublin to raise a new Irish regiment in the spring of 1900. It was perhaps only predictable that the cold and pompous John Morley should wreak private revenge in his reader's report. Yeats, who had also split and lost his Irish audience[62] by his actions, was forced back to A. H. Bullen, another publisher on the fringe, obviously because Smithers by then was bankrupt and beyond the pale.

Apparently there is every difference between the two Irish writers in 1900, Wilde, pro-Queen Victoria and anti-Boer, who felt he had 'died' in prison as a writer, and Yeats pro-Boer and anti-Queen Victoria, who had achieved international fame at last with the *Academy*'s prize for *The Wind Among the Reeds*. Yeats, however, was in a deep moral collapse and creative cul-de-sac, though few knew it at the time. Even so, these readers' reports and rejections give a broader focus to the positions Wilde and Yeats held, consciously, in the eyes of the publishing establishment.

A. J. A. Symons, bibliographer and publisher, set out in 1930 to examine 'no less an event than the origin of the book in its modern form'. The books of the Eighteen-Nineties, remained 'unnoted and forlorn', because they were —

> the outcome of a movement which, though by intention simply artistic, and as such detached from action, did nevertheless come into conflict with the moral and religious feeling of its time. The result of that conflict, which was provoked by an unhappy scandal, was a banishing, from bookshelves as from memory, of the offending works; and though, in the thirty years that have intervened, these vanished works have begun to be estimated, and even esteemed, as literature, their purely typographical virtue and significance remain unknown to all save the few collectors who cherish them.

The 'whole doctrine' behind the 'typographical renaissance' of the Nineties had fallen —

> into disgrace [...] was exorcised and cast out, because a single, though leading, advocate and exemplar of it was tried and convicted for an offence against morals. Just as Parnell's fault retarded peace in Ireland for thirty years, so the transgressions of Oscar Wilde delayed, for an equal period, due recognition for the work and worth of his friends and associates, in literature hardly less than in the more material sphere of printing.[63]

In 'Lord Arthur Savile's Crime' Wilde tells us that '[a]ctors are
so fortunate' —

> they can choose whether they will appear in tragedy or comedy
> [...]. But in real life it is different. Most men and women are
> forced to perform parts for which they have no qualifications.
> Our Guildensterns play Hamlet for us, and our Hamlets have to
> jest like Prince Hal. The world is a stage, but the play is badly
> cast.[64]

Yeats's Wilde as 'comedian' in a real life tragedy derives from
this observation. His downfall brought the end of Beardsley's
career at *The Yellow Book*.[65] Leonard Smithers, craving
respectability (according to Yeats), was prepared to lose money
on a new magazine and came to the rescue of these outcasts.
Yeats believed — few else would — that Symons made
Smithers promise to 'drop his secret trade in lascivious books'
and, even more remarkably, that he did just that. But the
tragic generation could not be squeamish. Leonard Smithers
who once boasted that he would publish 'anything that the
others are afraid of' (*Letters* 627n.) now found respectability in
disrespectability. The Sheffield solicitor and master book-
designer haphazardly bankrolled the counter-culture. The
cascade of Wilde's tragedy has its artistic shaping, but it is
also a chronicle play.

   Alone of the fine publishers, Smithers, the 'most
learned erotomaniac in Europe' provided in *The Savoy* a
vehicle for his new possession, Aubrey Beardsley and the self-
styled 'outlaws' (*Letters* 630-1). A candid reassessment of
antinomian publishing would recuperate Smithers, 'so
accustomed to bringing out books limited to an edition of three
copies, one for the author, one for yourself, and one for the
police' (*Letters* 737). Few since Vincent O'Sullivan have come
to his rescue.[66] None has taken up Wilde's sanction to Robert
Ross to write Smithers' biography (*Letters* pp. 729-30nn). His
son's life tells a scandalous tale without bitterness.[67]
Smithers's greatest books are invisible outside research
Libraries. Few can see the care and brilliance lavished on the
design and production of the Beardsley/Dowson/Vincent
O'Sullivan *Volpone* of 1898, or on *The Importance of Being*

*Earnest: A Trivial Comedy for Serious People By the Author of
Lady Windermere's Fan* (1899), and the Wilde limited editions
of 1899. Mason's bibliography records Smithers's struggle for
finish.[68] These books dared not speak their author's name,[69]
were 'boycotted by the press'. Wilde hoped 'the elect' would
buy them: Smithers had shown 'great pluck' (*Letters* 782).
Smithers and Wilde, two bankrupts in search of a chequebook,
collided in separate manoeuvres as the century foreclosed on
them. Wilde's last letter to him asks 'are the creditors
howling? If the wolf is at the door the only thing is to let him
in to dine' (*Letters* 834). Smithers, however, had financed the
remainder of Beardsley's life and work. He measured out
Dowson's financial lease. Yeats had thrown in his lot against
his dislike of Smithers. Beardsley began to design the fine book
neither Beardsley nor Yeats could finish: *The Shadowy
Waters*. When it did appear, with only a reused rose petal
design by the sinking Althea Gyles, it came from Hodder and
Stoughton, who never published another title for Yeats. But
Beardsley had been dead more than two years, Smithers was
bankrupt, and unable to match sales to demand for *The Ballad
of Reading Gaol*,[70] a matter which preoccupied him in pirate
editions after Wilde's death.

THE SCAPEGOAT
> Things thought too long can be no longer thought,
> For beauty dies of beauty, worth of worth. (*VP* 564)

In the preface to *The Oxford Book of Modern Verse* (1936) Yeats
rewrites the Wilde myth, shortly after he had defined his
early thought by the now-discarded disaster myth in the
Preface to *The Resurrection* and as he was writing the comic
Dramatis Personae, 1896-1902.

> Then in 1900 everybody got down off his stilts; henceforth
> nobody drank absinthe with his black coffee; nobody went mad;
> nobody committed suicide; nobody joined the Catholic Church;
> or if they did I have forgotten. Victorianism had been defeated
> [...]. (*OBMV* xi)

Yeats *chose* to forget. 1900 had marked the failure of the
movement, not the defeat of Victorianism, which was to

collapse in 1901 when Wilde and the Queen were dead. Yeats now 'stood in judgement upon Wilde': the 'man of action' is discovered a closet Victorian, 'overshadowed by old famous men he could not attack, for he was of their time and shared its admirations'. Wilde had 'tricked and clowned to draw attention to himself. Even when disaster struck him down it could not wholly clear his soul.' Wilde's poetry was 'an exaggeration of every Victorian fault, nor, except in the case of one poem not then written (*The Ballad of Reading Gaol*), has time corrected the verdict'.

Defining the canon, Yeats had assumed the black cap. 'Art can have but one subject', Yeats avers, trying vainly to liberate an Irish gallows ballad such as 'The Croppy Boy' from the overwritten *Reading Gaol*. Yeats found it a 'privilege' (*OBMV* vi-vii) to carve thirty-eight out of one hundred and nine stanzas, even removing the two refrain stanzas from the poem entirely, but offering them the meagre, exemplary hospitality of his polemical introduction. Wilde's poem is emasculated of its personal and political dimension in this unconvincing editorial compromise. Brendan Kennelly followed Yeats's overall decisions in *The Penguin Book of Irish Verse*.[71] More recently, Seamus Deane has chosen to cut twenty seven stanzas from Canto 3 for the text found in *The Field Day Anthology of Irish Writing*.[72]

Yeats's preface might have been prefigured in 'The Crucifixion of the Outcast'. In stripping rhetoric from *The Ballad* Yeats had to kill the thing he loved in life *and* loathed in poetry. No longer an outcast himself, Yeats nailed Wilde to the cross of Victorianism to assert the triumph of his own tradition. In eating Wilde's heart, he was prepared to devour his own myth.

APPENDIX: WILDE AND MACMILLAN

Macmillan received Wilde's *Fairy Stories with Illustrations* via Forbes Robertson on 26 January 1888, sent them out to be read on 6 February and received them back on 14 February, returning them to Wilde two days later (*B.L. Add. MS* 56017 f 42v). The Reader's Report is as follows:

5716 Fairy Stories (Oscar Wilde) ret. Feb. 16. 88.

> There is undoubtedly point and cleverness in the way in wh.
> these stories are told. The writer has, no doubt, the literary
> knack — the point and finish. You feel at once the hand of the
> man who knows how to write. Two or three of the stories are
> very pretty, but I can hardly say as a whole that they have any
> striking imaginative brilliance — nor do I think that they would
> be likely to rush into marked popularity. They are pretty and
> bright, but they hardly strike into the reader's mind. They are
> good and respectable. Whether they are more than that, I doubt.
> (*B. L. Add MS* 55941 f 56, unsigned, probably John Morley).[73]

There is no trace in any of these materials of a reading
of *The Picture of Dorian Gray*. Before it got into the process of
normal review by readers, Alexander Macmillan had sent the
following letter to Wilde:

> My dear Wilde,
> Thank you for letting me see your story, which I have read
> through. George is not here today, so I cannot give it him, but as
> you want it back so soon I think I ought not to keep it any
> longer and am returning it by hand with this note.
>   It is a weird tale and some of the conversation is most
> brilliant. I am afraid however that it would not do for us to
> publish. We have done very little in the way of such strong
> situations, and I confess there is something in the power which
> Dorian Gray gets over the young natural scientist, and one or
> two other things which is rather repelling. I dare say you do not
> mean it to be. I am sure it is not for us, and I do not like to keep it
> any longer.
>   Yours very truly,
>   Alexander Macmillan[74]

The story was published four days later in *Lippincott's
Monthly Magazine*, and a Press controversy ensued.

     Essays (i.e. what became *Intentions* with Osgood
McIlvaine in early 1891, see *Letters* pp. 287n., 288) was more
openly rejected.[75] The manuscript of *Essays* was sent out for
opinion by Macmillan on 22 October and returned on 4 November
(*B. L. Add. MS* 56017 f 72v). The report was not fair-copied
until after 20 November, according to the placement in the fair-
copy reports book, which is largely of Morley's reports
(unsigned) interspersed with signed specialist reports by
others. The report, probably by Morley, is as follows:

     Wilde (Oscar) 6960. Essays.

Five in number (1). Shakespeare and Acting Costume. (2). Pen, Pencil, and Poison. — being an account of Wainwright, an engraver, a critic, a forger, and a murderer. (3). Decay of Lying. (4) and (5). On The Art of Criticism.

1 and 2 are readable, but slight and fugitive. 3, Extremely clever, paradoxical and whimsical — and in itself perfectly readable.

Of 4 and 5 about the same may be said. On the whole, in spite of their cleverness and smartness, I doubt the success of these papers in a collected form. There is no unity of subject — and dialogue (into which 3, 4, and 5 are cast) is not a very attractive treatment nowadays.

Nor should we forget that the people who might well care for, and be amused by Mr Wilde's smart whimsicalities, have already seen them in the *19th Century*; and I cannot suppose many persons wishing to return to them.

Oscar Wilde has not, either, the sort of reputation — clever and accomplished writer as he is — that would help a volume of miscellanies from his pen.[76]

NOTES

1   Thus R. Ellmann defines 'the Age of Dorian' by its central character. See *Oscar Wilde* (London, Hamish Hamilton, 1987), p. 288. Hereafter *OW*. Quotations from the works of Wilde and Yeats are cited in-text using the following abbreviations: *AC, The Artist as Critic, Critical Writings of Oscar Wilde*, ed. R. Ellmann, (London, W.H. Allen, 1970); *CW, Complete Works of Oscar Wilde*, ed. V. Holland (London and Glasgow, Collins, 1948, 1986); *Letters, The Letters of Oscar Wilde*, ed. R. Hart-Davis (London, Rupert Hart-Davis, 1962); *Au, Autobiographies* (London, Macmillan, 1955); *AV A, A Vision, An Explanation of Life Founded upon the Writings of Giraldus and upon certain Doctrines attributed to Kusta Ben Luka* (London, privately printed for subscribers only by T. Werner Laurie, Ltd., 1925); *AV B, A Vision* (London, Macmillan, 1962); *E & I, Essays and Introductions* (London and New York, Macmillan, 1961); *LNI, Letters to the New Island: A New Edition (CEW VII)* edited by G. Bornstein and H. Witemeyer (London, Macmillan, 1989); *Mem, Memoirs: Autobiography — First Draft: Journal* transcribed and edited by D. Donoghue (London, Macmillan, 1972; New York, Macmillan, 1973); *Myth, Mythologies* (London and New York, Macmillan, 1959); *OBMV, The Oxford Book of Modern Verse 1895-1935*, chosen by W. B. Yeats (Oxford, Clarendon Press, 1936); *P & I, Prefaces and Introductions: Uncollected Prefaces and Introductions by Yeats to Works by other Authors and to Anthologies edited by Yeats (CEW VI)*, edited by W. H. O'Donnell (London, Macmillan, 1988); *UP1, Uncollected Prose by W. B. Yeats*, Vol. I, ed. J. P. Frayne (London, Macmillan; New York: Columbia University Press, 1970); *UP2, Uncollected Prose by W. B. Yeats*, Vol. 2, ed. J. P. Frayne and C. Johnson (London, Macmillan, 1975; New York, Columbia University

Press, 1976); *VP1, The Variorum Edition of the Plays of W. B. Yeats*, ed. R. K. Alspach assisted by C. C. Alspach (London and New York, Macmillan, 1966); (Cited from the corrected second printing of 1966.); *VP, The Variorum Edition of the Poems of W. B. Yeats*, ed. P. Allt and R. K. Alspach (New York, The Macmillan Co., 1957, 1966); *VSR, The Secret Rose, Stories by W. B. Yeats: A Variorum Edition*, ed. W. Gould, P. L. Marcus and M. J. Sidnell (London, Macmillan Academic and Professional, 1992); *Wade*, A. Wade, *A Bibliography of the Writings of W. B. Yeats*, third edition, rev. R. K. Alspach (London, Rupert Hart-Davis, 1968); *YT, Yeats and the Theatre*, ed. R. O'Driscoll and L. Reynolds (Toronto, Macmillan of Canada; Niagara Falls, New York, Maclean-Hunter Press, 1975).

2   'Melancholy [...] at the moment of triumph, the only moment when a man [...] can ask himself what is the value of life' (*P & I* 150).

3   V. O'Sullivan recalled that '[a]bout Parnell he repeated one of his favourite sayings: There is something vulgar in all success. The greatest men fail — or seem to the world to have failed.' See *Aspects of Wilde* (London: Constable & Co., 1936), p. 222.

4   He might have had the last laugh: see *VP1* 1176, lines 139-40.

5   T. B. Mosher, a pirate publisher. See *Arthur Symons: Selected Letters, 1880-1935*, ed. K. Beckson and J. M. Munro (London, Macmillan, 1989), pp. 171-2 (Symons to Thomas B. Mosher, 5 July 1904). Coulson Kernahan also tried unsuccessfully to dedicate a book to Wilde's memory shortly after his death. See his *In Good Company; Some Personal Recollections* (London & New York, John Lane, 1917), p. 189.

6   Unpublished letter to Lady Gregory, also *Au* 412 and *Iliad* Bk 19, Patroclus, who has been killed by Hector, is mourned by Briseis and other captive Trojan women:

> 'Alas, Patroclus [...] you were so gentle with me always. How can I ever cease to mourn You?' Thus Briseis wept, and the other women took up the lament, ostensibly for Patroclus, but each at heart for her own unhappy lot.

The Iliad translated with notes by T. A. Buckley (London, Bell and Daldy, 1870), was in Yeats's Library, see E. O'Shea, *A Descriptive Catalog of W. B. Yeats's Library* (New York and London, Garland Publishing, 1985), item 905.

7   'He had increased my admiration by his courage at the first trial which was just over, and I was soon to discover that my world, where historical knowledge had lessened or taken away the horror or disgust at his form of vice prevalent elsewhere in England, had many stories of his courage and self-possession' (*Mem* 79).

8   Later judgments did not vary this line: 'essentially a man of action, a writer by perversity and accident, [who] would have been more important as soldier and politician' (*Au* 285), the talker who 'played with the fundamental and insoluble' (*P & I* 148), whose 'fantasy had taken some tragic turn [...] meditating upon possible disaster' (*Au* 285).

9   'I have put all my genius into my life; I have put only my talent into my works': see A. Gide, *Oscar Wilde: A Study from the French*, with an introduction etc. by S. Mason (Oxford, Holywell Press, 1905), pp. 17, 49. Gide was to claim that the much quoted phrase had first appeared in print in his book. Yeats's memory of the antithesis, which goes back to 1888-9, is much more equivocal: see *Au* 135.

10   O'Sullivan, *Aspects of Wilde*, p. 28.

11   'We Irish are too poetical to be poets; we are a nation of brilliant failures, but we are the greatest talkers since the Greeks', Wilde had said before reading Yeats the proofs of 'The Decay of Lying' on Christmas Day, 1888 (*Au* 135).

12   R. Le Gallienne, *The Romantic '90s* (London, G. P. Putnam's Sons, 1925).

13   *Au* 300. Later he came to a tentative answer: Shelley more than Blake had shaped his own 'life, and when I thought of the tumultuous and often tragic lives of friends or acquaintance, I attributed to [Shelley's] direct or indirect influence their Jacobin frenzies, their brown demons' (*E & I* 424-5).

14   'A Literary Causerie: on a Book of Verses', *The Savoy* , August 1896.

15   D. Flower and H. Maas (eds.), *The Letters of Ernest Dowson* (London, Cassell, 1967), pp. 371-2.

16   Johnson's work 'mirrored a temperament so cold, so austere, so indifferent to our pains and pleasures, so wrapped up in one lonely and monotonous mood that one comes from it wearied and exalted, as though one had posed for some noble action, in a strange *tableau vivant*, that casts its painful stillness upon the mind instead of upon the body' (*UP2* 89).

17   Wilde's oral tale 'L'inutile résurrection', collected by G. de Saix in *Le Chant du Cygne* (Paris, Mercure de France, 1942), ends in a post-Resurrection stalemate, 'dans l'apathie des jours sans croyance et sans joie' (p. 172).

18   'Mr L. Johnson and certain Irish Poets', 27 August, 1898, see *UP2*, 113-118; *P & I* 111-112. See W. Gould, 'Lionel Johnson Comes the First to Mind: Sources for Owen Aherne' in G. M. Harper (ed.), *Yeats and The Occult* (Toronto, Macmillan of Canada, Maclean-Hunter Press, 1975), 255-284.

19   Re-reading *Marius the Epicurean* made Yeats begin 'to wonder if it, or the attitude of mind of which it was the noblest expression, had not caused the disaster of my friends', *Au* 302-3. On the influence of this book on Wilde, see M. Reeves and W. Gould, *Joachim of Fiore and the Myth of the Eternal Evangel in the Nineteenth Century* (Oxford, Clarendon Press, 1987), Ch. 7, pp. 166-74, 180-184.

20   *Aubrey Beardsley* (London, Unicorn Press, 1898).

21   'It was a profound thing which he said to a friend of mine [surely Yeats] who asked him whether he ever saw visions: "No", he replied, "I do not allow myself to see them except on paper." All his art is in that phrase' (*Aubrey Beardsley*, p. 15). Yeats and Symons offer apparently separate accounts of Beardsley's childhood vision of the bleeding crucifix (*Aubrey Beardsley*, pp. 11-2, cf. *Au* p. 329).

22   Cf. J. Ronsley's view in 'Yeats's Lecture Notes for "Friends of My Youth"', *YT* 61.
23   As Yeats admits in *Memoirs* 37, but denies in *Au* 165.
24   Which he took in Shelley's despite from Mary Shelley's 'Note on Prometheus Unbound'. See T. Hutchinson, ed., *The Complete Poetical Works of Percy Bysshe Shelley* (London, Oxford University Press, 1905, 1961), p. 271.
25   The drunken Willy Wilde was ready with blague about yachts in the Thames, £5000 and balloons, with Wilde ready to 'face the music, like Christ' (*Mem* 79-80); see also *Au* 288.
26   As R. Ellmann pointed out in his 'Oscar and Oisin' chapter of *Eminent Domain: Yeats among Wilde, Joyce, Pound, Eliot and Auden* (New York, Oxford University Press, 1967), p. 17. For the relevant echoes, see *AC* 311; *Au* 165, 270; *Myth* 333-4.
27   See also *Mem* 191, and the preface to Yeats's edition of *The Happy Prince and Other Fairy Tales* (1923), where Yeats goes 'back to the late eighties', remembering 'with pleasure [...] always the talker [...] either as I have heard him [...] or in some passage in a play, where there is a stroke of wit which had first come to him in conversation or might so have come'. Behind his words was 'the whole power' of 'that intellect [...] given [...] to pure contemplation' (*P & I* 148).
28   These subscription lectures at the Adelphi Club were held to raise money for the Abbey Theatre, after the withdrawal of Annie Horniman's support. Edmund Gosse presided, and banged his palm down upon a 'teacher's bell' with an air of barely suppressed outrage and loathing at the mere mention of dissipation and despair, according to William Carlos Williams', *Autobiography* (London, Random House, 1951) pp. 115-6. Gosse, a repressed homosexual, would 'always feel instinctively hostile' (as he had told Robert Ross). Gosse had virtually banned Ross from his house in a hypocritical letter of 17 May, 1895, and bid him seek consolation for the Wilde disaster in 'the infinite resources of literature'. He did, however, later defend Ross in public against Lord Alfred Douglas. See A. Thwaite, *Edmund Gosse: a Literary Landscape 1849-1928* (London, Secker and Warburg, 1984), pp. 359-362.
29   Yeats's telling note to himself concludes the section: 'Go on to describe Althea Gyles' (*Mem* 21-3, 92, 99).
30   'You did not realise that an artist, and especially such an artist as I ~~was~~ am, one, that is to say, the quality of whose work depends on the intensification of personality, requires for the development of his art the companionship of ideas, and intellectual atmosphere, quiet, peace, and solitude' (*Letters* 425).
31   Wilde was yet to review *The Wanderings of Oisin* (cf. *Au* 134), but did so anonymously, twice: see 'Some Literary Notes', *Woman's World* II: 17 (March 1889), 277-80 and 'Three New Poets: Yeats, FitzGerald, Le Gallienne' appeared in *The Pall Mall Gazette* XLIX: 7587 (12 July 1889), 3. Yeats's response to the latter review was acute. Wilde found 'populace' in '[a]nd a small and a feeble populace stooping with mattock and spade' (*VP* 58) to be 'infelicitous' (*AC* 151). Yeats substituted 'race' in

Poems (1895) but restored the infinitely stronger, contemptuous 'populace' in 1912.

32   Todhunter refuses to rise to Yeats's pert suggestion of a book issue with 'satirical designs and illustrations by Beardsley'(*Au* 281).

33   Agreeing with the single heckler in the audience that 'he and I are of exactly the same opinion, but what can we do against a whole house who are of the contrary opinion?' (*Au* 282).

34   *National Observer* 24 March 1894. See *VSR* 6-16. Wilde made amends by coming to the play another night, but they did not speak. See *Wade*, p. 32.

35   'The Master', published in April 1894 has certain affinities with Yeats's story. Yeats's story probably takes certain of its stylistic touches from Wilde's oral tales: e.g. 'I am myself the poorest, for I have travelled the bare road, and by the glittering footsteps of the sea; and the tattered doublet of particoloured cloth upon my back and the torn pointed shoes upon my feet have ever irked me, because of the towered city full of noble raiment which was in my heart' (*VSR* 15, 219-223 vv.).

36   V. O'Sullivan reads *Lord Arthur Savile's Crime* as having some psychobiographical 'basis in fact' (*Aspects of Wilde*, pp. 62-3). No doubt Wilde's superstition is well explained by the circumstances of Irish Protestantism ('I don't think I have any [religion]. I am an Irish Protestant' (p. 65)). See also R. Foster, 'Protestant Magic: W. B. Yeats and the Spell of Irish History', The Chatterton Lecture on Poetry, *Proceedings of the British Academy* LXXV, 1989, pp. 242-266.

37   On the concept in general see L. G. Christian, *Theatrum Mundi: The History of an Idea* (London & New York, Garland Publishing, 1987). See also W. Gould, 'A Crowded Theatre: Yeats and Balzac' in A. N. Jeffares (ed.) *Yeats the European* (Gerrards Cross: Colin Smythe Ltd, 1989), pp. 69-90.

38   O'Sullivan, *Aspects of Wilde*, p. 162.

39   'The nineteenth century, as we know it, is largely an invention of Balzac. Our Luciens de Rubempré, our Rastignacs, and De Marsays made their first appearance on the stage of the *Comédie Humaine*. We are merely carrying out, with footnotes and unnecessary additions, the whim or fancy or creative vision of a great novelist' (*AC* 309).

40   O'Sullivan says that perhaps he was 'born out of due time' (*Aspects of Wilde*, p. 28).

41   K. Thornton, *The Decadent Dilemma* (London, Edward Arnold, 1983), p. 79.

42   *The Decadent Dilemma*, p. 76.

43   'The Celt in London', 28 September 1889, *LNI* 13. Reviewing *A Woman of No Importance* in *The Bookman* in March 1895, Yeats had sharpened Walter Pater's judgement of *The Picture of Dorian Gray*. 'Mr Pater once said that Mr Oscar Wilde wrote like an excellent talker', said Yeats, 'and the criticism goes to the root' (*UP1* 354-5). Pater had written: 'There is always something of an excellent talker about the writing of Mr Oscar Wilde; and in his hands, as happens so rarely with those who practise it, the form of dialogue is justified by its being really

alive.' 'A Novel by Mr Oscar Wilde' (*The Bookman*, November
1891) is reprinted in J. Uglow (ed.), *Essays on Literature and Art
by Walter Pater* (London, Dent; Totowa, N. J., Rowman and
Littlefield, 1973), pp. 142-45.

44   No doubt these more affectionate memories of Wilde's earlier
books were invoked to soften Yeats's critique of Wilde's failure
to transcend 'the popular conventions, the spectres and
shadows of the stage' (*UP2* 355).

45   Cf. 'Romantic art deals with the exception and the individual'
(*AC* 240).

46   R. Ellmann twenty three years ago suggested an identification
between the artist and the criminal as the 'secret spring' of
Intentions (*AC* xix-xxiii). Ellmann is able to treat the issue of
homosexuality appropriately, and concludes that Wilde was 'a
genuine scapegoat' (xxiv).

47   *VSR* 151 vv.

48   W. Pater, *The Renaissance: Studies in Art and Poetry: The 1893
Text*, edited with Textual and Explanatory Notes, by D. L. Hill
(Berkeley, Los Angeles, London, University of California Press,
1980), pp. 18-19.

49   No 3, July 1896, which announces the end of quarterly,
beginning of monthly publication. Plate faces p. 54. The British
Museum copy was received on 27 June 1896.

50   Its last two numbers had been long filled up and Symons was
returning copy to contributors, including some already set. 'We
could not get it to pay its way; for as you know, the price was
reduced to meet the requirements of Smiths' bookstalls, and
Smiths' bookstalls behaved in the ridiculous way you
remember', Symons wrote to Richard Garnett. I am grateful to
Dr Bruce Morris for supplying me with a copy of this letter, the
present whereabouts of which I do not know.

51   V. O'Sullivan, *Opinions* (London, 1959), p. 203, claims that
anyone interested in the period and in *The Savoy* ought to look
at *The Senate*, but one look at that paper and one can see why
WBY contributed only 'O'Sullivan the Red to Mary Lavell' for
Vol. 3: 23 (March 1896), pp. 95-96.

52   Cf. R. Gagnier, *Idylls of the Marketplace: Oscar Wilde and the
Victorian Public* (London, Scholar Press, 1987), p. 11.

53   See also Reeves and Gould, *Joachim of Fiore...*, pp. 180-4.

54   Rather than from Nietzsche, though *The Savoy* (2-4) had
provided a bluffer's guide to Nietzsche in three articles by
Havelock Ellis: see Reeves and Gould, *Joachim of Fiore...*, pp. 232
& ff.

55   *Aubrey Beardsley*, p. 24. The debate led to some book titles.
Symons's *Images of Good and Evil* (London, William Heinemann,
1899) was followed by Yeats's *Ideas of Good and Evil* in 1903.
The latter takes its title from Blake. Yeats's own account of
Beardsley and the Vision of Evil, truncated no doubt in view of
Symons, asks 'who will thirst for the metaphysical, who have a
parched tongue, if we cannot recover the Vision of Evil?' (*Au*
326), and continues with his account of the doctrine of Art as
Victimage and the recovery through it of innocence (*ibid.* 330-3).

56   See Small, 'Oscar Wilde as a Professional Writer', *The Library Chronicle of the University of Texas at Austin*, 23:1, (1933), 33-49 at p. 34.

57   In 1894 Wilfred Hugh Chesson —

> saw a manuscript by a very well-known woman author lying — a new and purchased commodity — upon the table of a famous publisher [...] [who] turned over the preliminary pages and read these words: 'To Oscar Wilde, with admiration'. 'I'm not going to print that', he said, and a faithful pencil chained to his person pounced on the offending dedication and slew it.

Chesson's 'A Reminiscence of 1898' (*The Bookman* (New York), xxxiv (December 1911), 389-94) is reprinted in E. H. Mikhail (ed.), *Oscar Wilde: Interviews and Recollections*(London, Macmillan, 1979), p. 374. Small ignores the context of belle-lettristic contracts with Lane and the prudent Elkin Mathews which might have tempered the claim that the terms for *Poems* (1892) were 'outrageously hard' (Small, *loc. cit.*, pp. 44-5).

58   For full text see Appendix: Wilde and Macmillan, p. 183 ff.

59   The whole question of Macmillan's treatment of Irish writers including Yeats and Wilde is examined in my forthcoming *Yeats's Permanent Self: Textual Biography and the Shaping of the Canon.*

60   Leonard Smithers proved an early admirer, see *Letters* 221.

61   See Appendix: Wilde and Macmillan p. 183 ff for full text.

62   At moments when I have thought of the results of political subjection upon Ireland I have remembered a story told me by Oscar Wilde, who professed to have found it in a book of magic. 'If you carve a Cerberus upon an emerald', he said, 'and put it in the oil of a lamp and carry it into a room where your enemy is, two new heads will come upon his shoulders and all three devour one another' (*Au* 361).

63   A. J. A. Symons, 'An Unacknowledged Movement in Fine Printing: The Typography of the Eighteen-Nineties', *The Fleuron*, VII, 1930, pp. 83-119, at pp. 85, 116.

64   *Works*, p. 174. Yeats had reviewed the book for *United Ireland* on 26 September 1891. See 'Oscar Wilde's Last Book', *UP1* 202 & ff.

65   Wilde had found 'dull and loathsome' (*Letters* 354). Mrs Humphry Ward, who also seems to have worked behind the scenes 'to harden *The Times*'s libellous persecution' of Parnell, 'bullied Wilde's publisher, John Lane, into further hounding Aubrey Beardsley, so as to purge English culture of the infection of Yellow-bookery and sodomy'. See J. Sutherland, *Mrs Humphry Ward: Eminent Victorian Pre-eminent Edwardian* (Oxford, Clarendon Press, 1990), 191. André Raffalovich was refused Beardsley's frontispiece for *The Thread and the Path* in early June, 1895, by David Nutt. See H. Maas, J. L. Duncan and W. G. Good (eds), *The Letters of Aubrey Beardsley* (London, Cassell, 1970), p. 89.

66   Sydney Goodsir Smith seems to have presided over homage to Smithers and *The Savoy* in J. Singer's *The Holiday Book*

192 *Rediscovering Oscar Wilde*

(Glasgow, William McLellan, 1946), which included Smith's own 'A Publisher of the Nineties' on Smithers and the reprinting of a number of contributions from *The Savoy*, including 'The Binding of the Hair', a story from No 1 which Yeats included in *The Secret Rose* and subsequently abandoned: see *VSR* 177-81. James G. Nelson is compiling a bibliographical study. Peter Mendes is compiling a catalogue of 90s Erotica.

67   *The Early Life & Vicissitudes of Jack Smithers* (London, Martin Secker, 1939). There are robust defences of Smithers against the '[u]tterly selfish, idle' Wilde, 'a thief and a cadger to boot' (p. 22), largely in respect of his multiple sale of his copyrights, to Smithers and others. The little boy believed Wilde to have been in love with Alice Smithers and to have once spent the night on the doorstep of 6a Bedford Square (p. 18). For all of its manifest inaccuracy, Jack Smithers' tale is an overlooked document, its very innocence of perspective being a guarantee of sorts.

68   Examples of the twelve copies on full Japan vellum of this edition (bound in full vellum) and of *An Ideal Husband by the Author of Lady Windermere's Fan* (London, Leonard Smithers, 1899) are in the British Library.

69   'I see that it is my *name* that terrifies', Wilde commented to Smithers, January 9, 1898, concerning an American edition of *The Ballad* (*Letters* 698).

70   'My idea is *Reynolds*' [...]. It circulates widely among the criminal classes —to which I now belong — so I shall be read by my peer — a new experience for me' (*Letters* 663). Jack Smithers tells a touching tale of how he was forced to sign over the copyright in *The Ballad* to a London bookseller, possibly Siegle & Hill (*Early Life and Vicissitudes*, pp. 79-80, Mason p. 423).

71   Harmondsworth, Penguin, 1970, pp. 278-85.

72   Derry, Field Day Publications, 1991, II, pp. 731 & ff. Deane shares Yeats's view of Wilde's poetry, finding it 'vulgar in its facility of feeling and rhythmic automatism'. Whilst conceding that Wilde produced 'the outstanding synthesis of aesthetic nostalgia and popular ballad form', Deane nevertheless insists that 'as in all his work, the subversive, even radical, critique of society that is implicit in what he has to say, finds no release within the linguistic conventions which he mocked but which he remained imprisoned' (p. 721). For Deane, to be really modern one must be a Modernist.

73   Index refers also to an f. 10, presumably another report in another series of reader's reports, untraced.

74   ALS Alexander Macmillan to Wilde, 16 June 1890, MS Wilde, O. Recip., HRHRC, University of Texas at Austin. See I. Small, 'Oscar Wilde as a Professional Writer', *The Library Chronicle of the University of Texas at Austin*, 23: 1, (1993), 33-49 at p. 34, and also *Oscar Wilde Revalued: An Essay on New Materials and Methods of Research* (Greensboro, N. C., ELT Press, 1993), p. 79.

75   Again only one report seems to have survived. The reference in *Ad. MS* 56003 or 56017 (check) to a report at an f. 13 is untraced.

76   B. L. Add. MS. 55944 ff 39-40.

PLAGIARIST, OR PIONEER?

Merlin Holland

To determine one's own posthumous reputation from beyond the grave is a dangerous luxury not given to many literary men, but if anyone can be considered to have manipulated the vulgar constraints of time in this way (and to whom, after all, would one begrudge the gift less?) it is Oscar Wilde. If his relentless self-promotion during his life as a dandy, wit, conversationalist and writer of comedies has outlived any reputation he may have had as a scholar and a thinker, it is just as he would have wished it to be, the life taking precedence over the works, the genius, as he saw it, over the talent. If today there is a tendency among the general public to know him for *The Picture of Dorian Gray*, two volumes of fairy stories, five plays and *The Ballad of Reading Gaol*, the fault is in no small part his own. Twenty years ago I would even have gone so far as to prune the five plays down to two or three. Apart from the Ross edition of 1908 and the Collins *Collected Works* which first appeared forty years later, no collection for the general reader has offered his essays in their entirety and only recently has there appeared an anthology of his journalism — long overdue, for it contains some of his most sparkling prose. Wilde, even before the 1960s was an eminently marketable commodity, but as a lightweight, a humorist, even a romantic. A slim volume of *The Sayings of Oscar Wilde* was introduced only a short time back by an Oxford Professor of English Literature with the words: 'Wilde in his best art was not a serious person. Richard Ellmann's incomparable Life pays him the compliment he would have been the first to smile wryly at and set aside; that of taking him too seriously.' That is what the public expects to hear and naturally sees Oscar in the place of Lord Illingworth who remarks, 'vulgar habit that is people have nowadays of asking one whether one is serious or not. Nothing is serious except passion. The intellect is not a serious thing and never has been. It is an instrument on which one plays, that is all.'

The image of scintillating and paradoxical superficiality as well as a studied indifference to hard work was a myth which he was at pains to cultivate as early as his Oxford days. In a memoir written over sixty years later, the Rev. David Hunter Blair, who had been a contemporary of his at Oxford, wrote:

> Of course Wilde worked hard for the high academic honours which he achieved at Oxford. He liked to pose as a dilettante trifling with his books; but I knew of the hours of assiduous and laborious reading often into the small hours of the morning after our pleasant symposia in his rooms. I once told him that he reminded me of Blake, the brilliant scholar of St Ambrose's in Hughes' *Tom Brown at Oxford*, which we were all reading in the 'seventies: Blake, who after an evening of dissipation would bind a wet cloth round his throbbing brow, drink buckets of strong black coffee, and read Pindar until the chapel bells began to ring for morning prayer. Oscar did a great amount of reading in his small and stuffy bedroom, where books lay in apparently hopeless confusion, though he knew where to lay his hands on each in every corner.[1]

Moreover, he goes on to quote the now famous words which, significantly are seldom prefaced by the question which prompted them:

> 'You talk a lot about yourself, Oscar', said [William] Ward, 'and all the things that you would like to achieve. But you never say what you are going to do with your life. You, Oscar, who have twice as much brains in that ridiculous head of yours as both of us put together — what are you going to do with them? What is your real ambition in life?'
> 'God knows', said Oscar, serious for a moment. 'I won't be a dried-up Oxford don, anyhow. I'll be a poet, a writer, a dramatist. Somehow or other I'll be famous, and if not famous, I'll be notorious.'[2]

But beneath the apparent nonchalance, careful reading of his letters and a study of such contemporary accounts reveal a firm streak of ambition. Without being able to give it definite direction, he unquestionably has ideas about the course he wishes his life to take and of how he intends to succeed. He was going to burn with Pater's hard gem-like flame and do it within the context of his own century.

In May 1877, after his rustication from Oxford for returning nearly four weeks late for the Easter Term, he busied himself writing poetry and a review of the Grosvenor Gallery opening. The review, his first prose work to be published, appeared in *The Dublin University Magazine*[3] — an obvious choice given his past connections. Two of the poems were despatched, one cannot help feeling, as pretexts for writing to their recipients, both of whom were household names of the time. To William Gladstone, then in Liberal opposition, he sent his sonnet 'On the Massacres of the Christians in Bulgaria' hoping that Gladstone might use his influence to have it published.[4] Gladstone's pamphlet *Bulgarian Horrors and the Question of the East* in which he was severely critical of the Government's Eastern policy, had been published the year before. An exchange of letters ensued but the sonnet had to await publication until its inclusion in the *Poems* four years later. In July the same year he wrote to Lord Houghton,[5] whom he had already met in Dublin, about an ugly bas-relief memorial by the tomb of Keats in Rome and included his sonnet 'Keats' Grave'. Houghton had published his *Life, Letters and Literary Remains of John Keats* in 1848 but more significantly he knew anyone of note in politics and the arts and was present at almost every great social gathering. Houghton disagreed with much of what Wilde said but the letter had not gone unanswered. A copy of the Grosvenor Gallery article was sent to Walter Pater and elicited exactly the desired response — fulsome praise and an invitation to make his acquaintance.[6]

On his arrival in London two years later he immediately made it his business to court the friendship of the day's leading actresses, attending their first nights and writing sonnets to them. Within a few months of first writing to Ellen Terry in September 1880 with a copy of his play *Vera*, she has become 'Dear Nellie' and he 'your devoted admirer and affectionate friend'.[7] He also realised soon enough the importance of a regular income, and as early as 1880 is soliciting Oscar Browning's help to secure a position as an Inspector of Schools. It is advice which he was to pass on to one of his correspondents some years later:

> As regards your prospects in literature, believe me that it is
> impossible to live by literature. By journalism a man may make
> an income, but rarely by pure literary work. I would strongly
> advise you to try and make some profession, such as that of
> tutor, the basis and mainstay of your life, and to keep literature
> for your finest, rarest moments. Remember that London is full of
> young men working for literary success, and that you must
> carve your way to fame. Laurels don't come for the asking.[8]

Invited in 1883 by one of his mother's friends to spend some time
in Rome, he resists the temptation and replies to her: 'I am
deep in literary work and cannot stir [...] till I have finished
two plays. This sounds ambitious but we live in an age of
inordinate personal ambition, and I am determined that the
world shall understand me.'[9]

    Much of this may be familiar, but we should remember
that almost all these facts were unknown before the publication
of Wilde's *Letters* in 1962. Since then there have been only two
biographies of note; Ellmann's in 1987 which is unquestionably
the best we have and Montgomery Hyde's in 1976, a lopsided
affair which predictably devoted over a third of its pages to
the trials and the imprisonment. Ellmann treats the works in
more detail than Hyde but still the main emphasis is on
Wilde's life, a fact which must have been conditioned by
commercial considerations if the phenomenal world-wide sales
are any indication. Despite this it is not an easy book for the
general reader, and, dare I say it, I fear that many thousands of
copies languished ostentatiously on coffee-tables before finding
their way, half-read, to the book-case. The old smoke-screen
remains; the public wants Oscar but they still want him in the
brilliantly outrageous, witty and life-enhancing form that he
persuaded them to take a century ago and still he tries to
dissuade us parasepulchrally (how tiresome that we have no
good English equivalent for *outre-tombe*) from looking behind
the scenes. Even the academic world has not escaped, for it is
essentially only in the last twenty-five years that he has been
accepted as worthy of serious post-graduate research.

    If we are to re-assess, re-discover even, as the title of
this conference suggests, Wilde's contribution to late
nineteenth-century literature and perhaps, just as important, to
the history of twentieth-century culture and ideas, the impetus

must come initially from the academic world. Richard Ellmann has made a fine start but there is a startlingly large amount of source material still to be evaluated. In many cases it has been overlooked by researchers as too trivial for consideration, and I for one will instantly plead guilty to returning to an archive after several years and wondering why on earth I had overlooked the significance of certain papers. Our preconceptions of the man are deeply ingrained and there are aspects of both his life and his work which we need to approach from an entirely new standpoint. We may ultimately reach many of the same conclusions, but Wilde can only gain in stature and complexity as a result.

I did not embrace an academic career, or perhaps it would be more accurate to say that an academic career did not embrace me, a characteristic which would appear to run in the family. In consequence I have sat, often uneasily, between the obscure '-isms' of modern literary research and the over-simplified popular views of Oscar's life. It is a position made no easier by the weight of emotional baggage with which each generation unwittingly lumbers its descendants. I did not know my grandfather, and cold logic tells me that I have no more reason to defend or criticise him than my neighbour; and yet there is an intangible link perhaps vicariously through my father's suffering as a child which is difficult to ignore. In his autobiography in 1954 he made an intensely personal appeal:

> As people recede further and further into the past, they are apt to assume the aspect of effigies from which all humanity has departed; and when other people write about them, they hack them about to make them fit into a pattern of their own making until no flesh or blood remains. This is especially true of Oscar Wilde. Most of the people who have written about him have treated him like a beetle under a microscope, to be examined and dissected and analysed as a psychological problem — not as a human being at all.[10]

In retrospect it has been heeded almost too well, for in concentrating so much on the man we have been in danger of overlooking a remarkable intellect.

In 1976, I was approached by two American scholars requesting my permission to obtain photocopies of certain Wilde manuscripts from the Clark Library in Los Angeles.

These manuscripts were Wilde's notebooks kept while he was an undergraduate at Oxford and the researchers would like, they said, to edit them for publication. There seemed no good reason to refuse for there was little in them which could be sensationalized in the manner which was characteristic of all too many books about my grandfather around that time. However, I am ashamed to admit I harboured the uncharitable thought that to put into print such a ragbag of diffuse scribblings was to serve up barrel scrapings as *haute cuisine* instead of leaving them to be tipped, as I believed properly, into the stock pot. There was also a nagging fear that the book, when published,[11] might show Wilde up in an unfavourable light. He himself had warned Whistler on the dangers of self-interpretation after his famous 'Ten O'Clock Lecture':

> Dear Butterfly, by the aid of a biographical dictionary I discovered that there were once two painters, called Benjamin West and Paul Delaroche, who recklessly took to lecturing on Art. As of their works nothing at all remains, I conclude that they explained themselves away. Be warned in time, James; and remain, as I do, incomprehensible.[12]

In the event its subtitle 'A Portrait of Mind in the Making' told all. It was a work of considerable scholarship and understanding and one to which I owe at least part of the genesis of this address. Not only did it contribute to the growing re-evaluation of Wilde as a serious thinker but it examined the influence his reading was to have on his later works.

Plagiarist or pioneer? Both emotive words and both perhaps too strong, which is a lesson in not ascribing titles to papers before they are finished. However, to plagiarise Gwendolen and to spare you any possible disappointment, I think it only fair to tell you quite frankly beforehand that I am fully determined to sit on the fence.

From the moment that Wilde's *Poems* were ridiculed from the floor of the Oxford Union by the 20 year-old classical scholar Oliver Elton, it was inevitable that all his future works would be scrutinized for derivations. They were described as 'thin', 'immoral', and 'for the most part not by their putative father at all but by a number of better known and more deservedly reputed authors'.[13] The volume which had been solicited by the Librarian was returned. A dislike of Wilde's flamboyant style and growing reputation as an aesthetic poseur was undoubtedly at the root of this farce. Why else would a second year undergraduate have taken notice of what was otherwise a fairly routine acquisition? Envy clothes itself in curious forms; taking a Second in Mods earlier in the year and mindful that this Irish peacock had distinguished himself with a double First cannot have helped. But he was not alone. Already the public had come to expect originality from the self-proclaimed Professor of Aesthetics and all they had got was 'the trash of a man of a certain amount of mimetic ability' as *The Spectator* described the collection.[14] 'Imitation of previous writers goes far enough seriously to damage their originality', chided *The Athenaeum*.[15] 'Mr Wilde may be aesthetic', sneered *Punch*, 'but he is not original. This is a volume of echoes — it is Swinburne and water, while here and there we note that the author has been reminiscent of Mr Rossetti and Mrs Browning.'[16] It was hardly an auspicious start to a literary career. There are undoubtedly very clear echoes of Swinburne, of Wordsworth, of Keats but it is scarcely surprising since his Oxford years had been filled as much with the reading of them as with the Classics, and according to Hunter Blair he was given to 'dropping into poetry, spouting yards of verse, either his own or that of other poets whom he favoured, and spouting it uncommonly well'.[17] There are instances when he came perilously close to justifying the critics as for example with a biblical quotation most probably culled from Pater's *Studies in the History of the Renaissance*.[18] Jonathan confesses to his father Saul, 'I did but taste a little honey with the end of the rod that was in mine hand, and, lo, I must die', and Wilde renders it into the wonderful cadences of:

> lo! with a little rod
> I did but touch the honey of romance —
> And must I lose a soul's inheritance?

Clever craftsmanship with words, but no substitute for originality in the eyes of those who were anxious to see him trip over his silver tongue. In another poem 'Ye shall be Gods' his debt to Swinburne is clear. Wilde's poem begins:

> Before the dividing of the days
> Or the singing of summer or spring,

and Swinburne's from *Atlanta in Calydon*:

> Before the beginning of the years
> There came to the making of man.

Even the metre is imitated, but in his defence 'Ye shall be Gods', one of his earliest poems dating from Trinity, Dublin, remained wisely unpublished.[19] Imitative his poetry may have been but directly plagiaristic it was not. Nonetheless Wilde remained conscious of the accusations until many years after when he was correcting the proofs of *The Ballad of Reading Gaol* and was concerned that his phrase 'Grey Hunger and green Thirst' might seem an echo of Swinburne's 'Green pleasure and grey grief'.[20] In the event he changed it to 'lean Hunger and green Thirst' doubtless to forestall any nitpicking critics who would be waiting, hatchets sharpened, for his first post-prison offering.[21] However visionary Wilde was, though he could not have anticipated the arrival of *The English Poetry Full Text Database 600-1900* on CD-ROM in 1994 when the question of derivation, imitation, call it what you will, may be solved once and for all. I suspect that Oscar may still have the last laugh for in the few comparisons I have made, his unique feeling for the music of words has invariably improved on his source.

If Wilde's early poetic borrowings were mainly stylistic imitations, his next attempts bear more evidence of what was to become his very individual style, but they also show clear signs of a tendency to lift whole phrases if not paragraphs from writers more established than he. The years between 1882 and 1888 were largely filled with journalistic work and lectures. America for nearly a year was his initiation, but the notice he was given was short and his first lecture had not even been prepared by the time he docked in New York at the beginning of January 1882. Within ten days 'The English Renaissance' had been written and delivered for the first time. It was long and over-erudite for his American audience and underwent numerous revisions before being given for the last time on 8 February. A considerable amount of work was done on the genesis and texts of 'The English Renaissance' as well as his other two American lectures 'The Decorative Arts' and 'The House Beautiful' by Kevin O'Brien as early as 1973 and from it one fact is clear: he borrowed heavily and shamelessly from Ruskin, Morris and Pater, including verbatim passages from all.[22] When the *Collected Works* was published in 1908 and included the text of the lecture, Robbie Ross, Wilde's longtime friend and literary executor who was responsible for the edition, either excised the relevant passages or had the good sense to attribute them to their rightful authors. A combination of time, or rather the lack of it, and distance from his original sources may have encouraged Wilde to waive literary integrity in this way. Style, as he loved to maintain was the thing, and content merely a vehicle for it.

On his return Wilde lectured to the British on 'Value of Art in Modern Life', 'Dress' and his 'Impressions of America'. The latter for once seems to be entirely original, based as it is on his year-long lecture tour and, apart from some of his correspondence, is probably the nearest we shall ever come to hearing his legendary conversation. As for the other two, I hope that as part of our re-evaluation of his literary development, research will be done textually into both of them and into the itineraries. Apart from filling in a sparsely documented period in his life it will tell us how far he dared to repeat the literary thefts of the American tour once he was back on home ground.

It was on this very home ground that Wilde made the mistake of purloining the ideas of one of the more remarkable painters but also one of the most acerbic personalities of the period, James Whistler. Invited to address the students at the Royal Academy in 1883 he turned to Whistler for suggestions. The two men had been friends in a good-natured bantering sort of way, since Wilde had moved to London in 1879 and Whistler seemed happy to oblige. He was somewhat vexed, though, that Wilde did not play the proper disciple, openly recognising his master, as Herbert Vivian, a journalist on *The Sun* recalled some years later:

Oscar was invited to deliver an important lecture on art and wishing to give it the newest possible flavouring, he went to the fountain head and consulted Mr Whistler who welcomed the passport to publicity and good naturedly devoted his dinner hour to an exhaustive exposition of all his views on art. Now Oscar has a memory like one of Edison's phonographs and his lecture left nothing to be desired in point of accuracy, but he unfortunately committed the indiscretion of belauding Impressionism and not Mr Whistler whereat the full vials of the Master's indignation were poured upon the devoted head of his unfortunate disciple. Oscar was invited to a large dinner party and plied with questions across the full length of the table with reference to his lecture. 'Now Oscar, tell us what you said to them', mine host would repeat inflexibly and the poor fellow had to trot out all his points again. As each was enunciated, Whistler got up and made a solemn bow, with his hand across his breast, to show his sense of the compliment paid him by the reproduction of his theories. It was at this party that Whistler's famous *mot* first saw the light. Whistler having got off some poignant epigram, Oscar called out gushingly, 'Oh Jimmy! I wish I had said that!'. 'Never mind Oscar, you may be sure you will', was the crushing retort and everyone shook with merriment.[23]

Two years later Whistler avenged himself by delivering his famous 'Ten O'Clock Lecture' on Art in which his criticism of Wilde was thinly disguised:

The Dilettante stalks abroad. The amateur is loosed. The voice of the aesthete is heard in the land, and catastrophe is upon us. And there are curious converts to a weird *culte*, in which all instinct for attractiveness — all freshness and sparkle — is to give way to a strange vocation for the unlovely.[24]

But the matter was far from over. Wilde's review, complimentary at face value was penned, tongue firmly in cheek occasioning more public correspondence in the columns of the press. 'What has Oscar in common with Art? except that he dines at our tables and picks from our platters the plums for the pudding he peddles in the provinces', he wrote to the *World*.[25] The final insult, as far as Whistler was concerned, was Wilde's blatant use of his joke, 'Oscar — has the courage of the opinions... of others!' in 'The Decay of Lying' in 1889. This fact was only drawn to his attention by Herbert Vivian's article in November that year but Whistler had clearly had enough. He wrote to the Editor of *Truth*: 'Among your ruthless exposures of the shams of today, nothing, I confess, have I enjoyed with keener relish than your late tilt at that arch-impostor and pest of the period — the all-pervading plagiarist! How is it that, in your list of culprits, you omitted that fattest of offenders, our own Oscar?'[26] And with that, any possible hope of reconciliation came to an abrupt end.

When Robert Ross brought the publication of the *Collected Works* to an end with the volume of 'Miscellanies' he included a number of Wilde's letters to Whistler, 'with', as he said, 'greater misgiving than anything else in this volume'. He acknowledged his friend's debt to the painter, but rightly makes the point that 'the tedious attempt to recognise in every jest of his some original by Whistler, induces the criticism that it seems a pity that the great painter did not get them off on the public before he was forestalled'. Verbal plagiarism? Any reasonable coroner would return an open verdict.

There is, at the Clark Library, an exercise book containing what is described as an 'Essay on Chatterton'.[27] Christopher Millard makes note of it in his bibliography and assumes, since Issue 4 of *The Century Guild Hobby Horse* in October 1886 announced the unavoidable delay of Mr Wilde's article on Chatterton, that it was intended for publication. It was apparently never published. Wilde told Herbert Horne in a letter that he had given it as a lecture before an audience of 800 at Birkbeck College in November 1886[28] and agreed to give it in Bournemouth in April 1888 but does not mention it again. Whether he had prepared it as an article or as a lecture, I found it profoundly disturbing when I first saw the manuscript, for spread throughout the pages is a litter of cuttings taken from two printed books both 'Lives' of Thomas Chatterton by Daniel Wilson in 1869 and David Masson in 1874. Cursory examination shows the reason for most of them. They are largely quotations from Chatterton's poems or from 18th century accounts ascribed correctly to their authors, but a dozen or so pages are simply the biographical work of Wilson or Masson themselves. I tried regarding them as simple *aide-mémoire* but was defeated on finding that Wilde had actually fitted his own manuscript around one and deleted superfluous adjectives in another to suit his style. Whatever the proposed destination for the piece he was clearly going to use several thousand words of someone else's research in his piece. I was sympathetic to the short-cut of pasting in his quotations, for unlike us he did not live in an age of photocopiers; I was concerned to find such blatant evidence of plagiarism; but what shocked me most of all was the mutilation of the books, which, as objects, seem to rank second only to lilies in his esteem. Maybe they were only printers sheets but I fear not.

The Picture of Dorian Gray is the work of Wilde's which has probably given more enjoyment to literary sleuths than any other. At a conservative count there are 15 books which are said to have had a major influence on the plot or the depiction of the characters and it is certainly beyond the scope of such a paper as this to discuss them. (I note, incidentally, with delicious anticipation that we are to be treated during the conference to yet another potential source by Isobel Murray.) If critics at the time of its publication in both periodical and the later expanded book form intimated that Wilde was not altogether original in his choice of plot it was most certainly fuelled by preconception based on his past record as an author. But to accuse Wilde of truly plagiarising a plot whose roots may be considered to go back to Dr Faustus and perhaps beyond is a weak case. There is, however, well-known plagiarism in the descriptions of musical instruments in Chapter 11 with whole sentences lifted from the South Kensington Museum Art Handbooks. It was noted by the *Punch* reviewer in 1890.[29] Ingleby in 1907 points out similar borrowings[30] from Lefébure's book on embroideries[31] which Wilde reviewed for the *Woman's World* in 1888. Lord Henry borrows freely from Pater. It is already 1891, four years from the virtual end of Wilde's literary career and, to put it vulgarly, he's still at it.

There is no doubt in my mind that Wilde was, at least superficially, happiest writing for the theatre. It combined everything which he as a showman could have wanted. The success was immediate; he only had to present himself at the theatre to be in touch with his adulatory public. The 'red and yellow gold', as he loved to call it, poured in by the sackful to finance his increasingly extravagant style of life. In short, both literary gratifaction and material reward were instant. By contrast selling books slowly through the trade was a dull business. To amuse several hundred people an evening with one's wit was to dominate the largest drawing-room in the world.

It is not surprising, then, to find that the plots tend to have been dismissed as secondary to the brilliance of the dialogue. Once again it is a preconception which has come down over the years with Oscar's unmistakable stamp on it warning us to take nothing seriously except the frivolous behind which, inevitably, is concealed the serious. To talk of messages and morals at this stage is to preempt some of the theatrical research which is being done today, but as the tiny pieces, apparently insignificant on their own, fit into the puzzle, I think it will be no surprise to find Wilde far more deeply aware of the power of the theatre and more concerned in consequence with social issues that we have given him credit for.

And so to the point at which to slot my own piece into the jigsaw which I hope will draw together some of the long threads of this apparently disjointed paper. About the time that I read Oscar's *Oxford Notebooks*, I obtained a photocopy of the Tite Street sale catalogue.[32] It was a sheriff's sale of all his possessions and it took place, you will remember, when he was in prison awaiting his first trial. The majority of items by far was his books, a total of nearly two thousand volumes, and primed by Professors Helfand's and Smith's work which evaluated the influence of Wilde's reading at Oxford on his later work, I determined to piece together as much as I could of that library. Apart from the first 16 lots catalogued sufficiently well to identify the books accurately, the remainder was worse than useless, finishing with lot 114 'French novels, about 100 volumes' which sold for 35 shillings. Over the next two years, from later booksellers catalogues, from auction records and from diverse correspondences and other sources, I amassed a list of some 380 titles which had unquestionably passed through Wilde's hands. The search led me into unexpected by-ways, one of the most fascinating of which was a file containing the creditors' claims at the time of his bankruptcy.[33] It was a file of precisely the type to which I referred earlier — available, perused for the grander biographical details and dates, yet with the minutiae apparently overlooked. In Oscar's writing there is much which is uncannily prophetic but I doubt he could have foreseen that it would take a hundred years to realise the significance of 'it is only by not paying one's bills that one can hope to live in the memory of the commercial classes'. I have to say that I felt like one of those 'trash-can' journalists in America, sifting through the refuse of the famous in a sort of amateur forensic way to recreate a mode of life — a voyeur with a difference. But the life I recreated — my God what style! There are some fascinating footnotes for future biographers — imagine receiving 3000 personal newspaper cuttings in the course of a year.[34] One claim was a detailed account from David Nutt, bookseller and publisher of *The Happy Prince* for all the books which Wilde had purchased and on which dates between June 1888 and April 1895. Some were Nutt's own publications but many were foreign and amongst the latter were Series 4-8 of Jules Lemaître's *Impressions de Théâtre*. Lemaître was one of the foremost literary critics of the time and in addition, a playwright. In the first volume which Wilde purchased on 21 November 1889, Lemaître is sent by the editor to review his own play *Révoltée*. He gives an account of the plot.[35] The Comtesse de Voves is married to a man she does not love and by whom she has a son. Twenty years before she had a second child, a daughter, by a man who was not her husband. The daughter, Hélène, is brought up in a convent believing her mother to be dead and the Comtesse to have been her mother's closest friend. Mme de Voves manages to marry Hélène off to a pedestrian professor of mathematics with whom she is now as bored as her mother was in her own marriage. Hélène is on the verge of taking a lover. Mother, terrified at seeing her daughter repeat her own mistake reveals her secret to both her son and daughter independently, tearing up Hélène's letter to her lover. All the familiar elements of Wilde's society comedies are there; the fallen woman; the dramatic revelation; the intercepted letter. It was something noted at the time by A. B. Walkley in his 1892 review of *Lady Windermere* in *The Speaker*[36] but largely ignored since. What is even more significant than the plot is Lemaître's own criticism in *Impressions de Théâtre*. He recognises that the *dénouement* in the last act is as weak as it is melodramatic and records the advice of Ludovic Halévy, another playwright, not to weigh down the end with the death of the brother in a duel and to lighten the whole with touches of comedy. There is also the advice he sought from Alexandre Dumas:

> Je me souviens cependant que, lorsque M. Dumas eut la bonté d'écouter, il y a deux ans, la lecture de mon manuscrit, il me dit très nettement:
> - Trop d'aveux! Il n'en faut qu'un.
> - Et à qui doit-il être fait? Au fils ou à la fille?
> - Au fils.

The single indirect revelation is naturally a far stronger device. They were both pieces of advice which Wilde used to good effect in *Lady Windermere's Fan* two years later but partly ignored in *A Woman of No Importance* — perhaps the weakest of the 'big four'. Plagiarism? Hardly, just creative manipulation of a basic idea and the free, albeit secondhand, use of Dumas' advice. There is 'plagiarism' in the plays but of a very different sort; Wilde is now stealing openly from himself. Curiously it is not something on which the contemporary reviewers seem to have remarked. This may be in part because eighteen months elapsed between the production and the publication of the first two plays and unless a theatre critic, by sheer coincidence, had been reading *The Picture of Dorian Gray* the very night before attending *A Woman of No Importance*, it is unlikely he would have noticed. Also, on his guard for true plagiarism, the last thing the critic would expect is to find Wilde lifting clever dialogue from his own writings. And besides is there anything morally reprehensible in reviving one's own witticisms? Is 'She looks like an *édition de luxe* of a wicked French novel', any less funny in *Lady Windermere's Fan* because one has read it before in *The Picture of Dorian Gray*? Only perhaps to the student who reads the *Collected Works* for a weekly tutorial which can hardly have been in Wilde's mind when he re-used it.

Nor was Wilde one to waste the opportunities of a well-turned phrase or paradox. Which of us can honestly say that he has not done the same? His letters in this respect are revealing. Several favourites reappear at regular intervals. 'Greek and gracious' is applied variously to Roland Atwood, Bosie Douglas and his own handwriting. The 'streets are paved with brass' in New York and several times in Paris. It is noticed occasionally by Rupert Hart-Davis in his 1962 edition of the *Letters*, but he is quick to point a finger at convenient re-use of 'many phrases' from Wilde's article 'The Tomb of Keats' in his letter to Lord Houghton, where in fact he repeats one sentence only and, so it seems to me, takes particular care to paraphrase rather than to copy the rest.[37] When found out he is disarmingly frank. Late in 1898 he writes one of his many begging letter to Robbie Ross asking for money, ostensibly to pay an hotel bill at Nogent before the inn-keeper sells his clothes. Ross's reply, although it has not survived, must have been sharp and to the point. Wilde's next letter starts: 'My dear Robbie, I am so sorry about my excuse. I had forgotten I had used Nogent before. It shows the utter collapse of my imagination and rather distresses me.'[38]

It has been suggested that there was an ingenuous side to Oscar Wilde, a Peter Pan who was often unaware of the consequences of his actions. It is one of the only explanations, alongside his infatuation for Alfred Douglas which can possibly explain his disastrous action against Queensberry. For a man of Wilde's intelligence to imagine that the defence's plea of justification would be based on his relationship with Douglas alone, when the others were an open secret, seems unthinkable. We are forced partly to the conclusion that in his supreme and misplaced self-confidence he believed that 'society', worshipping his talent, would never harm him. It is equally false to see him, as he undoubtedly was on occasions, as a simple plagiariser, imagining that he could submit the result to public scrutiny and hope that he would not be discovered. Wilde was a literary magpie with a love of glittering language. Mundane considerations of 'respect' for the origins of a phrase or a plot yielded before the potential which they offered; his reading was prodigious and he used it to supplement his own creative imagination. I am not implying that he was intellectually amoral but more that he seemed to believe in a sort of communism of language and ideas on which to draw, justifying it in the name of style. 'In all important matters', as he said, 'style, not sincerity, is the essential. The modern novelist as Wilde describes him in *The Decay of Lying* 'has not even the courage of other people's ideas, but insists on going directly to life for everything'. His fascination for example with Chatterton and his forgeries is the admiration for the artist who, 'may not have had the moral conscience which is truth to fact but he had the artistic conscience which is truth to beauty'.[39]

There are echoes here too of his old tutor, Mahaffy's *Principles of the Art of Conversation*:

> There is such a thing in society — Aristotle saw it long ago — as being overscrupulous in truthfulness. Even a consummate liar, though generally vulgar and therefore offensive, is a better ingredient in a company than the scrupulously truthful man who weighs every statement, questions every fact and corrects every inaccuracy. In the presence of such a social scourge, I have heard a witty talker pronounce it the golden rule of conversation to know nothing *accurately*. Far more important is it, in my mind to *demand* no accuracy. There is no greater or more common blunder in society than to express disbelief or scepticism in a story told for the amusement of the company. High moral worth and extreme truthfulness, though lending the speaker dignity, must not be allowed to tyrannise.[40]

In the realm of the imagination, for Oscar Wilde, Art transcends Morality; or is that too dangerous and too glib an interpretation?

I have an uneasy feeling, like the fairground huckster with the two-headed sheep, that someone will shout 'Fraud' and demand a refund, for the animal as I have presented him thus far has but one and the second has been no more than implied, a reflection in the mirror. To have entitled this address 'Plagiarist, or Pioneer?', was, I see in retrospect, vastly ambitious. Either of these two aspects of Oscar Wilde could be dealt with at far greater length than in a simple conference paper and, in itself, that is indicative of the amount of research which is still to be done. The source material to do so is available, in some cases has been available for many years and now needs to be re-evaluated.

But there are three days before us and if I touch only briefly on Wilde as innovator and raise more questions than I answer and rather speculate on things which never were but which, from further tiny pieces of the puzzle, we can legitimately conjecture might have been I hope that you will see it in the spirit of this conference which is 'Rediscovery'.

Among the books which Wilde purchased from David Nutt was one in September 1888 entitled *Autour du Divorce*. Its author, who went by the pseudonym of Gyp, was the Comtesse Sibylle Gabrielle Marie Antoinette de Martel de Janville who, it seemed, was one of the editors of a popular magazine *La Vie Parisienne*. The book, written in dialogue form, tells the story of Paulette, one of the characters appearing weekly in *La Vie Parisienne*, and who, bored with her husband decides to divorce him. But how? Simple. She goes to the bookseller on the Place Dauphine and buys every available book on the subject. From these she learns that sufficient grounds are insults and ill-treatment by her husband before witnesses and, having goaded the poor man beyond endurance into committing them — *la voilà divorcée*! However, it was less the comic aspect in the book than the emancipated French woman which interested Wilde. Gyp published more than seventy volumes of such social sketches and dialogues, most between 1885 and 1900 and that Wilde was aware of her influence on French life is shown in the telegram which he sent to Ada Leverson in 1893:

> Your dialogue is brilliant and delightful and dangerous. What the Comtesse Gyp has done in France for Life, you have done in England for Art. Nothing pains me except stupidity and morality.[41]

Wilde's views on women have come down to us piecemeal through his correspondence, through what we can read into his editorship of the *Woman's World* and the moral standpoint he adopts to the 'scarlet women' of his plays. It is not enough to dismiss his obvious interest in women as the sterile interest of the effeminate for the feminine, nor to take his sexist quips at face value. His interest in woman's place in society was far greater, I believe, than we give him credit for.

Wilde as a social reformer may seem a tenuous proposition based on little more than *The Soul of Man under Socialism*, an admiration for Morris and a nodding acquaintance with Shaw[42] but he preserved a keen interest in the subject until his last days. His friend George Ives appears to have sent him a copy of Edward Carpenter's *Civilization; its Cause and Cure* late in 1900 which he admits to 'reading constantly'.[43] When Christopher Millard (Wilde's bibliographer under his pseudonym Stuart Mason) went to Paris in 1904, he visited the Hôtel d'Alsace with Robert Sherard who recalls that among some three hundred volumes of Wilde's which the proprietor, Dupoirier, has still kept, 'he seems to have collected and to have read everything that he could lay his hand upon which treats of prison life in England'.[44] An obvious interest given his past circumstances and to speculate further would perhaps smack of 'Cleopatra's Nose'. I would though dearly love to lay my hands on the copy of Carpenter's book which Millard brought home and described to his friend Walter Ledger: 'I found [and have] among OW's books in Paris, the same author's [Carpenter] work on *Civilization* with OW's pencil marginings.'[45]

Wilde the thinker and scholar must eventually take his place beside Wilde the entertainer and jester. The literary establishment will scoff and the public will object that the cosy little niche into which they have put their 'wit, homosexual martyr and playwright' is not big enough to accommodate another more serious side to his character. It will not be easy for he still manages posthumously to intertwine his life with his art, to blur the edges and confound our attempts to dissect it all and label the parts. Try as his critics will to pin him down, he remains too elusive. But as he trusts us to look behind the scenes and not to misinterpret what is undoubtedly there, the profound learning and scholarship, it can only add to his stature as an author. The magic will not be dispelled, for we will find that there is not one but a multiplicity of masks as he continues to slip mockingly between fiction and fact, challenging us like the conjuror to believe what is illusion and when we will not, showing us that it was, in fact, reality after all — always one step ahead, with a grain of truth in every paradox.

NOTES

1   Rev. D. H. Blair, 'Oscar Wilde as I Knew Him', *Dublin Review*, 406 (1938), p. 94.
2   H. Blair, p. 93.
3   *Dublin University Magazine*, 90 (1877), pp. 118-126.
4   *The Letters of Oscar Wilde*, edited by R. Hart-Davis, (London, 1962), p. 37.

5   *Letters*, p. 41.
6   *Letters*, pp. 46-47.
7   *Letters*, p. 74.
8   *Letters*, p. 179.
9   *Letters*, p. 146.
10   V. Holland, *Son of Oscar Wilde* (London, 1954), p. 198.
11   *Oscar Wilde's Oxford Notebooks*, edited by P. E. Smith and M. S. Helfand (London, New York, 1989).
12   J. Whistler, *The Gentle Art of Making Enemies* (London, 1892), p. 163.
13   H. Newbolt, *My World as in My Time* (London, 1932), pp. 96-7.
14   *Spectator*, 13 August 1881, pp. 1048-50.
15   *Athenaeum*, 23 July 1881, pp. 103-4.
16   *Punch*, 23 July 1881, p. 26.
17   H. Blair, p. 93.
18   W. Pater, *Studies in the History of the Renaissance* (London, 1873), p. 195.
19   Now in the Berg Collection, New York Public Library.
20   A. Swinburne, 'A Match', *Poems and Ballads* (London, 1866).
21   *Letters*, p. 680.
22   See K. O'Brien, *Oscar Wilde in Canada* (Toronto, 1982).
23   H. Vivian, 'The Reminiscences of a Short Life', *The Weekly Sun*, 17 November 1889, p. 4.
24   Whistler, *The Gentle Art*, p. 152.
25   Whistler, *The Gentle Art*, p. 164.
26   Whistler, *The Gentle Art*, p. 236.
27   Clark Library, UCLA. MS Finzi 2440.
28   *Letters*, pp. 191-2; *More Letters of Oscar Wilde*, ed. by R. Hart-Davis (London, 1985), p. 73.
29   In particular: C. Engel, *A Descriptive Catalogue of the Musical Instruments in the South Kensington Museum*, 2nd edition (London, 1874), pp. 69-81; A. H. Church, *Precious Stones Considered in Their Scientific and Artistic Relations* (London, 1883), pp. 56-72; W. Jones, *History and Mystery of Precious Stones* (London, 1880), pp. 10-17.
30   L. C. Ingleby, *Oscar Wilde* (London, 1907), pp. 313-15.
31   E. Lefébure, *Embroidery and Lace: Their Manufacture and History from the Remotest Antiquity to the Present* (London, 1888), especially pp. 40, 44, 53, 88, 91, 132, 137, 144.
32   In the collection of Lady Eccles.
33   Public Record Office, London. File B9/428.
34   Ibid., Newspaper Extract and Special Information Agency.
35   J. Lemaître, 'Révoltée', *Impressions de Théâtre*, Série (1889), pp. 111-124.
36   *Speaker*, 27 February 1892, pp. 257-8.
37   *Letters*, p. 41 and n. 2.
38   *Letters*, p. 763.
39   Chatterton MS, Clark Library.
40   J. P. Mahaffy, *Principles of the Art of Conversation* (London, 1887), p. 78, para. 27.
41   *Letters*, p. 347.
42   In his epilogue to Frank Harris's *Oscar Wilde: His life and Confessions* (London, 1938), p. 334, Shaw tells the story about

how he tried to get signatures for a petition to reprieve the Chicago anarchists in 1886: 'The only signature I got was Oscar's. It was a completely disinterested act on his part; and it secured my distinguished consideration for him for the rest of his life.'

43   *Letters*, p. 835.
44   R. H. Sherard, *Twenty Years in Paris* (London, 1905), p. 456.
45   C. Millard, TLS to Walter Ledger, 11 April 1905. Bodleian Library, Ross 13/1-5.

WILDE IN THE GORBALS: SOCIETY DRAMA AND CITIZENS THEATRE

Joel H. Kaplan

During the 1890s when Oscar Wilde's comedies were first played to fashionable audiences in London's West End, the Gorbals, a working class district of Glasgow on the wrong side of the River Clyde, was already notorious as one of the worst slums in Europe.[1] A century later, the Gorbals, still a depressed urban centre, has become the unlikely site for a reappraisal of Wilde's achievement as a society playwright. To understand the paradox is to understand something of the aims and methods of Glasgow's Citizens Theatre, a regional company unique in Great Britain, both for its continental repertoire and its belief in exuberant theatricality as a means of exploring social issues. Formed by Glaswegian playwright James Bridie, with the hope of establishing a Scottish National Theatre, the Citizens has since 1945 performed at the 600 seat Princess's Theatre, a late Victorian playhouse near Gorbals Cross. The troupe's international reputation, however, dates from the 1970s with the appointment of Giles Havergal as artistic director, and the subsequent emergence of a production executive consisting of Havergal, designer-director Philip Prowse, and playwright-dramaturg Robert David MacDonald. Under this triumvirate the Citz, as it has affectionately been called, has all but abandoned Bridie's nationalist dream, choosing instead to bring new readings of British and European plays to a broad public at consistently low prices. The company has, in the process, embraced a programme both elitist and egalitarian. Its commitment to community involvement is bodied forth in a series of free previews, generous concessions, and seat prices low enough to attract one of the youngest audiences in Europe.

Recent surveys place at 43% the number of spectators under 21. Such populism also extends to the troupe's uniform pay scale and the organization of its playbills, each of which lists alphabetically all members from directors to custodial staff. At the same time, the company has turned its back upon the type of kitchen sink realism that, in Britain at least, still characterizes much regional theatre. Indeed, under the Havergal regime, the Citizens' celebration of its own illusion making, its determination, in the words of theatre historian Anthony Jackson, to '*assert* artifice, rather than disguise or apologize for it', has become its distinguishing mark.[2]

The individual most readily identified with the articulation of a Citizens' style is Philip Prowse, who since 1971 has served as the company's resident designer. Trained in London at the Slade School of Art, and engaged briefly as a design assistant at Covent Garden, Prowse is something of an anomaly in British theatre, a director who comes to his craft from a technical rather than a performance background. At Glasgow his influence has been pervasive. The highly sculptural sets he has created for his own productions as well as those of fellow directors Havergal and MacDonald, have placed upon the Citizens' stage a succession of gilt frames, plush curtains, frosted mirrors, and textured walls that have been able to evoke with breath-taking versatility environments Jacobean, contemporary, and *fin-de-siècle*. Since 1982 when Prowse effectively stopped designing productions other than his own, his propensity for a hard-edged opulence bordering on 'camp' has found a natural home in the chicly bohemian worlds of Genet, Coward, and Oscar Wilde. A highly acclaimed staging of Coward's *Vortex*, brought to London in 1989, set that play's crucial encounter between a socialite and her drug-addicted son on a vast plain of satin bedsheet, their grapplings reflected in a huge overhead mirror. The device helped to harness the work's Oedipal energies to comment more broadly upon what Prowse has characterized as Coward's 'yuppie' sensibility.[3] A 1982 Genet retrospective, consisting of back to back productions of *The Balcony* (*Le Balcon*), *The Blacks* (*Les Nègres*) and *The Screens* (*Les Paravents*), worked to replicate on the Citizens' stage the Victorian details of its auditorium. When, in *The Balcony*, Genet's brothel materialized through an assembly of bidets, sinks, couches, and whips, the image seemed both *outré* and strangely familiar. Perhaps, though, the most successful instances of what critic Michael Coveney has called the Citizens' 'obsessional theatrics' have come out of Prowse's 1980s encounters with Oscar Wilde.[4] As a designer, Prowse had in the seventies twice built costumes and scenery for Citizens' revivals of *The Importance of Being Earnest*, including a 1977 mounting of the play's earlier four-act draft. In his capacity as director-designer, however, Prowse has chosen to steer clear of *Earnest* — as, indeed, he has of *Salome* — exploring instead the less travelled terrain of Wilde's three society comedies: *Lady Windermere's Fan* (1892), *A Woman of No Importance* (1893), and *An Ideal Husband* (1895).

What has been described, with the benefit of hindsight, as an Oscar Wilde ring, cycle, or mini-festival, began in the fall of 1984 with Prowse's Glasgow staging of *A Woman of No Importance* — a production that, seven years later, would become the basis for his Royal Shakespeare Company debut. The most recalcitrant of the society dramas, *A Woman of No Importance*, first presented at the Haymarket in 1893, has been diagnosed as suffering from acute schizophrenia. The play's melodramatic plot, with its bad baronet, wronged woman, and bastard child, sits uneasily, we are told, with the epigrammatic exchanges through which Wilde winks at his audience. For Prowse, however, this very doubleness was part of the play's attraction. Assured of the work's essential subversiveness, he went about preparing a stylistic common ground upon which the conventions of genteel society might meet those of moral fable. A first act, set on the lawn at Hunstanton Chase, offered spectators a walled garden of brushed gold, with ornamental urns, daffodil banks, and a large circular carp pond. It was, Irving Wardle would later note, a pastoral from which nature had been painted out.[5] Here to the strains of Elgar's cello concerto, Ladies Hunstanton and Caroline Pontefract policed the niceties of best circles manners with the rigour of a hanging court. The effect was to create a kind of Wildean meta-world, a triumph of art over nature complete enough to admit a complex of puns and citations from Wilde's life and previous work. On curtain rise — a front curtain was reinstated for the event — a young man, bearing an uncanny resemblance to Lord Alfred Douglas, mimed his way through a bout of imaginary croquet. In the scenes that followed, Lord Illingworth, who cribs most of his best lines from *Dorian Gray*'s Lord Henry Wotton, conspicuously sported the yellow gloves Wilde had specified for his prototype. A high neck-band worn by the vacuous Lady Stutfield likewise echoed the velvet neck-band her namesake had to wear to hide the mark of Wilde's Canterville ghost. In such a world, aesthetically playful, inter-textual and self-referential, the moral integrity of the betrayed Mrs Arbuthnot became a pose as studied as the rest. The decision compelled viewers to take the play's wit and sentiment with equal measures of earnestness and triviality.

It was, in the end, an inspired ploy. Not only did it permit Prowse to 'throw away' some of Wilde's most revered *bon mots*, it allowed him to fracture the work's emotional crises, presenting them simultaneously from opposing points of view. When, in Acts II and III, Mrs Arbuthnot faced her seducer in Lady Hunstanton's splendid drawing room, her fear of social embarrassment was as fully registered as her sense of moral outrage. For Illingworth, having to meet, as social equals, his former mistress and illegitimate son, presented a problem as real as Mrs Arbuthnot's accusations. By allowing spectators to experience both sensations, Prowse permitted them to judge Illingworth without subscribing to the morality of his opponents. Curiously, the tactic also reclaimed for late twentieth century viewers a number of the work's initial effects. Chief among these was the sensuality of Mrs Arbuthnot. Created in 1893 by the smoky voiced Mrs Bernard Beere, who played Acts II and III in a black gown with a plunging neckline, the role was seen by Wilde's contemporaries as intruding a troubling sexuality into the modishness of a butterfly world. Prowse not only reproduced the effect, but used it to undermine the cadences of Mrs Arbuthnot's Old Testament rhetoric. The complexity of response required was suggested by the production's handling of Wilde's final scene. Set by Prowse in a tomb-like vicarage, conjured up by crepe curtains and an overplus of black chairs, Wilde's duologue between Mrs Arbuthnot and son Gerald was used both to upend the values of

Hunstanton Chase, and show how the alternatives to it were equally unpalatable. 'Wearing her shame', in the words of *Observer* critic Michael Ratcliffe, 'with an arrogance as striking as any of the aristocratic assumptions on parade elsewhere' (9 September 1984), Wilde's woman-with-a-past set forth in chilling terms the perversity of 'a mother's love' built upon festering hatreds. When at the scene's close, Lord Illingworth arrived, only to be struck in the face with one of his own yellow gloves, viewers were asked to see a blow delivered in righteous fury received primarily as social insult. Illingworth might be hissed from the stage, as he was on a number of evenings, yet small comfort remained for Mrs Arbuthnot. It was, in the end, a bleak post-modern conclusion in which Prowse's own ambivalences were neatly aligned with those of his author, setting Wilde's belief in the redemptive powers of love and forgiveness against an equally Wildean disdain for smug coteries intent largely upon forgiving themselves.

The critical acclaim, and full houses, to which the production played, encouraged the Citizens, two years later, to tackle *An Ideal Husband*, the last and least congenial of the society dramas. Opening at the Haymarket in January 1895, and taken off in mid-run after Wilde's arrest, the play is almost impossible to disentangle today from our knowledge of its author's trials and imprisonment. Not only is Lord Chiltern, the work's central figure, a man of position fearing public exposure, but bitter passages attacking tabloid journalists, double standards, and public morality seem to point with prescient clarity to the events of the months to come. Indeed, the parallel was one Wilde himself sought to exploit in his post-prison years, identifying himself with Lord Goring, the play's dandy philosopher. Revising proofs for the Smithers edition of 1899, Wilde even provided Goring with a Louis Seize cane identical to one he himself was known to carry, describing him, in a passage that echoes his self portrait in *De Profundis*, as one who stood 'in immediate relation to modern life'. It is to Prowse's credit that he was able to side-step such after-the-fact correspondences, while capturing something of the fatality that still hedges the work. By refusing to present audiences with a Goring made-up to resemble Wilde, a temptation few of the play's recent producers have been able to resist, he managed both to protect Goring's integrity as a stage figure, and retain a long, disagreeable but thematically central speech in which Goring declares (and Lady Chiltern repeats) that a man's life is worth more than a woman's.[6] At the same time Prowse's keen eye for period detail enabled him to catch in more disturbing ways the play's sense of gathering doom. His Chilterns, to begin with, were brutally gauche. Their Octagon Room in Act I was pompous and vulgar, a vast cavern of kitsch swathed in black, red, and gold, with gilded balustrades, marble plinths, and ormolu bowls filled with black and gold fruit. Not only did such sensibility betray a *nouveau* spirit that underscored Lord Chiltern's moral bankruptcy, but the party with which the play opens became, in such surroundings, the outward sign of a society gone both morbid and predatory. Michael Billington, in his *Guardian* review, documents a world in which 'elegant women pass[ed] out dead drunk on the sofa', while 'evening-dressed men parade[d] in front of them as in a sexual meat market' (1 September 1986).

In Mrs Cheveley, the play's backbiting villainess, Prowse allowed such gaucherie to collapse into coarseness. Taking his cue from Shaw, who had praised Wilde's powers of discernment in making his adventuress 'selfish, dishonest, and third rate' (*Saturday Review*, 12 January 1895), he set forth a *décolleté* mercenary who, while struggling to remove an incriminating bracelet, hissed out a clearly audible four letter expletive. The episode, which offended some of Prowse's critics, was a fair enough handling of the unspecified *'curse'* Wilde tells us *'breaks from [Mrs Cheveley's] lips'* when she loses her composure. Its deliverance, at any rate, helped to suggest the *'distorted'* face *'dreadful to look at'* that Wilde insists lies beneath her mask. Mrs Cheveley's exit at the act's end, bearing a note that she hopes will compromise Lady Chiltern, became part of the reading. Her path blocked by Lord Goring, Wilde has Mrs Cheveley ring for Goring's man servant, Phipps, whose arrival makes it awkward for Goring to stop her escape. Finding the social dynamics of the situation inaccessible to modern viewers, Prowse had her rip open her bodice — in effect, crying 'rape' — then stride triumphantly out past shamefaced master and scandalized man.[7] If such outbursts shocked Glasgow audiences, they worked to reinforce Prowse's equally scathing view of Lord and Lady Chiltern. The former became in his hands a pushing *parvenu*, behaving as politicians are wont to behave, the latter, a stupidly good woman disillusioned by her marriage. It was, however, in the production's final moments that Prowse moved most decisively to re-problematize a work Wilde's contemporaries had held to be a problem play. Lord Chiltern, who has responded to blackmail by, once again, behaving ignominiously, blaming Lady Chiltern when all else has failed, appears on stage alone with his wife. To his final line: 'Gertrude, is it love you feel for me, or is it pity merely', Wilde has her reply: 'It is love, Robert. Love, and only love. For both of us a new life is beginning.' Leaving Chiltern's question unanswered, Prowse concluded the play with a slow fade, as husband and wife stared silently at one another across an expanse of gold-splattered drawing room.

Similar liberties were taken in 1988 with the Citizens' staging of *Lady Windermere's Fan*. Here, however, Prowse's readjustments had the effect of restoring to the play something of its original force. When Wilde had begun work on *Lady Windermere*, in the summer of 1891, he had intended to delay until Act IV the disclosure of the play's central secret, that Mrs Erlynne, its scheming villainess was, in fact, mother of the puritanical Lady Windermere. His purpose, he explained in a letter to George Alexander, his producer and leading man, was to challenge easy assumptions about 'good' and 'bad' behaviour. Initially called *A Good Woman*, his script was designed to present a traditional adventuress inexplicably sacrificing herself to save the reputation of a 'good' wife gone astray. Let viewers know too early, Wilde argued, that the pair are mother and daughter, and a potentially disturbing plot becomes a conventionally sentimental one. Alexander, unwilling to risk alienating his audience, compelled Wilde to alter his action. After a single performance, the revelation of Mrs Erlynne's identity was shifted to Acts I and II, where it has remained to this day.[8] Prowse, sensing a flintier work beneath the surface of Wilde's published text, removed the half-dozen lines Wilde had added to satisfy his manager. The result, simply enough wrought, surprised even those critics who knew something of the play's pedigree. Michael Coveney, in the *Financial Times*, saw the excisions as an overdue adjudication in Wilde's favour, 'restoring' to the play after some ninety-six years 'a dynamic bite and tension' (9 May 1988). *Times* critic Robert Dawson Scott spoke of a 'toughening up' that 'reinvented the play' for contemporary viewers (18 May 1988), while Mary Brennan of the *Glasgow Herald* observed how 'the slight textual cuts that kept the secret of [Lady Windermere's] birth until the final act' helped 'to realize the tensions beneath the equivocating superficiality of Wilde's leisured society' (7 May 1988). The most telling comments came from the *Guardian*'s Michael Billington, who noting how 'completely [the production] revises our notion of how to play early Oscar' twice placed the work in the company of Ibsen's *Doll's House*, reminding readers of Max Beerbohm's claim for Wilde as 'a thinker and weaver of ideas' (9 May 1988).

On stage Prowse's 'tough' new text provided the opportunity for a particularly lush Citizens' revival. Operating, in 1988, on greatly increased grants from the Strathclyde and Glasgow District Councils, the company found itself able to build sets and costumes the *Times* pronounced 'sumptuous even by Prowse's standards' (18 May 1988). The Windermeres' town house, a cool study in gold, cream, and du Barry rose, became, like the Chilterns' ballroom, an index of its inhabitants. The keynote here was patrician reticence, embodied in the Windermeres' May-December marriage. Taking his cue from Lady Windermere's Act I announcement of her birthday ball, Prowse cast Wilde's action as a two-part rite of passage. For his second act the Windermere terrace was transformed into a dazzling fairy-land 'lit up with naked bulbs like Brighton pier' (*Guardian*, 9 May 1988). An enormous cake, wheeled on and applauded by her guests, marked Lady Windermere's coming-of-age. The Whistlerian palette of both scenes stood in marked contrast to the crimson glare of Lord Darlington's chambers, a sinister den of crushed velvet, plush drapes, and wall-to-wall Fragonards. When in Act III Lady Windermere ventured in, Prowse made it clear that she had embarked upon an infernal journey that would necessarily estrange her from her world. Returned to her parlour, her reputation intact, she resembled one of Eliot's Magi, uneasy among her household gods. The magnitude of her distress was powerfully registered in her Act IV exit. At the play's close, Lord Windermere, aware of Mrs Erlynne's manœuvrings but ignorant of her sacrifice, confides to Lord Augustus, her husband-to-be, that he is 'certainly marrying a very clever woman'. Lady Windermere, in possession of a very different secret, corrects him. Lord Augustus, she maintains, is 'marrying a very good woman'. Producers have, in the past, used the parallel to draw the Windermeres cozily together, reconciled in a mutual ignorance. Prowse chose instead to stress the antithesis of the exchange. When his Lord Windermere conceded with a sneer the fact of Mrs Erlynne's 'cleverness', Lady Windermere crossed up stage and struck him smartly in the face. Her assurance to Lord Augustus that he was 'marrying a very good woman' was followed by her immediate exit, leaving Windermere, to cite *The Observer* once again, standing 'alone in the Belgravian twilight turning to stone from fury and shame' (15 May 1988). It was, in context, a withering indictment of a world whose surfaces Prowse (like Wilde) had both celebrated and mocked. Bringing to a close the most inventive attempt this century to stage, in tandem, all three of Wilde's society plays, it seemed to argue with pointed eloquence, Wilde's potential as a playwright of some importance for our own *fin-de-siècle*.

NOTES

1   I am indebted to members of the Citizens Theatre, especially Philip Prowse, Giles Havergal, Lyn Pullen, and Kenny Miller, for their assistance in the preparation of this paper. The company is, of course, in no way implicated in my observations or conclusions. A companion piece to the present essay 'Staging Wilde's Society Plays: A Conversation with Philip Prowse' appears in *Modern Drama* 37:1 (March 1994).

2   G. Rowell and A. Jackson, *The Repertory Movement: a History of Regional Theatre in Britain*. Cambridge, Cambridge University Press, 1984, p. 140.

3   At the time Prowse had characterized *The Vortex* as 'a yuppie piece then, and [...] a yuppie piece now'. M. Coveney *The Citz: 21 Years of the Glasgow Citizens Theatre*. London, Nick Hern, 1990, p. 175.

4   For a compact eyewitness account of Prowse's Wilde productions for the Citizens see Coveney, pp. 176-179.

5   Writing for *The Independent on Sunday*, Wardle was describing
           the RSC's Barbican production. By 1991 Prowse had made the
           effect literal by placing upstage an immense golden frame
           containing two panels from a Fragonard landscape (6 October
           1991).
6   The passage, often curtailed in performance, was entirely
           eliminated from recent productions at London's Westminster
           Theatre (1989) and Manchester's Royal Exchange (1992). In
           both instances the cuts were designed to win sympathy for a
           Goring bearing a marked resemblance to Wilde himself. For
           Wilde's own defence of the speech see his post-production
           interview in the *Sketch* (9 January 1895).
7   To critics, like *The Glasgow Herald*'s Mary Brennan, who
           complained that Mrs Cheveley was 'too markedly common to
           pass in polite society' (Coveney 177), one might reply that
           Prowse had reclaimed for his audience another of Wilde's
           initial effects. Reviewing Lewis Waller's 1895 Haymarket
           production, the critic for *The Illustrated Sporting and Dramatic
           News* had similarly wondered whether Mrs Cheveley (Florence
           West) had the necessary 'polish' to move freely in good society
           (12 January 1895). *The Lady's Pictorial* found her 'vulgar' and
           'undignified' (12 January 1895), *The Morning Post* 'stagy' (4
           January 1895), and *The Saturday Review* 'overdressed for her
           part' (12 January 1895). In the play itself, we might recall she is
           described as wearing 'far too much rogue [...] and not quite
           enough clothes', a combination Lord Goring reads as 'a sign of
           despair in a woman'.
8   For the particulars of the dispute see J. H. Kaplan 'A Puppet's
           Power: George Alexander, Clement Scott, and the Replotting of
           Lady Windermere's Fan', in *Theatre Notebook* 46:2, pp. 59-73.

OSCAR WILDE'S *SALOME*: SYMBOLIST PRINCESS

Patricia Kellogg-Dennis

I can never think of Oscar Wilde without remembering the time twenty-five or more years ago when I took a summer ride up a ski lift at Mount Killington in Vermont, the purpose being to hike down the montain. There at the top was a plaque celebrating the fact that Oscar Wilde had climbed Killington and spent the night there. Oscar Wilde on Mount Killington? The Dandy of the Strand? Bunburying in the wilds of America? Several years later, when I began to delve into treatments of the Salome figure in latteral European and British nineteenth-century literature and art, I had a similar reaction when I read Wilde's *Salomé* (1893). Oscar Wilde writing about the *femme fatale* of Symbolist/Decadent literature and art? The master of comedy? In French? I was convinced he had found *Salomé*, fully birthed, in a suitcase in Victoria Station.

In a way he had. The biblical story had already been treated by a number of writers and artists after Heinrich Heine, drawing on folklore versions of the dancing decapitator, put her, in his 1835 long poem *Atta Troll*, into a procession of classical *femmes fatales*. Whether given the name of Herodias or the name of Salome, she had already inspired not only Heine but also Flaubert, Mallarmé, and Laforgue to use her as an 'objective correlative'. These literary works were paralleled by a number of painters who found in her story a way of expressing their understanding of woman, muse, and sexuality: Puvis de Chavannes, Gustave Moreau, Gustav Klimt, and Edvard Munch, to mention a few. Stir in also Richard Strauss's 1905 opera. And you could add Massenet's music for Mallarmé's *Hérodiade*. The Salome/Herodias figure was almost as popular among nineteenth-century artists as the Virgin Mary was among medieval artists.

Although Wilde referred to *Salomé* with seriousness in *De Profundis* — he regrets that he hadn't written more 'beautiful coloured musical things' like it (*Portable* 549) — and André Gide recalls that Wilde confided to him that it did him a lot of good to know that *Salomé* was playing in Paris during his term in prison (27), it is difficult to know how seriously Wilde actually felt about the play when he first wrote it. The famous story of the play's hasty inspiration and writing[1] does not preclude that Wilde was genuinely trying to write a serious drama in a lyric mode, but it seems more plausible that he was consciously or unconsciously parodying and criticizing French Symbolist literature. If we accept Stanley Weintraub's perspective that Wilde was primarily a critic, and, thus, all of his works are extensions of that talent, and, if we accept Shaw's perspective that Wilde's 'real forte' was comedy (in Ellmann 100), then one can view Wilde's *Salomé* as a brilliant pastiche of turn-of-the-century Decadent art, a pastiche which I think Aubrey Beardsley's illustrations put into relief.

Contemporary, and later critical reactions to the play, are mainly positive in their acceptance of it as a serious piece of literature. Gide's and Joyce's as well as most of Wilde's critics' and biographers' reactions are ones of enthusiastic applause. Even Yeats, who judged it 'thoroughly bad' in a 1906 letter to Sturge Moore (8), reflected the influence it had on him in two of his verse plays, *The King of the Great Clock Tower* (1934) and *A Full Moon in March* (1935). The twentieth-century Symbolist scholar, Philippe Jullian, calls it 'one of the most famous and one of the worst of [...] [Wilde's] works' (246). Mario Praz has been more circumspect in his treatment of it:

> [*Salomé* is] humoristic, with a humour which one can with difficulty believe to be unintentional, so much does Wilde's play resemble a parody of the whole of the material used by the Decadents and of the stammering mannerisms of Maeterlinck's dramas — and, as a parody, *Salome* comes very near to being a masterpiece. Yet it seems that Wilde was not quite aiming at this. (298)

Most importantly, as Camille Paglia asserts, it 'capsulizes the French decadent tradition of the *femme fatale*' (562). Paglia also points out that it reads much better in its original French than it does in its English translation by Lord Alfred Douglas because of its 'incantatory style', far more suitable to French than to English (563).

Its stage history reflects a range of reactions to it. Banned in Britain in 1892 because of its biblical theme, it was first staged by Lugné-Poe in Paris in 1896. A Max Reinhardt production of it in the early 1900s in Berlin had a 'longer consecutive period in Germany than any play by any Englishman' (Ross V). Although poorly received during its first British and American productions in 1905, *Salome* was performed and successfully received in almost every major European city between 1902 and 1912 despite the fact that its first operatic appearance with Strauss's music at the Metropolitan Opera so shocked the audience on 22 January 1907 that it was dropped from the repertory after only one performance. More recently, the play has received some interesting interpretations. In 1972, the PBS, in a series called 'International Performances', presented Maurice Béjart's original French version of *Salomé*, an Expressionist production which highlighted the dance. The Italian producer, Carmelo Bene, borrowed from both Flaubert and Wilde in 1973 to create a Surrealistic spectacle of grotesque decadence. The Salome of this movie is a nubile, bewitched, impassive, naked androgyne; Herod a pop-art satyr; John the Baptist, a Bermuda-shorts' clad ranting Italian peasant. Lindsey Kemp's 1975 production of *Salome (based on the play by Oscar Wilde)* with the New York Theatre Ensemble was a camp presentation with an all-male cast and insisted on a homosexual approach to the play.

Some recent assessments of the play, spurred by Jane Marcus's argument in 1974 that Wilde's purpose in writing *Salome* was to present a vision of the New Woman, do not seem convincing. Marcus argues that Wilde was out to 'de-mystify' the image of the whorish virgin and turn her into a 'real person' (96). Marcus calls Wilde's ending, in which Salome is slaughtered by Herod, a 'bold stroke of genius' and 'the most important piece in the puzzle of the meaning of the play' (97). She claims that Salome, through her martyrdom, is raised above the status of the Baptist who is comparable to Lovborg in Ibsen's *Hedda Gabler*, an 'autonomous' artist whom the female, frustrated by a male society, justifiably decides to destroy.

Feminist criticism should not attempt to rewrite what has been written; rather, it should attempt to understand what has been written. Oscar Wilde's *Salome* is clearly a product of male — in Wilde's case bisexual — attitudes about women. The fascination of Wilde's depiction of Salome lies in his synthesis of western — and many eastern — ways of stereotyping women. Three female archetypes from biblical, classical, and Celtic culture inform Wilde's figure of Salome. We find each of them represented in Heine's *Walpurgisnacht* scene in *Atta Troll.* Like Heine's Herodias, she is a castrator; like Heine's Diana, she is a flirt; and, like Heine's Fee Abunde, she is a nitwit. All three of these figures are dangerous figures in Heine. All three of these figures are implicitly associated in Heine with the moon by which the poet/narrator of *Atta Troll* sees their progression, an experience which marks his heroic descent into an underworld of sorts.

But Wilde did not really need Heine's suggestion that the moon, the feminine, the erratic, and the mysterious were inextricably linked. Nor did he need Moreau's obsession with the Salomé figure to present her as a virgin drugged by her own sensuality. Neither did he need Laforgue's presentation of her as a silly schoolgirl testing her powers. These attitudes toward women had long been in the atmosphere, but it is fascinating to observe how Wilde arrives at making his Salome more mythic than conventional, more quirky than usual.

The play opens with the most dominant image in the play, the moon. The Young Syrian — whose fascination for Salome ends in his self destruction — and the Page of Herodias are discussing Herod's stepdaughter:

THE YOUNG SYRIAN. How beautiful is the Princess Salome tonight!
THE PAGE OF HERODIAS. Look at the moon. How strange the moon seems! She is like a woman rising from a tomb. She is like a dead woman. One might fancy she is looking for dead things.
THE YOUNG SYRIAN. She has a strange look. She is like a little princess who wears a yellow veil, and whose feet are of silver. She is like a princess who has little white doves for feet. One might fancy she was dancing.
THE PAGE OF HERODIAS. She is like a woman who is dead. She moves very slowly.[2]

Later on, Salome's obsession with purity, paradoxically the cause of her lust for Iokanaan[3] the pure, is expressed in a chant to this same moon which she compares to 'a little piece of money, a little silver flower' (59). The moon as symbol of the feminine is stressed in the following speech by the repetition of the pronoun *she*:

> SALOME. How good to see the moon! [...] She is cold and chaste. I am sure she is a virgin. [...] She has never defiled herself. She has never abandoned herself to men, like the other goddesses. (60)

After this apostrophe to the moon (reminiscent of Mallarmé's Hérodiade's exaltation of cold chastity in the 'Scène' of his poem), Salome is distracted by the voice of the prophet, and she exercises her wiles on the Young Syrian, Narraboth, to get what she wants — a look at the prisoner. The cistern in which the Baptist is incarcerated appears to Salome 'like a tomb' (14) recalling the Page of Herodias' earlier association of the moon with death. To this association of woman, death, moon is added the association of the cistern or well. We know today that the cauldron or chalice was formerly associated with the earth mother figure and was, in many cultures, a symbol of regeneration. The character of Herod in Wilde's *Salome* summarizes what this complex set of associations had come to mean by the end of the last century:

> HEROD. The moon has a strange look to-night. Has she not a strange look? She is like a mad woman [...] seeking everywhere for lovers. She is naked too. [...] The clouds are seeking to cover her nakedness, but she will not let them. She shows herself naked in the sky. She reels through the clouds like a drunken woman. (27-8)

Only Herodias, a stereotype of the bitchy wife, sees nothing in the moon but the moon: 'the moon is like the moon, that is all' (28). Herodias is straight out of one of Wilde's comedies; as Jack says of Lady Bracknell in *The Importance of Being Earnest*, 'she is a monster, without being a myth.'

Wilde's stage directions for the finale call for a 'great cloud' to obliterate the moon and, against this eclipse, Salome rhapsodizes about having kissed the bloody head which she

holds in her hands (66). A ray of moonlight i
enraptured girl.[4] Herod orders his soldiers
woman!' (67). Thus both symbolically and litera
is extinguished by the male, but the image of a
hence castrating (Freud 212), female is far more powerful than
that of the cloud erasing the moon or of Herod ordering
Salome's death. One is reminded of two lines from Swinburne's
'Hermaphroditus II' of 1863:

> But on the one side sat a man like death,
> And on the other a woman sat like sin.[5]

Joyce, writing about *Salome*, argued that at the centre of
Wilde's concern there was always a strong concept of sin (59).
Wilde, in *De Profundis*, wrote that the sinner represented 'the
nearest possible approach to the perfection of man' because,
through his repentance, he reaches the most real of all
moments, 'the moment of initiation' (in Ellmann, 549-50).
However, Wilde does not grant his Salome that realization of
initiation; she is killed by Herod's soldiers before she can
realise what she has done. She is sin itself.

Wilde's decision to kill Salome at the end of his drama
represents his most innovative contribution to the story,
although there is precedent for Herod's order to execute her in
Laforgue's tale. Therein she tries to throw the severed head of
the Baptist off a cliff, miscalculates, and ends up like
Iphegenia in some versions of whatever happened at Aulis, by
falling off the cliff herself.

It seems probable that Wilde, in his finale, was
making use of the magnificent irony of Laforgue's disposal of
Salome at the end of his tale. The suggestion that Wilde was
simply pandering to a moralistic audience in the finale
(Daffner 309) doesn't seem plausible. Perhaps more plausible
seems Ellmann's theory that Wilde felt a necessity to kill off
both Salome and the Baptist because, in so doing, he was
killing off the two most important influences in his aesthetic
development, the sensuous Pater and the puritanical Ruskin.

But Oscar Wilde was a brilliant dramatist with a
classical understanding of the distinctions between comedy —
ends in marriage —, and tragedy — ends in death. Wilde

subtitled his play *Salome* 'A Tragedy in One Act'. And, if he did not have Salome killed at the end simply because he saw himself as writing a tragedy, he was perhaps influenced by the final statement of Villiers de L'Isle Adam's Axel: 'Live? Our servants will do that for us.' Having consummated a moment of classical crime and decadent ecstasy, Salome would have needed a *deus ex machina* to save her from Wilde's ending because, most plausibly, Wilde was outmannering the Mannerist conventions of Symbolist/Decadent art and literature.

What he gave us is a Salome who, like Strindberg's Miss Julie, probably had a death wish, who, like Ibsen's Hedda Gabler, probably would have destroyed all of John the Baptist's Essene manuscripts could she have laid her hands on them, and, who, like Cecily in *The Importance of Being Earnest*, probably kept a diary about what her ideal lover should be.

Oscar Wilde's Salome wasn't a New Woman; she is a paradigm of the symbolist *femme fatale*.

NOTES

1   Purportedly, Wilde, inspired by Flaubert's *Hérodias* and a *Salomé* of Gustave Moreau's, created the play verbally one day in a Paris café for Adolphe Retté, Stuart Merrill, and others. Returning to his room, he noticed a blank writing pad on his desk and sat down to write the piece in one great furious splash of inspiration, in French. Several hours later, just as he had come to the dance part, he realized that he was hungry and went to the *Grand Café* at the corner of the Boulevard des Capucines and the Rue Scribe where a gypsy orchestra was playing; Wilde then asked Rigo, the leader, to play something in harmony with the mood of the play he was writing. Satisfied by Rigo, he returned to his room and completed *Salomé*. (Zagona 122)

2   All citations from the text come from *Salome: A Tragedy in One Act*: Translated from the French of Oscar Wilde by Lord Alfred Douglas: Pictured by A. Beardsley (New York, Dover Publications, 1967).

3   Wilde followed Flaubert's spelling of the Baptist's name.

4   Ellmann, 'Ouvertures to *Salome*', in *Oscar Wilde: A Collection of Critical Essays* (74), suggests that a 'dramatic poem called *Salome* published in Cambridge, Mass., in 1862, by a young Harvard graduate named J.C. Heywood, and subsequently republished during the 1880's in the form of a trilogy', is Wilde's source for the kissing of the severed head rather than Heine.

5   'Hermaphroditus', incidentally, is one of the first pieces of
     homosexual literature in the late nineteenth century. B. Reade,
     'Introduction' to *Sexual Heretics* (13-14) writes that it 'stood
     alone in being the first openly published English poem on such a
     subject since the seventeenth century in which the "argument"
     was sensual and not satirical nor [...] sentimental'.

REFERENCES

Daffner, H. *Salome: Ihre Gestalt in Geschichte und Kunst*. Munich, H.
     Schmidt, 1912.
Ellmann, R. 'Ouvertures to *Salome*' in *Oscar Wilde: A Collection of
     Critical Essays*. Ed. R. Ellmann. New Jersey, Prentice Hall, 1969.
Freud, S. *Sexuality and the Psychology of Love*. New York, Collier Books,
     1972.
Gide, A. *Oscar Wilde, In Memoriam (Reminiscences) De Profundis*. Trans.
     B. Frechtman. New York, Philosophical Library, 1949.
Joyce, J. 'Oscar Wilde, The Poet of *Salome*'. In *Oscar Wilde: A Collection
     of Critical Essays*.
Jullian, P.. *Oscar Wilde*. Trans. V. Wundham. New York, Viking Press,
     1969.
Marcus, J. 'Salome: The Jewish Princess was a New Woman'. *Bulletin of
     the New York Public Library* (Autumn 1974), 95-113.
Paglia, C. *Sexual Personae: Art and Decadence from Nefertiti to Emily
     Dickinson*. Yale University Press, 1990.
Praz, M. *The Romantic Agony*. Trans. A. Davidson. New York, World
     Publishing Company, 1968.
Reade, B. *Sexual Heretics*. New York, Coward-McCann, 1970.
Ross, R. 'Preface' to *Salomé, la sainte courtisane*. London, G.P. Putnam's
     Sons, 1915.
Yeats and T. S. Moore. *Their Correspondance, 1907-1937*. Ed. U. Bridge.
     Oxford University Press, 1953.
Zagona, H. G. *The Legend of Salome and the Principle of Art for Art's
     Sake*. Genève, Librairie E. Droz, 1960.

LOSING ONE'S HEAD:
WILDE'S CONFESSION IN *SALOME*

Melissa Knox

Oscar Wilde remarked that he 'lived in fear of not being misunderstood', a quip that can be taken as an epigraph for *Salome*, his drama of operatic fame. His strong desire to confess yet at the same time conceal everything expressed itself in witty ambiguities, verbal conundrums that amused, yet confused his audiences, and made him a master of the quotable but impenetrable epigram. He lived in fear of **being** understood. He knew that in every line he wrote he revealed the secrets of his soul, 'for out of ourselves', he observed, 'we can never pass, nor can there be in creation what in the creator is not.' Indeed it fits his *Salome* when he remarked, 'man is least himself when he talks in his own person. Give him a mask and he will tell you the truth.'[1] The Byzantine setting of the play, the strange, biblical language borrowed from *The Song of Songs*, the utterings of Delphic obscurity lifted from various Old Testament prophets mask a confession that he feared would be all too easily understood. The more the characters in the play question the meaning of Iokanaan's strange prophecies, the more Wilde hints at his fear: that the public will recognize his own confession behind his mask of wit or obscurity. The play reveals, in one bloody statement, a confession that he wanted to make, even though he knew that to confess would destroy him.

Wilde's effort to be misunderstood seeps through every detail of the play. Why did he write a drama in French? He seems to be imitating French Symbolist poets by using a strange, private symbolism. Why is the moon — who is constantly identified with Salome — compared to a woman 'rising from the tomb', a woman with 'feet of silver', a 'shadow of a white rose in a mirror of silver'? And why is the moon like 'the hand of a dead woman who is seeking to cover herself with a shroud' (557)? Why did Wilde transform the politically motivated execution of John the Baptist into a lust-murder by a young girl who has tried to seduce the prophet? Why does Salome appear at times to be just a little girl, wondering why Iokanaan wouldn't look at her, and at other times like a Dracula, tasting with relish the bloody lips of the severed head?

Salome is the least easy to understand of all his dramas, but, as I think, it reveals Wilde's early experiences and his sexual development. The gruesome behaviour of Salome — the young princess with a seemingly cannibalistic lust for the severed head of the prophet Iokanaan — has always aroused curiosity and consternation. Critics and audiences have wavered between taking Wilde seriously and feeling that he was only making a grotesque joke. One of Wilde's friends, W. Graham Robertson, inadvertently offended him by laughing when Wilde read the play to him out loud. Robertson took the play as a burlesque of Maeterlinck. 'I thought I was safe and laughed approvingly [...] "That's a funny bit". Wilde reacted with great disappointment.'[2]

I have often wondered about aspects of the story which are indeed not easy to understand: when Salome, who is introduced as a young and beautiful girl, tells Iokanaan that she would like to kiss him, he rebuffs her with great disgust. Why is she interested in this strange man covered with filth and rags? Curiously, although he denounces women and sexuality, she appears not to hear or understand him, guilelessly announcing herself: 'I am Salome, Daughter of Herodias!'. Why does she want this man so isolated from the outside world, and who appears to be feared by her parents? With a child's unpredictable impetuosity, she just wants him. She is not concerned with his responses — indeed she barely hears them — she is concerned with her desires. Do you ask a doll whether it wants to be kissed? He is a doll for her, an important one because her parents fear him, and because he rejects her and therefore becomes more desirable.

Iokanaan is also a puzzle. A man imprisoned in a dark, dirty cistern, isolated from the outside world until he sees her, his violent refusal is the last reaction I would expect. Of course, he is a holy man. And that might, for many, be enough explanation. We know that Salome is exceptionally alluring, since neither Herod nor Narraboth, the young Syrian, can tear their eyes away from her. Indeed, Narraboth eventually falls on a spear and kills himself when he has to listen to her insist that she will kiss Iokanaan's mouth. Salome stares at the prophet Iokanaan. The more insistently she demands that he let her kiss his mouth, the more he denounces not only this desire, but beyond that he denounces all women and their sexuality. He violently rejects heterosexual adventures: 'Back! Daughter of Babylon! By woman came evil into the world,' he cries when Salome asks to touch his body.

The tone of the drama has been difficult to understand because the sexuality of Salome appears to be bizarre. She seems chillingly cruel when Iokanaan refuses her advances and she demands his head on a silver platter. When she gets it on a silver platter she responds with a taunt: 'Ah! thou wouldst not suffer me to kiss thy mouth [...] Well! I will kiss it now. I will bite it with my teeth as one bites a ripe fruit' (573). But her next lines, 'But wherefore dost thou not look at me? Art thou afraid of me?' are a clue to the whole character: she has no understanding of the permanence of death. What seems like cruelty is only a mood of the moment, a blow dealt by infantile frustration, not out of a desire to gratify a sadistic impulse: she just wants to punish Iokanaan for rejecting her. And how can she fulfil her desire to kiss him unless she has his head in her hands? Holding the bloody head, she still wonders why he won't open his eyes. She expects that he will stand up again and — having learned the error of his ways — he will finally kiss her. Her persistent demands, her lack of fear of the events she is causing, are frightening in an adult or teenager. But in the play of children one can easily encounter them.

The childish longing for his love, the inability to comprehend his death, shows itself in her questions. A sadist would experience satisfaction and feel happy to see in the blood that drips from Iokanaan's neck the proof that he really suffered. But Salome feels no satisfaction: she only wants to know why he won't look at her. Her questions betray her pathetic surprise, a child's wonder and a fear that she begins to feel when he does not wake up and look at her.

She equates love with looking and being looked at: 'If thou hadst looked at me, thou hadst loved me', summarizes her interest in him. Salome expresses all her sexuality through the orality of the child: 'I am hungry for thy body; and neither wine nor apples can appease my desire.' She never alludes to the sexual organs. The strong emphasis on oral incorporation of the beloved is of course characteristic of early childhood. In *Three Essays on the Theory of Sexuality* Freud describes this early pre-genital sexual organization, the 'oral, or cannibalistic' phase: 'Here sexual activity has not yet been separated from the ingestion of food, nor are opposite currents within the activity differentiated. The sexual aim consists in the incorporation of the object.'[3] Salome's desire to kiss and to bite the lips of the head is the natural culmination of the child's love for Iokanaan. The final insult for her was that he did not look at her, not even when she was dancing: 'Well, thou hast seen thy God, Iokanaan, but me, me, thou didst never see. If thou hadst seen me thou hadst love me. I saw thee, and I loved thee.'

When the head ignores her final threat — to throw it to the dogs and the birds of the air — her true lament begins. She yearns for the beauty of his body, she longs for him to look at her again, she feels entirely bewildered: 'Well I know that thou wouldst have loved me, and the mystery of Love is greater than the mystery of Death.' The mystery of death is that he didn't get up and live again after being beheaded — a mystery that all children eventually solve when they begin to grow up and understand reality. The mystery of love, that Iokanaan is not aroused by her the way she is aroused by him, preoccupied Wilde all his life. In one of his comedies, *Lady Windermere's Fan*, a character confesses that he is a mystery to himself, adding: 'I am the only person in the world I should like to know thoroughly; but I don't see any chance of it just at present' (403). Wilde did and did not want his homosexuality to remain the mystery that it was to himself; he longed to talk about it, to make it clear to himself — and yet he foresaw the consequences.

The childish, the childlike Salome — an adolescent behaving like a girl of four or five — gave me another clue. The mask of Wilde the cosmopolitan *roué* hid a child. Essentially he did remain a child all his life — a highly educated and sophisticated child, full of the charm, the naive kindness, demonstrativeness and exhibitionism that characterize childhood. Both Salome and Wilde possess the qualities that he attributed to another young girl in his comedy *An Ideal Husband*: 'the fascinating tyranny of youth, and the astonishing courage of innocence' (483) — fascinating because it is something that reality forces adults to relinquish. The typical child possesses a megalomanic self-confidence as he constantly experiences — but tries to stave off — his powerlessness.

Only in early childhood is the mind so open to the unconscious — so prone to allowing wishes to mask themselves as realities. Growing up inevitably distances the mind from the unconscious. Wilde's lifelong closeness to his unconscious, together with his phenomenal success as a playwright, allowed him to retain the fatal megalomania that provoked his downfall. His closeness to the unconscious, which also gave him access to the sources of creativity, is what inspired him perhaps to describe *Salome* as 'so like a piece of music'.[4] He had suggested that music is the 'perfect type of art', asserting 'music can never reveal its ultimate secret' (1031). Music has the curious quality of revealing and defending against revelation. By revealing emotion in sounds it keeps the sources of emotion from being verbalized. Consciousness requires verbalization; music does not. Perhaps sensing this, the journalist Richard Le Gallienne prophetically remarked in 1893 that Salome 'seems built to music. Its gradual growth is like the development of a theme in music.'[5] Wilde gratefully wrote to him, 'you have got into the secret chamber of the house in which Salome was fashioned, and I rejoice to think that to you has my secret been revealed.' What was that secret?

There had never been any question in my mind that Iokanaan, who so strongly senses the highly active and highly dangerous sexuality of the girl-child Salome and so excitedly rejects her, must represent a conflict of the author. Like Wilde, Iokanaan feels no sexual attraction to women. Unlike Wilde, Iokanaan easily resists sexual temptation. Wilde, who boasted with typical bravado, 'I can resist anything — except temptation' admired the ability of John the Baptist to say 'no' to Salome. In *De Profundis*, the long letter he wrote from prison

to his lover, Lord Alfred Douglas, Wilde summed up his own
weakness in yielding to the influence of Lord Alfred with this
significant statement: 'I lost my head.'[6] Like Iokanaan, Wilde
considers himself a prophet, announcing a new way of life for
believers. Certainly he is a kind of John the Baptist, now
considered both martyr and mascot for Gay rights.

Once we have recognized that Iokanaan in a way
represents Oscar Wilde, it is easy to see his parents, Sir
William and Lady Wilde, in the characters of Herod and
Herodias. Wilde's Herod and Herodias, like Wilde's parents,
revel in the sensuality Iokanaan denounces. The young Oscar,
introducing his mother to a college friend, remarked: 'My
mother and I are founding a society for the suppression of
virtue.' As well they might. Lady Wilde, known for her
eccentric, literary salon, exhibited a carefree lasciviousness.
Once, someone asked to bring a guest, a 'respectable' person.
'Respectable!' Lady Wilde thundered, 'Never use that word
here. It is only tradespeople who are respectable.'[7] Asked by a
visitor, 'How do you manage to get together such a lot of
interesting people!' Lady Wilde answered, 'It's quite simple.
All one has to do is to get all sorts of people — but no dull
specimens — and take care to mix them. Don't trouble about
their morals. It doesn't matter if they haven't any.'[8] If one
listens, with these remarks of Lady Wilde's ringing in one's
ears, to Oscar's description of the orgiastic banquet of Herod
and Herodias, one feels that he didn't have to look further
than his own mother's salon for inspiration: 'there are Jews
from Jerusalem who are tearing each other in pieces over their
foolish ceremonies, and barbarians, who drink and drink, and
spill their wine on the pavement, and Greeks from Smyrna
with painted eyes and painted cheeks, and frizzed hair curled
in twisted coils, and silent, subtle Egyptians, with long nails of
jade and russet cloaks, and Romans, brutal and coarse, with
their uncouth jargon.'

In her sixties, Lady Wilde remarked to a young man,
'When you are as old as I, young man, you will know there is
only one thing in the world worth living for, and that is sin.'[9]
She sounds like Salome's mother, Herodias, who 'gave herself
unto the captains of Assyria [...] hath given herself to the

young men of Egypt' (557-8) etc, etc, — the description of her lustful propensities goes on quite a while.

Lewdness is not the only trait shared by Lady Wilde and Herodias. They also dress alike. Queen Herodias wears 'a black mitre sewn with pearls' (553), and other assorted jewels, and '[her] hair is powdered with blue dust'; Oscar's mother is no less outlandish. One of Lady Wilde's guests remarked on her 'white-powdered blue-black head [...] invariably crowned with a gilded laurel wreath'. Others recalled that 'sometimes she would dress in white, her [...] hair hanging down her back, like a druid priestess. At other times she would be seen in purple brocade, with a towering headdress of velvet decorated with white streamers[10] — and lots of jewelry, far too much to describe.

There is one other similarity between the two women, perhaps the most poignant. Herodias' dissatisfaction with her husband, who is cheating on her, is obvious. Oscar's father, a well-known physician, fathered at least three illegitimate children, and was rumored to have spawned 'a family in every farmhouse'.[11] Herod's lecherous glances so disturb Salome that she runs away from his banquet hall. He follows her relentlessly. Oscar's father was equally persistent with one of his young lovers, a nineteen-year-old patient of his. He was like Herod, lavish in offers to his lover. Like Herod he was offering her anything — even the half of his kingdom.

The play opens with a curiously morbid association of the Moon and the Princess Salome. The Moon is 'like a woman rising from the tomb [...] like a dead woman. You would fancy she was looking for dead things [...] like a woman who is dead' (552). Wilde continues to attribute to both Salome and the moon a deathlike quality: she is 'like a little princess whose feet are of silver [...] so pale [...] like the shadow of a rose in a mirror of silver [...] a little princess whose eyes are of amber' (552-6). As if she were also a very young child, Salome has 'little white doves for feet [...] little white hands fluttering like doves [...]. They are like white butterflies' (552-4). Where does all that come from?

The Wildes had a daughter, a younger sister of Oscar, whom he adored. She died. She died at the young age of nine. Oscar was eleven or twelve. He kept a lock of her hair in an envelope he had lovingly decorated. Years later, reciting to a friend a memorial poem composed to his sister when he was twenty, Oscar said he remembered her 'dancing like a golden sunbeam about the house'.

Wilde's young sister Isola played a crucial role in his life. In several of his poems, he associates a young girl's death with erotic longing or seduction. An early poem, 'Ballade de Marguerite', concerning a forester's love for a princess, concludes with Wilde's thinly disguised wish to lie down beside his sister in the grave:

> O mother, you know I loved her true:
> O mother, hath one grave room for two? (774)

His memorial poem to his sister, 'Requiescat', closes with the lines,

> All my life's buried here,
> Heap earth upon it.

In his poem, 'The Harlot's House' he describes the seduction of a young girl by prostitutes. The memory of a frightened but erotically eager young girl dominates the poem. Wilde describes the prostitutes as 'phantoms', 'strange mechanical grotesques', 'wire-pulled automatons', and 'skeletons'. I think that the seductive little sister comes alive in these phrases.

The chaotic family background of the Wilde home suggests that the children's parents were too preoccupied to give them enough care and affection; Oscar and Isola, I assume, turned increasingly to each other for love and emotional support, which would have quickly ripened into a childish sexual intimacy. This kind of erotic activity between children, when later practiced by adults, has the flavour of perversion, and in the case of Wilde can be found glorified in his drama *Salome*. Salome, with her 'little feet' and hands and her childish wish for the eyes in Iokanaan's severed head to open and look at her, behaves like a child of four or five, much younger than her approximate age of fourteen. Childhood relationships, distorted or disguised, reappear in the later relationships of the adolescent and the adult. Wilde appears to have had a dim sense that such early experiences indelibly stamped him. In a letter of early 1886 he wrote: 'Our most fiery moments of ecstasy are merely shadows of what somewhere else we have felt, or of what we long some day to feel'[12] — a remark that invites us to look for a model for Salome in his early life. Oscar's intensity of grief for Isola, that lasted all his life, derived from the guilt he felt as a young boy. He had allowed himself to be seduced by his little sister — had probably agreed to infantile sexual play — and then she was the one who — as Wilde must have felt — was punished by death.

The young princess Salome, whose sexual invitations are rebuffed with great verbal violence by the imprisoned prophet Iokanaan, ultimately demands and gets his severed head. Wilde certainly lost his head more than once in his life. Dreams, as we have learned from Freud, use concrete imagery to express abstractions, and *Salome* certainly appears to the audience as a dream, even quite aside from its language and the characterizations of its personalities. The metaphoric sense of the term 'losing one's head' is expressed in the beheading of Iokanaan in Wilde's drama. This concretising in the language of the dream frequently possesses the characteristic of a joke. Freud, describing such concrete imagery in dreams, mentioned a patient who dreamed that his 'uncle had given him a kiss in an auto[mobile]', an image conveying the idea of 'auto-erotism'.[13] Iokanaan gets decapitated: this is how Wilde in the style of dreams confesses his rash behaviour and guilt. But the story, at bottom one of two little children, a brother and sister, playing doctor, exploring each others bodies with pleasure, is extremely ordinary. Why should this childish scene be a source of great conflict in Wilde's life, a part of the fragment of a great confession uttered in *Salome*? Probably his realistic conflict — to show or to conceal his homosexuality — intensified the vestiges of guilt he felt about his early sensual exploits with little Isola; the burden of guilt he carried for their childish erotic experiments inspired a longing for punishment. Who knows — the experience with his little sister may have contributed to the development of his homosexuality. At least, he may have thought so. His guilt may have contributed to his fear of women, and by that to the development of his homosexuality.

Wilde's quip, 'I often betray myself with a kiss',[14] is a hint that helps to unravel the secret of the play. If Freud is right in suggesting that relationships often begin and end with identifications, we can surmise that Wilde's early attachments to his overwhelming mother and his seductive younger sister got stuck in the phase of identifying with them because they could not be developed in reality, or if they were partially developed the resultant guilt would have been too much to bear. The relationships therefore had to end. He retreated into an unconscious feminine identification: like his mother and sister, he too would be sexually approachable by a male. His Salome becomes his anima in Jung's and Freud's sense of the innate bisexuality of the human being. His incestuous feelings provoked a great deal of guilt and his sister's death could only have seemed to confirm the idea that he was guilty and deserved punishment. In the beheading of Iokanaan he expresses his crime of losing his head to his sister, and the punishment of decapitation that he feels he deserves for that crime and for being homosexual. He had to keep his homosexuality a mystery from the world, but at the same time he wanted to declare it from the rooftops.

Where could his confession through the drama of *Salome* lead Wilde? Where did he think it would lead him? His identification with Iokanaan, John the Baptist, the prophet and the soldier of Christ, reveals that the play is a moment in his planned life drama. He was going to cast himself as Christ, to die as a martyr for gay rights — and in his famous or infamous trial he did it. Even after he went to prison he greatly expanded on the comparison of himself to Christ: the long letter he wrote from prison, *De Profundis*, is filled with admiration for Christ attempts to imitate him. Wilde's need to confess had been enormously intensified by a crucial event in his life. Just before writing *Salome*, he had met Lord Alfred Douglas, known as 'Bosie', the fatally attractive young man for whom Wilde martyred himself, who prepared the way for Wilde to crucify himself. The blonde, beautiful Bosie, twenty years younger than Wilde, revived — by his childlike appearance and impulsive behaviour — Wilde's earlier love for the little sister who died, and in letters Wilde frequently called Bosie 'child', 'my delicate flower, my lily of lilies', language very reminiscent of *Salome* and *The Song of Songs*, whose language Wilde appropriates in *Salome*. From prison, Wilde promised in a letter to Bosie that 'even covered with mud' — we can understand that to mean in the grave — 'I shall cry to you'.[15] Such words, such intense, worshipful love as this, are reminiscent of the feelings he expressed for his sister. A remark in his novel, *The Picture of Dorian Gray*, intimates that his love for Bosie was a revival of his love for his sister: 'Romance lives by repetition', Wilde writes, 'We can have in life but one great experience at best, and the secret of life is to reproduce that experience as often as possible' (149).

The weird, surreal, middle-eastern world of *Salome* seems far removed indeed from the middle-class Dublin of the 1850s in which Wilde was born and grew up. This exotic piece of theatre does reveal, however, in distorted symbols and dreamlike disguises, the turbulent boyhood loves and terrors of Oscar Wilde, and the family problems that contributed to his development as a wit who attempted through his unsurpassed humour to overcome and control what tore him apart all his life. Wilde himself invites us to recognize the autobiographical elements of his art, to recognize that we cannot understand it without interpreting its hidden depths: 'Art [...] shows us [...] our own soul, the one world of which we have any real cognizance. And the soul itself, the soul of each one of us, is to each one of us a mystery. It hides in the dark and broods, and consciousness cannot tell us of its workings' (1194). And in spite of his fear of being understood and caught red-handed, he felt compelled to confess. As he once remarked, 'Autobiography is irresistible'.

NOTES

1   Oscar Wilde , 'The Critic as Artist', in *Complete Works of Oscar Wilde*, ed. V. Holland (London, Collins, 1986), p. 1045. Hereafter, page numbers to this edition will be given in the text.

2   W. G. Robertson, 'Of Oscar Wilde', in *Time Was* (London, Hamish Hamilton, 1931), p. 130-8, rpt. *Oscar Wilde: Interviews and Recollections*, vol. I, ed. E. H. Mikhail, p. 212.

3   S. Freud, *Three Essays on the Theory of Sexuality*, in *The Standard Edition of the Complete Psychological Works of Sigmund Freud*, (VII) trans. J. Strachey (London, The Hogarth Press, 1981), p. 198.

4   *The Letters of Oscar Wilde*, ed. R. Hart-Davis (New York, Harcourt, Brace & World, 1962), p. 475.
5   Incidentally Wilde borrowed this remark from Walter Pater. In 'The School of Giorgione', Pater writes that 'all the arts in common [are] aspiring towards the principle of music; music being the typical, or ideally consummate art, the object of the great *Anders-streben* of all art, of all that is artistic, or partakes of artistic qualities. *All art constantly aspires towards the condition of music.'. The Renaissance.* Ed. D. L. Hill, pp. 105-106.
6   *Letters*, p. 430.
7   R. Sherard, *The Real Oscar Wilde* (London, T. Werner Laurie Ltd, no date), pp. 65-66.
8   H. Wyndham, *Speranza: A Biography of Lady Wilde* (New York, Philosophical Library Inc., 1951), p. 76.
9   R. Ellmann, *Oscar Wilde* (London, Hamish Hamilton, 1987), p. 13.
10   H. Wyndham, *Speranza*, pp. 76-77.
11   G. B. Shaw, 'My Memories of Oscar Wilde', in F. Harris, *Oscar Wilde: His Life and Confession* (New York, Covici, Friede, 1930), p. 388.
12   *Letters*, p. 185.
13   S. Freud, *The Interpretation of Dreams*, in *Standard Edition* (V), pp. 408-409.
14   *Letters*, p. 373.
15   *Letters*, pp. 397-398.

OSCAR WILDE AS A MODERN DRAMATIST AND ACTOR

Jacques de Langlade

When Bernard Shaw told Frank Harris that Wilde would not escape his trial, on board the 'Jolly Roger', because he could not play the part, he knew that all his life Wilde had been not only a playwright but also an actor.

The first part of Oscar Wilde as an actor on the stage of the world was probably played in the fashionable circle of his mother in their home in Dublin. He was then about sixteen or eighteen years old, and already fascinated by his wonderful mother, the Passionaria of Ireland, Speranza. There he met numerous writers, artists, actors and actresses. He also began to study his appearance, his manners, his character. In 1878 he first met Sarah Bernhardt when she arrived in Folkestone. He never forgot her in *Phèdre* and wrote a poem to celebrate her genius, her beauty. Then he thought it fashionable to fall in love with the beautiful Lily Langtry, the mistress of the Prince of Wales. In fact, he always said that he would have married with pleasure, either Queen Victoria, Sarah Bernhardt or Lily Langtry. His second part was played in 1878 on the stage of the Sheldonian theatre at Oxford, when he read 'Ravenna', his poem which won the Newdigate Prize.

His third part took place after he left Oxford, when he walked down Piccadilly, followed by young boys and girls in Greek tunics, holding a sunflower in his hand and asking for a glass to water his flowers. In 1881, Gilbert and Sullivan produced the musical comedy *Patience*. Dante Gabriel Rossetti and Oscar Wilde were the main personages of the play which was a satire of the aesthetic movement. If Dante Gabriel Rossetti was rather angry of being thus portrayed, Wilde on the contrary was delighted especially because this sudden notoriety opened to him the doors of the United States where he toured for almost one year, lecturing from New York to Nebraska, on different stages, trying to educate the people of America. He never succeeded, but discovered the *immediate applause* of the public, and understood that only the stage could offer such an applause.

He had already written a play, *Vera*, which could not be performed for political reasons. For Mary Anderson he then wrote *The Duchess of Padua* which proved to be another failure. Yet his numerous remarks on the theatre, on the scenery, on the actors and critics, show at that time how his ideas on the theatre were topical. He perfectly knew, and wrote, that Art is the scientific result of an emotional desire for beauty. If this is not closely considered then art means nothing. And, presently the aim of the theatre is to propose to the public, as far as Vitez, Vilar, Terzieff... are concerned, more an intellectual pleasure than a mere amusement. In the same way, Wilde was very attentive to the actors as long as he knew that they were artists as well.

Then Wilde was a playwright and we find in his plays another aspect of him which shows his modernity. André Gide saw it perfectly well:

> Certes je n'en suis pas venu à considérer ces pièces comme des oeuvres parfaites, mais elles m'apparaissent aujourd'hui que j'ai appris à mieux les connaître, comme des plus curieuses, des plus significatives et, quoi qu'on en ait dit, des plus neuves du théâtre contemporain [...]. Éclairées sous ce jour et, pour ainsi dire, par en-dessous, les pièces de Wilde laissent apparaître, à côté des mots de parade scintillants comme des bijoux faux, quantités de phrases bizarrement révélatrices et d'un intérêt psychologique puissant. C'est pour ces dernières que Wilde écrivit toute la pièce, n'en doutez point.

In short he says that the main interest of Wilde's theatre is to be found between the lines, in the avowals that one may find behind the jewels and the ornaments which are here only for the show. And this is specially true in *A Woman of No Importance*, who is obliged to hide her past, to fear the horrible sneers of the world, exactly as Robert Chiltern is obliged to hide his own shameful past from his wife, and in the same way as Wilde himself had to hide his from Constance, his devoted wife. This is what he says in *A Woman of No Importance*:

> For her there is no joy, no peace, no atonement. She is a woman who drags a chain like a guilty thing. She is a woman who wears a mask, like a thing that is a leper. The fire cannot purify her. The waters cannot quench her anguish. Nothing can heal her! No anodyne can give her sleep! No poppies forgetfulness! She is lost!

And to her son, she says:

> It is my dishonour that has made you so dear to me. It is my disgrace that has bound you so closely to me. It is the price I paid for you — the price of soul and body — that makes me love you as I do [...] child of my shame, be still the child of my shame.

And this is written in 1893, when Wilde knew that his love for Alfred Douglas was to end in a tragedy, and that Bosie was to be the child of his shame!

And what to say of *Salome*, banned by the Chancellor during the rehearsals and proscribed for quite a while, until Richard Strauss turned it to music and made a triumph out of it.

In fact we see in Iokanaan, the first announcement of the humanity of Christ, which Wilde dwells upon in the *De Profundis*. And the Salome of the Gospel becomes with Wilde a woman in love with Iokanaan, while the Prophet himself is afraid of the charms of the Princess of Judea. Many recent pictures or plays did consider in the same way that Christ, after all, was a human being even if this may be thought sacrilegious. Though moderate and attentive, Wilde's views, as expressed in *Salome* or in *De Profundis*, are absolutely modern. As regard the game of the actors, the production, the scenery, we discover in Wilde a real talent of producer, a part which our modern playwright leave too often to the producer. Let us see for example, what he writes to George Alexander in February 1892, during the reherseals of *Lady Windermere's Fan*:

> I heard by chance in the theatre today — after you had left the stage — that you intended using the first scene a second time — in the last act. I think you should have told me this, as after a long consultation on the subject more than four weeks ago you

agreed to have what is directed in the book of the play, namely Lady Windermere's boudoir, a scene which I consider very essential from a dramatic point of view. My object, however, in writing is not to reproach you in any way — reproaches being useless things — but to point this out. If through pressure of time, or for reasons of economy, you are unable to give the play its full scenic mounting, the scene that has to be repeated should be *the second*, not *the first*. Lady Windermere may be in her drawing-room in the fourth act. She should not be in her husband's library. This is a very important point.

In the same way he wrote to Mary Anderson in March 1883, about *The Duchess of Padua*:

As regards the characters, the Duke is a type of the Renaissance noble: I felt that to have made him merely a common and vulgar villain would have been *banal*; he is a cynic, and a philosopher; he has no heart, and his vileness comes from his intellect; it is a very strong acting part as you see, and must be given to an experienced actor. To write a comedy one requires comedy merely, but to write a tragedy, tragedy is not sufficient; the strain of emotion on the audience must be lightened; they will not weep if you have not made them laugh.

As for his views on the theatre and his opinion on the critics we must refer to his interview to *The Sketch*, which he gave after the first night of *An Ideal Husband*, where he says:

The colour of a flower may suggest to one the plot of a tragedy; a passage of music may give one the sestet of a sonnet; but whatever actually occurs gives the artist no suggestion. Every romance that one has in one's life is a romance lost for one's art. To introduce real people into a novel or a play is a sign of an unimaginative mind, a coarse, untutored observation and an entire absence of style [...]. Everything is of use to the artist except an idea.

As for the critics, whom Wilde never thought useful, he said in the same interview:

The critics have propounded the degrading dogma that the duty of the dramatist is to please the public. Rossetti did not weave words into sonnets to please the public, and Corot did not paint silver and grey twilights to please the public. The mere fact of telling an artist to adopt any particular form of art in order to please the public makes him shun it. We shall never have a real drama in England until it is recognized that a play is as personal and individual a form of self-expression as a poem or a picture.

In his prime Oscar Wilde was a poet. Then a critic, a novelist and recognized as thus. But the playwright, so successful in his time, is presently almost ignored, in any case in France, where *Salome* is produced almost every year in the same dreadful way.

It was about time to show that the great modernity of Wilde lies in his opinions and achievements as a dramatist.

THE GOTHIC WILDE

Donald Lawler

As the 1880s were ending and the Aesthetic Movement modulating into the Decadence, Oscar Wilde was concluding a series of essays, later to be collected as *Intentions*, that contributed a radical aesthetic to this movement of which he had become the unacknowledged leader. Having made a case for aestheticizing Victorian manners and mores in 'The Decay of Lying', Wilde began turning the tables on art in 'The Portrait of Mr. W. H.', by offering a fictional resolution to the problem of Shakespeare's sonnets, showing that faith alone brings art to life, whereas empirical demands for proof cause faith to become deceitful, seeking foolish correlatives of itself in forgery. Wilde's gothic transactions with aestheticism that were to follow in the early 1890s, invite critical inquiry that addresses both their revisionary and gothic character. This paper brings into focus Wilde's uses of the gothic[1] in three major works, in three different structural genres: *Dorian Gray*, a novel; *Salome*, a one-act play; and a long poem, *The Sphinx*. From a critical perspective, they form an odd sort of trilogy, connected by shared interests, common themes, and treatments — especially a gothicized aestheticism whose obsessive beauty-worship expresses itself in a symptomatic fixation with art's decorative character — and sharing a reliance on the gothic as expressing, determining, and resolving the artistic requirements of each work.[2]

Wilde appropriated gothic resources of expression, effect, even genre-framing for exploring the limits and contradictions of his own arguments for aestheticizing life. In this series of works the once 'Great Aesthete' explores the destructive effects of art, especially in the familiar romantic idealization of beauty as well as in a synaesthesia of art for life, an advanced form of Romantic idealism's disillusion with worldly commerce.

I propose to begin as did Wilde with *Dorian Gray* in which he first explored and reshaped the expressive resources of the gothic for telling the story of Dorian Gray.[3] In so doing, Wilde displayed his exceptional powers of inventive synthesis, theatrical intuition, and stylistic ingenuity to their best advantage. The gothic informs every important aspect of the novel to the extent that references will be limited to a few representative instances of the novel's more innovative and influential gothic features.[4]

Wilde's contribution to exploring new worlds of gothic influence and revelation was to gothicize art in *Dorian Gray*. More precisely it was the romantic aesthetic worship of art and beauty that he gothicized, locating it at the juncture between the two great forces of the revised, 1891 novel: the archetypal moral allegory of the wages of sin complemented by an aesthetic allegory that interrogates two, art-related delusions. The first is Basil's artistic error of painting a confessional portrait that proclaimed his own love for his subject. The second is Lord Henry's aesthetic doctrine that living may be refined into an art-form. Dorian's supplement to that axiom is the delusion that Henry's aesthetic vision is achievable with a wish-fulfilled perpetual youth stolen from Basil's portrait and by aestheticizing life through art, leading to a spiritualization of the senses.

The encryption of the gothic begins with Basil Hallward's romanticized portrait that awakens a narcissism in Dorian, who sees himself through the eyes of the artist's 'idolatry'. Basil's admission to Henry that he had erred artistically by putting too much of himself into the painting includes his aesthetic apologia exposing a more ambitious motive of the artist for his subject than an invitation to vanity. Dorian has 'suggested to me a new manner in art,' and Basil then adds, 'I can now recreate life in a way that was hidden from me before' (14). That statement departs from Romantic idealism to foreshadow the gothic world.[5] Unlike previous gothic stories, the invention of the gothic world in this one is a cooperative venture in three stages, dispersed over the first three chapters. Basil provides the occasion in a life-size, realistic portrait of his ideal Dorian. Henry adds the catalytic temptation in his philosophy of pleasure declaimed as Dorian poses on Basil's platform, while the painter adds the final touches to the picture. These remaining brush strokes are critical because they are a record of Dorian's expression as he recognizes in his repressed appetites ways to a knowledge of good and evil with the power of transforming his life. Basil paints on, 'conscious only that a look had come into the lad's face that he had never seen before' (20), as Dorian experiences a conversion to Henry's philosophy of self-realization through affirmation and pursuit of appetites: 'The only way to get rid of a temptation is to yield to it' (21). Dorian is easily caught in the network of Henry's epigrams — 'Nothing can cure the soul but the senses, just as nothing can cure the senses but the soul.' The novel makes no claims about Dorian being smart, but he had a perfect profile, which after all both Henry and the author preferred to mere intelligence in their favorites.

Thus, Basil's portrait of an ideal Dorian becomes a recording of Dorian's fall from innocence and grace. These are the strange combinations and conjunctions of influences reflected in the portrait that were to have such a profound and lasting influence on Gray. Henry's temptation speech established the basis for Dorian's legitimizing his appetites by redefining them as questing for experience and therefore as a kind of knowledge rather than as matters for denial, repression, and shame. In gothic terms, Gray's wish to exchange lives with the portrait is his expression of the classic desire of the gothic protagonist/antagonist to re-create himself, this time by bartering his soul for a life in art, appropriating the appearances of the artist's icon, while his soul animates the picture that will then begin to age. The painting's reflecting the true condition of Gray's soul is the price of his admission to the gothic world.

Dorian Gray never does understand the rules of the world he hoped to live in, but they are obviously not what he expected. In the gothic world, they never are. The interactive magical picture is not merely the focus of the gothic world in the novel: it *is* the gothic world and with its invention Wilde gothicizes art and the beauty-worship of aestheticism, just as Mary Shelley gothicized science and the mad scientist in

Frankenstein.[6] The consequences of Dorian's wish that gothicizes art resonate throughout every remaining action of the novel. Nothing is left untouched by it.

Dorian's new opinions of art, mostly appropriations from Lord Henry, nonetheless diverge from his mentor's even as early as the Sibyl Vane affair. Dorian's rejection of Sibyl is the direct result of her abandonment of a life or more accurately a love in art for the real thing, once she had experienced it. Her declaration as a contemporary Lady of Shalott strikes at the heart of Dorian's aesthetic idealism. With the loss of Sibyl's influence and his gradual estrangement from Basil, Gray indulges his appetites, believing his sins justified by his quest for self-understanding and self-fulfillment. These may have been precepts of Henry's philosophy of the Dandy; but once acted upon, understanding becomes self-loathing. Dorian also enacts and therefore transforms Henry's doctrine of aestheticizing life, only Dorian really attempts it as an extended exercise in redesigning his instinctive behaviour, sense impressions, and even the structure of both brain and mind through art.[7] This is the main purpose of the notorious eleventh chapter, of its central location, of its literal cataloguing of the exotica of art, and of its position immediately preceding Basil's murder. Chapter eleven presents two contradictory views of Dorian's extended experiments in self-reconstruction. First, it implies that Gray artificially controls and refines his responses. Second, it shows that Gray's method for applying art to life and recreating himself is a delusion. He is, rather, a collector and a dilettantish one at that. His only artistic creation, most ironically, is his gothic revision of Basil's portrait, which Gray achieves through his misbehaviour, contextualized in the diary of his life as updated daily in the picture (120).

Even Gray's delusions of a life in art are permanently gothicized after he reveals the condition of his soul to Basil in the gothic portrait and then murders him. Gray who once had lived to savour and raise every new experience to the level of a sonnet, a fugue, or a watercolour could think of nothing thereafter but escape from guilt and of course his emblematic conscience, even if that meant abandoning art and dandyism for ugliness, violence, and crime.[8] Gray is hounded by an impressive variety of secularized, contemporary Wildean furies in addition to the portrait: from the avenging but luckless James Vane to the various arts in which Gray seeks both consolation and escape. Gray's fascination with the painting quickly becomes a morbid obsession, and as other gothic hero-villains, he becomes the enthralled captive of the gothic world he has created, ending in hysteria and near-madness.

The phrase 'Gothic art' is used by Wilde but once and in Chapter eleven of the novel, prefaced by Dorian's conviction that 'life itself was the first, the greatest of the arts, and for it all the other arts seemed to be but a preparation' (100) and contextualized by Dorian's increasingly hallucinated mental state (102). In the story of Gray's failure to aestheticize the life of a dandy, Wilde represents art as having been transformed into the talisman of gothic thinking in which the moods and atmospheres created by art recreate, reinforce, and sustain the nightmare originating in the picture. Once Dorian's imagination has been gothicized, he cannot free himself from it. Instead of promoting the ideal of Dorian's 'new scheme of life', elaborated in Chapter eleven, 'that would have its reasoned philosophy and its ordered principles, and find in the spiritualizing of the senses its highest realization' (101), gothicized imagination subverts Gray's agenda for aestheticizing life and spiritualizing the senses into parodies as foul as the picture of Basil's original icon of beauty and inspiration had become.[9]

* * *

After finishing *Dorian Gray*, Wilde turned his attention to other projects: another essay, perhaps a reparational homage to Ruskin in 'The Soul of Man under Socialism' and the first of his derivations of the French well-made play that became *Lady Windermere's Fan*. His work on that social comedy was soon interrupted by *Salome*, a topic that Wilde had been considering for more than a year. In addition to obvious and well-recognized French influences and Wilde's decision to write out of his system a sexual tragedy before completing a more polite sexual and social comedy, it appears that he was also interested in exploring further potentials of gothicized art for three related interests represented but not foregrounded in the novel: sexual passion (unfulfilled, repressed, and perverse), the supernatural (especially the scriptural and prophetic), and the tragic.[10]

The controversies surrounding the play must have exasperated even the showman in Wilde since its performance was limited to the original French version in Paris during Wilde's lifetime.[11] Nevertheless, *Salome*, without doubt, was intended by Wilde to be shocking and controversial, and in that he could not have been disappointed. In the play, Wilde extends the influence of gothicized art to scripture, dramatizing freely from the narratives of Matthew (14:1-12) and Mark (6:14-29). Wilde wants his scriptural materials to exercise influences in the play roughly analogous to myth or legend in Greek tragedy, within the context of a gothic mode modulated by the rich economy of symbolist drama. Together they develop the mood and tonal unity of the drama, transforming the biblical account of Salome and the death of John the Baptist from an erotically charged imbroglio of mismatched desire into a gothically inverted worship of death. Herod's recoil at Salome's necrophilic foreplay with the head of the Baptist as the stage empties and darkens may be the most subtly complex dramatic action Wilde invented, and its power, drawing upon the convergence of the play's gothic elements, is superbly theatrical.[12]

The decorative and descriptive symbolism Wilde uses repeatedly in the play forecasts an approaching gothic storm of sexual emotion and reaction. The repetitive technique may have been inspired by Maeterlinck, but it also derives surely from the uses of aesthetic and decorative effects in *Dorian Gray*.[13] In *Salome*, subtle dramatic variations and inversions of dialogue, scenery, lighting, acting as dramatic equivalents of balladic refrains (according to Wilde), promote premonitions of the gothic. It is not necessary to recognize these as patterns repeated from the novel, partly because foreknowledge of events leading to Salome's dance and its outcome for the Baptist bears a parodic similarity to dramatic irony — the gothic is a parodic form — producing resonances for the audience with every word and action of the characters.

The argument from unrequited or denied sexual passion involves the major players of the drama in a complex dance of transformations, leading to the deaths of all but the original guilty parties, Herod and Herodias, whose incestuous marriage occasioned the arrest of the Baptist for preaching against Herodias's adultery. The overlapping romantic entanglements among characters produce several perverse and inverse passions that build toward Salome's awakened lust for the prophet. It is her sudden, irresistible passion that Wilde requires of his biblical Juliet, whose virginal innocence is attested by the other characters in that stylized dialogue Wilde uses to frame the symbolist associations he unpacks from some of his earlier stories.[14] Wilde required Salome's passion to flame out of an early indifference to the attentions that her budding sexuality wins for her. Even Herod's leering admiration that awakens a sense of her own sexual power does not affect her beyond making her more wary. Rather than appearing intimidated by Herod's amorous interest, Salome realizes that a weakness of character expressing itself in voyeurism gives her a degree of power over him that she will soon exploit. Would Salome and Herodias have discussed Herod's Inclination? Salome remains coyly indifferent to the attentions of Narraboth, the young Syrian captain of the guard; but then she is a princess, and Wilde never has her forget it. Her detachment matches that of Dorian Gray at the beginning of the novel, a quality the author apparently found attractive and perhaps personally challenging. And yet she responds immediately to the sound of Iokanaan's chthonic voice, a monotone that intimidates Herod if not Herodias, who suffers no illusions that the Baptist speaks with any supernatural authority. The appearance of the Baptist evokes Salome's libido, moving her to adopt the language and manner of an aggressive courtship of the prophet. Young and impetuous, Salome grows more perverse with each rebuffed advance. Acceleration of Salome's enthralled passion for the prophet can be measured by the Baptist's features that her passion fetishizes: the black hair, the white body, and finally the red lips. Salome's contradictory passion and denial statements express youthful petulance and confusion at failing to arouse even Iokanaan's human interest in her let alone an erotic response. Her passion focuses at last upon the lips of the prophet as the symbol of his power and prophetic office.[15] Thereafter, Salome is obsessed with kissing the mouth of the Baptist. His contemptuous rejection of her as unworthy of notice seems to motivate her the more, as it warps her judgment.

Salome's immortal dance is the central action of the play, her art gothicized by a purpose we foreknow to be death, but which turns out to be something even worse. Salome dances for the head of the Baptist, a man she loves so madly that she will take his life in order to possess him. That desire beckons the gothic entry into the drama, an arrival more anticipated than experienced.[16] The dance is a powerful scene in any venue, and yet it is all but unwritten in the play. The unveiling of the scorned woman dancing her temptation before the enthralled desire of Herod is left, like the sins of Dorian Gray, to the reader's (and the dancer's) powers of invention. Salome's dance becomes the first measure of her moral insanity — once a category of psychology understood by Victorians. Moreau's image of Salome dances also before our mind's eye, a visual double and another painted allusion, as Wilde's image performs her own version of this most intentional of dances. And yet, if this be the obligatory scene of the play, it is neither the climax nor the quintessentially gothic scene that biblical history teaches us to expect, a point that confirms Wilde's theatrical instincts.

There are three powerful scenes yet to follow in which the gothic character of the play defines itself. In another of Wilde's bargaining scenes, Herod's haggling over the promised reward neatly reverses the power roles of the King and his step-daughter. In her monotonal responses, interrupted by Herod's prolix, Pilate-like attempts at saving both face and conscience, Salome assumes the imperative style of the Baptist, thereby parodying it. The final scene begins with the head of Iokanaan brought to Salome on a charger, in payment of Herod's debt and the double revenge of two scorned women, Herodias and her daughter.

Having altered the scriptures thus far for dramatic effect, Wilde places his personal imprint on the Salome legend in the conclusion, producing an unusual climax for a gothic plot. Salome's dramatic apostrophe to the severed head and missing body of the Baptist is indeed worthy of a prose Browning.

Salome's perverse eroticism, outdoes even Swinburne in the gothic power of its interrogation of the Baptist's prophetic and implicitly Christian asceticism by Salome's Dionysian carnality. In a sense, Salome's monologue was prefaced by her awakened libido at the sight of the Baptist, who represents power, supernatural authority, her own lost innocence and frustrated desire. More than one reader has remarked on the parallelism between Salome and Iokanaan, and that sense of shared identity emphasizes Wilde's gothic representation of the revulsion of the flesh at what is described in *Dorian Gray* as 'this monstrous soul-life'. Iokanaan had spiritualized his senses by denying and demonizing them and the world to which they belong. Salome apparently wins her monologistic debate with the Baptist but at the price of becoming enough like him to suggest the transposition of Dorian and his picture.

The play ends with two more strong dramatic moments. First we hear the voice of Salome sounding like the disembodied voice of the Baptist in her Maenad-like, triumphant peroration: 'They say that love hath a bitter taste. [...] But what of that? What of that? I have kissed thy mouth, Iokanaan.' Only in possessing the head of the Baptist does Salome think to possess his lips of power and prophecy, both metaphors of the man. Herod's disgusted, and fearful reflex is one of those moments of ironic and even cynical reversal that Wilde loved to construct in his prose poems: 'Kill that woman!'. The genius in that reflexive instant lies in the way Wilde forces dramatic recognition of both the appropriateness of the sentence and concurrently its impulsive, arbitrary, and hypocritical wrongness. The play closes with Salome crushed to death but thereby released by Herod from a state of Dionysian sexual frenzy that has disgusted the Tetrarch (although apparently not Herodias, whose last words are 'I approve of what my daughter has done') and is supposed to appall the audience as well. The conclusion like that of other gothic plots remains ambiguous, inviting revisionary, even contradictory interpretations. Nor should we mistake the play's and the gothic's heteroglossal preferences, if I may appropriate Bakhtin's ingenious and fashionable term.[17]

*   *   *

The Sphinx, Wilde's long unfinished poem, had its beginnings in Paris, according to Ellmann, in 1874 (36, 90-91), inspired by Poe, Swinburne, and Browning. The idea was put aside but taken up again at Oxford in 1878, after Wilde had finished 'Ravenna', when it would have suited his purpose of establishing himself as a young poet of promise to follow the Newdigate Prize poem with another from a similar perspective: a set piece featuring youthful, Byronic reflections on a vaguely classical subject graced by curious historical and learned ornamentation. Though ambitious enough for fame, a youngish Wilde perhaps sensing unrealized potentials put it back in the trunk. He may have had another go at it in the early eighties while back in Paris but with no better result. Finally, some time in the early nineties, probably following the publication of the original *Salome*, Wilde completed the poem, in Paris, of course.

I suggest that Wilde returned for this last time to his unfinished sphinx because he saw how it could be revived and completed by applying a gothic aesthetic that had produced such sensational effects in both *Dorian Gray* and *Salome*. The gothic provided the means for realizing the unfulfilled potentials of the various drafts, and this revised, final version of *The Sphinx* was published at last in an ornate edition designed by Charles Ricketts in 1894, at least a year after it was completed.

Although Wilde's *Sphinx* is more Greek than Egyptian in form, both mythic traditions are mingled together freely in the poem. Hermaphroditic, the sphinx symbolizes a pagan ideal of uniting a primitive animism with animal worship, an early representation of mystery religion, and a forerunner of the great mystery religion, Christianity, bridging the historic evolution of mind and soul. Wilde connects the mythological sphinx — perhaps for contemporary and later readers a relic of an incredible age of monsters out of the fossil rocks, somehow symbolized by the early generations of Greek and Egyptian gods, swarming with monstrous mutations — to the Old and New Testaments in which the land of Egypt, a refuge for Joseph and Israel only to become a slave state, later serves as a haven for the holy family fleeing the tyranny of another Herod.

Wilde's sphinx dwells in a private Victorian collection of antiquities, a curiosity, a silent messenger of Greco-Egyptian myth and the chaos that informed it, surrounded by the upholstery of late Victorian imperial England. It is a displacement that inspired Victorian and later stories of supernatural terror and whose gothic potentials are obvious. The location is also a metaphor for the aestheticized history of the sphinx, a fantastic biography of mythic and legendary rumours, appropriately chaotic and contradictory, whose primary effect is the gothicized, nightmare-like state of an overly stimulated imagination, such as we encounter in *Dorian Gray* and *Salome*. Indeed, our interlocutor's late descriptions of the sphinx have the distinct flavour of Wilde's gothicized art.[18] The characteristic heaping up of aesthetic ornamentation also serves purposes similar to the gothicized art of *Dorian Gray*. Different forces creating the gothic world of each work, however, do indeed produce related but different effects. Dorian's intentional wish creates his gothic world of art, but it is the speaker's enthralled, perverse sexual fantasies that lead him into the sphinx's circle of desire and devolution.

The speaker's long, monologic interview with the sphinx, the many questions put to the mute statuette whose mythic voice has not been heard in twenty centuries, seem to break an enchantment of silent isolation and bring the symbol back to a kind of life, at least in the gothicized imagination of the speaker.[19] The sphinx yet has power, it seems, of speaking as a gothic artifact through the imagination of the questioner. In this respect, Wilde's sphinx appears to be a significant departure from Rossetti's reflections on the great bull that Layard had excavated from Nineveh and brought as the spoils of science to the British Museum. Wilde wants the sphinx to be a relic of an altogether different sort of history, not natural but mythic and pre-human. *The Sphinx* offers a gothic archaeology of a human soul rather than of a city, and the secret of the sphinx's savage antiquity lies in the imagination of the speaker as a primitive retention of pre-conscious mind. The life of the sphinx is stored in the imagination of the speaker rather than at a national gallery or in his private collection. The statuette speaks to those who understand its unconscious iconography.[20]

The interrogation of the sphinx produces a fantastic psychoanalysis of the god's ancient promiscuous life. The probing questions and increasingly morbid emphasis on the sphinx's mythic indiscretions gradually reveal to the reader the erotic fantasies of the speaker in the guise of an inquiry into the perverse sexual preference of sphinxes in which passion is linked with cruelty and even murder, both aspects of erotic passion in *Dorian Gray* and *Salome*, and both traditionally energizing forces of the gothic. However, grotesquely, the sphinx symbolizes for the speaker a demi-god at liberty to indulge in its impulses and appetites freely and without guilt, as matters of preference and involving nothing of moral restraints or absolute prohibitions, both of which, when viewed by Wilde's contemporary anthropology, were considered decayed remnants of tribal taboos.

The speaker's renunciation of the sphinx as false in a complex echoing of Keats raises questions about our speaker's stability, similar to those about Gray. First, the rejection is also a self-indictement of one whose imagination has been gothicized by the sphinx's seductive silence, ancient at the crossroads of historic and cosmic time yet revenant in its power to energize our speaker's imaginative avatar. The sphinx seems therefore relevant historically as gothicized imagination: not merely its symbol but its reification, realized in the monstrous archetype from which the speaker cannot completely escape. Yeats's famous concluding lines to 'The Second Coming' may have a special relevance, perhaps even special reference to Wilde's revenant sphinx: 'what rough beast, its hour come round at last...' We also have license to recall Herod's reflexive dismissal of Salome's necrophilia.[21]

Wilde's connection of the sphinx with Christianity may not be as gratuitous as Ellmann suggests. Developing from *Dorian Gray* and *Salome*, it anticipates Wilde's later meditations on the aesthetic Christ as an artist of religion. Each symbol — the sphinx statuette and crucifix — exercises power over the speaker's imagination in this poem, although the crucifix is rather a latecomer. Yet each symbol betrays albeit differently the humanism that was at this point in Wilde's life central to his speculative thinking. The primitive animistic power of the sphinx in its chaotic mixture of animal and human pre-consciousness becomes historically parallel to the irrational, that is to say, the historically unfulfilled archetype of the crucified god whose humanity and divinity appear locked in unresolvable antithesis. In the poem if the sphinx is too savage to lift the narrator above the primitive avatar of human imagination, the crucifix is too complex a symbol of the human in the divine and the divine potential of the human to be realizable. Claims by both symbols offer the speaker little to choose but a cold conscience, itself the remnant of tribal guilt. At the centre of the circle of fear and desire are the contradictory symbols: the woman/animal and the man/god, each representing a now gothicized myth, one ancient and bestial the other historical and divine through which, Wilde's interlocutor implies, human imagination has been tangled in problematic contradictions. Arousing himself from his gothic reveries, our speaker, still a student in his 'students cell', finds himself obliged to choose between the loathsome mystery of the sullen sphinx whose power to 'wake in me each bestial sense' and the powerless crucified God who 'weeps for every soul that dies, and weeps for every soul in vain'. Can there be escape from this nightmare if the sphinx must be renounced by a dying or poisoned soul? The waking world appears to offer only despair in place of guilt, suggesting that the difference between two worlds linked by imagination is insufficient to relieve the burden of a gothic life of desire that eventually kills the soul.

*   *   *

Wilde's uses of the gothic mode in three major works helped produce two masterpieces and transformed an unfinished work into a dramatic monologue of the conflicted presentations of carnal passion and spiritual enervation.

Wilde's first deployment of the gothic mode seems to have arisen from the inspiration for *Dorian Gray* to deconstruct Wilde's own aesthetic philosophy of life as represented in his stories and essays of the late eighties and early nineties. To a significant extent, the foundations of *Dorian Gray*, *Salome*, and *The Sphinx* as decadent masterpieces seem dependent upon Wilde's decision to use the gothic as the most effective means for resolving artistically the competing claims of the aesthetic, sexual, tragic, and supernatural aspects of works representing portions of his own inner life. Since the works were to be realized through sequences of effects, like the phasmatropic projection of Victorian picture cards set into a synchronized motion, Wilde required a form that emphasized powerful engagement of reader reaction through his manipulation of imagery, symbols, legendary or mythic structures and secondary or imagined emotions. Traditionally, appeals of this kind have been especially suited to the gothic because the genre offered models for expressing those hidden, complex relationships among the sexual, psychological, and supernatural declensions of mind encoded in the exotic and decorative powers of art.

Wilde's use of the gothic was a brief, brilliant episode in an experimental phase of his career during which he assayed and reshaped conventions of the major structural genres *en route* to his greatest success as a comedic dramatist. Wilde was not to return to the gothic. Perhaps after prison and social martyrdom, reflected so powerfully in *The Ballad of Reading Gaol*, neither the gothic nor the tragic were available options to his art because he had experienced both real tragedy and the fulfillment of his own imagination of disaster. As Lord Henry once put it: 'the only things that one can use in fiction are the things that one has ceased to use in fact' (64).

NOTES

1   Given the persistence of a critical superstition that the gothic novel died in the 1820's, I am obliged to declare such reports have been grossly exaggerated and to affirm its survival despite critical interment: 'it had a limited run (nearly everyone dates it from *Otranto* in 1764 to either *Melmoth* in 1820 or Hogg's *Confessions of a Justified Sinner* in 1824)' (Geary 2).

Day's definition of gothic literature identifies characters' experience of an enthralled state of fear and desire as the distinctive power of the genre, and it will serve our needs in this essay. Although emphasizing the fate of characters in gothic plots, this approach is a variant of reader-response in the Aristotelian tradition. The primary cause of the characters' enthralled condition is a kind of hubris: the desire for something contrary to nature, often associated with the supernatural or forbidden sex.

In his Preface to the second edition of *The Castle of Otranto*, H. Walpole explained that his new type of romance had been invented to energize the fiction of his age by representing two powerful, instinctive forces omitted from contemporary novels: the will to believe in a supernatural (and the fear of it at the same time, most often expressed as dread of the demonic) and the desire for a sexual freedom proscribed by social mores and religion. The gothic internalized the conflict of these forces through the power of romance or fantastic narrative to engage readers' primary emotions of awe, fear, wonder, and desire. Walpole also established alliances with the tragic and the didactic, traits that have remained affiliated with the gothic ever since.

The transmission of the gothic to the present has produced too many distinct sub-types even to mention let alone discuss, but these discrete species range from gothic science fiction (*Frankenstein* to *Jurassic Park*) to gothic fantasy (*Varney the Vampire* to *Twin Peaks*) and include domesticated gothics like *The Picture of Dorian Gray*, and exotics like *Salome*, and *The Sphinx*.

2   The premise of this approach of *Dorian Gray*, *Salome*, and *The Sphinx* is that they are each in the gothic mode, meaning that they commonly share an experimental use of the gothic in conjunction with other well-documented formal elements of plotting and style. Wilde's use of the gothic has been noted, albeit in passing, by many scholars (Buckler, Charlesworth-Gelpi, Cohen, Ellmann, Hyde, Kohl, Nassaar, Régnier, San Juan) but not formally addressed. It seems to me that many features of Wilde's three works that have perplexed critics as 'strange' (a favoured term) and even ineffable are more readily understandable as expressive of the gothic.

3   References in my text are to the revised, 1891 version of the novel. However, in the original, *Lippincott's* version (1890), gothic sensationalism amplified the effect of the moral allegory, of Dorian's growing depravity and eventual indirect suicide. Although it was not Wilde's intent, his original use of the gothic contributed to a widespread misinterpretation of that finale as the despairing but repentant act of a justified sinner: a misreading Wilde himself realized his text supported. The revised version, although it does not close out moral allegory, reinforces the relationship between art and the gothic world of nightmare and anxiety.

4   Wilde selected the gothic because he needed a literary mode that would promote the best features of a complex narrative that included a fantastic premise with supernatural resonances (the soul-bargaining and the magical picture), a complex allegory (moral, aesthetic, historical, autobiographical), and multivalent sexual passions while producing a more tragic than pathetic or sentimental impression. Wilde developed his gothic fantastic treatment of the living painting to emphasize his ingenious scheme of gothicising art and everything associated with art in the novel, but especially the decorative uses of art. The result of these and the other conjunctions within the context of a gothic narrative was to produce a style of discourse, design, and symbolic emphasis that was immediately identified as the

distinctive idiom of British Decadence. The key to this idiom, I
believe, is Wilde's gothic treatment of art and its many
associations, but especially as an intensely decorative and
ornamental mode.

5   'To recreate life' is the gothic signature of such over-reachers as
Drs Frankenstein and Jekyll. It does not matter to the gothic that
Basil intended no more than recreating life aesthetically. The
tragic pattern is already established for Dorian to complete,
proving Basil's error fatal not only for the painter but also,
eventually, for Sibyl Vane and Dorian.

6   Wilde gothicizes art in the novel and in the other texts we
examine only for the duration of the plot and not in some
ontologic sense. Nevertheless, Wilde's vision of the gothic
potential of art does take its place permanently in the repertory
of the gothic. Just as *Frankenstein* defines the condition of gothic
science, so does *Dorian Gray* establish a gothicized art that is
retained as a resource in the genre.

7   It is probable that Wilde derived Dorian's method of attempting
to spiritualize the senses from contemporary thinkers like G. H.
Lewes and Wilhelm Wundt. We find traces in references to
Henry's quasi-scientific studies of individual and group
behaviour, the importance of hereditary influences on Dorian
equated with personal influences (Henry, Basil, and Sibyl) and
the influences of art. These reflect theories of Lewes and Wundt
on parallel psychic and physical causation that informed their
debate with Huxley and the Darwinists over a purely
materialist model for development and influence of human
consciousness.

The key notion for Lewes was 'psychic causality', an
idea that first Henry and then Dorian mis-appropriate as a
formula for reconstructing an aestheticized self, built up by
repeated exposures to artistic effects that would produce
acquired dispositions. Unfortunately for Gray's scheme of
becoming the artist of his own life, since art had been gothicized
in the painting by his own wish, everything aestheticized
becomes thereby gothicized as well.

8   See *Dorian Gray* 143: to Dorian the image of the closed circle of
hallucinated desire and fear is an apt representation of his
gothicized mind. At this point art enthrals rather than enchants
because the linkage of art with evil, of dandyism and
aestheticism with the gothic world has become a self-replicating
pattern.

9   A few representative examples will do: the morning after
Basil's murder Gray awakens peacefully in his sunlit bedroom,
then but 'gradually the events of the preceding night crept with
silent, bloodstained feet into his brain' (125). The bloodstains
foreshadow the changes in the picture. Later, when Gray seeks
escape from consciousness in London's opium dens, 'the moon
hung low in the sky like a yellow skull' (142). This moment
comes just before he encounters his nemesis, James Vane. It may
be worth an aside to note that Wilde's idea for costuming
Salome was to dress the entire cast in yellow.

10   Themes of perverse sexual passion, supernaturalism of one sort or another, and tragic deaths have been associated with the gothic novel since *The Castle of Otranto* and were also linked in some of Wilde's poetry and later stories like 'Mr W. H.' and those in *A House of Pomegranates*.

11   The text I use is the English language translation, originally botched so badly by Alfred Douglas that Wilde finally did a complete revision, after having rejected Aubrey Beardsley's offer to make a new translation of his own. In a somewhat more radical if eccentric way, the play's transmission history forms the rough equivalent of mediated narratives in gothic stories.
        Refusal to approve a license for the English version while the play was in rehearsal caused a great controversy over censorship, and drew from Wilde a threat to renounce his English citizenship and defect to France where he would be free from interference. Had he done so rather than heed George Archer's counsel not to leave under fire, he would have left an intellectual hero, at least in Europe, and literary and cultural history would have been changed. It is tempting to speculate how different Wilde's life could have been. As it was, Wilde stayed, and a similar motive later kept Wilde from taking his chance to leave England for France after the collapse of the first trial.

12   It should be noted that *Salome* performed is far more effective than *Salome* read, although admittedly the experiences differ. For instance the theatrical effect of the repetitious, stylized dialogue, punctuated by the symbolist imagery encountered in the speech of every character but Herodias and Iokanaan can be mesmerizing in the theatre, especially as the erotically and gothically derived tensions build toward a culturally foretold climax. Indeed, no small portion of the play's success is the result of Wilde's genius for playing his characters against his audience's expectations derived from both scriptural authority and other artistic representations.

13   Wilde's gothic invasion of the world of art from the novel to the play included the power to gothicize the imaginations of those who invoke emotionally charged decorative effects or seem obsessed by them: allusiveness is an attribute of genres. This helps to account for the otherwise gratuitous foreboding shared by the choric characters with the principals. Hence anything that a gothicized art may incorporate either directly or by association becomes a rumour of some aspect of the gothic world.
        The power of gothicized art, as we have already seen, haunts the imagination of the characters and, thereby, affects the reader's imagination. By using the power of a gothic aesthetic, Wilde had at his disposal for drama a proved and effective way for exercising an audience's response and for energizing their imaginations without need of explanations. Gothic appeals to readers' secondary fears and desires, for example, are experienced as reflexes of imagination, needing no conceptual recognition.

14   Those parodic prose-poems with biblical subjects were given in
        Wilde's aestheticized, archaic idiom. The moon that serves
        symbolic duty in poems, stories, and the novel, rises to the level
        of influence in *Salome* and serves also as a thematic barometer,
        changing from white to red to black. There is the symbolism
        associated with Salome's little white feet — possibly imported
        from 'The Fisherman and His Soul' because of their sexual
        fetishism there — that fascinate the Syrian captain and even his
        gay admirer, the 'Page of Herodias'. Flower and bird symbols
        abound in 'The Nightingale and the Rose', and a bird out of *The
        Happy Prince and Other Tales* may have precursed the white
        doves associated with the early, virginal Salome before the
        moon turns red.

15   Iokanaan hardly engages Salome in dialogic exchange; and he
        does not have a pleasant word to say to or about anyone. He
        offers only a few words about the Christ who is to follow but
        who remains distantly off stage. The Baptist appears as the last
        Old Testament prophet.
        Salome, however, finds him irresistible, perhaps, because he
        denies himself to her, or perhaps for no reason at all beyond an
        inexplicable attraction. It is the sort of tragic fatality about
        which Basil speaks in the novel. If the fisherman (of 'The
        Fisherman and His Soul') could fall in love with a woman's feet
        because the mermaid had none and Dorian be enchanted by
        Henry's voice, it would not be uncharacteristic in Wilde for
        Salome to be smitten by Iokanaan's voice, hair, skin, and at last
        mouth.
        Religion is not so much gothicized in *Salome* as marginalized.
        However, scripture in its translated discourse, to the extent that
        it is aestheticized in the play, does reveal a parodic, gothic
        potential for Wilde as it did in the prose poems. Matthew and
        Mark are, after all, revised by Wilde for a gothic, dramatic
        purpose.

16   Here is another instance of Wilde's innovative use of gothic
        conventions or practice.

17   Perhaps the literary and dramatic conclusions need to be
        critically separated for the moment. As the performance ends,
        the audience is supposed to agree with Herod's outrage at
        Salome's necrophilia and blasphemy but be shocked at his
        arbitrary order to kill Salome — at least this may be assumed
        about the majority of Wilde's contemporary audiences. Readers
        who dramatize the text internally enjoy the burden of electing to
        reread the conclusion where they will find not only signs of
        authorial sympathy for the admittedly mad Salome but traces of
        another working myth — that of Cupid and Psyche — behind
        the Dionysian construction that is foregrounded.
                There is, then, more than one irony to Herod's
        command. Salome has ended her monologue: 'If thou hadst
        looked at me thou hadst loved me, and the mystery of love is
        greater than the mystery of death. Love only one should
        consider.' What a lesson for him! Perhaps what Salome thought
        she was getting in Iokanaan was a god to equal her passion
        rather than a desiccated prophet. Herod's response is to deplore

Salome's 'crime against an unknown God'. It is a statement with more reflexive than direct meanings. In the myth of Cupid and Psyche, Cupid was the unknown god.

Historically, another Herod was to pass another death sentence, this time on the very unknown god this Herod condoles. And, of course, the 'unknown God' alludes to St Paul's famous 'Areopagus Sermon' in Athens (Acts 17:22-31) that led to the conversion of many.

18   Wilde reintroduces from *Dorian Gray* the drawing room of a collector of ancient and fabled curiosities, especially ones that would have been associated with anthropological study of primitive customs, religious rituals, and sexual rites that James G. Frazer had just analyzed in *The Golden Bough. The Roots of Religion and Folklore* (1890). Wilde's interlocutor may remind us of Gray in both his youth and debauched imagination, but there seems something of the amateur anthropologist in him also, more like the Victorian gentleman-scientist of Robert Browning's 'A Tocatta of Galuppi's', perhaps, than Wilde's decadent brat. Once again Wilde imports a work of art to be wished into a kind of hallucinated, gothic life that then reflects the true condition of the protagonist's guilty soul.

In the 1944 MGM film adaptation of *Dorian Gray*, not only does the sphinx appear in Basil's studio, in the painting, and in Dorian's study but also the poem is quoted several times as a basis for representing the statuette as one of the gods of Egypt with the power of granting Dorian Gray's wish for endless youth and for exercising an ancient evil influence over the lad in what was a rather creative reversal of the historical declension of influences in the texts.

19   The sphinx has long since turned to stone and has no longer a voice of her own. Her previously reputed conversations with humans having been riddling invitations to death make us wonder whether this her silence is now another form of riddle.

20   In *Dorian Gray*, this very argument for the survival of imagination and conscience as transformed remnants of the emotional and irrational life of primitive cultures is one phase of the theme of gothicized influence. The idea fascinated Wilde, perhaps because he was one who had learned to search for and recognize influences that had shaped his own life, especially we may suppose, his sexual life. This interest may have originated with Pater and later been reinforced by the growing influences of post-Darwinist psychology and the newer cultural and primitive anthropology. The theme appears in stories like 'Lord Arthur Savile's Crime', 'Mr. W. H.', and *Intentions* before it became gothicized in *Dorian Gray, Salome*, and *The Sphinx*.

21   Wilde's reversal of the argument of *Salome* in the poem is worth noting. Instead of the female princess who is the victim of the gothic world created by her sick desire for Iokanaan, the speaker's morbid and carnal curiosity elaborated through his double-edged confessional interview, exercises in him appetites so feral that no human of Wilde's class could have entertained them without shame, even in a conditional state.

REFERENCES

Behrendt, P. F. *Oscar Wilde. Eros and Aesthetics*, New York, St Martin's Press, 1991.

Buckler, W. 'The Picture of Dorian Gray. An Essay in Aesthetic Exploration', *Victorians Institute Journal* 18 (1990), 135-174.

Charlesworth-Gelpi, B. *Dark Passages: The Decadent Consciousness in Victorian Literature*, Madison, University of Wisconsin Press, 1965.

Cohen, P. K. *The Moral Vision of Oscar Wilde*, Cranbury, New Jersey and London, Associated University Press, 1978.

Day, W. P. *In the Circles of Fear and Desire*, Chicago, University of Chicago Press, 1987.

Ellmann, R. *Golden Codgers*, New York, Oxford University Press, 1973.

—. *Oscar Wilde*, New York, Knopf, 1988.

Gagnier, R. *Idylls of the Marketplace*, Palo Alto, Stanford University Press, 1986.

Geary, R. F. *The Supernatural in Gothic Fiction*, Lewiston, New York, Mellon University Press, 1992.

Hyde, H. *Oscar Wilde*, New York, Ferrar, 1975.

Kohl, N. *Oscar Wilde. The Works of a Conformist Rebel*, trans. D. H. Wilson, New York, Cambridge University Press, 1989.

Nassaar, C. S. *Into the Demon Universe. A Literary Exploration of Oscar Wilde*, New Haven, Yale University Press, 1974.

San Juan, Jr., E. *The Art of Oscar Wilde*, Princeton University Press, 1967.

Walpole, H. 'Preface', *The Castle of Otranto*. Ed. W. S. Lewis, Oxford, Oxford University Press, 1969.

Wilde, Oscar. *Complete Works*, London, Collins, 1969.

—. *Letters*, Ed. R. Hart-Davis, London, Hart-Davis, 1962.

—. *The Picture of Dorian Gray*, Ed. D. Lawler, New York, Norton, 1987.

Worth, K. *Oscar Wilde*, New York, Grove Press, 1983.

OSCAR WILDE:
THE ONCE AND FUTURE DANDY

Jerusha McCormack

> *Dandy*: 1780 (perhaps a shortening of *Jack-A-Dandy*, the last element of which may be identical with *Dandy*, pet-form of *Andrew*).
> A.1. One who studies ostentatiously to dress elegantly and fashionably; a fop, an exquisite.
> *Dandy*: *Anglo-Indian* 1865 (Hindi *dandi*, f. *dand* staff, oar.)
> 1. A boatman on the Ganges.
> From *The Shorter Oxford English Dictionary* (1973), Vol. I.

Oscar Wilde once said: 'The future belongs to the dandy. It is the exquisites who are going to rule.'[1] He was wrong: in the sense that few today would even know what a dandy was, much less recognize in him a figure of power.

To most people, the dandy is merely a man of fashion, albeit one who made an almost heroic commitment to style. But such a definition vitiates the force of dandyism not merely as a concept, but as a creed, one which transforms the way one looks at life.[2]

The most lucid exposition of this creed is by Charles Baudelaire, who inscribes dandyism as 'an institution outside the law'.[3] He understands that the dandy's pursuit of style is not a mere act of homage to fashion but, in fact, a passionate revolt against convention itself. Revolt is not repudiation. Its potency relies on the force of what it repudiates. As another exponent of dandyism, Barbey D'Aurevilly, observed: 'Dandyism, while still respecting the conventionalities, plays with them. While admitting their power, it suffers from and revenges itself upon them, and pleads them as an excuse against themselves; dominates and is dominated by them in turn.'[4] It is this reciprocity of turn and counterturn, the implicit structure of an act of provocation and revenge, upon which I wish to focus in the performance of Wilde's dandyism.

Politically (Baudelaire notes), 'dandyism appears especially in those periods of transition when democracy has not yet become all-powerful, and when aristocracy is only partially weakened and discredited' (p. 421). At such a time of insecurity, conventions become elevated into ideals, deriving their authority from a kind of communal team-think which masks pervasive double standards.

Such a scenario graphically describes what was known as 'society' in late Victorian England. Constructed as a veritable cathedral of bourgeois denial and doublethink, its unparallelled degree of conformity was enforced by a policy of exclusion. Given over to the tyranny of niceness and order, it was an airless world built on the rejection of all which threatened — or seemed to threaten — its uneasy security. As Wilde's heroines are eloquent testimony, ostracism from such a society constituted a fate worse than death.

Into this scenario the dandy arrives: a leisured outsider who conceives of himself (in the words of Baudelaire) as 'establishing a new kind of aristocracy' (p. 421). Despising the society into which he seeks initiation, the dandy takes his revenge by creating himself in its image, miming its clothes, its manners and mannerisms. ('Imitation', as Wilde observed, 'can be made the sincerest form of insult.'[5]) Inherently exaggerated, such mimicry exposes the fissures of its own performance: the double standards on which it rests. What the dandy performs is a kind of psychic jujitsu — he 'throws people' by using the force of their attitude to defeat them. In effect, by means of his performance the dandy gets his audience to share his contempt for itself.

In this respect, the strategies of Wilde's dandies anticipate the Dada principle of provocation or the procedures of the Theatre of Cruelty.[6] In the larger world of the British Empire, they might also be taken as anticipating the principled actions of another of its children, Mohandas Gandhi. It is one of the coincidences of history that Gandhi arrived in London from India in October 1888 to study law at the Inner Temple. Like Wilde, he had taken note of the work of the Fabian Society and was to be crucially influenced by the work of John Ruskin. And, like Wilde, he refashioned himself as a dandy. In the chapter of his autobiography entitled 'Playing the English Gentleman', Gandhi recounts how his new-found 'punctiliousness in dress' led him to exchange his disasterous white flannel suit for a chimney-pot hat and an evening suit made in Bond Street.[7] He sent home for a double watch-chain of gold and mastered the art of tying a tie. In the same cause he undertook courses in dancing and the violin; then lessons in French and elocution. Gandhi finished his law course three years later and was called to the English Bar in June 1891. Leaving London to return to India immediately thereafter, Gandhi missed by several years Wilde's own virtuoso performance as dandy during the trials which concluded with his conviction in 1895.

From the perspective of that conviction (and with a certain poetic licence) we may note the similarities of their campaigns of dissent. Both Wilde and Gandhi were from the margins of the British Empire. Both, in their separate ways, sought to be included in the centre. Both took their careers from their sense of exclusion. Both worked a very public method of provocation: for Wilde, the stage and later the court dock; for Gandhi, the public staging of his mass protests. Finally, both thoroughly understood how to exploit popular media to the fullest extent in making their symbolic protests. Without embarrassing the comparison further, I would like to suggest that Wilde used the figure of the dandy to register protest in much the same way as Gandhi registered his.

Underlying the strategies of Wilde's dandyism and of Gandhi's later political career are a kind of ritual provocation that effectively hands control over to the audience. Apparently innocuous ('nonviolent' in Gandhi's terms) their strategy of protest is designed to elicit powerful response. Gandhi's protests succeeded in provoking actual violence, thus revealing the iron fist under the velvet glove of imperialist paternalism. Wilde's target was equally the doublethink of the Empire at home: 'It is the spectator, and not life', he asserted, 'that art really mirrors.'[8] By turning the audience's language upon itself, Wilde's dandy engages in a mime of its ritual cant which exposes it as cant.[9] By its laughter, Wilde's audience betrays recognition while denying implication. In making Wilde's dramas a success, his audience (as Wilde pointed out) declared itself a success.[10] When it turned on

Wilde, his audience did so with the ferocity of those betrayed by a figure of their own making: to use Wilde's own phrase in another context, their reaction was the 'rage of Caliban seeing his own face in a glass'.[11]

Such strenuous, potentially lethal, interaction between the dandy and his audience is the logical consequence of its intimacy. By accepting the conventionalities of his audience even while subverting them, Wilde's wits operated within a closed circle of response. How many of Wilde's texts — from *The Picture of Dorian Gray* and 'Pen, Pencil and Poison' through *Salome* to *The Ballad of Reading Gaol* — may be construed as variations on this cycle of reciprocity: of murder becoming, in effect, suicide? Not only does this appear to be the emotional circuit implicit in Wilde's drama but also that of the larger drama which was his life. A great deal of the Wilde *mythos* tacitly or explicitly invokes the concepts of 'victimization' and 'martyrdom', implying an act of unprovoked violence against him. Wilde himself never underestimated the rage of the artist nor the force of his scorn, even while acknowledging it to be predicated upon a reciprocal and answering violence.[12] Until his dandyism is interpreted in terms of protest and provocation and even in terms of larger political dissent, it may not be possible to understand the full implications of Wilde's claim that he stood in symbolic relation to the art and culture of his age.

NOTES

1   H. Jackson, *The Eighteen Nineties: A Review of Art and Ideas at the Close of the Nineteenth Century* (New York, Capricorn Books, 1966), p. 105.

2   For the purposes of this paper, I intend to use 'dandy' to designate not only the insolently witty figures of Wilde's comedies, but also to specify the personae Wilde created in his prose fictions and as voices for his critical essays. Dandyism, as such, has to do with a certain linguistic style deployed in a certain context and may thus be extended to Wilde's invention of himself, as I argue in a previous essay, 'Masks Without Faces: The Personalities of Oscar Wilde', *English Literature in Transition*, vol. 22, no. 4 (1979): 253-69.

3   'The Painter of Modern Life: The Dandy', *Baudelaire: Selected Writings on Art and Artists*, translated by P. E. Charles (Harmondsworth, Middlesex, England: Penguin Books; 1972),

p. 419. Following quotations from Baudelaire derive from this source.

4   *Dandyism*, p. 23, quoted in R. Gagnier, *Idylls of the Market-place: Oscar Wilde and the Victorian Public* (Aldershot, Scolar Press, 1987), p. 221. While Gagnier expertly locates Wilde within the cultural context of dandyism, both English and French, she understands the dandy as a product of the market place: an economic commodity, rather than a political phenomenon.

5   'The Decay of Lying', *Intentions* (New York, Brentano's, 1912), p. 42.

6   Gagnier makes an illuminating parallel between the theatre of Artaud and Alfred Jarry and that of Wilde, pp. 109-117. As yet (to my knowledge) nothing has been written about Wilde and Dadaism.

7   M. K. Gandhi, *An Autobiography: or The Story of My Experiments with Truth* (Harmondsworth, Middlesex, Penguin Books, 1929), pp. 60-63. The following details are taken from this source.

8   Oscar Wilde, 'The Preface', *The Picture of Dorian Gray* edited by I. Murray (London, Oxford University Press, 1974), xxxiv.

9   Cf. J. McCormack, 'Masks Without Faces', pp. 263-69, on the use of this kind of doubletalk. It is also discussed at length by Gagnier, especially pp. 29-31.

10   Cf. Wilde's curtain speech after the first performance of *Lady Windermere's Fan*, his first real commercial success: 'I congratulate you on the *great* success of your performance, which persuades me that you think *almost* as highly of the play as I do myself.' R. Ellmann, *Oscar Wilde* (New York, Alfred Knopf, 1988), p. 366.

11   'The Preface', *The Picture of Dorian Gray*, xxxiii.

12   Note particularly Wilde's portrayal of Christ as a prototype of the artist in the letter to Robert Ross from prison (first published under the title *De Profundis*), saying: 'The cold philanthropies, the ostentatious public charities, the tedious formalisms so dear to the middle-class mind, he exposed with utter and relentless scorn.' *The Letters of Oscar Wilde* edited by R. Hart-Davis (London, Rupert Hart-Davis, 1963), p. 486.

FROM MISS PRISM TO MISPRISION: OSCAR WILDE AND CONTEMPORARY THEORY

Bart Moore-Gilbert

In 1968 Richard Ellmann remarked that Wilde 'laid the basis for many critical positions which are still debated in much the same terms, to which we like to attribute more ponderous names'.[1] This paper seeks to sketch out some of the ways in which Wilde's critical essays, especially 'The Critic as Artist', anticipate the arguments of one contemporary critical 'school' in particular, that associated with 'reader-' or 'audience-oriented' theory. Since space is short I will rely on Elizabeth Freund's definition of its main preoccupations to set the framework for subsequent discussion:

> In one mode or another, the swerve to the reader assumes that our relationship to reality [and the art object] is not a positive knowledge but a hermeneutic construct, that all perception is already an act of interpretation, that the notion of a 'text-in-itself' is empty, that a poem cannot be understood in isolation from its results, and that subject and object are indivisibly bound [...]. Reader-response criticism probes the practical or theoretical consequences of the event of reading by further asking what the relationship is between the private and the public, or how and where meaning is made, authenticated and authorised, or why readers agree or disagree about their interpretations. In doing so it ventures to reconceptualize the terms of the text-reader interaction.[2]

In one sense, of course, concern for the reader and the reception of the work of art is as old as aesthetic theory itself, as reference to Plato and Aristotle in 'The Critic as Artist' suggests. But the long tradition of criticism which asserts the instrumental potential of the arts (to change society or 'improve' the reader), usually constructs the reader as something to be acted upon, rather than acting, in the process of reading. In contrast, 'The Critic as Artist' seeks to reverse the subordination of the reader intrinsic to the classical paradigm. It suggests three specific ways that criticism can be seen as creative, all of which anticipate the manoeuvres of contemporary 'reader-oriented' theory. The first step is to enact 'the death of the author' by denying authorial intentionalism as the source of textual meaning. Gilbert's assertion that criticism 'does not confine itself [...] to discovering the real intention of the artist and accepting that as final',[3] is premised on the argument that the finished work has 'an independent life of its own, and may deliver a message far other than that which was put into its lips to say' (874). The work of art 'whispers of a thousand different things which were not present in the mind' of the artist (874). Moreover, the very qualities which enable artists to create, according to Gilbert, disable them from being good critics. He cites the mutual misunderstandings of the Romantic poets to substantiate his claim that the 'very concentration of vision that makes a man an artist, limits by its sheer intensity his faculty of appreciation' (894).

Secondly: 'The critic occupies the same relation to the work of art that he criticises as the artist does to the visible world of form and colour, or the unseen world of passion and of thought' (875). Criticism, then, 'works with materials, and puts them into a form that is at once new and delightful. What more can one say of poetry?' (872). Victorian art-criticism is one example adduced by Wilde to argue his case. 'Pen, Pencil and Poison' praises Wainewright as 'one of the first to develop what has been called the art-literature of the nineteenth century, that form of literature which has found in Mr Ruskin and Mr Browning its two most perfect exponents' (848). 'The Critic as Artist' cites the work of Pater, which according to Gilbert 'treats the work of art simply as a starting-point for a new creation' and by 'its equal beauty' comes to stand as a new work of art in its own right (873). Indeed, Gilbert estimates Ruskin's criticism as being, in certain respects, greater than the painting of Turner which inspired it. In his blurring of the distinction between creative and critical discourse, as both theoretical project and in his own practice, Wilde anticipates a key tendency in contemporary theory. Gilbert's suggestion that criticism will one day escape its traditionally subordinate, secondary role, is answered in the euphoric claim of Josue Harari in 1979 that 'criticism has reached a state of maturity where it is now openly challenging the primacy of literature. Criticism has become an independent operation that is primary in the production of texts.'[4]

Thirdly, and perhaps most radically, Gilbert insists on the 'incompleteness' (875) of the text prior to the reader's response to it. Criticism, in his opinion, 'fills with wonder a form which the artist may have left void, or not understood, or understood incompletely' (874). The choice of Aristotle's *Treatise on Poetry* to illustrate his thesis is particularly apposite since it consists of 'notes jotted down for an art lecture, or of isolated fragments destined for some larger book' (864). Gilbert's critique synthetically draws the fragments into a 'richer unity' (875) than exists in the original, by expanding the 'notes' into something more coherent. Wilde consistently conceives of the text as essentially fragmentary. Thus Pater's work is represented as a 'mosaic' (863) and Browning has the 'incompleteness of the Titan' (859). It is in the act of criticism alone 'that Art becomes complete' (875). In this respect, Wilde anticipates the work of figures like Ingarden and Iser, who see the work of art as interrupted by 'spots of indeterminacy', 'gaps' and 'blanks', which must be resolved, filled in or 'concretised' by the reader before the text has meaning.[5]

While Wilde insists that criticism can create a 'richer unity' (875) in the work of art, as with Ingarden and Iser,[6] there is no suggestion that any reader can impose on it some final coherence. In this respect 'music is the perfect type of art. Music can never reveal its ultimate secret' (875). Gilbert alludes to the 'thousand different things' that *Tannhauser* speaks to him of and concludes: 'Beauty has as many meanings as man has moods' (874). 'The hermeneutic circle' can never be definitively completed, moreover, because the reader is irreducibly fissured and plural. Like Dorian Gray, Wilde seems to 'wonder at the shallow psychology of those who conceive the Ego in man as a thing simple, permanent, reliable, and of one essence. To him, man was a being with myriad lives and myriad sensations, a complex, multiform creature that bore within itself strange legacies of thought and passion.'[7] Wilde's textualisation of the reader explodes the idea of a unifying perceiving subjectivity in a manner which anticipates Roland Barthes, who was himself preoccupied in his later career with theorising the reader's role in the production of the text: 'This "I" which approaches the text is already itself a plurality of other texts, of codes which are infinite or, more precisely, whose origins are lost.'[8]

Given these premises, it is inevitable that Wilde's conception of critical practice differs radically from the mainstream, particularly as represented by a contemporary like Arnold. Wilde is particularly hostile to Arnold's polemic on behalf of 'disinterestedness' and objectivity in critical practice: '[The] more strongly [...] personality enters into the interpretation, the more real the interpretation becomes, the more satisfying, the more convincing, and the more true' (877). Much contemporary 'reader-oriented' theory is equally convinced that criticism is neither desirable, or even perhaps possible, if the text is approached with a mind which attempts to be truly 'open' or innocent, even if such a state could ever actually be attained. In this respect 'The Critic as Artist' foreshadows Gadamer's rehabilitation of prejudice in *Truth and Method* (1960), where it is seen as a precondition of understanding and, indeed, a primary means of articulating an historically grounded critical response.[9]

Wilde goes beyond Gadamer, however, in proceeding to suggest that criticism also necessarily involves a calculated 'misreading' of the text in hand. Far from trying to 'see the object as in itself it really is', as mainstream critics from Arnold to Leavis have insisted is the critic's duty, 'The Critic as Artist' claims that criticism 'need not necessarily bear any obvious resemblance to the thing it criticises' (874). Instead, Gilbert encourages the reader to recreate the object and put it into 'a form that is at once new and delightful [...] no ignoble considerations of probability [...] affect it ever' (872). This element of Gilbert's argument can be viewed as an early version of the contemporary theory of 'misprision', powerfully argued in Harold Bloom's *The Anxiety of Influence* (1973) and *A Map of Misreading* (1975).[10]

The pre-eminent place given to the reader's involvement in producing the text governs Wilde's evaluative hierarchies for the arts. Wilde privileges 'decorative' forms which tend to both foreground their status as art and engage the reader more deeply in constructing their meaning. Music is paradigmatic of the highest art because its meaning is always 'indefinite' (858). Poetry is preferred to prose and within prose, romance and fantasy are set above the novel. And the more 'realistic' novels are, the lower they are in the scale. Literary realists are 'far too intelligible [...] they do not stir the imagination, but set definite bounds to it' (874-5). In discriminating between art which invites the reader's active participation from that which constrains the reader, Wilde again anticipates contemporary 'reader-oriented' theory. Barthes's distinction in *S/Z* between 'readerly' and 'writerly' texts, or that between 'rhetorical' and 'dialectical' works in Stanley Fish's *Self-Consuming Artefacts* (1972), similarly subvert traditional notions of the text's unity and self-sufficiency, and the artist's authority as guide to the work's meaning, in order to emphasise the reader's productive role in constructing the text.

The principal problem faced by 'reader-oriented' theory has been the question of where, if at all, the limits of the reader's freedom are to be drawn. The danger, in Freund's view, is to progressively enfranchise the reader 'until the irksome dichotomy of reader/text is abolished by the assimilation of the text into the reader or the reader into the text. The outcome of this turn of events is to undermine the reader-response project, for when the discrete concepts of "reader" and "text" lose their specific difference the *raison d'être* for both a *text*-centred and a *reader-* or *self*-centred criticism is undone.'[11]

Many 'reader-oriented' theorists have sought to prevent their project collapsing by counterbalancing the freedom they seek on the reader's behalf with a variety of normative models of 'literary competence'. Richards's 'Good Sense', Culler's 'ideal reader', Ingarden's distinction between 'adequate' and 'inadequate' concretisations, Fish's model of 'interpretive communities' — all are designed to avoid the critical anarchy inherent in totally enfranchising the reader. At times, Wilde appears to reject any such constraints; Gilbert bluntly asserts that criticism is 'the purest form of personal impression' (872) and 'is in its essence purely subjective' (873).

But, in practice, Wilde seems well aware that this argument threatens the project of criticism itself. Since, in the end, criticism must always be of something, or it ceases to be criticism, the essays backtrack, readmitting norms of interpretation which they were ostensibly aiming to abolish.

For example, having sought to abolish the author as a standard by which to interpret the work, Gilbert reinstates him, to some degree, as a constraint, since one of the purposes of criticism is 'to realise the experiences of those who are greater than we are. The pain of Leopardi crying out against life becomes our pain' (883). Similarly, having just insisted that criticism 'is no more to be judged by any low standard of imitation or resemblance than is the work of the poet or sculptor' (871), Gilbert withdraws: 'Some resemblance, no doubt, the creative work of the critic will have to the work that has stirred him to creation' (875).

The readerly competence such constraints help define is not, for Wilde, the product of an 'interpretive community' understood in the narrow sense of the academic institution. In the formation of the critical sensibility, 'the dullness of tutors and professors matters very little' (891). Nonetheless, his frequent allusions to the 'elect' imply the existence of a group whose norms in practice provide a framework for the interpretive process. For the 'elect', critical competence begins with exposure from an early age to the beautiful in all its forms and is, according to 'Pen, Pencil and Poison', 'made perfect by frequent contact with the best work' (847). This facilitates internalisation of the best principles of aesthetic form: 'The harmony that resides in the delicate proportions of lines and masses becomes mirrored in the mind [...] the marvels of design stir the imagination. In the mere loveliness of the materials employed there are latent elements of culture' (892).

Such an education, according to Gilbert, will develop 'that unnerring instinct that reveals to one all things under their condition of beauty' (893). But 'instinct', it transpires, must be complemented by a formidable amount of contextual knowledge relating to the work in question. If, as 'Pen, Pencil and Poison' argues, 'the first step in aesthetic criticism is to realise one's own impressions' (847), the second involves something much more conventional. Thus in 'The Portrait of Mr

W. H.', we find Cyril Graham attempting to complete his initial 'synthetic' impression of the true identity of W. H. by corroboration from the sonnets themselves, with all the subordination to biographical, textual and historical evidence that this implies. 'The Critic as Artist' sets exacting standards for this second kind of response which it terms 'analytic' criticism (876):

> And he who desires to understand Shakespeare truly must understand the relations in which Shakespeare stood to the Renaissance and the Reformation, to the age of Elizabeth and the age of James; he must be familiar with the history of the struggle for supremacy between the old classical forms and the new spirit of romance, between the school of Sidney, and Daniel, and Johnson, and the school of Marlowe and Marlowe's greater son; he must know the materials that were at Shakespeare's disposal and the method in which he used them, and the conditions of theatric presentation in the sixteenth and seventeenth century, their limitations and their opportunities for freedom, and the literary criticism of Shakespeare's day, its aims and modes and canons; he must study the English language in its progress, and blank or rhymed verse in its various developments; he must study the Greek drama, and the connection between the art of the creator of the Agamemnon and the art of the creator of Macbeth; in a word, he must be able to bind Elizabethan London to the Athens of Pericles, and to learn Shakespeare's true position in the history of European drama and the drama of the world. (886-7)

Far from being totally free in his interpretation, as this formidable series of prerequisites suggests, the reader is now constituted as a series of 'pre-understandings' which are necessary to adequate response. In this light, the competent reader can now be seen to embody a whole series of cultural codes which are called into play by the text, so that while the text was formerly seen as something constituted by the reader, the reader now appears to be 'produced' by the text.

By following the 'swerve' to the reader to the end of its trajectory, Wilde inevitably returns to the position he started from. In Freund's view such self-cancellation typifies modern 'reader-oriented' theory as well. Its 'complex and interminable dialectic [...] persists in trying — but repeatedly fails — to negotiate the question whether reading is a transitive or intransitive verb: does the reader control the text or does the text control the reader?'.[12] But if Wilde is no more successful than many contemporary theorists in escaping this aporia, his foundational attempt to turn the critical focus away from the text's relationship with author and world to its relationship with the reader nonetheless requires critical history to be rewritten. Archivists of modern 'reader-oriented' theory as various as Freund, Stanley Fish and Jane Tompkins, locate the origins of this critical tendency in the work of I. A. Richards.[13] I hope that I have shown that we should now more properly be looking to Wilde.

NOTES

1   R. Ellmann, 'The Critic as Artist as Wilde' in ed. H. Bloom, *Oscar Wilde* (New York, Chelsea House, 1985), p. 94.

2   E. Freund, *The Return of the Reader: Reader-Response Criticism* (London, Methuen, 1987), pp. 5-6.

3   Oscar Wilde, 'The Critic as Artist' in *The Complete Works of Oscar Wilde* (London, Hamlyn, 1963), p. 873. Further page references in text.

4   J. V. Harari, 'Critical Factions/Critical Fictions' in ed. J. V. Harari, *Textual Strategies: Perspectives in Post-Structuralist Criticism* (Ithaca, Cornell University Press, 1979), p. 70.

5   In his work of 1931, *The Literary Work of Art: An Investigation on the Borderlines of Ontology, Logic and Theory of Literature*, (Evanston, Northwestern University Press, 1973), Ingarden argues that all representations are, in contrast to real objects, characterised ontologically by 'spots of indeterminacy' (246-54). Thus 'we can say that [...] every literary work is in principle incomplete and always in need of supplementation' (251). Ingarden distinguishes between 'the purely literary work of art as it exists in itself, independent of its concretizations, and these concretizations. The literary work 'is a *schematic* formation in which [...] various elements persevere in a characteristic *potentiality* [...] only when the literary work of art attains *adequate* expression if a concretization is there — in an ideal case — *a full establishment, an intuitive exhibition, of all these qualities*' (372). In 'The Reading Process: A Phenomenological Approach', in ed. J. P. Tompkins, *Reader-Response Criticism* (London, Johns Hopkins University Press, 1980), W. Iser suggests that 'the reader [...] actually causes the text to reveal its potential multiplicity of connections. These connections are the product of the reader's mind working on the raw material of the text, though they are not the text itself — for this consists just of sentences, statements, information, etc' (p. 54). Iser illustrates the process thus: 'The "stars" in a literary text are fixed; the lines that join them are variable [...] thus, by reading we uncover the unformulated part of the text, and this very indeterminacy is the force that drives us to work out a configurative meaning while at the same time giving us the

necessary degree of freedom to do so' (pp. 57, 62). A much more detailed elaboration, with practical exemplification, is provided by Iser in *The Act of Reading: A Theory of Aesthetic Response* (London, Routledge, 1978).

6   See Ingarden, *The Literary Work of Art*, p. 341 and Iser, 'The Reading Process: A Phenomenological Approach', in ed. Tompkins, *Reader-Response Criticism*, p. 60.

7   Oscar Wilde, *The Picture of Dorian Gray* (Harmondsworth, Penguin, 1973), p. 159.

8   R. Barthes, *S/Z*, trans. R. Miller (London, Cape, 1975), p. 154.

9   In *Truth and Method*, second edition (London, Sheed & Ward, 1989), H.-G. Gadamer argues that 'the fundamental prejudice of the Enlightenment is the prejudice against prejudice itself' (p. 270). According to Gadamer it is in prejudice, which is social rather than private in character, that the historicality of the individual is articulated and he asks: 'Does understanding in the human sciences understand itself correctly when it relegates the whole of its historicality to the position of prejudices from which we must free ourselves?'(p. 282). If 'the hermeneutical situation is determined by the prejudices that we bring with us [and] constitute, then, the horizon of a particular present' (p. 306), it is not the task of criticism to efface these prejudices but rather to bring them out during the critical act, which then confronts the critic's 'horizon' with that of the work in question. Cf. Iser: 'The sacrifice of the real reader's own beliefs would mean the loss of the whole repertoire of historical norms and values, and this in turn would entail the loss of the tension which is a precondition for the processing and for the comprehension that follows it.' *The Act of Reading*, (p. 37).

10   Like Wilde, Bloom's *A Map of Misreading* (New York, Oxford University Press, 1975) deliberately blurs the categories of reader, critic and artist. Thus the 'misreading, or misprision, that one poet performs upon another [...] does not differ in kind from the necessary critical acts performed by every strong reader upon every text he encounters' (p. 3). According to Bloom every 'reader' belatedly faces the fullness of the text in question. If he is to originate a new text 'the poet-reader begins with a trope or defense that is a misreading [...] a poet interpreting his precursor, and any subsequent interpreter reading either poet, must *falsify* his reading' (p. 69). In this way 'an intolerable presence [the precursor's poem] has been voided, and the new poem [or critical act] starts in the *illusion* that this absence can deceive us into accepting a new presence' (p. 71). Bloom's argument here provides a revealing gloss on his own treatment of Wilde in *The Anxiety of Influence*, which is little less than critical parricide.

11   E. Freund, *Return of the Reader*, p. 10.

12   E. Freund, *Return of the Reader*, p. 104.

13   E. Freund, *Return of the Reader*, pp. 9 and 25; J. P. Tompkins, 'An Introduction to Reader-Response Criticism' in ed. Tompkins, *Reader-Response Criticism*, p. x; S. Fish, 'Literature in the Reader: Affective Stylistics' in ed. J. P. Tompkins, *Reader-Response Criticism*, p. 90.

OSCAR WILDE IN HIS LITERARY ELEMENT: YET ANOTHER SOURCE FOR *DORIAN GRAY*?

Isobel Murray

> The search for sources of Wilde's *The Picture of Dorian Gray* is unending, but here is another...
> Richard Ellmann

Wilde's culture, the medium in which he might be said to float, is a very rich and varied one, and he is always aware of it, as he is always aware of himself and his reader, constantly making open or covert reference to the marvellous and ever-flowing tradition in which he exercises his individual talent. He treats all the great writers he knows as in some sense his contemporaries, to whom he can bow in appreciation, or with whom he can continue to debate. He also treats many now little known writers of his own day, as cheerfully, as some kind of impetus or provocation to write.

This very catholicity — and perhaps his genial good humour — saved him from the patricidal urges Harold Bloom has seen as characteristic of the 'strong poet'. Interestingly, Bloom considers, discusses and rejects Wilde in the first pages of *The Anxiety of Influence*, before naming a single one of the 'strong poets' he means to write about. Does Wilde's nonconformity embarass modern theories of influence?

Undeterred by the question, I wish to investigate yet another source for *Dorian Gray*, perhaps the first significant female writer cited, apart from Speranza. Louisa May Alcott is currently claimed by Elaine Showalter as producing 'the American female myth' in *Little Women*, but her more sensational, often pseudonymous novels have less to offer as feminist models. *A Modern Mephistopheles* was first published in 1877, before Huysmans published *A Rebours*. It was published under the author's name for the first time posthumously in 1889. I suggest it had a significant part in the mysterious process of 'inspiring' *Dorian Gray*, and in particular that her character Jasper Helwyze, who dominates the handsome younger man Felix Canaris, has a significant power of suggestion for Lord Henry Wotton, mentor of Dorian Gray.

Wilde had met Alcott in New York, where they were fellow guests of honour at a reception, in 1882, five years after she first published *A Modern Mephistopheles* anonymously.[1] While he is unlikely to have had any suspicion of her double life as A. M. Barnard, writer of lurid sensation stories full of *femmes fatales*, revenge, and opium or hashish experiences, he is likely to have been aware of her prodigious writing output under her own name, which included a serious novel called *Work* (1872) as well as torrents for female juveniles. He also inevitably knew *of* her, of her father Bronson Alcott's Transcendentalism, and his friendship with Emerson, Hawthorne and Thoreau. Whether or not they discussed it on 8 January 1882, Alcott and Wilde shared a passionate and lifelong admiration for Emerson, whom Alcott had described as 'the god of my idolatry', and whom Wilde quoted, echoed and elaborated on throughout his writing life.[2] But on this occasion Oscar soon deserted Alcott for the actress Clara Morris, whom he hoped to inveigle into a production of *Vera*: I suggest he only seriously encountered Alcott posthumously, in 1889, when a number of factors rendered him susceptible to the second edition of her novel *A Modern Mephistopheles*, the first with her authorship acknowledged. At this point the fact of her recent decease, combined with the fact that the novel was not being published for the first time, meant that it was not too celebrated: Wilde was able to find it inspirational without loud cries of 'Plagiarism!' from the fiction reviewers. This is clear from the fact that *Dorian Gray* was reviewed for *Lippincott's* by Nathaniel Hawthorne's son Julian, who had been raised in the same Transcendental circles as Alcott. He immediately succumbed to the temptation of source-hunting, and cited Balzac, Stevenson, Disraeli and Bulwer-Lytton, with no mention of Alcott, although he describes Lord Henry as 'a charming, gentle, witty, euphemistic Mephistopheles'.[3]

I cannot establish for sure that Wilde did not read this novel when it first appeared in 1877, in the new 'No Name Series', or in the intervening years: but there is no reason to suppose that he did. By 1889 its very title must have been attractive to Wilde, who was in some stage of pre-composition of 'The Fisherman and His Soul' and *Dorian Gray*, both variations on the Faustian theme. And the writer's name, given in 1889, would have its own interest in such an unexpected context. The first few pages would strike chords. Alcott's novel opens with a dramatic scene in which a desperately disappointed young writer attempts suicide, destroying himself along with his manuscript in a haze of charcoal fumes. The pathetic situation of the young writer is one Wilde had touched on himself in 'The Happy Prince', where the Prince sends the Swallow with one of his emerald eyes to save a beautiful young playwright in a garret, too cold and hungry to write more. It also reminded Wilde inevitably of this situation acted out in real life: on 9 September 1889 Amy Levy, perhaps the most talented of the young writers Wilde had encouraged to write for *The Woman's World*, had taken her own life in the same way, aged only 27. It was on 17 December 1889 that J. M. Stoddart of *Lippincott's* received a letter from Wilde:

> I have invented a new story, which is better than 'The Fisherman and his Soul', and I am quite ready to set to work at once on it. It will be ready by the end of March.[4]

I have suggested elsewhere that, whatever other inspirations fed Wilde's imagination, Edward Heron-Allen's *Suicide of Sylvester Gray* came to hand at a very timely hour, when Wilde was committing himself to the novel, and gave him some suggestions, particularly for his creation and treatment of Dorian.[5] And similarly I wish now to show that Alcott's *A Modern Mephistopheles*, newly published for the first time under her own name, supplied him, in the character of Jasper Helwyze, with a very suggestive model for Lord Henry Wotton.

The novel has had very little attention. Where American feminist critics have reinstated *Little Women* as the 'American feminist myth', and found in some readings of the

sensation stories with dangerous women characters themes of
authorial frustration and rebellion, the Gladys of *A Modern
Mephistopheles* has no such appeal.[6] Innocent, candid and
'born for self-sacrifice', she combines the missionary attributes
of David Copperfield's Agnes, always pointing upward, with
the girlish attractions of the heroine of Crockett's *The Lilac
Sunbonnet*, the all-too-appropriately named Winsome
Charteris.[7]

I suggest that the title of the novel points us accurately
to its central concern — not the young man performing Faust's
role, nor the young woman cast as Margaret, but the callous and
ultimately wicked figure who shadows Goethe's
Mephistopheles, Jasper Helwyze. (Nothing over-subtle in the
choice of his name, any more than there was with Felix
Canaris, the happy young man with associations of happiness,
bright colour, soft feathers, singing and gold.)

Nonetheless, Wilde respected it enough to learn from
it, I contend. And since it is particularly hard to come by, let me
describe it, briefly, with particular reference to aspects Wilde
was to echo. The first chapter is not only dramatic, but
extremely pared down and economical. The poignant scene of
the suicide of young Felix Canaris is interrupted by Jasper
Helwyze, and juxtaposed with a happy scene only a month
later in Helwyze's home, a place of luxury and culture, taste
and discrimination, where Felix has regained his spirits and
the fullness of his beauty.

Alcott is determined the reader should not miss the
Faustian point. The book's epigraph is from the very end of
Goethe's *Faust*:

> The Indescribable,
> Here it is done:
> The Woman-Soul leadeth us
> Upward and on!

And hints of the true nature and identity of Helwyze abound.
His first words, as he enters the suicide chamber are, 'The
devil!'. When the youth pleads, 'for God's sake, stay!' he
replies, already sounding like a prefiguring of Lord Henry, 'for
my own sake, rather: I want excitement.' Again on the next page
Felix asks, 'what good angel sent you, sir?' and is informed,

'your bad angel, you might say, since it was the man who damned your book' (*MM* 10). Alcott employs the pervasive theatrical metaphors that are also a feature of *Dorian Gray*:

> The stranger read the little tragedy at a glance, and found the chief actor to his taste; for despite his hard case he possessed beauty, youth, and the high aspirations that die hard, — three gifts often peculiarly attractive to those who have lost them all. (*MM* 11)

Inside five short pages we have learned much of the basic situation. Then comes the translation to the 'noble library' and 'a dream of luxury'. We are not allowed to forget *Faust* — Helwyze has a copy in his hand — but we are invited to admire Felix, who was 'scarcely less beautiful than the Narcissus in the niche behind him': a connection frequently made in *Dorian Gray*. He is in short:

> a wonderfully attractive young man, whose natural ease and elegance fitted him to adorn that charming place, as well as to enjoy the luxury his pleasure-loving senses craved. (*MM* 15)

Helwyze muses over his Goethe:

> Youth surely *is* the beauty of the devil, and that boy might have come straight from the witches' kitchen and the magic draught.

And at once we are alerted to his plan to dominate Felix:

> Of all the visions haunting his ambitious brain not one is so wild and wayward as the fancy which haunts mine. Why not play fate, and finish what I have begun? (*MM* 15)

This foreshadows Lord Henry's musings about Dorian in Chapter III of Wilde's novel:

> He was a marvellous type, too, [...] or could be fashioned into a marvellous type, at any rate. There was nothing that one could not do with him. [...] He would seek to dominate him — had already, indeed, half done so. He would make that wonderful spirit his own. (*OAOW* 75)

Helwyze is not, like Lord Henry, the first to make his victim conscious of his own beauty — Felix is already vain, and responds to compliments. But what Helwyze temptingly offers, in return for 'a year of your liberty', is the chance of fame. Felix is intensely susceptible, as we see in his fervent response, delivered with 'passionate energy'; a speech surely parallel in many ways to the mysterious and crucial 'prayer' that Dorian utters over the picture:

> You have divined my longing. I do hunger and thirst for fame; I dream of it by night, I sigh for it by day; every thought and aspiration centres in that desire; and if I did not still cling to that hope, even the perfect home you offer me would seem a prison. I *must* have it; the success men covet and admire, suffer and strive for, and die content if they win it only for a little time. Give me this and I am yours, body and soul; I have nothing else to offer. (*MM* 17)

They shake hands on it, and the pact is made. Alcott continues the economy of this first chapter. She introduces two female characters, the young Gladys and the still-beautiful Olivia, formerly faithless mistress to Helwyze and now his emotional slave, but she keeps the narrative simple. Most of the chapters concern just two characters. So Chapter II sees Felix's thoughtless wooing of Gladys in an idyllic garden setting. Felix's beauty and sensuousness are repeatedly underlined:

> Too beautiful for a man he was, and seemed to protest against it by a disdainful negligence of all the arts which could enhance the gracious gift. A picturesque carelessness marked his costume, the luxuriant curls that covered his head were in riotous confusion; and as he came into the light he stretched his limbs with the graceful abandon of a young wood-god rousing from his drowse in some green covert. (*MM* 20)

For most of the novel Felix remains a heartless, self-sufficient 'beautiful boy', of the kind described by Camille Paglia as 'one of the west's most stunning sexual personae',[8] and only the tragic loss of his wife and baby will finally teach him what Gladys in her lifetime had begun, — teaching him 'to love her with the love in which self bears no part' (*MM* 231). So clearly he is not a close model for Dorian Gray, either as heartless boy or as true lover.

In this chapter Felix tells Gladys of his past despair, and how 'when he called on death, Helwyze came' (*MM* 27).

Unaware that Helwyze is eavesdropping, Felix goes on to confide his master's secrets. His past is the tale of 'a wonderfully free, rich life' until age thirty, then 'a terrible fall'. The ambiguity is important, but the fall has been physical, whatever else, and Helwyze has had ten years of daily pain and will suffer another ten if his 'indomitable will' holds out (*MM* 29).

This provision of some kind of 'excuse' for Helwyze's behaviour seems to me to weaken it: compassion for his suffering can confuse the reader's attitude to the cold-blooded cruelty of his manipulations. Certainly Wilde did not choose to adopt any alibi for Lord Henry, and I find *Dorian Gray* the stronger for this reason.

In Chapter III Helwyze and Olivia spell out in conversation the possibility of comparing Faust and Margaret, Mephistopheles and Martha with Felix and Gladys, Helwyze and Olivia. Further Helwyze declares that 'the accidental reading of my favourite tragedy, at a certain moment, gave me a hint which has afforded amusement for a year' (*MM* 36). Like Lord Henry, Helwyze enjoys being a spectator of life, and also yields to the temptation to intervene and manipulate. 'The danger is the charm. I crave excitement, occupation.' Olivia intuits that Felix is bound to Helwyze by fear, but Helwyze complacently describes him as a Greek slave — 'I bought my handsome Alcibiades, and an excellent bargain I find him' (*MM* 38). Olivia again intuits that Helwyze will tire of Felix — implicitly as his boyish good looks fade — but in that case, returns Helwyze, he will give the boy to her as 'a charming plaything'. In return, he asks her to give him Gladys.

There are a number of passages in this chapter which underline Helwyze's curiosity and need for amusement, and also his willingness to interfere and mould lives, and his enjoyment of manipulation. He declares: 'I promise myself much satisfaction in observing how this young creature [Gladys] meets the trials and temptations life and love will bring her' (*MM* 41). He has no fears of Gladys, because she is so young: 'I can mould her as I please, and that suits me.' And when Olivia warns Gladys may influence Felix, he is unimpressed and full of further plans:

> Felix suits me excellently, and it will only add another charm to
> the relation if I control him through the medium of another. My
> young lion is discovering his power rapidly, and I must give him
> a Una before he breaks loose and chooses for himself. If matters
> must be complicated, I choose to do it, and it will occupy my
> winter pleasantly to watch the success of this new combination.
> (*MM* 44-5)

Perhaps most telling here is a passage containing
images of playing people like stringed instruments, which
seems to stand behind Lord Henry's meditation in Chapter III
of *Dorian Gray*, which begins: 'Talking to him was like playing
upon an exquisite violin. He answered to every touch and thrill
of the bow' (*OAOW* 74-5). When Dorian falls in love, Lord
Henry is conscious — with pleasure —

> that it was through certain words of his, musical words said
> with musical utterance, that Dorian Gray's soul had turned to
> this white girl and bowed in worship before her. To a large
> extent the lad was his own creation. (*OAOW* 91)

Alcott already had a recurrent image of Helwyze as unnatural
musician:

> Leaning in the low, lounging chair, Helwyze had listened
> motionless, except that the fingers of one thin hand moved
> fitfully, as if he played upon some instrument inaudible to all
> ears but his own. A frequent gesture of his, and most significant,
> to any one who knew that his favourite pastime was touching
> human heart-strings with marvellous success in producing
> discords by his uncanny skill. (*MM* 40)

We will see these fingers moving again at important points in
the narrative.[9] Dorian Gray, we recall, was early susceptible to
the hands of Lord Henry Wotton:

> His cool, white, flower-like hands, even, had a curious charm.
> They moved, as he spoke, like music, and seemed to have a
> language of their own. But he felt afraid of him, and ashamed of
> being afraid. (*OAOW* 63-4)

The long conversation with Olivia serves to establish
her, as under Helwyze's domination but still insightful, and
morally aware. Helwyze stresses his aims to her:

> Yes; to study the mysterious mechanism of human nature is a most absorbing pastime, when books weary, and other sources of enjoyment are forbidden. Try it, and see what an exciting game it becomes, when men and women are the pawns you learn to move at will. (*MM* 46)

Olivia here highlights Helwyze's lack of conscience, and does not hesitate to warn, to disapprove, and to use striking condemnatory imagery. Helwyze's intended subjugation of Gladys she sees as vivisection. This image is also used of Lord Henry in *Dorian Gray*: 'and so he had begun by vivisecting himself, as he had ended by vivisecting others' (*OAOW* 90). Olivia tells Helwyze:

> In your hands she will be as helpless as the dumb creatures surgeons torture, that they may watch a living nerve, count the throbbing of an artery, or see how long the poor things will live bereft of some vital part. Let the child alone, Jasper, or you will repent of it. (*MM* 47)

And it is possible to read Gladys' early death as stemming indeed from Helwyze's debilitating intervention in her life.

The rest of the book can be more briefly sketched. In Chapter IV Helwyze requires Felix to marry. Marriage, says Helwyze, anticipating Lord Henry, 'need not change your life, except to make it freer, perhaps happier' (*MM* 53), and he argues that it will ensure that Felix will continue to enjoy public attention. At this, Felix succumbs to the tempter, with the recurrent image of musical instrument in the hands of a musician: 'as a skilful hand touched the various chords that vibrated most tunefully in a young, imaginative, ardent nature' (*MM* 56). Helwyze wishes Felix to marry Gladys, with whom he has been casually flirting, while she has fallen deeply and permanently in love with him: but Felix is currently infatuated with the older Olivia. Helwyze is almost totally convinced that Olivia will spurn the young man, so allows him to speak: 'therefore you are free to try your fate before you grant my whim and make Gladys happy' (*MM* 59). Helwyze is left alone to muse, 'suspense is a new emotion; I will enjoy it' (*MM* 61).

Helwyze persuades Gladys to work for him as sick man's companion, and, gently ridiculed by Olivia, Felix returns to courting Gladys, though he does not love her; all of this with intermittent interventions from Helwyze, who 'sat as if at a play' watching the 'pretty postoral [*sic*] enacted before him' (*MM* 80). This is the same deadly metaphor — and the same deadly attitude — that we see in Lord Henry, when he successfully persuades Dorian to regard Sibyl Vane's death as no more than a scene in a play (*OAOW* 123-5).

It is perhaps time to remind the reader that I am not concerned here to trace some single direct line of influence from Alcott's novel to *Dorian Gray*, but rather to indicate that her novel is one of a range of 'influences' available to Wilde at the time of composition. Any reader might well prefer to see Balzac, for example, as a 'source' here. Balzac was one of Wilde's favorite writers, and Lucien de Rubempré one of his all-time favorite characters. The character of Dorian clearly owes more to Lucien than to Felix.[10]

Felix does occasionally suffer from better feelings, but his love of luxury and his subjection to Helwyze carry the day, and when he thinks Helwyze may marry the girl himself he hastens 'to make his own the thing another seemed to covet' (*MM* 91). Gladys loves him, and determines to convert him, but Helwyze mocks his half-hearted efforts to act honourably by her, as Lord Henry will mock Dorian over his good resolutions about Hetty Merton: 'Marry when and how you please, only do not annoy me with another spasm of virtue' (*MM* 99). He similarly quenches Felix's 'noble emotion' later, recognizing 'the old passion under a new name. May your virtuous aspirations be blest!' (*MM* 116).

As Alcott develops the character of Helwyze, it is important to remember that her novel predates not only *Dorian Gray* but also Huysmans' *A Rebours* (published 1884), for Helwyze has traits in common with Des Esseintes, beyond their sharing delicate health, as well as with Lord Henry and the maturely corrupted Dorian. The housebound Helwyze has created different ambiances for himself, as Des Esseintes will do more elaborately:

> Here and there she came upon some characteristic whim or arrangement, which made her smile with amusement, or sigh with pity, remembering the recluse who tried to cheer his solitude by these devices. One recess held a single picture glowing with the warm splendour of the east. A divan, a

Persian rug, an amber-mouthed *nargileh*, and a Turkish coffee service, all gold and scarlet, completed the illusion. (*MM* 105)

Helwyze's collected treasures ('rich stuffs, curious coins, and lovely ornaments') also predate those of Des Esseintes. But little Gladys is hard to corrupt: although tempted by luxury, she is armoured in faith and her love for Felix. She successively refuses a beautiful gauzy scarf, a bracelet carved with the Nine Muses, and 'a collection of Hindoo gods and goddesses' (*MM* 129), and goes on to defend her beliefs earnestly against Helwyze's total lack of belief. Gladys is neither reflected nor developed in *Dorian Gray*, except that her Christian name is used for the Duchess of Monmouth,[11] unless she is seen perhaps as one aspect of Sibyl Vane, who appears so fleetingly, and might have been an influence for good. Dorian told Lord Henry that Sybil's voice made him forget 'you and all your wrong, fascinating, poisonous, delightful theories' (*OAOW* 105). In *A Modern Mephistopheles* the girl continues to strive for the hero's soul, and saves him at last, Beatrice-like, from beyond the grave.

Gladys's moral force wins a curious battle in Chapter X, when she insists the new poem should be re-written so that the hero does not die ignominiously but 'ends by living well'. In the event, this is what happens, both in the poem and in the novel as a whole — but ironically Gladys is quite unaware that the poem she admires so much is written (and rewritten) by Helwyze, not her husband. One more 'advance echo' here: when the poem has been read aloud, and Helwyze asks if it should be destroyed, as Felix had first suggested, Gladys says emphatically, 'it would be like burning a live thing' (*MM* 149). Only a short step from here to Dorian defending his portrait against Basil's knife and exclaiming, 'don't, Basil, don't! It would be murder!' (*OAOW* 68).

By this time, what was serviceable to Wilde in the novel has really been covered, although some of it will be repeated. In the part of the story Wilde ignores as unsuitable for his purpose, Felix overcomes temptations and begins to love Gladys, but is only saved from an overwhelming temptation to murder Helwyze in his sleep by Gladys's intervention. At last he confesses his secret shame to her, acknowledging that

Helwyze is the true author of the highly praised poems of Felix Canaris. Helwyze, whose chief characteristic is after all curiosity, administers hashish to the unsuspecting Gladys, and thus releases a much more ardent young woman, who presents tableaux and songs with Olivia, singing unusually passionately and in (for her) a state of near undress. At last Helwyze does 'an evil thing' (*MM* 204). 'He deliberately violated the sanctuary of a human soul': he forces Gladys in her tranced state to admit that she and Felix will be free only when Helwyze dies, and that she fears his growing love for her. In the end Gladys's baby dies and she follows him to Heaven, pausing only to require that Felix and Helwyze forgive each other, and to remind Felix that after he pursues his destiny of 'living well' she and the baby will be waiting for him. She is also seen in Tennysonian terms, while Helwyze is compared to Hawthorne's Roger Chillingworth.[12]

Helwyze's punishment is unmeasurable. He now truly loves Gladys, and has lost her to Felix in this life and to a Heaven he cannot believe in in the next: so as he says, his life changes from Purgatory to Hell. Moreover, the ruthless author visits him with a paralytic stroke, and he hears the doctor's verdict — that it may take years, but that his brain will eventually be destroyed also.

So if one were to attempt to summarize Wilde's temporary engagement with and attachment to *A Modern Mephistopheles*, it might be something like this. The most important way in which the Alcott novel offers suggestion to the author of *The Picture of Dorian Gray* is in her development of the character of Jasper Helwyze. Whether or not he has read Pater (and we are not told, although he possesses many books the narrator lists as potentially dangerous to Gladys), he is certainly 'for ever curiously testing new opinions and courting new impressions'. His chosen role as spectator of life, his enjoyment of influence over others, his obsessive curiosity, potentially fatal to his chosen specimens, are all destined to appear again to some extent in Lord Henry Wotton.

But if Helwyze is inspirational for Lord Henry, Wilde changes the character crucially. Most centrally, while Helwyze uses Felix and Gladys as his specimens for observation, and plans to manipulate their lives for his amusement, Lord Henry goes further. He teaches Dorian Gray not only about his youth and beauty and their brevity, and the New Hedonism: he teaches Dorian to take up spectatorship himself, to view Sibyl's death as merely 'a strange lurid fragment from some Jacobean tragedy, as a wonderful scene from Webster, or Ford, or Cyril Tourneur' (*OAOW* 125). For this reason the books soon part company, for in *A Modern Mephistopheles* Helwyze remains the most important and interesting character, while in *Dorian Gray* the centre shifts from Lord Henry to the developing Dorian himself, and is concerned to chart his corruption, by Lord Henry's doctrines, by the beauty of the portrait, by the 'poison book' that completes the process. So the focus is very different. In *A Modern Mephistopheles*, there is a longterm antagonism and rivalry between Jasper Helwyze and Felix Canaris, which develops into their rivalry for Gladys, unspoken but menacing in Helwyze's case. No such rivalry exists in *Dorian Gray*, although the penultimate chapter seems to demonstrate the limitations of friendship between two such egotists, and the account of Dorian's progress is more concentrated and convincing.

NOTES

1   See L. Lewis and H. J. Smith, *Oscar Wilde Discovers America*, New York, 1936 repr. 1964, pp. 44-45.

2   Alcott quoted in E. Showalter, *Sister's Choice: Tradition and Change in American Women's Writing*, Oxford, 1991, p. 44. See I. Murray, 'Oscar Wilde and Individualism: Contexts for *The Soul of Man*', in *Durham University Journal*, Vol. LXXXIII, No 2, July 1991, pp. 202-207.

3   See K. Beckson (ed.), *Oscar Wilde: The Critical Heritage*, 1970, pp. 79-80.

4   R. Hart-Davis (ed), *More Letters of Oscar Wilde*, 1985, p. 87.

5   See my Introduction to the Oxford English Novels edition of *The Picture of Dorian Gray*, 1974, pp. xxi-xxiv.

6   Alcott scholarship and criticism are mushrooming. For the basics, see M. Stern (ed.) *Behind a Mask: The Unknown Thrillers of Louisa May Alcott* (1975), and *Plots and Counterplots: More Unknown Thrillers of Louisa May Alcott* (1977). Elaine Showalter produced *Alternative Alcott*, a judicious selection of the writer's prolific output with an illuminating introduction in 1988, and wrote an introduction to *Little Women* which as '*Little Women*: The American Female Myth' became one of the Clarendon Lectures published in 1991 as *Sister's Choice*.

7   *A Modern Mephistopheles*, 1877, p. 31. Further references are given in brackets after quotations in the text as 'MM 00'. Because of its scarcity, this novel will be quoted much more often than *Dorian Gray*, but when Wilde's novel is quoted it will be in the Oxford Authors edition, and cited in the text as 'OAOW 00'. Where Alcott's novel *has* been noticed, attention has tended to focus on the Faust theme, where 'a young writer bargains with the Devil in order to become a famous poet' (*Alternative Alcott*, Introduction, p. xxxix), or on the scene where Helwyze deliberately administers opium or hashish to the innocent Gladys, and goes on to rape her mind of its worst fears. Apparently Alcott herself, lover of 'lurid style', was dependent on opiates.

8   C. Paglia, *Sexual Personae: Art and Decadence from Nefertiti to Emily Dickinson*, Harmondsworth, 1991, p. 15 and *passim*.

9   See *MM* 66 and 139.

10   In *Splendeurs et misères des courtisanes* (1847), Lucien's relationship to the dominant master criminal Vautrin foreshadows Dorian's with Lord Henry, and Felix's motivation resembles his: in *Les Illusions Perdues* (1843), a friend writes of him, 'Lucien would willingly sign a pact tomorrow with the devil himself if this pact promised him a few years of brilliance and luxury' (*Lost Illusions*, trans. H. J. Hunt, Harmondsworth, 1971, p. 510). And here, anticipating both Helwyze and Lord Henry, Vautrin declares, 'I myself love power for power's sake! I shall always be happy to see you enjoying the things which are forbidden to me. In short, I shall live in you!' (p. 650). Here too, Lucien's mistress Coralie is more suggestive for Sibyl Vane than the pious Gladys. Like Sibyl she is an actress, and in chapter 38 her love and her art are in conflict; she is 'unskilled in the insincerities common to actresses' and when she knows the reality of love she can no longer act it. See also *The Decay of Lying* (OAOW 222), and *Reviews* 1908, pp. 77-79.

11   If this is conscious and deliberate, it is surely as ironical as Lord Henry's erring and emotional wife, with her passion for pianists, sharing her Christian name with Queen Victoria.

12   Alcott's novel quotes Shelley, Spenser, Emerson and Aeschylus, as well as Goethe and Shakespeare. But the importance of Gladys's sexual purity is underlined by the tableaux from Tennyson's *Idylls* performed by Vivien and Gladys, the latter as the innocent Enid, the betraying Vivien, a devout novice and the deserted Elaine. And Gladys and Helwyze have a lengthy discussion of Roger Chillingworth in *The Scarlet Letter*, whom Gladys condemns for 'the unpardonable sin', quoting Hawthorne on 'the want of love and reverence for the human soul, which makes a man pry into its mysterious depths, [...] from a cold, philosophical curiosity' (*MM* 241).

EROS AND THANATOS IN
THE PICTURE OF DORIAN GRAY

Sylvia Ostermann

> Aesthetics are higher than ethics. They belong to a more
> spiritual sphere. To discern the beauty of a thing is the finest
> point to which we can arrive. Even a colour-sense is more
> important, in the development of the individual, than a sense of
> right and wrong.[1]

The one-sided determinations of Oscar Wilde as a dandy, as a
personification of a decadent life-style and fighter against
bourgeois conformism block the view of the integrated structure
of the novel. I shall try to point out that within the narrative
strategy there is a discourse on art and morality and a discourse
on the rigidity of Victorian sexual principles. Oscar Wilde
debunks the hypocritical sexual morality of the Victorians by a
concept of sublime eroticism. The relation of Eros and Thanatos
is revealed by the self-assertiveness of the androgynous
aesthete Dorian Gray who tries to legitimize his sexual
inversion by his aesthetic sensibility.

Eroticism, the longing for love, is a term for all
physical and spiritual shapes of love.[2] It includes the aspect of
sexual appeal as well as sensual pleasure. In so far eroticism
means, first of all, the art of love as an individual sublimation
of the instinctual. There is an artistic transformation of sexual
ambitions in behaviour, fashion, art and literature. In
particular this way eroticism works as a means of expression in
personal communication. The aim of erotic art of life is not the
difference between moral allowance and prohibition but the
experience of pleasure itself and its inherent qualities, its
refined perception and transformation.

Plato's idea of erotic fulfillment as a procreation
within the 'beautiful' has essentially determined Oscar
Wilde's representation of eroticism. Like Plato he proclaims an

erotic education that enables the personality to progress from a love of physical beauty to the love of a beautiful soul and finally to the performance of beauty itself which is equally the true and the good. Plato's theory of eros is the beginning of the history of the subject which discovers the truth of being in its desire. The turning from physical to spiritual eros, justified already by Plato, is excellently described in *The Picture of Dorian Gray*. Wilde's aestheticism was challenged by the idea that artistic creation, related to that contemplative life celebrated by Plato, was the highest form of action. In 'The Decay of Lying' Wilde points out 'that Life imitates Art far more than Art imitates Life',[3] and instead of art mirroring nature, nature mirrors art.[4] The preface to *Dorian Gray* declares: 'It is the spectator, and not life, that art really mirrors.'[5] The portrait is to mirror Dorian's external beauty but mirrors in fact his internal ugliness. In so far the novel mirrors Wilde's alienation from Victorian society. To create identity outside the bourgeois hierarchy of values was only possible in art or in an aesthetic sublimity of life. He always combines beauty with decay, joy with suffering. This is why I shall try to reveal the close relation of eros and death.

Wilde's enthusiasm for France with its climax of erotic lifestyle at the end of the eighteenth century was at the same time contrasted by the bourgeois ideal of marriage in Victorian England. The prevailing mood of puritanism with its theory of asceticism limited an erotic life. Erotic passion before or outside marriage was declared a moral guilt or sin which had to be punished. The limitation of erotic love to heterosexual relations resulted in a criminilization of homosexual practices. Homosexual ambitions were regarded as something pathological that had to be treated medically. The erotic art of early societies was replaced by a science of sexuality.

Oscar Wilde was a commited enemy of the prohibited and repressed erotic impulses he observed everywhere. The conception of *Dorian Gray* is determined by overstepping the mark concerning Wilde's own erotic behaviour. To show one's homoerotic relations in public or private resulted in a conviction of two years in England at the end of the 19th century.[6] It was the Criminal Law Amendment Act of 1885 which punished gross indecency between males, the same law that Oscar Wilde fell victim to ten years later. It is quite interesting that he used the theme of eroticism only in terms of unhappiness. The three main characters he declared as parts of his own identity:

> Basil Hallward is what I think I am: Lord Henry what the world thinks me: Dorian what I would like to be — in other ages, perhaps.[7]

Between the pictures, Basil Hallward had painted, and Dorian exists an autoerotic relation which is connected with the fear of growing older and the longing for eternal youth. The connection between death and eros is already indicated in the first two chapters. It reveals what Sigmund Freud later describes in terms of impulse of life and impulse of death, Eros and Thanatos. Consequently he develops types of libido, the erotic, the compulsive, and finally the narcissistic type. The last one is essentially negatively characterised. The excessive love or admiration for oneself favours being loved instead of loving.[8] In artistic anticipation Dorian Gray is both, the erotic and the narcissistic type. Particularly the wish of being loved is the main force of life which is combined with an immense potential of aggression:[9] 'Youth is the only thing worth having. When I find that I am growing old, I shall kill myself', said Dorian.[10] When Basil in a dark premonition is going to destroy the picture he is prevented by Dorian: 'Don't Basil, don't! [...] It would be murder! [...] I am in love with it, [...]. It is part of myself' (*DG*, 27).

The picture becomes the idealised object of his desire of eternal youth. To be loved by Basil means nothing to him compared with his self-love. When Basil confesses his love to Lord Henry: 'He [Dorian] is absolutely necessary to me [...] if you only knew what Dorian Gray is to me!' (*DG*, 14), and 'my life as an artist depends on him' (*DG*, 17), Dorian transforms Lord Henry's theory of new Hedonism into life: 'Be always searching for new sensations. Be afraid of nothing [...]. A new Hedonism — that is what our century wants' (*DG*, 23).

Dorian tries to live out practically the pure theoretical statements of Lord Henry:

> The aim of life is self-development. To realize one's nature
> perfectly — that is what each of us is here for. People are afraid
> of themselves, nowadays. They have forgotten the highest of all
> duties, the duty that one owes to one's self.
> (*DG*, 19)

Dorian is not afraid and he realizes the Hellenic ideal to give
free rein to one's natural impulses, because 'the only way to get
rid of a temptation is to yield to it' (*DG*, 20). Here already the
subversive thought is revealed, that renunciation to the erotic
instinct is closely connected with an increase in destructive
power.

With the Sibyl-Vane action the misanthropic
influence of Lord Henry becomes obvious. The aim of the
aesthetic programme is pleasure and self-development by
intensifying the ability to experience and to enjoy oneself.
Dorian is fascinated by the actress not by the woman Sibyl
Vane. In art her beauty is absolute, in life she is nothing to
Dorian. Art is confronted with life, beauty with love. Art and
beauty are the highest values of experience despite the moral
responsibility and contrasted to life and love. According to
Walter Pater the intensification of experience can only be
achieved by art: 'for art comes to you professing frankly to give
nothing but the highest quality to your moments as they pass,
and simply for those moments' sake.'[11] Love is not intended, but
the sublimity of the senses. What Walter Pater suggested is
realized in Dorian's thinking after the suicide of Sibyl Vane:

> Its aim, indeed, was to be experience itself, and not the fruits of
> experience, sweet or bitter as they might be. Of the asceticism
> that deadens the senses, as of the vulgar profligacy that dulls
> them, it was to know nothing. But it was to teach man to
> concentrate himself upon the moments of a life that is itself but a
> moment. (*DG*, 101)

Sin itself is not criticised but regarded as an extension of
experience: 'Sin is the only real colour-element left in modern
life' (*DG*, 28).

The love of Sibyl Vane, according to Dorian, is in its
end 'vulgar profligacy' that had to be repressed and forgotten.
Eros and death are closely connected here too. Only the picture
reflects Dorian's immorality and he enjoys it. In spite of

recognizing Lord Henry's poisonous theory, Dorian is enthralled by it. Dorian's remorse and sadness after Sibyl's death is dominated by Lord Henry's idea of goodness: 'When we are happy we are always good, but when we are good we are not always happy' (*DG*, 63). That is nearly the same idea that Walter Pater proclaimed: 'One is not always happy when one is good; but one is always good when one is happy.'[12] The death of Sibyl Vane does not really affect him:

> It seems to me to be simply like a wonderful ending to a wonderful play. It has the terrible beauty of a Greek tragedy, a tragedy in which I took a great part, but by which I have not been wounded. (*DG*, 80)

Dorian's increasing egotism is in fact the unconscious fear of death. The longing for curious sensations is fulfilled for a moment, which is underlined by Lord Henry who wished that he had ever had such an experience (*DG*, 80) and that there is something to him quite beautiful about her death (*DG*, 81).

The cynical valuation of that death is accompanied by Lord Henry's image of women who 'appreciate cruelty [...] more than anything else [...]. We have emancipated them, but they remain slaves looking for their masters [...]. They love being dominated' (*DG*, 81). That Lord Henry knows nothing about women and their longing to emancipate themselves from male dominated values is quite obvious. His contempt for women is a universal misanthropic attitude and finally a contempt of himself. The destructive power of such an attitude is underlined by the fact that he is left by his wife. An ethic of difference is alien to his nature, because it requires to acknowledge the specific male and female perspective including the different erotic pleasure and body-consciousness.[13] Love is stylized to art itself. Basil's passionate love for Dorian is revealed in a sublime eroticism:

> The love that he bore him [...] had nothing in it that was not noble and intellectual. It was not the mere physical admiration of beauty that is born of the senses, and that dies when the senses tire. It was such love as Michael Angelo had known. (*DG*, 93)

Despite the fact that Dorian recognized this real love, it is too late for him. His moral profligacy with its destructive potential has gone already too far. With the 'yellow book' (*DG*, 96) Lord Henry dominates Dorian completely. Dorian refines his erotic appeal by the perfection of external beauty what the narrator comments: 'Like Gautier, he was one for whom "the visible world existed" [...] to him life itself was the first [...] of the arts' (*DG*, 100). Fashion and Dandyism were an attempt 'to assert the absolute modernity of beauty' (*DG*, 100). His eroticism is increasingly determined by an uncertain feeling of death:

> To him, man was a being with myriad lives and myriad sensations, a complex multiform creature that bore within itself strange legacies of thought and passion, and whose very flesh was tainted with the monstrous maladies of the dead. (*DG*, 111)

The inner decay is irresistible. The homicide of Basil is a horrible crime after that he felt strangely calm. In view of his beauty he still feels the terrible pleasure of a double life. But eros and death fight against each other: 'His soul [...] was sick to death' (*DG*, 142). Ugliness that had been hateful to him he realizes now as 'the one reality [...] more vivid [...] than all the gracious shapes of Art' (*DG*, 143).

According to his teacher Lord Henry, Dorian 'never searched for happiness', he 'searched for pleasure' (*DG*, 151) only. As he confessed, he found it too often, and lost at the same time his libido expressed by the desire: 'I wish I could love' (*DG*, 156). The fatal contradiction of his life becomes obvious to him. The fight of the two essential forces eros and death is according to Freud's theory of impulses[14] the basis of the desperate effort to maintain his youth. The loss of his libido is the gain of his destructive impulse. Aggression is in terms of Marcuse the manifestation of the death impulse.[15] Dorian is at the end both afraid of death and of life (*DG*, 153). The death-force-energy dominates his life-force: 'It is the coming of death that terrifies me' (*DG*, 156). The relation of crime and art developed by Lord Henry reveals the failure of the aesthetic philosophy and the failure of Dorian Gray:

> All crime is vulgar, just as all vulgarity is crime [...] I should fancy that crime was to them [the lower orders] what art is to us, simply a method of procuring extraordinary sensations. (*DG*, 162)

When Oscar Wilde proclaims: 'All art is immoral'[16] or as he does in his preface: 'All art is quite useless' (*DG*, 4), he does it for provocative purposes. In his letters he confesses the intention of Dorian Gray:

> All excess, as well as all renunciation, brings its own punishment. The painter, Basil Hallward, worshipping physical beauty far too much [...] dies by the hand of one whose soul he has created a monstrous and absurd vanity. Dorian Gray, having led a life of mere sensation and pleasure, tries to kill conscience, and at that moment kills himself [...]. Yes, there is a terrible moral in Dorian Gray [...] which will be revealed to all whose minds are healthy.[17]

Supposing my own mind is healthy, I agree with the idea that art and life, aesthetic behaviour and moral consciousness are here in a contradiction that cannot be solved.[18]

One way out could have been Marcuse's later developed theory of 'libidinous reason'[19] that anticipates a utopia of a non-repressive society, in which the conflict between Eros and Thanatos is reconciled. A new tendency against the non-sublimity of eroticism is the 'androgynous revolution'.[20] The problem of the difference of sexes is removed from the ideal of a psychological and social equality. The new androgynous human being could replace an eroticism based on tender friendship instead of constraints and difference of man and woman.

Dorian Gray is in a certain way the type of an 'androgynous aesthete'[21] if he were able to develop his ability to love and to exert critical and unsentimental thinking. If he had been able to overcome his own narcissism and to accept the tragically limited nature of human existence,[22] he would never have sold his soul and he would never have become the victim of the constraints between Eros and Thanatos which can only be reconciled by love itself.

NOTES

1   R. Ellmann, *Oscar Wilde*, Alfred A. Knopf, New York, 1988, p. 305.
2   *Brockhaus Enzyklopädie*, Bd. 6, Mannheim, 1988, p. 542.
3   Oscar Wilde, 'The Decay of Lying', in: A. B. Lawler, L. Lawler, *Oscar Wilde, The Picture of Dorian Gray*, Norton critical edition, New York, London, 1988, p. 319. Abbreviation *DG*, all quotations refer to this edition.
4   Ibid., p. 320.
5   Oscar Wilde, *The Picture of Dorian Gray*, Norton critical edition, p. 3.
6   H. Montgomery Hyde (ed.), *The Trials of Oscar Wilde*, London, 1948, p. 357.
7   *Selected Letters of Oscar Wilde*, ed. by R. Hart-Davis, Oxford, 1979, p. 352.
8   S. Freud, *Essays*, Bd. III, 1920-1937, Berlin 1988, p. 297.
9   Ibid.
10   Oscar Wilde, *The Picture of Dorian Gray*, Norton critical edition, p. 26.
11   Cf. E. Warner, G. Hough (eds.), *Strangeness and Beauty*, Cambridge, 1983, vol. 2, p. 33.
12   R. Ellmann, *Oscar Wilde*, Alfred Knopf, New York, 1988, p. 306.
13   Comp. K. Millet, *Sexual Politics*, New York, 1970 and L. Irigaray, *Fünf Texte zur Geschlechtsdifferenz*, Frankfurt am Main, 1987.
14   S. Freud, *Triebe und Triebschicksale*, in: *Essays*, Bd. 2, ed. Dietrich Simon, Berlin 1988, p. 9f.
15   H. Marcuse, *Triebstruktur und Gesellschaft*, Frankfurt am Main, 1968, p. 266.
16   Oscar Wilde, 'The Critic as Artist', in: Norton critical edition, p. 316.
17   Oscar Wilde, *Selected Letters*, ed. R. Hart-Davis, Oxford, 1979, p. 259.
18   N. Kohl, *Oscar Wilde, Das Literarische Werk zwischen Provokation und Anpassung*, Carl Winter Verlag, Heidelberg, 1980, p. 286.
19   H. Marcuse, *Triebstruktur und Gesellschaft*, Frankfurt am Main, 1968, p. 220 ff.
20   E. Badinter, *Ich bin Du*, Die neue Beziehung zwischen Mann und Frau oder die androgyne Revolution, Frankfurt am Main, 1987.
21   M. Pfister, Oscar Wilde, *The Picture of Dorian Gray*, W. Fink Verlag, München, 1986.
22   E. Fromm, *Haben oder Sein*, München, 1976, p. 163.

DECODING *THE BALLAD OF READING GAOL*

Norman Page

The Ballad of Reading Gaol, Wilde's last major work, is a surprise ending to his literary career. As he admitted even before it was finished, it is written in a 'new style' in which he was 'out-Henleying Kipling' — hardly the models that his career to that date would have rendered predictable, and not a change of style that he persisted in, for within a couple of months he was declaring, with a slight variation of the earlier phrase, 'I will never again out-Kipling Henley'. The other literary projects of the last years of his life came to nothing, though at one stage there was to have been a companion-poem to *The Ballad*, celebrating freedom rather that mourning imprisonment: it would have been titled *The Ballad of the Fisher-Boy*, and Wilde recited three stanzas of it to Frank Harris but seems to have got no further. Meeting Laurence Housman in Paris, Wilde told him he would never write again.

In more than one way, then, *The Ballad of Reading Gaol* occupies a distinctive place among his writings. It was a poem that had to be written and was completed relatively quickly. What I shall be suggesting is that its urgency and personal significance derive from its precise biographical context, but that at the same time its method is one of obliqueness and indirection. It thus contrasts with and complements the other major product of his prison experiences, *De Profundis*, which is more directly autobiographical and confessional. The poem aspires to an impersonality (not fully realized in the event) for which the ballad form was an appropriate medium; its 'new style' is not the result of a mere whim or itch for novelty but a necessary newness.

Let us consider for a moment Wilde's situation in the summer of 1897. He had been released on 19 May, the manuscript of *De Profundis* being handed to him as he left prison. Within less than two weeks he was already at work on *The Ballad*. His pen was busy in the first days of his freedom, and twenty letters survive, including a very long one to the editor of the *Daily Chronicle*, from the first two weeks. Freedom, including the freedom to write as many letters as he wished, was clearly a powerful stimulus. But it is also clear that *The Ballad* was demanding to be written, and one letter he had received may throw light on his state of mind. His wife Constance had sent a reply to a letter he had written her 'full of penitence' (as she told her brother), and her reply contained a refusal to grant his wish to be reunited with his sons. As he told Ross:

> She sends me photographs of the boys [...] but makes no promise to allow me to see them: she says *she* will see me, twice a year, but I want my boys. It is a terrible punishment, dear Robbie, and oh! how well I deserve it.

The first draft of the poem was written quickly, but revision and expansion took longer. Well before the end of July he was able to tell Ross that the poem was 'nearly finished'; it was, however, to be finished more than once as it passed through various drafts and grew in the process. In late August he sent it to Smithers, describing it as still unrevised, and only in October was he able to claim that it was 'finished at last' — though later in the month he was still sending Smithers some additional stanzas. In short, although Wilde later told Ross that 'the idea of *The Ballad* came to me while I was in the dock, waiting for my sentence to be pronounced', and although it embodies the experience of two years' hard labour, it is the product of a specific moment: the first days of his freedom, embittered by the realization that his family life, and especially his relationship with his sons, had very possibly been destroyed for ever.

What we find on turning to the poem, however, is not a direct confrontation of this personal tragedy but an objectifying and displacing of his experience. The protagonist of *The Ballad* is — like the protagonist of Kipling's great ballad *Danny Deever* (first published by Henley) — a soldier sentenced to be hanged for murder. The dedication identifies its central character as a former 'Trooper of the Royal Horse Guards', and the poem's opening line refers to his 'scarlet coat'. This links him with the redcoats and condemned prisoners of the most recent of all the likely literary influences on Wilde's *Ballad*: Housman's *A Shropshire Lad* had appeared in the previous year, and Housman had sent Wilde a copy upon his release from prison. There is, however, evidence that Wilde was already aware of the poem, since Ross told Housman many years later that 'when he visited his friend in jail he learnt some of the poems by heart and recited them to him'. (The pronouns here are perhaps slightly ambiguous, but Wilde's acquaintance with at least parts of the poem seems likely.) There is no poem in Housman's collection that uses the same stanza-form as *The Ballad*, but *A Shropshire Lad* IX describes the harrowing all-night wait for 'the stroke of eight' and the morning execution in terms quite close to those used by Wilde.

For a metrical model we probably need to turn to two poems that would have been very familiar to his first readers. Though mainly cast in four-line stanzas, Coleridge's *Rime of the Ancient Mariner* has a number of six-liners that must have been in Wilde's mind and ear; it too is of course a tale of guilt and atonement. Hood's 'The Dream of Eugene Aram' tells a story of crime, remorse and punishment, and its stanzas have a very similar movement to many of Wilde's, though it is much shorter than *The Ballad* and has less variety of tone as well as less subtlety of structure and point of view. For *The Ballad* combines a simple but strong narrative with a considerable amount of reflection, generalization and propaganda as well as displacing personal experience onto a persona in a somewhat similar way to that adopted by Isherwood in his Berlin stories. Wilde was troubled by its modulations from one manner to another, telling Ross that 'the poem suffers under the difficulty of a divided aim in style'. Arthur Symons observed acutely in a review that while it possessed 'the value of a document' it was essentially 'a sombre [...] reverie, and it is the subcurrent of meditation, it is the asides, which count, not the story'. An opposite view was taken by Yeats, who, anthologizing the poem, shortened it so as to omit most of the 'message'. Changes introduced after the first draft seem to have been designed to strengthen the didacticism rather than to heighten the

narrative and dramatic effects, and it must be said that not all
the revisions and additions were well-advised. In the final
version there is a kind of instability most evident in the
fluctuations of diction: on the one hand, there are graphic
visual touches of an almost novelistic or cinematic kind, such as
the traces of lime on the warders' boots after the hasty burial
of the hanged man; on the other hand, there is much
poeticizing and recourse to capitalized abstractions — during
the night before the hanging; for instance, the prisoners' cells
are haunted by 'crooked shapes of Terror' which keep a 'tryst',
and 'with mop and mow' dance a 'saraband' involving
'arabesques'. These sharp variations in emotional pressure seem
to reflect an indecision on Wilde's part as to what kind of poem
he really wanted to write and find a rough parallel in similar
inconsistencies in Isherwood's prose style.

It is, then, a poem based upon the most intense
experience of Wilde's life, but at the same time a very literary
poem, almost a pastiche, in what one might have supposed *a
priori* to be a deeply uncongenial style; and it is a poem whose
different elements seem to be in conflict with each other.
Furthermore, it is a poem of self-concealment that is
simultaneously one of self-disclosure. For it is easy to take for
granted the inevitability of the narrative, and an effort of
defamiliarization is called for. With his prison experiences
only days behind him, one might have expected Wilde to use
his new-found literary freedom to give direct expression to that
ordeal. What he does instead is to take a figure of whom he
knew little and had seen even less — and, moreover, one whose
tragedy already belonged to the past, for Trooper Wooldridge
had been hanged on 7 July 1896. The central narrative tells of
the man's confinement, trial, sentencing, last days, execution
and burial, but at the same time moves between objectivity and
self-identification and between an individual response to
Wooldridge's fate and a group response. The author of *The
Picture of Dorian Gray* knew about the literary possibilities of
the double, and there are moments when the condemned
criminal seems to be Wilde's other self; at other times his
preoccupation with his own guilt gives way to the consciousness
of sharing a communal experience of guilt.

The opening stanza affirms at once that the protagonist is different from the other prisoners in the nature of his crime as well as the peculiar horror of the punishment that awaits him. Yet to identify himself with a wife-murderer would have called for no great imaginative leap on Wilde's part, since he had before him Constance's letter reminding him that he had destroyed his domestic and family life. Within half-a-dozen stanzas, learning that the man is to die, he immediately enters into his situation:

> Dear Christ! the very prison walls
> Suddenly seemed to reel,
> And the sky above my head became
> Like a casque of scorching steel;
> And, though I was a soul in pain,
> My pain I could not feel.

> I only knew what hunted thought
> Quickened his step, and why
> He looked upon the garish day
> With such a wistful eye;
> The man had killed the thing he loved,
> And so he had to die.

And at this point the murderer, no longer rendered unique and an outcast (like the Ancient Mariner) by the nature of his deed, becomes representative:

> Yet each man kills the thing he loves,
> By each let this be heard,
> Some do it with a bitter look,
> Some with a flattering word,
> The coward does it with a kiss,
> The brave man with a sword!

The phrases may be more charged with personal feeling than at first appears, for Wilde had been prodigal with kisses and flattering words, just as (to refer to phrases in the next two stanzas) he could be said to have 'strangle[d] with the hands of Lust' and to have entered a sexual underworld in which 'some sell, and others buy'. At such points, while apparently describing a shared experience, Wilde seems to be writing his personal history in a simple code.

As he himself saw it, Wilde too had killed the thing he loved, at least metaphorically; at this stage he was not to know that Constance would be dead within less than two months of the poem's publication, though not before being 'frightfully upset by this wonderful poem of Oscar's'. He recognizes kinship with the wife-murderer but at the same time a crucial difference: while 'each man kills the thing he loves', yet 'each man does not die'. There follow seven stanzas each of which begins 'he does not', which, by a familiar trope, assert the essential similarity between the convicted murderer and the man guilty of any crime, including Wilde's own. We may note here the curious absence in the poem of any sense of injustice, of the barbarism that was the subject of one of Housman's poems (probably referring to Wilde's fate) having the refrain 'They're sending him to prison for the colour of his hair'. Wilde attacks prison conditions but not the laws that sent him there; indeed he declares near the end of the poem 'I know not whether Laws be right, / Or whether Laws be wrong'. One explanation of this (and there are obviously other possible explanations) is that he was anxious to insist on the kinship of all who suffered in prison: to define their crimes would be to differentiate between them, and his main point is that the murderer's guilt, and his fate, is scarcely different from his own.

Yet ultimately the poem turns its back on kinship to insist on the otherness of the condemned man's appalling fate: the drama of the poem is the drama of his last days and the immediate aftermath of the hanging, and his separateness from the community of prisoners is all-important. (It was a separateness that the newly-released Wilde was perhaps beginning to experience.) This necessarily reduces the narrator, whom most readers will be ready to identify with Wilde himself, to the status of an observer, and again this aspect of the poem's distinctive strategy may be compared with that adopted by Isherwood in a story such as 'On Ruegen Island', the third section of *Goodbye to Berlin*. Here too painful autobiographical material is transformed and objectified: Isherwood's turbulent relationship with Otto is displaced onto a third party, thus enabling the Isherwood-character in the story to adopt an observer's and commentator's stance. Wilde for his part was not inexperienced in effecting this kind of coding: the plays have persuasively been interpreted as concealed expositions and explorations of his own secret life at the time of their composition. What is distinctive about *The Ballad of Reading Gaol* is the adoption of an alien poetic genre and style. Kipling's *Barrack-Room Ballads*, published in 1892, had contained a number of poems with titles that began *The Ballad of...*, and readers of the Nineties may have been struck by the parallel and by its unexpectedness. In 1890 Wilde had observed of *Plain Tales from the Hills* that reading it 'one feels as if one were seated under a palm-tree reading life by superb flashes of vulgarity'. In the obvious relationship of *The Ballad* to a popular tradition, Wilde himself had in a literal sense courted vulgarity, and if the experiment did not altogether succeed it remains extraordinarily daring. A last and not least unexpected touch is provided by the fact that, of all Wilde's writings, it was *The Ballad* that furnished the inscription for his tomb in Père Lachaise.

WILDE & TWO WOMEN: UNPUBLISHED ACCOUNTS BY ELIZABETH ROBINS & BLANCHE CRACKANTHORPE

Kerry Powell

Bound together in the Fales Library of New York University are two unpublished documents containing recollections and reflections on the life of Oscar Wilde by two important women of the 1890s. One is a typescript copy of a letter of 1895 by Blanche Alethea Crackanthorpe, written near the end of Wilde's criminal trial for homosexuality. It is addressed to Elizabeth Robins, who refers to the letter in her own fragmentary, 12-page memoir of Wilde written late in life. The Crackanthorpe letter and the fragmentary memoir are contained in a single folder of the Fales Library's vast collection of Robins's unpublished as well as published writings. Unknown to biographers as far as I have been able to determine, these two documents reveal several unchronicled yet telling episodes and perspectives, while at the same time they disclose a conflicted attitude toward Wilde on the part of women who espoused 'advanced' social and aesthetic ideas in the mid-1890s.

Blanche Crackanthorpe, the mother of fiction writer Hubert Crackanthorpe, was an early supporter of the plays of Ibsen and an advocate of birth control and reproductive rights for women. A writer herself, she authored a play called *The Turn of the Wheel* which dealt uncompromisingly with abortion and was denied a license for performance by the Examiner of Plays. She was part of a group of women — including Mrs W. K. Clifford, Constance Fleming, Florence Bell, and Elizabeth Robins herself — who sought to transform the British theatre of the 1890s into a forum for addressing and correcting the oppression of women in Victorian society. Robins herself created a sensation by introducing *Hedda Gabler* to England, and later producing as well as acting in plays by Ibsen and others which represented women as capable of power and even violence, to the consternation of many in her audiences. I have shown elsewhere how she attempted to enlist Wilde in her project of a 'Theatre of the Future' — a theatre in which gender equality and cooperative, noncompetitive endeavour would inaugurate an era of aesthetic renewal of the drama and eventually moral renewal of the nation. Robins and Crackanthorpe were thus public figures who organized their efforts single-mindedly toward aesthetic and social reform. To them, Oscar Wilde was an enigmatic personality, appealing in his iconoclasm and personal qualities of wit and generosity, but disturbing in his reluctance to commit whole-heartedly to what they regarded as great causes. His wit seemed self-indulgent, uncommitted to truth or even meaning, and his appetite for luxury jarred with the ascetic sense of duty which energized the lives of women like Robins and Crackanthorpe.

This mixture of sympathy and tension between Wilde and what might be called late-Victorian feminism is evident in the unpublished documents in the Fales Library. They make clear that Robins, Crackanthorpe, and like-minded women talked and agonized over Wilde at the time of his public disgrace. 'What you say of the Wilde affair finds an echo here', writes Blanche Crackanthorpe to Elizabeth Robins on April 9, 1895. 'I can think of little else. That is, it comes back upon me at intervals during the day, and when I wake in the night.' Sympathy for Wilde thus informs the first part of the letter, apparently reflecting earlier conversations or letters on the subject between the two women. 'Montague [Blanche Crackanthorpe's husband, himself a lawyer who attended the trial] told me that he never was present at anything so horrible as the last day of O. W.'s cross examination by Carson, Q. C. The man was like a tortured, hunted animal.'

Suddenly, however, the letter turns from expressions of sympathy for Wilde to concern for his wife Constance, and in general for standards of morality which must be upheld at any cost:

Mrs Clifford told me she had heard [...] that it was feared Mrs
Wilde's mind might give way — her distress is beyond all
words. She asked me, hearing I had written to her, should she do
the same [she knows her very slightly]. I told her 'Yes, yes, most
certainly!'. This is the moment when sympathy may save her
from the overwhelming shame and humiliation, and Mrs
Clifford promised me she would. It seems that the police have
known of the whole thing for a long, long time, but with the
timidity of officials and the slow working of the machinery of
'departments', have done nothing but 'wait and watch' [...].
There was an idea on Sunday that many other arrests would
follow — I only hope they may — nothing would do so much to
purge schools and universities — and sorely they need it — as
sentences which should strike terror and dismay into the hearts
of the offenders. 'Light, light, more light.'[1]

Elizabeth Robins's unpublished memoir of Wilde,
called *Oscar Wilde: An Appreciation*, was prompted or at least
deeply informed by the letter that Blanche Crackanthorpe sent
her in April 1895. Many years later, near the end of her own
long and eventful career, Robins still found it unsettling to look
back on the catastrophe that engulfed Wilde in 1895 — 'bitter'
and 'shattering' are the adjectives that she employs to describe
its effect on her. 'It is difficult even at this long distance of
time', she writes in her fragmentary memoir of Wilde, 'to look
back at the days of his fiercely lime-lit trial, with its
aftermath of solitary imprisonment and degrading exile'. So,
difficult, in fact, that Robins seems unable to manage it alone,
recalling and quoting at length 'a friend's letter' — the letter
from Blanche Crackanthorpe — to put the events of April 1895
into perspective. But she quotes that portion of her friend's
letter that is most sympathetic to Wilde, then turns to lengthy
quotations from another friend, theatrical critic and reformer
William Archer, for further help. 'Through all his physical
suffering, his humiliation, his self-reproach,' she writes, citing
Archer's review of *De Profundis*, 'he was manifestly sustained
by the consciousness of being the protagonist in a strange
tragedy, the victim of an almost unexampled reverse of fortune,
the leading performer in an unique and thrilling episode of the
great mundane Mystery-Play.'[2] Could his suffering, then, have
been to Wilde's observing self a thing of beauty, even joy? As if
such a question were unanswerable, for her at least, Robins
halts halfway through the next sentence and abondons her
memoir of Wilde. She could not, in the final analysis, make

sense of the events of 1895 or even narrate them except through
the eyes and with the words of others.

Despite its compromised ending the avowed purpose of
Robins's memoir is to pay a 'debt' to a man whose personal
kindness and professional encouragement made a difference in
her early years as a London actress newly arrived from
America. As an example she refers to an apparently lost letter
from Wilde:

> One especially heartening, which I still treasure, in which he
> says that he hopes some day he may be 'fortunate enough to
> have so subtle and fascinating an artist' to interpret some 'part'
> of his. 'You know what pleasure your art always gives me.'[3]

After expressing her gratitude for his support of her theatrical
enterprises, especially the landmark production of *Hedda
Gabler*, Robins expresses her delight in Wilde's conversation,
which he raised, she says, to a 'fine art' unknown in the
twentieth century :

> There was nothing at that time, nor I believe since, the least like
> Oscar Wilde dominating a London dinner table. He did what he
> liked with people: he could make them shine, he could make them
> shrink — a king among his subjects for that hour [...]. Oscar
> [was] tall, broad, already a little ponderous, brilliant beyond
> the power of report, overbearing yet urbane, unless crossed,
> and then most alarming.

He was at home among artists and critics, Robins recalls, but
equally so 'in that world of the leisured, a company slightly
stiffened by some admixture of Army and Navy spiced with a
dash of officialdom'.[4]

Mixed with this admiration and affection for Wilde in
Robins's memoir is an underlying uneasiness, even a sense of
estrangement from the man to whom these pages were written
in homage. Like Blanche Crackanthorpe's letter, only in a
different way, Robins's memoir singles out Wilde's
relationship with his wife Constance as a way of giving form to
these misgivings. Robins tells of visiting Wilde's house in Tite
Street, carrying with her a manuscript on which she hoped he
would comment. What followed has never been related, I
believe, except in Robins's unpublished memoir:

Mr Wilde was not at home. But Mrs Wilde was — in white
muslin with a blue sash round her waist, insisting that I should
came in. She was like a grave, beautiful school girl, dressed for
an Occasion, ready to welcome distraction till the party should
begin. It was one of those bitter days that I have thought only
the vaunted English spring can provide. In my outdoor wraps I
sat in the fireless drawing room and shivered, while Mrs Wilde,
no doubt acustomed to a visitor with a carefully done up packet
under one arm, told me that if I had brought something for her
husband, she would see that it was given to him.

I had no mind to leave my manuscript without first
seeing Wilde; but, gently, his wife persisted that she would take
care of it. I found myself explaining what it was and why I
wanted to see him. Should I wait till he came in? She looked
serious at that, but seemed not to want to be rid of me. She
apologized for having no fire. 'We never have a fire after 1st
May', she said. Perhaps I had stared at her midsummer frock.
'My husband likes me to wear white', she said gravely. What he
would not like, she seemed to think, would be that I should have
come with something for him and not have left it. She would take
care, she repeated [...]. 'You don't think he will be in soon,
then?' No, she didn't think so. 'How long did she imagine he
would be?' She couldn't be sure. 'He *is* in London, I suppose?'
No. I opened my eyes. She thought he was in Paris [...] and there
she sat in white muslin, without a fire, waiting [...]. I left my
manuscript behind.[5]

This poignant scene — Wilde's indefinite absence from the
chill drawing-room in which his white-clad wife follows out
his wishes — leaves Robins vaguely troubled as well as
surprised. The unspoken sense of something gone wrong with the
man she liked and admired continues in the ensuing paragraphs
of the memoir, in which Robins recounts Wilde's triumphs as a
writer almost dismissively, hardly pausing to comment except
disparagingly, referring, for example, to 'his Poems which
never touched me, or *Dorian Gray* which I disliked'. The
memoir, which began with the purpose of acknowledging
'appreciation and gratitude' to Wilde, then moves to a
description of Robins's last meeting with him, one that occurred
in late 1894 or early 1895, just before the collapse of his career.
Robins's description of this final visit from Wilde —untold, as
far as I know, except in her typescript memoir — at first
confirms the reader's sense of her growing estrangement from
the man she had meant to honour. He was overfed and reticent;
and when he stood up to go, Elizabeth Robins was glad. But in

the moment of their final parting, something extraordinary occurred:

> The great bulk of him seemed to fill the little room and shut out the light. As we shook hands, we both glanced at the window and saw the room grow duller, greyer. Rain was coming down in sheets. 'You can't go just yet', I said, commiserating. No, he would have to wait another minute or two, he said, turning away to stare at the picture over the mantelpiece — Michael Angelo's 'Fortune on her Wheel', which Gerturde Bell had given to me. The rain drummed, the panes streamed. Wilde turned round, but still loomed there, blocking out my small fireplace with his blackness. The only colour anywhere seemed to be a blob of blue, the scarabaeus from Old Nile that seemed at home on the huge pale hand holding the lapel of his frock coat.
> But now he was talking — about Form and about working in a new genre. Did I know that nothing says so much as the words that say little, and say even that little under a cloak? Symbol... He was no longer generalizing; you would say he was reciting, but for the reflective look, the occasional slight hesitation the little changes, trying the phrase again with a faintly amused self-consciousness, then catching my intent look, going on. He saw I was excited.
> Was this prose, or was it poetry in a new measure? A sense of his mastery of the strange instrument held me in a stillness of delight. When he had ended, the rain was quiet too. But he began again. He was smiling now, we were happy. On and on, the pure diction, the delicate imagery that veiled and yet revealed the Sadness that was under the Cloak.
> There were more of these Fables, as he called them, than I ever saw published, and I blessed the rain that had given me that hour, given it to him, as I realized later.[6]

This transcendent interlude in Robins's memoir gives way to further regrets — an observation, for example, in the next paragraph that Wilde's published fables and poems in prose were nothing in comparison to the spontaneous artistry of his talk in her darkened drawing-room. In his actual work, she asks, 'what had become of the poetry? These mannered exercises, written down in cold blood, were colder than the print. Cold? They were dead.'[7]

For all that, Robins's memoir is kinder and more thoughtful than the letter from Blanche Crackanthorpe, dated 9 April 1895, which lies beside it in a manuscript file at New York University and may well have inspired Robins to attempt her own assessment of Wilde. Yet one finds disappointment and occasional bewilderment in the few pages that Robins was able to produce before giving up her biographical task altogether. More than Crackanthorpe's letter on Wilde's criminal trial, Robins's memoir of his life displays affection and sympathy for one whose spectacular career ended in 'solitary imprisonment and degrading exile'. Wilde's talent and potential for greatness can at times overwhelm the author of *Oscar Wilde: An Appreciation*, but his failure, in her eyes, to realize that potential leaves her crestfallen and even resentful. For a growing number of women in the 1890s — 'advanced' women like Robins and Crackanthorpe — the artist's mission was a disciplined endeavour toward social betterment which left no room for self-indulgence or indeterminacy of meaning. Wilde in Robins's memoir is figured to a large extent by absence and silence, and his flashes of brilliance are finally insufficient to redeem or even explain the great paradox of his life. Robins stopped writing the memoir in the middle of an unsuccessful attempt to find something 'real', some 'profound mystery', that would explain and give meaning to the catastrophe that ended Wilde's career. This effort ended in midsentence, the last disappointment and perhaps the most eloquent silence in Robins's remarkable essay.

NOTES

1   Typescript copy of a letter from Blanche Crackanthorpe to Elizabeth Robins, 9 April 1895, MS. Fales Library, New York University, pp. 1-2.
2   E. Robins, *Oscar Wilde: An Appreciation*, MS. Fales Library, New York University, pp. 10-12.
3   *Ibid.*, pp. 1-2.
4   *Ibid.*, p. 3.
5   *Ibid.*, pp. 4-5.
6   *Ibid.*, pp. 6-7.
7   *Ibid.*, p. 8.

LADY WILDE 'SPERANZA': A WOMAN OF GREAT IMPORTANCE

María Pilar Pulido

> LORD ILLINGWORTH. All women become like their mothers.
> That is their tragedy.
> MRS ALLONBY. No man does. That is his.[1]

By the time of Oscar Wilde's birth, Lady Wilde had already gained a place in Irish Nationalist Literary History under the *nom de plume* of 'Speranza'. If her political views are to be judged according to the patriotic verse she wrote for *The Nation* from 1847 until its closure the following year, there can be no doubt that her sympathy and love for Ireland was anything but genuine and deeply felt. Her dedication 'To Ireland' in her book of poems published in 1871 as well as the preface to her *Ancient Legends of Ireland* (1888) bear eloquent testimony to a profound sense of patriotism. Nevertheless, despite her claim that the conservatism of the Ascendancy to which she belonged had not succeeded in taming her 'rebellious nature', the contents of her private correspondance, during her revolutionary period and beyond, point to 'Speranza' taking a dim view of the success of an armed insurrection. Equally revealing was her pride in Sir William's knighthood, and her acceptance of a pension from the very same Empire she had wished to topple.

Writing for a revolution suited her air of *grandeur*. She, at all times, sided with the underdog by coming to the rescue of the fatherland — pining as it was for the coming of a hero — by denouncing the bondage of women down through the centuries[2] and by lending an ear to all the young poets who crowded her *salons littéraires* in Dublin and London. The sympathy she felt for the oppressed, tinged as it was with a touch of narcissism, shows a personal commitment to causes that through 'Speranza'

319

take on a sacred dimension, thus becoming a sort of personal crusade.

'Speranza' represented her innermost aspirations and around that pseudonym she weaved her own legend as a poet of the nation: she claimed descent from Dante, she probably changed her name from Frances to Francesca, and surrounded her persona with the gloss and glamour of the anecdotal, opening with her conversion to nationalism and closing with her often quoted interruption at Gavan Duffy's trial at which she cried out: 'I am the culprit!', words, which as she confessed later, she never actually uttered: 'I was quite amused at that imputed heroic act of mine becoming historical. Posterity will not believe it and I shall leave it so — it will read well 100 years hence and if an illustrated history of Ireland is published no doubt I shall be immortalised in the act of addressing the Court.'[3] Once the danger was over, the fervour, with which Miss Elgee's imagination had been fired, cooled considerably :

> At last I think his [Duffy's] trials are over. I was in quite an alarm lest I should have to appear as witness; however, I wrote a letter acknowledging the authorship, and the Court said they must believe me, so that there was then really no case against Mr D. Still the whole affair has thoroughly unsettled me against politics — our grand Revolution ending in shielding itself with a lady's name.[4]

Irresistible it had proved to her, the image of the patriot as a young poet whose magic words would stir the country into action for, like her son Oscar, 'Speranza' found youth and beauty enthralling. The poem 'The Young Patriot Leader' was inspired by a Young Irelander, Thomas Meagher :

> In his beauty and his youth, the Apostle of the Truth,
>   Goes he forth with the words of salvation,
> And a noble madness falls on each spirit he enthralls,
>   As he chants his wild Paeans to the nation.
>
> As a tempest in its force, as a torrent in its course,
>   So his words fiercely sweep all before them,
> And they smite like two-edged swords, those undaunted
>   thunder words,
>   On all hearts, as tho' angels did implore them.[5]

Although she is perfectly aware of the prophet's doom,[6] at no stage does she hesitate in offering him the bitter chalice of death. For the 'Speranza' of the nation, what Ireland needed were martyrs and the spilling of the victim's blood just as much as the tyrant's. Indeed, self-sacrifice was the hero's greatest virtue, and its cleansing power had also an effect on the possessors of the artistic temperament or of the 'feminine soul' for whom suffering brings about redemption; thus, Lady Wilde's reaction to Oscar serving a two-year prison sentence with a laconic 'it will do him good' seems, if not apparently logical, at least consistent with her beliefs. Oscar Wilde himself during his stay in prison, somehow, attuned to his mother's faith and found solace in the cleansing effect of suffering: 'during the last few months I have, after terrible struggles and difficulties, been able to comprehend some of the lessons hidden in the heart of pain. Clergymen, and people who use phrases without wisdom, sometimes talk of suffering as a mystery. It is really a revelation.'[7]

On his American lecture tour, Oscar Wilde introduced himself as the son of 'Speranza'[8] and he praised highly the work of the '48 revolutionary poets and that of his mother. Years later, in *De Profundis*, Oscar referred to the bitterness that his inability to live up to his mother's name and expectations had added to his own tragedy.[9] It was, thus, hardly surprising that Oscar's first play, *Vera, or the Nihilists*, was a political play that depicted a country, Russia, downtrodden by a royal tyrant, and on the brink of a revolution backed by a group of people (led by a woman) determined to bring about the establishment of a republic or to die in the attempt.[10] The ressemblance between the play and the ambiance that reigned in pre-'48 revolutionary Ireland is striking. Even the internal differences with regard to the effectiveness of a bloodless revolution echo the divergence in political strategy that had brought about the split between Young Ireland and 'The Liberator'. In the play, Michael is blood thirsty, 'there should be none here but men whose hands are rough with labour or red with blood',[11] and he opposes the Professor's philosophy of merely restricting nihilism to revolutionary pamphlets: 'My forte is more in writing pamphlets than in taking shots.'[12] Dimitri's moving narration

of his conversion, 'I thought I could free Russia. I heard men
talk of Liberty one night in a café. I had never heard the word
before. It seemed to be a new God they spoke of. I joined them',[13]
reminds us of the event that transformed Miss Elgee into a 'new
volcano of sedition'. She had been brought up as Oscar told an
American audience, 'in an atmosphere of alien English thought,
among people high in Bench and Senate and far removed from
any love or knowledge of those wrongs of the people to which
she afterwards gave such passionate expression. And one day in
1845, standing at the window of her lordly house, she saw a
great funeral pass in its solemn trappings of sorrow down the
street.'[14] As C. J. Hamilton so aptly puts it, 'she got hold of a
book, *The Spirit of the Nation*, containing poems by D'Alton
Williams, and her imagination took fire from it, and she
became a poetess and a patriot.'[15]

The nationalist ideology of the Young Irelanders,
despite its proclaimed pan-Hibernian temper, never ceased to
be elitist and was of little appeal to the masses. In Oscar's
play, Vera, the vestal of freedom,[16] describes the lack of
sympathy between their political claims and the peasants:
'[...] though these dull Russian peasants care little for our
proclamations, and less for our martyrdoms. When the blow is
struck, it must be from the town, not from the country.'[17] She
herself was concerned with the dignity of Ireland as an
imaginary unit and not so much with the welfare of the middle
of the road Irishman. Like Carlyle, she abhorred democracy:
'No Democracy. Why should a rude, uncultured mob dare to
utter its voice? Let the best reign, Intellect and Ability.'[18]
'Speranza' had a romantic vision of the revolutionary like her
son, who had gone bail for John Barlas, a Scottish anarchist
poet who had fired a shot in the Houses of Parliament. Artistic
genius above all, Oscar's politics were determined by
aesthetics; thus, his defence of an individualistic socialism,
his dislike of capitalism and his contempt for the masses. Lady
Wilde's 'aristocratic' republicanism, however, did not stop her
from enjoying the balls and receptions given at Dublin Castle:

> I went to the last Drawingroom at the Castle and Lord
> Aberdeen smiled very archly as he bent to kiss my cheek, which
> is the ceremony of presentation. I smiled too and thought of
> 'Jacta Alea Est'.[19]

Neither did her husband's knighthood displease her nor the pension she received from Her Majesty after Sir Williams's demise in 1876. Once again, Vera's ambiguity[20] concerning politics is clearly depicted by the attraction she feels for Alexis, his manners and noble spirit, even before she knows who he really is: 'Why does he make me feel at times as if I would have him as my king, Republican though I be? Oh, fool, fool, fool . False to your oath! Weak as water! Have done! Remember what you are — a Nihilist, a Nihilist.'[21]

Vera's words about the man she loves, only second to her country, echo 'Speranza''s epistolary declaration about a Scotsman who despite his criticism of her literary persona, or precisely because of it, captured Miss Elgee's tameless heart, 'now is this Justice to Ireland, has a Scotchman any right to come over here and prove that 'Speranza' is no divine Priestess after all — merely a lamp-holder in the Court of the Gentiles [...] but after all, like a true woman, I love to be a slave when I find a real king.'[22]

Her marriage to Doctor Wilde in 1851 put an end to her personal literary ambitions. As she drifted from the political to the social sphere, she looked back on her nationalistic period considering it to be 'an abnormal state', though well worth living. Lady Wilde had not accomplished her destiny yet and, after Willie's birth, she transformed her former hero-worship into hero-rearing, 'I will rear him a Hero' she wrote to a friend; although, it was Oscar who was to take the necessary steps into making her dream come true.

The idea of opening a *salon littéraire* came to her as early as 1859: 'I am going to establish weekly *conversazioni* at my own house (if I can) and agglomerate together all the thinking minds of Dublin.'[23] Willie and Oscar were soon allowed to gather among the groups of celebrities and mediocrities that crowded mummy's bohemian 'at homes'.[24] Needless to say, it was in Lady Wilde's salons that Oscar developed his conversational skills and where he was granted a heaven-sent opportunity to master the paradoxes and epigrams which made of him an *assidu* to the most important drawing rooms of the time. Professor Mahaffy, Dr Tisdall, Mr H. J. Fitzpatrick, and Dr Shaw proved excellent limestones for sharpening Oscar's wit, a talent that for Lady Wilde was 'the rarest, the best gift' a writer could possess. Brilliant conversation was what Lady Wilde demanded of her guests among whom she posed, happy as always to be the centre of attention; posing, quite naturally, was to become part of Oscar's personality.

Surrounded by her literary court, the 'Irish Madame Récamier' displayed her extravagance of manner and attire in an artificial semidarkness. 'I called at Merrion Square late in the afternoon', commented Miss Henriette Corkran, 'for Lady Wilde never received anyone till 5 p.m., as she hated what she called "the brutality of strong lights"; the shutters were closed and the lamps had pink shades, though it was full daylight.'[25] Pink shades seem to prove most effective when it comes to concealing one's age, as Mrs Erlynne points out in *Lady Windermere's Fan*: 'Besides, my dear Windermere, how on earth could I pose as a mother with a grown-up daughter? Margaret is twenty-one, and I have never admitted that I am more than twenty-nine, or thirty at the most. Twenty-nine when there are pink shades, thirty when there are not.'[26] Lack of precision about one's age was to become a maxim for both Lady Wilde and Oscar; as Lord Illingworth stresses: 'One should never trust a woman who tells one her real age. A woman who would tell one that, would tell one anything.'[27]

For a certain time, conscious of his own popularity and eager to promote his mother's *salon*, Oscar became his mother's lion and played a role which, according to the illustrious French tradition, that Lady Wilde so proudly claimed to uphold, implied a bond between the *salonnière* and her paramour that often went beyond the realm of the intellect.[28] Believing herself to be a representative of a species in extinction, she regretfully confessed her disappointment that women of genius 'no longer cast their influence on society as brilliant thinkers and talkers' and that 'a literary *salon*, ruled over by some dazzling queen of intellect, some splendid woman of wit and learning, exists in London no more'.[29] Lady Wilde staunchly defended the role a high-bred woman is called to play in society where her mastery of the art of conversation would allow her to exert a life-long power: 'She may lose the attractions of youth, but the fascination and charm of manner and conversation still remain.'[30]

The drawing room is a recurrent setting in Oscar Wilde's plays: at Lady Windermere's last reception before Easter in Bentinck House where 'it was said that at one time the supper-room was absolutely crammed with geniuses',[31] Lord Arthur was informed of his destiny by the hostess's pet, a palmist; the first act of *A Woman of No Importance* opens at a party held at Lady Hunstanton's country house; in *An Ideal Husband*, Lady Chiltern receives her guests at the top of the staircase. In his only novel, *The Picture of Dorian Gray* which its author described as 'all conversation and no action', Basil and Dorian met for the first time at one of Lady Brandon's parties.

Encouraged by Lady Wilde in that art of sparkling conversation for conversation's sake that in real life constituted Oscar's genius and that his literary talent moulded into his works, the greatest author of the nineties was bound to find in drama the best ground for displaying his dazzling literary skills.

NOTES

1   Oscar Wilde, *A Woman of No Importance*, Act III, *The Complete Works of Oscar Wilde*, London, Collins, 1948.
2   She wrote several articles about the subject: 'Bondage of Woman', 'Genius and Marriage', 'Social Graces', 'Venus Victrix', and 'American Women', among others, published under the title of *Social Studies*, London, Ward and Downey, 1893.
3   Lady Wilde, letter to unknown correspondent dated 7 April 1858, Reading University.
4   Lady Wilde, letter to unknown correspondent dated 1848, Reading University.
5   'Meagher is about 22, handsome, daring, reckless of consequences, wild, bright, flashing eyes, glowing colour and the most beautiful mouth, teeth and smile I ever beheld, but he has not judgement for a leader. His mission is to give the daring energetic impulse: other must guide the direction of it. I was present at his trial. Nothing could exceed the sympathy he excited ; he is a person of good fortune and though sprung from the trading class yet is refined and high-bred looking. He was brought to see me at his particular desire. Those lines of mine "The Young Patriot" were meant for him.' Lady Wilde, letter to unknown correspondent dated 18 June 1849, Reading University.

6   'I cannot think an insurrection would ever be successful against
         the mighty English power.' Lady Wilde, letter to unknown
         correspondent dated 1849, Reading University.
7   Oscar Wilde, *De Profundis*, ibid.
8   'In spite of the lessons of Pater and Mahaffy, Oscar remained
         very much the son of "Speranza".' P. Jullian, *Oscar Wilde*,
         London, Granada, 1968 (rep. 1981), p. 53.
9   'If it is painful to her to read such an indictment against one of
         her sons, let her remember that my mother, who intellectually
         ranks with Elizabeth Barrett Browning, and historically with
         Madame Roland, died broken-hearted because the son of whose
         genius and art she had been so proud, and whom she had
         regarded always as a worthy continuer of a distinguished
         name, had been condemned to the treadmill for two years.'
         Oscar Wilde, *De Profundis*, ibid., p. 942.
10   When Oscar penned this play, he had regretfully given up
         poetry, a genre that 'Speranza' looked upon with approval and
         that was later to become of vital importance in Wilde's
         relationship with Lord Alfred. Perhaps, Oscar's enthusiasm for
         Bosie's lyric talent was reminiscent of his mother's ambition
         that was never truly fulfilled.
11   Oscar Wilde, *Vera, or the Nihilists*, ibid., Act I.
12   Oscar Wilde,*Vera, or the Nihilists*, ibid., Act III.
13   Oscar Wilde,*Vera, or the Nihilists*, ibid., Prologue.
14   T. De Vere White, *The Anglo-Irish*, London, Victor Gollancz
         Ltd, 1972, p. 198.
15   C. J. Hamilton, *Notable Irishwomen*, Dublin, Sealy, Bryers &
         Walker, 1904, p. 176.
16   'Here, on thy altar, O Liberty, do I dedicate myself to thy
         service; do with me as thou wilt!' Oscar Wilde, *Vera, or the
         Nihilists*, ibid., Act III.
17   Oscar Wilde, *Vera, or the Nihilists*, ibid., Act I.
18   Lady Wilde, letter undated to unknown correspondent, Reading
         University.
19   'Jacta Alea Est' was the seditious article written by 'Speranza'
         and published on 29 July 1848 in *The Nation* resulting in the
         closure of the weekly.
20   As Philippe Jullian states in his assessment of the play: 'Wilde's
         Vera is interesting in so much as the only female, the Vera of the
         title, cannot control her weakness for the very regime she
         wishes to overthrow.' P. Jullian, *Oscar Wilde*, London,
         Granada, 1968, p. 81.
21   Oscar Wilde, *Vera, or the Nihilists*, ibid., Act I.
22   Lady Wilde, letter to unknown correspondent dated October
         1849, Reading University.
23   Lady Wilde, letter to unknown correspondent dated 10
         February 1859, Reading University.
24   'Both children from the time they were able to keep awake at
         night had been admitted to the parties and *conversazioni* in the
         parlour of the handsome mansion at 1 Merrion Square.' F.
         Winwar, *Oscar Wilde and the Yellow Nineties*, London, Harper
         and Brothers, 1941, pp. 8-9.

25   Miss Henriette Corkran from her book *Celebrities I have Met* as quoted by C. J. Hamilton, *Notable Irishwoman*, Dublin, Sealy, Bryers and Walker, 1904, p. 183.

26   Oscar Wilde, *Lady Windermere's Fan*, ibid., Act IV.

27   Oscar Wilde, *A Woman of No Importance*, ibid., Act I.

28   'L'amitié amoureuse' linked forever the names of Mme Récamier and Chateaubriand to l'Abbaye-Au-Bois, Benjamin Constant and Mme de Staël, Jules Lemaître and Mme de Loynes and also, Anatole France and Mme de Caillavet, among others. F. Wagener, *Madame Récamier*, Mesnil-sur-l'Extrée, Ed. Lattès, 1986.

29   Lady Wilde, 'Social Graces', *Social Studies*, London, Ward and Downey, 1893, pp. 53-77.

30   Lady Wilde, 'Social Graces', *Social Studies*, London, Ward and Downey, 1893, pp. 53-77.

31   Oscar Wilde, *Lord Arthur Savile's Crime*, ibid., p. 168.

WILDE AND EUROPEAN THEATRE

Peter Raby

Wilde chose the London theatre as the context for his Hibernian or Celtic plays, and there is an aura of Englishness about some aspects of his drama: an Englishness which is slightly, perhaps deliberately, misleading on his part, but which has tended to cling to the way his plays have been received. The Wilde revaluation, which this conference explores, has only recently begun to redefine the context in which both the comedies and *Salome* properly belong.

As the centenary of *The Importance of Being Earnest* approaches, Wilde's plays are once again dominant in London's West End. A sense of *déjà vu* arises. The 1993 spring productions of *An Ideal Husband* and *The Importance of Being Earnest* were playing to full houses. A year earlier, *A Woman of No Importance*, in Philip Prowse's production for the Royal Shakespeare Company, made a triumphant return to the Haymarket. The Glasgow Citizens' theatre has already provided the context for Prowse's regeneration of the three society comedies. Even *Salome*, in Steven Berkoff's re-staging, has been hauled back from the opera house, where it can somehow be conveniently overlooked by English critics that Wilde had very much to do with it, and reclaimed for the London theatre: not just any theatre but, after suitable preliminaries at the Gate Theatre, Dublin, and Edinburgh, the Royal National Theatre. It has taken a hundred years for Wilde's dramatic achievement to be so emphatically recognized; and the opportunities for reappraising his work offered by this sequence of high-profile productions has made it less bizarre to see Wilde as a major playwright in both British and European terms, in contrast to the limited and rather grudging English estimate which once prevailed: the writer of one brilliant farce and some smartly packaged but essentially flawed boulevard entertainments. This higher status may come as no surprise to students of Wilde, or lovers of theatre. It certainly startled the collective of London theatre critics, who, with a few honourable exceptions, reacted much as their predecessors had done in the 1890s.

A common feature of the recent productions mentioned above is their enthusiastic reception by audiences. The critics frequently allude to the box-office pull of Wilde, as though this is somehow to his discredit; but there is surely only a cast-iron connection in the case of *The Importance of Being Earnest*.

There cannot be many greater distances, superficially, than that between the milieu of the society dramas and Glasgow's Gorbals; yet the plays under Prowse's direction were as well-received there as the Peter Hall and Nicholas Hytner productions have been in London's West End. The reaction was not solely to the wit, or the style, but to the content; instead of seeming safely distanced, much of it had a disturbingly contemporary ring. The smooth immorality of the London political world, for example, anatomised in *An Ideal Husband*, required no updating to hit its target. There are more reservations, naturally, among the reviewers; almost all of them, for example, contrived to praise Berkoff's *Salome* while damning Wilde's contribution to the proceedings. But over the course of five years' exposure, serious critics have been confronted by the combined intelligence of the directors, designers and performers of these plays, and have responded by gradual if somewhat guarded revaluation. Michael Billington suggested that Prowse's production of *Lady Windermere's Fan* 'completely revises our notion of how to play early Oscar'; he reminded his readers of how closely the London *première* followed that of *A Doll's House*, and praised Prowse for rescuing the play from being 'a quilted divertissement'.[1] Other critics were more cautious: John Gross, with representative caution, wrote of *A Woman of No Importance*: 'As soon as it's over, you realise that it is the stilted period piece that you always thought it was; but it is oddly moving while it lasts.'[2] A year later, describing *An Ideal Husband* as 'a very stagey affair' but also 'an eminently stageable one', he concluded: 'All in all, a singularly satisfying evening and, at its high points, a rather moving one.' John Peter used both productions to contrast

Wilde with Shaw, praising *A Woman of No Importance* as 'almost, if not quite, as lethal as *Mrs Warren's Profession*'; in responding to *An Ideal Husband*, he confronted the familiar question of the melodrama: 'The melodramatist arranges the blood-curdlingly improbable coincidences and displays them to brilliant advantage; the wit throws off his coruscating jokes to destabilise the whole operation. It is an example of schizophrenia unparalleled in the theatre, except by Shaw — with the difference that Wilde knew precisely what he was doing, whereas Shaw was not only willing to sell a serious argument for a good laugh, but he did not even know he was doing it.'[4] Reviewing Tom Stoppard's *Arcadia*, Benedict Nightingale described Harriet Walter's Lady Croom as 'a Lady Bracknell with sex appeal', and commented that 'its creative team would seem to involve the founding fathers of chaos theory and Oscar Wilde'.[5] Ibsen; Wilde as *moving;* Wilde as Shaw's master; Wilde as reference point for Stoppard's creative aim, 'the perfect marriage of ideas and high comedy': Wilde is clearly in danger of being recognized, even by the English, as a classic.

Wilde occupies an unusual position among contemporaries such as Ibsen and Shaw in that, once Alexander had persuaded him to complete *Lady Windermere's Fan*, he wrote successfully and immediately for commercial managements in his own country, and was usually closely involved in the rehearsal process. The exception was the decidedly unEnglish *Salome*, Wilde's first great gesture towards the theatre of Europe. By courtesy of the English censor, this became a continental work, realizable only in Paris or Germany or Moscow. Written in French, and for a French actress, it demonstrates Wilde's instinctive awareness of the potential of a new kind of theatre. The genesis of *Salome* is located within Wilde's response to his experience of Paris, and to French culture and art. His choice of Bernhardt for the role of Salome was astute. What English actress could have taken the part at that point in the development of the English theatre? When *Salome* was eventually produced in England, William Archer suggested that the whole company should have been sent by special train to Berlin before attempting the play; and even then Miss Darragh would have been an impossible

Salome, executing the dance with all the propriety of an English governess; Max Beerbohm, flinching at the dread name of the London venue, the Bijou, gives a vivid impression of the Englishness of this Salome: 'To think that a young English lady in the twentieth century could have been so badly brought up as to behave in so outrageous a manner! We looked severely at her mother. Was she not ashamed?'[6] The English theatre, even of 1905, was decidedly not ready for this experiment.

There seem to have been three possible French productions: Paul Fort was reported to have considered a production at Le Théâtre de l'Art. Even as late as October 1894, Wilde had realistic hopes of a Paris *première* for *Salome* with Sarah Bernhardt in the title role: she announced its inclusion in a number of probable productions for a subscription season. Finally, Lugné-Poe included *Salome* in a sequence which included *Peer Gynt* and *Ubu Roi*. Wilde wished to involve Charles Ricketts as designer for the Lugné-Poe production: Ricketts proposed a black floor, upon which Salomé's feet could move like white doves, while the author conceived a Salomé clothed in green like a curious poisonous lizard. Lugné-Poe finally achieved the first realisation of *Salome*, sending a copy of Toulouse-Lautrec's programme to London as a kind of token; Wilde, in prison, asked Ross for a *résumé* of the French reviews, and for word of 'any new tendency in the stage of Paris or London'.[7] Lugné-Poe became a fierce defender of Wilde's interests. He wrote to More Adey in 1896 about a projected, and unauthorised, production of *La Passante*, which he thought might be *Une femme de peu d'importance* in disguise: a French provincial company was hoping to cash in on the scandal; but Wilde, he suggested, might find protection from the French society of authors: since the staging of *Salome*, Wilde had the right to be treated 'comme auteur français'.[8]

William Archer described Salome as 'an oriental Hedda Gabler', and the play has usually been kept separate from Wilde's comedies in critical discussion. What the recent productions of Wilde's more obviously Ibsen-like plays has achieved is to reveal them as infinitely more subtle, multilayered and ambiguous than they have been usually regarded; less specifically English, more European in their frame of reference. With *Salome*, late Victorian society, in the person of the Censor, knew that something subversive was being suggested: it was immoral, blasphemous, decadent and should be swiftly exported on the Blue Train to Hamburg or Vienna, the destination of other irreformable women such as Mrs Erlynne or Mrs Cheveley. In the case of Wilde's comedies, and especially *The Importance of Being Earnest*, there was little danger. The English had swiftly contrived their own method of coming to terms with Ibsen's drama: it was marginalised, by making it the province of the Independent Theatre movement; unfashionable theatres, subscription *matinées*, uneven casts, financial obstacles: the triumphs of Elizabeth Robins brought few other than artistic rewards, even though, as Tracy Davis has shown,[9] the early productions featuring Janet Achurch and Robins were more financially viable, and the audiences more broadly-based, than has usually been accepted. As with the decadent 'French' messages of *Salome*, the serious, Nordic significance of Ibsen for English audiences was as crystal clear, and equally unwelcome. In *A Doll's House*, in *Hedda Gabler*, with so many of Ibsen's moments of comedy filtered out in the process of translation, the 'issues' stood out in stark relief. In contrast, Wilde's plays, apparently constructed upon familiar and traditional frameworks, and written in a style which invited audiences to laugh, were thought enjoyable but insubstantial trifles. The general impression has survived, contributing to the myth that Wilde did not care about his dramatic writing, a myth that seems unsustainable to anyone who has had to wrestle with the complexity of the texts of his plays. Yet now in the 1990s Wilde's plays, seemingly concerned with a narrow and unrepresentative stratum of society, function as a critique quite as incisive and far-reaching as Ibsen's. The connections between Wilde and Ibsen have been argued for some years by dramatic critics, most recently and persuasively by Kerry Powell in *Oscar Wilde and the Theatre of the 1890s*; that critical position is now being given a substantial stage dimension within contemporary theatre practice, freed from the particular glories of the Gielgud tradition.

Wilde had several opportunities for first-hand experience of Ibsen in 1893. Although he was not present at the first night of Elizabeth Robins' spring production of *The Master Builder* (he was in Devon, sending off copies of *Salome* to his friends and pretending to Shaw that *The Quintessence of Ibsenism* was his bedside reading), he went up to London to see it: 'Michael Field' observed him there, watching the stage 'impassively but with intentness'. Later that summer, Wilde shared the same London stage with Ibsen. Beerbohm Tree, of all the London commercial managers, had the closest encounters with Ibsen. Elizabeth Robins, in her frustrating negotiations for a place on the London stage, aroused his interest in lending his theatre for a *matinée* of *Ghosts* so long as Tree could play Osvald Alving himself.[10] Then he shifted his sights to *The Master Builder*, if he could play Solness and change his profession to sculptor. Once *A Woman of No Importance* was successfully launched in April, Tree mounted a production of *An Enemy of the People*, which he presented, initially, at a *matinée*. Several of his cast were already appearing in Wilde's play: Charles Allan, Wilde's Member of Parliament Kelvil, acted of Peter Stockmann, Mayor and Chief of Police; and Holman Clark, Wilde's Sir John Pontefract, was Billing. Lily Hanbury, the first Lady Windermere, played Petra Stockmann and Tree moved from Lord Illingworth to Dr Stockmann. The same kind of grudging recognition apparent in 1990s reviews of Wilde's society plays appears in notices of Tree. He 'brings all his earnest and picturesque power to bear upon the task of endowing the medical enthusiast with vitality and interest. Sometimes he almost succeeds, though it would seem that when he does so he is wandering furthest from the true Dr Stockmann of Ibsen's allegory.'[11] Hesketh Pearson comments that 'Tree played Dr Stockmann in a humorous manner that would have surprised Ibsen'.[12] Shaw and Archer, fiercely protective of Ibsen, expressed strong misgivings about Tree's interpretation: Shaw, so easy with himself about re-writing Ibsen, called Tree's characterisation 'the polar opposite' of Ibsen's Stockmann; Archer allowed it to be a sketch which gave every promise of developing into a brilliant portrait. The elements of comedy, irony, even farce which Tree found in the play seem entirely in keeping with the Ibsen of modern criticism; Ludvig Josephson, who had worked so closely with Ibsen, a more objective and better qualified critic than either Shaw or Archer, called Tree's 'the best Ibsen performance' he had seen for many a day. Between *An Enemy of the People* and Wilde's next play, *An Ideal Husband*, which he began to write that summer in Goring, there are a number of points of contact: the theme of the corruption at the heart of public life; the idea that the majority is never right; and the subtle interplay between truth and lying, the truths which are so elderly that they are practically senile, and can hardly be told from lies. The Ibsen *matinée* was not an isolated performance. Tree continued the series, and by the end of July had moved *An Enemy of the People* into evening performances, so that for a short period it was effectively playing in repertory with *A Woman of No Importance*. *The Illustrated Sporting and Dramatic News*, which had previously labelled this 'drama of drains' 'dull and didactic', reported that a cry of 'Three cheers for Ibsen!'[13] was heard, and answered.

One key member of Wilde's cast for *An Ideal Husband* was also deeply involved with Ibsen that summer: Lewis Waller, Wilde's future Sir Robert Chiltern, acted Rosmer, and Solness. As Rosmer, *The Pall Mall Gazette* commented: 'He was very earnest, but after all it is of the very essence of Rosmer that he was not after all earnest...'[14] When Wilde came up to London for the last night of *A Woman of No Importance*, Max Beerbohm reported seeing him at supper afterwards with, a final Ibsen touch, vine-leaves in his hair...

Wilde dismissed criticisms that he was in debt to Scribe and Sardou, preferring to cite *The Family Herald* as a source. Of course, he made use of the conventions and motifs of French drama, as did Ibsen; he knew how to exploit and adapt popular forms, and how to make them interact with supposedly 'serious matters'. He demonstrates this supremely in the near-farcical pattern of Act 3 of *An Ideal Husband*, where the series of unforeseen arrivals, the disposing of embarrassing visitors in different rooms, the alternations of master and servant, the business with the letters, provide a comic and physical counterpoint to the 'high' moral issues. That pattern forms an elaborate framework, the playwright's equivalent of a mask; and the heightened sense which the artifice brings only serves to make one more aware of the moral and social agenda. The world Wilde describes is manipulated into a form made familiar on the stage; the tone and even the incidents themselves bear an unsettling resemblance to life, as lived or as reported. The pages of *Vanity Fair* from the summer of 1893 convey a brittle commentary on the smart twitchings of English 'society': 'The season died brilliantly last week [...] Lord Curzon dined without his wife, and Lady Helmsley dined without her husband [...] Lady Howe had her jewel-case stolen, while staying with Lord and Lady Dorchester at Portsmouth.'[15] The age Wilde creates is an age of surfaces, as Lady Bracknell points out. It survives on an elaborate and highly coded set of gestures, which appear to have the authority of absolute moral value behind them. You are defined by them; you break them at your peril, or for your salvation. Some of them are trivial, to do with buttonholes and neckties, with sizes in gloves and the angle of chins. Others occupy the middle ground, such as a wife cutting open her husband's bankbook, or a married woman visiting a male friend's rooms in the evening. A few are seriously grave, selling a state secret, or being an unmarried mother.

This examining and playing with social gesture and convention, and their underlying meanings is, I would argue, what Wilde absorbed from Ibsen. He reveals the inherited Victorian and colonial value system as deeply flawed. Buoyed by the recognition of audiences who saw themselves, if subtly distorted, in the looking-glass of the stage picture, Wilde's portraits of a specialised segment of society may have seemed for a moment disarmingly, even charmingly, English. But there was an angry edge to the laughter. A hundred years on, his merciless reading of society, freed from the straitjacket of naturalistic detail, comes across as an even sharper and yet more generalised critique of manners and values at the very end of an era.

Images from recent productions evoked, for this spectator, not only the clear vision of Ibsen but the ironic perspectives of Chekhov. *A Woman of No Importance*, with its autumnal country-house setting, struck a particularly resonant chord in Prowse's production: the extended conversations on the terrace, waiting for the next meal; the isolation of the characters, and especially the women; the pattern of movement as they drift through picture gallery and terrace, searching for distraction; the sense of something more important happening elsewhere; Gerald's frustration at life defined by a small town provincial bank; the opposition between the older generation, and the young, between the old order and values, and the new. Prowse introduced a ghostly prologue: a young man, Lord Alfred Rufford as it transpired, dressed in white, self-absorbed — Dorian Gray, Lord Alfred Douglas — playing croquet silently against himself on the Hunstanton lawns as if he had strayed from a production of *The Seagull;* while from the unseen garden came the startling scream of a peacock. When Lady Hunstanton called on Mrs Arbuthnot in the last Act, and made her way out through the garden, she was momentarily halted in her tracks by the ominous caw of a crow. Those sounds seemed to define, and to signal the end, of an era: to suggest that the play is as much about loss, about the exhaustion of a way of life, as about new beginnings and ideals.

The peacock, with its echo of *Salome,* re-appeared in Bob Crowley's design for *The Importance of Being Earnest,* dominating the garden of The Manor, Woolton, Hertfordshire: it formed, indeed the whole garden, a decadent exercise in topiary which knocked any notions of pastoral firmly on the head. Yet even here there were echoes of Chekhov, with a Governess who specialised in German (in Wilde's first scenario, he even thought of pairing Miss Prism with the local doctor), the constant traffic to and from the railway station, and a resigned Merriman who had grown old in the service, a more reticent version of Firs.

One thing that the passage of time, and the development of a fresh approach to staging, can achieve is to break down the rigid compartments of genre, and style, and free plays which have seemed locked in by preconception. A dramatist at once so professional and yet so playful as Wilde is especially resilient, and repays experiment. Ibsen and Chekhov, too, revealed themselves to their producers and directors slowly.

Wilde's career as a playwright was cut short, when he had only recently found his distinctive voice, and begun to work in constructive collaboration with the theatre of his time. Writing to Alexander with the first scenario of *The Importance of Being Earnest,* and half quoting the American manager Palmer, Wilde described *Earnest* as a play 'with no real serious interest — just a comedy';[16] the irony faded, and the self-mockery was taken at face value, and applied to all Wilde's plays. Only now, perhaps, has the theatre found the confidence to give full realisation to Wilde's originality, to prise him loose from an inward-looking Englishness of reference and presentation, and to place him within the wider frame of a European perspective. Wilde's remark, 'I think the theatre should belong to the Furies', seems less wishful now. His plays have acquired a new cutting-edge in the theatre of the 1990s, even if his characteristic sound is not the breaking string, dying away, but the cadences of an off-stage piano or the explosion of a temperance beverage. Wilde's last play, like Chekhov's, is a comedy in which the characters seem to invent themselves. Charlotta in *The Cherry Orchard* conjures up a baby from the luggage; Miss Prism, a Victorian Fury, makes a baby disappear in a cloakroom. In the plays of Wilde, as in Chekhov, you can feel the emptiness; you hear in the background the thudding of the axe; and in both, the servants drink the champagne.

NOTES

1   *Guardian*, 9 May 1988.
2   *Sunday Telegraph*, 6 October 1991.
3   *Sunday Telegraph*, 15 November 1992.
4   *Sunday Times*, 15 November 1992.
5   *Times*, 15 April 1993.
6   Max Beerbohm, *Around Theatres*, 1953, p. 379.
7   Letter of 10 March 1896, *The Letters of Oscar Wilde*, 1962.
8   Letter of Lugné-Poe to More Adey, 4 October 1896, Clark Library.
9   T. C. Davis, 'Ibsen's Victorian Audience', *Essays in Theatre*, Vol. 4, No 1, November 1985, pp. 21-38.
10   E. Robins, *Both Sides of the Curtain*, London, 1940, p. 260.
11   *The Illustrated Sporting and Dramatic News*, 24 June 1893.
12   H. Pearson, *Beerbohm Tree*, 1956, p. 72.
13   *The Illustrated Sporting and Dramatic News*, 29 July 1893.
14   *Pall Mall Gazette*, 1 June 1893.
15   *Vanity Fair*, 27 July 1893; 10 August 1893.
16   P. Raby, 'The Making of *The Importance of Being Earnest*: an unpublished letter from Oscar Wilde', *Times Literary Supplement*, 20 December 1991.

RE-DISCOVERING WILDE IN TRAVESTIES BY JOYCE AND STOPPARD

Gerd Rohmann

Oscar Wilde, the great aphorist and aesthete, has become a personified legend. Both, his personality and his work were re-discovered in the intertextual[1] literary genre *par excellence*, in travesty,[2] for what makes an artist's reputation more intriguing than paradoxical sayings like:

> Women are pictures. Men are problems. If you want to know what a woman means — which, by the way, is always a dangerous thing to do — look at her, don't listen to her.[3]

or,

> The happiness of a married man depends on the people he has not married.[4]

or,

> Women represent the triumph of matter over mind — just as men represent the triumph of mind over morals.[5]

and finally,

> One cannot be too careful in the choice of one's enemies.[6]

Most tragically, Wilde chose provocation instead of following his own wisdom.

My paper concentrates on two important rediscoveries of Oscar Wilde in *Ulysses* (1922) and *Travesties* (1974). Joyce and Stoppard create intertextual relationships with Wilde's aestheticism and comedies of manners.[7]

The dramatic dialogue of the 'Circe' chapter shows a kaleidoscope of dream travesties. It is inspired by the performance of *The Importance of Being Earnest* at Zürich, on 29 April 1918, directed by James Joyce.

> When the play was over Carr [who had acted Algernon Moncrieff] with rage began to dance, saying I want twenty Quid for them there dandy pants.[8]

In fact Claud Sykes and Joyce had founded the 'English Players' in spring, a team of professional and amateur actors. Henry Carr, an employee of the British Consulate, was chosen to play the part of Algernon Moncrieff, because of his good-looking figure in pants. In *Travesties* Stoppard has him called 'smart-arse'.[9] After the first night of *The Importance of Being Earnest* Carr was so proud of having mainly contributed to the success of the play that he felt merely tipped by the SFr. 10 amateur pay. He also asked Joyce to remunerate him for the trousers he had bought to wear in Wilde's play, which Joyce refused. An insulting threat followed:

> You are a cad. You have cheated me and pocketed all the proceeds for yourself, you are a swindler. If you don't leave the room at once I'll fling you down the stairs; when next I meet you in the streets I shall wring your neck.[10]

Joyce must have thought to face a vulgar version of Algernon Moncrieff who lives in luxury at the full expenses of his relatives under the motto:

> Relations are simply a tedious pack of people who haven't got the remotest knowledge of how to live, nor the smallest instinct about when to die.[11]

Wilde's good-for-nothing honestly utters the thoughts of Victorians and many others, whereas Joyce and Carr sued each other before the Zürich District Court. Carr was fined to pay five theatre tickets, SFr. 60, and the court fees, Joyce triumphed over Carr and H. M. Consul Percy Bennett —

> The bully British Philistine once more drove Oscar Wilde [...].
> They found a Norse solicitor to prove that white was black [...].
> So, farewell bruiser Bennett [...].[12]

But he continued the law-suit for a threat of violence which could not be proved, with the consequence that Joyce had to pay Carr's expenses, his lawyer and the court fees, a sum of ca. SFr. 200. This humiliation was reason enough for the Irish novelist to take a literary revenge on British diplomats in Switzerland. The persons with whom Joyce had been at law all configurate in the chapters of *Ulysses* written shortly after he finally lost his case on 11 February 1919:

> Henry Carr, his opponent
> Dr. Wettstein, Carr's solicitor
> Frank Smith and Joe Gann, the Consulate employees who had witnessed against him
> Percy Bennet, His Majesty's Consul at Zürich
> Sir Horace Rumbold, British Minister in Bern.

I found the first bad memories mentioned in the 'Wandering Rocks' chapter where dead Paddy Dignam's son is mirrored reading the following announcement of a boxing-match:

> Myler Keogh, Dublin's pet lamb,
> will meet sergeantmajor Bennett,
> the Portobello bruiser,
> for a purse of fifty sovereigns, [...].
> (*Ulysses*, 206)

According to the *Freeman Journal*, M. L. Keogh's fight really took place, but against a 'Garry of the 6th Dragoons', on 28/29 April 1904.[13] The evening of 29 April 1918, was the first night of Wilde's *The Importance of Being Earnest*, directed by James Joyce, which caused the quarrel about the price of Algernon Moncrieff's trousers with Henry Carr and his boss Arthur Percy Bennett. Bennett the bruiser in *Ulysses* comes from Portobello Barracks, an English military camp on the Southern outskirts of Dublin.

In the 'Circe' chapter, Henry Carr, who had boasted in Zürich of his brilliant career as a military officer, is degraded to 'Private Carr'. He gives his address as 'Portobello barracks canteen' (*Ulysses*, 368), the Consulate being thus reduced in the novel to a military fast food establishment. A few lines later he fraternizes with his boss: 'Bennett? He's my pal. I love old Bennett' (*Ulysses*, 369). The fictitious Carr, consequently, is a soldier of the lowest rank who loves the company of bruisers. Joyce further insinuates that Bennett the Consul made common cause with his employee. This was suspicion enough for Joyce's complaint that the British Consulate boycotted more performances of Wilde's play. In Puritan-minded, provincial Switzerland the most extravagant exiles Lenin, Tzara the Dadaist and Joyce himself had found temporary homes during the First World War, but Wilde's moral reputation remained deadly or fatal there.

In 1909, on the occasion of the performance in Trieste of Richard Strauss's opera *Salome*, Joyce had written an article on 'Oscar Wilde: The Poet of *Salome*'. Here, Joyce explicitly deals with Wilde's moral banishment and imprisonment.

> His fantastic legend, his opera — a polyphonic variation on the rapport of art and nature, but at the same time a revelation of his own psyche — [...]. He deceived himself into believing that he was the bearer of good news of neo-paganism to an enslaved people. [...] Wilde, far from being a perverted monster who sprang in some inexplicable way from the civilization of modern England, is the logical and inescapable product of the Anglo-Saxon college and university system, with its secrecy and restrictions. [...] he undoubtedly was a scapegoat. His greater crime was that he had caused a scandal in England, and it is well known that the English authorities did everything possible to persuade him to flee before they issued an order for his arrest. [...]. After having mocked the idols of the market place, he bent his knees, sad and repentent that he had once been the singer of the divinity of joy.[14]

In his monumental *Habilitationsschrift* on *Oscar Wilde: The Literary Work Between Provocation and Conformity*,[15] Norbert Kohl confirms that, most tragically, Wilde mistook the theatre goers' applause and amusement for assent and acclaim of his own extravagant and provoking life style by the Victorian bourgeoisie.

Joyce's revenge on his amateur actor Henry Carr is even fiercer than his literary slander of Consul Bennett and Minister Rumbold. Private Carr and his fellow hooligan Private Compton swagger tight into nighttown and 'burst together from their mouths a volleyed fart' (*Ulysses*, 351). Their 'tunics blood bright' identify them as 'redcoats', i. e. British soldiers. Cissy Caffrey, a bawd, takes Stephen Dedalus for a parson, as he tipsily utters Latin quotations. The whole night scene is a fantastic play travestying events from Wilde's life and work, a summary of *Ulysses* and far outdoing *The Importance of Being Earnest*, the travesty of the Victorian *double standard* where: 'Style, not sincerity is the vital thing.'[16]

The cross-examination of Bloom in Nighttown bears many traits of Joyce's lawsuit against Carr at Zürich, Barrister O'Molloy's statement proves the contradictions of discourse and truth: 'We are not in a beargarden nor at an Oxford rag nor is this a travesty of justice' (*Ulysses*, 383). After all — it was! Sir Horace George Mantagu Rumbold, British Minister in Switzerland 1916-18, who had not even reacted on Joyce's written request to keep Bennett from boycotting his 'English Players' and to stop Carr's threats of violence, re-appears in the 'Cyclops' chapter as barber Rumbold applying for the job of hangman to the High Sheriff of Dublin. In a clumsy letter of reference written by himself Rumbold is introduced into *Ulysses*:

> In the abovementioned painful case I hanged Joe Gann [...] and I was assistant when [...] Billington executed the awful murderer Toad Smith.
> And a barbarous bloody barbarian he is too, says the citizen. (Ulysses, 249)

This comment on Rumbold's introduction is a summary of the Irish novelist's revenge on Wilde censorship by the British minister. Billington is a historical figure as F. Smith, employee of the Zürich Consulate whose name became Toad because he licked Carr's boots. Joe Gann, also employed by the British Consulate, was the only witness present when Carr threatened to wring Joyce's neck.[17] He refused as well to inform the court against Carr and is literarily hanged for lying.

Near the end of the 'Circe' episode, when the dream play is nearly over, we meet Joyce's ex-actor of Algernon Moncrieff again, as Private Carr, the violent, royalist, nationalist British common hooligan soldier who bullies poor Dedalus.

PRIVATE CARR (*his cap awry, advances to Stephen.*) Say, how would it be, governor, if I was to bash in your jaw? [...] What's that you're saying about my king?
[...]
STEPHEN. I seem to annoy them. Green rag to a bull.
(*Ulysses*, 480, 481, 483)

The Irish 'show the green' to demonstrate their spirit of liberty. On the first night of *Lady Windermere's Fan*, Wilde had opened his play with a green carnation in the buttonhole, which released the scandal when the coloured flower was discovered to be the distinguishing mark of homosexuals. Irish shamrock and Irish green have the effect of red rags to John Bull, who is represented by King Edward VII and by his vilest subject in Nighttown, Private Carr. The scene is full of victimizations, evoked by Wilde's self-victimization and Joyce's unhappy memories after his performance of *The Importance of Being Earnest*. The King witnesses Rumbold's Masterpiece, the cruel hanging of Ireland's hope, the croppy boy, whilst Carr rants at Stephen:

(*tugging at his belt*) I'll wring the neck of any fucker says a word against my fucking king. [...] (*loosening his belt, shouts*) I'll wring the neck of any fucking bastard says a word against my bleeding fucking king. [...] (*with ferocious articulation*) I'll do him in, so help me fucking Christ! I'll wring the bastard fucker's bleeding blasted fucking windpipe! [...] (*breaks loose*) I'll insult him. (*He rushes towards Stephen, fist outstretched, and strikes him in the face. Stephen totters, collapses, falls, stunned.* [...]).
(*Ulysses*, 486, 488, 490, 491)

Algernoon Moncrieff, the 'dandy extérieur', is only a proselyte of Wilde; Henry Carr, who slipped into his role, a mere fetishist of well-cut trousers and of a sportive figure with a latent proneness to hooliganism.

How deeply the lost lawsuit and uncompensated humiliation hurt Joyce's ego is proved by the facts that he assumes the beaten Dedalus's role and that, in taking his literary revenge, develops Henry Carr into the worst character of *Ulysses*. Joyce does not miss the opportunity to send a curse after Consul Bennett who, in the novel is, as he was in real life, vulgar Private Carr's officer.

PRIVATE COMPTON (*tugging his comrade.*) Here. Bugger off,
   Harry. Here's the cops! [...] (*pulling his comrade*) Here, bugger
   off, Harry. Or Bennett'll shove you in the lockup.
PRIVATE CARR (*staggering as he is pulled away.*) God fuck old
   Bennett. He's a whitearsed bugger. I don't give a shit for him.
(*Ulysses*, 491, 492)

The only mentioning of the word 'travesty' except in
the title of Tom Stoppard's play *Travesties* (1974) alludes to
the result of Joyce's legal proceedings against Carr after the
performance of *The Importance of Being Earnest* as 'a travesty
of justice'.[18] Both plays are comedies of errors. In Stoppard's
'memory play'[19] Henry Carr (1894-1962) is an old man with a
broken remembrance of things past. Wilde's drama, similar to
Worthing's and Moncrieff's *bunburying*[20] is exclusively enacted
in Old Carr's memory. Scenes of *The Importance of Being
Earnest* which were never performed, have shaped Carr's
character. Only Gwendolen and Cecily appear on stage as
offshoots from Gwendolen Fairfax and Cecily Cardew, but in
changed roles. In Wilde's play, Gwendolen is Lady Bracknell's
daughter, who, on Cecily's confession with a country-girl's
innocent honesty that 'When I see a spade I call it a spade',
satirically pretends to be of such elevated social status that
she is glad to say: 'I have never seen a spade.'[21]
   Carr, in Stoppard's play pretends to be the Dadaist
Tzara's brother. Moncrieff in *The Importance of Being Earnest*
pretends being Worthing's brother. The ending proves that this
is true, and that truth is never simple. Both Moncrieff and
Worthing escape the Victorian social decorum by pretending
that they have to assist a fictitious friend, Bunbury,
respectively a fictive brother, Ernest. There is no importance at
all of being earnest. In his slanderous introductions of the main
characters, Stoppard took information from Wilde and style
from the inter-text of *Ulysses*. Carr is introduced by —

CECILY. [...] I'm about to puke into your nancy straw hat, you
   prig! You swanking canting fop, you bourgeois intellectual
   humbugger, you *artist*!
(*Travesties*, 77.)

and by

> TZARA. [...] You bloody English philistine — you ignorant
> smart-arse bogus bourgeois Anglo-Saxon prick!
> (*Travesties*, 47.)

Stoppard would have known nothing about Carr's behaviour after Wilde's play without Joyce's criticism in *Ulysses* and Richard Ellmann's biography.[22] Even the quarrel is revived in the introduction of Joyce to the play by —

> CARR. [...] an essentially private man who wished his total
> indifference to public notice to be universally recognized —
> in short a liar and a hypocrite, a tight-fisted, sponging,
> fornicating drunk not worth the paper, [...].
> (*Travesties*, 23)

The allusions to avarice and to Joyce's affair with Martha Fleischmann are clearly related to the Zürich events.[23] Their first dialogue proves that Carr has no understanding for Joyce and his work.

> CARR. [...] something about you suggests Limerick.
> JOYCE. Dublin, don't tell me you know it?
> CARR. Only from the guidebook, and I gather you are in the
> process of revising that.
> (*Travesties*, 47-48)

Through Joyce, Stoppard clearly takes Wilde's side, for Joyce from Dadaist chaos conjures a white carnation, alluding to the flower which morally broke Wilde's neck. This is but another detailed proof of the textual interlocking of *Travesties*, in this case, with *Lady Windermere's Fan*.

Both, Joyce and Stoppard, take their literary revenge on Carr and on philistinism, Joyce by turning him into Private Carr, Stoppard by presenting him as a senile madman in *Travesties*.

> CARR. [...] I got my wires a bit crossed here and there, [...]. (64)

Joyce's modern prose epic in the manner of Homer, the greatest intertextual novel of the century, was inspired by Oscar Wilde and casts light on *Travesties* with a theory of art about which it is important to be earnest.

JOYCE. An artist is the magician put among men to gratify —
capriciously — their urge of immortality. [...] What now
about the Trojan War if it had been passed over by the
artists's touch? Dust. A forgotten expedition [...]. It is a theme
so overwhelming that I am almost afraid to treat it. And yet I
with my Dublin Odyssey will double that immortality, [...].
(*Travesties*, 62)

Ulysses and *Travesties* cannot be fully understood by
the traditional philological approaches to parody and
persiflage. These genres fluctuate, their historical pretexts
being unknown. The rediscovery of Wilde travestied by Joyce
and Stoppard, however, inspires their literary creativity.
Wilde's work and the legend of his life make modern and post-
modern literature break boundaries between historical and
fictional worlds.

NOTES

1   Intertextuality can be defined as communicative potential
     acquired in the process of reading: 'Tout texte est absorption et
     transformation d'un autre texte', J. Kristeva, *Semeiotiké* (Paris,
     Seuil, 1969), p. 144.
2   A literary travesty is an intentional or unintentional
     caricature-like treatment of another work in a different form. cf.
     Kleines literarisches Lexikon, vol. 3: Sachbegriffe, eds., H.
     Rüdiger, E. Koppen (Bern, München, Francke, 1966) *Wörterbuch
     der Literaturwissenschaft*, ed. C. Träger (Leipzig, VEB
     Bibliographisches Institut, 1986), p. 520. 'James Joyce's *Ulysses*
     is partly a travesty of Homer's *Odyssey*', C. Baldick, *The
     Concise Oxford Dictionary of Literary Terms* (Oxford, New
     York, Oxford University Press, 1990), p. 229.
3   Oscar Wilde, *A Woman of No Importance* (London, New York,
     A. R. Keller, 1907), p. 107.
4   Oscar Wilde, *A Woman of No Importance* (London, New York,
     A. R. Keller, 1907), p. 109.
5   Oscar Wilde, *A Woman of No Importance* (London, New York,
     A. R. Keller, 1907), p. 107.
6   From 'Phrases and Philosophies for the Use of the Young'.
7   There are many allusions to Wilde's concept of Anti-
     Victorianism in his theory of 'l'art pour l'art', but not in the
     sense of travesty listed in D. Gifford, *Ulysses Annotated*, 2nd
     edition (Berkeley, Los Angeles, London, University of
     California Press, 1989).
8   R. Ellmann, *James Joyce* (New York, London, Oxford University
     Press, 1976), p. 445.
9   T. Stoppard, *Travesties* (London, Boston, Faber, 1975), p. 47.

10   Information by A. Dutli, who inspected the court files, in: Th.
        Faerber and M. Luchsinger, *Joyce und Zürich* (Zürich,
        Schweizerische Bankgesellschaft, 1982), p. 41.
11   Oscar Wilde, *The Importance of Being Earnest*, ed. J. Bristow
        (London, New York, Routledge, 1992), p. 44.
12   R. Ellmann, *Joyce*, p. 459.
13   Th. Faerber and M. Luchsinger, op. cit., p. 50.
14   Originally as 'Oscar Wilde; Il Poeta di *Salome*', *Il Piccolo della
        Sera*, Trieste, 24 March 1909. Quoted in translation from: K.
        Beckson (ed.), *Oscar Wilde: The Critical Heritage* (London,
        Routledge & Kegan Paul, 1970), pp. 56-60.
15   N. Kohl, *Oscar Wilde: Das literarische Werk zwischen
        Provokation und Anpassung* (Heidelberg, Winter, 1980), p. 440:
        'Er verwechselte auf folgenschwere Weise Applaus und
        Amusement der Theaterbesucher mit Zustimmung und Billigung
        seiner extravaganten und provokanten Lebensart durch den
        viktorianischen Bourgeois.'
16   N. Kohl, *Oscar Wilde*, p. 422.
17   Th. Faerber and M. Luchsinger, op. cit., p. 51.
18   T. Stoppard, *Travesties*, p. 64.
19   M. Brunkhorst, 'Der Erzähler im Drama: Versionen des *memory
        play* bei Fry, Shaffer, Stoppard und Beckett', *Arbeiten aus
        Anglistik und Amerikanistik*, 5 (1980), pp. 225-240. M.
        Brunkhorst, 'Die Hosen des Algernon Moncrieff bei Wilde,
        Joyce und Stoppard', in: M. Brunkhorst, G. Rohmann, K. Schoell
        (eds.), *Klassiker-Renaissance: Modelle der Gegenwartsliteratur*
        (Tübingen, Stauffenburg, 1991), pp. 149-160.
20   N. Kohl, *Oscar Wilde*, p. 435.
21   Oscar Wilde, *The Importance of Being Earnest*, p. 67.
22   R. Ellmann, *James Joyce*, p. 426 ff.
23   Th. Faerber and M. Luchsinger, op. cit., pp. 41-42.

RE(DIS)COVERING WILDE FOR LATIN AMERICA: MARTÍ, DARÍO, BORGES, LISPECTOR

Roy Rosenstein

> One never outgrows one's early enthusiasms: one merely denies them.
> Peter Ackroyd, *The Last Testament of Oscar Wilde*.

In memory of Edouard Roditi (1910-1992)

'I shall never make a new friend in my life, though perhaps a few after I die.' The enemies Oscar Wilde made in his lifetime, including those in his immediate circle who betrayed him, are wellknown; less studied are those waves of readers and other friends who have admired him in each generation before and following his death. Over the years we have learned how Wilde came to be an inspiration to modernists and anarchists in Spain (Davis), more recently of Wilde's role in the introduction of modernism in Russia (Moeller-Sally), even of his reception in China, Japan and Mongolia (Bonnie McDougal, Yone Noguchi, and John R. Krueger in Mikhail). And of course today we are rediscovering Wilde in Monaco, not at all inappropriately.

My own focus rests squarely beyond Europe. It has been widely acknowledged that 'the Continental critics began to see what was important in Wilde's thought sooner than the English and American critics' (Harris 461). Thus 'the Germans were the first to take Wilde as a figure seriously and to treat the man and his work in a responsibly scholarly manner'(Fletcher 53). No doubt other critics would think also of France, an immediate source of Wildean inspiration and an early *terre d'asile* to his genius, but where to this day, in 1993, *l'homme* still generates more interest than does *l'oeuvre* (e.g., Charrière). On the other hand, as early as 1904 in Russia, whether studied in the original, available in translation, or simply read about in secondary sources, 'Oskar Uajl'd', his writings and his *zhiznetvorchestvo* or concept of life as art 'had become a nexus of contention between the modernists, who hailed him as one of their own and considered his life "instructive", and the conservatives, who disapproved of them all' (Moeller-Sally 465). Similarly the discussion of Wilde in Spain did not wait for the various translations into Spanish that came in the twenties. But in Spain, unlike Russia, those who would champion or simply defend Wilde in the first decade of our century were few if any: in short, any debate there remained one-sided and unfavourable to Wilde, much as it was across the Bay of Biscay and the English Channel. All the more surprisingly, then as we shall see, the reception of Wilde in Latin America, if we contrast it with his fortunes across Europe in general and in Spain in particular, is from the first more personal and above all more cordial.[1] Indeed, when scholars note that the English and American critics were the last to appreciate the importance of reading Oscar, they refer to North Americans only. If Wilde was lambasted on the Continent and elsewhere before and especially after his fall, he was welcomed more warmly in spirit in South America than he had been received in person in North America. Wilde may well have found among a handful of Hispanics his first, most devoted, and most diverse readership abroad. Before Latin American modernism and ever since, Wilde has not fallen from favour among his Latin American audience, which includes first and foremost his fellow writers.[2]

In this brief overview I will speak to several critical highpoints in Wilde's reception in Latin America over more than a century. For Latin America, Wilde's importance was recognized in 1882 by José Martí, the critic and journalist who would become Cuba's national hero; in the 1890s in the criticism and memoirs of Nicaragua's Rubén Darío, the most influential poet Spanish America has yet produced; from the first decade of this century in the works of Argentina's Jorge Luis Borges, the most universal of Latin American authors; ultimately in the introduction to a translation of *Dorian Gray* by Brazil's Clarice Lispector, her country's and her continent's leading woman writer. Their homage to Wilde effectively represents four stages in his reception in Latin America: Martí's appeal that Wilde be heard out; the personal esteem of Darío; a fellow writer's admiration from Borges; Wilde's enthusiastic sanctioning and diffusion for all audiences by Lispector.

José Martí (1853-1895) was read as a literary critic and political journalist long before he was venerated as Cuba's national hero. In 1882 he was in New York to hear Wilde; his articles on him appeared immediately in Havana and soon after in Buenos Aires. Martí's admiration for Wilde's aestheticism prompted a comparatist plea for Latin America to look beyond its national traditions, to Slavic, Germanic and Anglo-Saxon literatures. Among such foreign figures, Wilde figures prominently, in the company of Flaubert, Pushkin, Keats, Emerson, Whitman. 'Look at Oscar Wilde', he says repeatedly, 'listen to Wilde!'. In Martí's words, Wilde 'has purchased with his economic independence the right to intellectual independence'(67). Martí recognizes in him a brother who champions artistic *independence,* the key word for the Cuban who will devote his life to freeing his country from colonial domination. Martí's portrait of Wilde seems to anticipate a common martyrdom in the service of libertarian causes. For Martí, '[Wilde] broadcasts his faith. There have been others who died for it. We will soon come to that' (66). When Martí was fatally wounded leading his troops into battle in 1895, it was in the same year Wilde also fell. Because Wilde was widely perceived as a dandy and little more in January 1882, Martí's stirring harangue is all the more striking. Wilde was as yet little known as writer, but Martí hails him passionately as a fellow free thinker and independent spirit voicing, as he says, 'our shared thoughts'(71).

Eleven years later, in 1893, when Martí was lecturing in New York, his audience included the Nicaraguan poet Rubén Darío (1867-1916) (Lida 221; Fay 641; Bodet 104-5). Darío was already reading and writing about Wilde; they would later meet in *fin-de-siècle* Paris. Both had begun to make a mark: Wilde first achieved literary recognition in May 1888 with *The Happy Prince,* in the same year that Darío published his epoch-making collection *Azul* in Chile (Ellmann 282). This well-travelled Latin American diplomat and cultural ambassador, whose hedonistic poetry has been compared to

Swinburne's, responded favorably also to Wilde and his verse. Darío's reaction must have seemed remarkably supportive in the 1890s amid the widespread condemnation that surrounded Wilde in life and after his death. Darío was not alone among Spanish-language writers in Paris to have met Wilde: continental figures like Pio Baroja and Antonio Machado had also encountered him there in the nineties (Davis 1973, 141-43). But where many pre-modernist Spaniards (except Galdós: Dendle 135) were then intolerant of Wilde, the Nicaraguan found in him a fellow poet and critic whom he cites and defends repeatedly. Continental Spanish writers, including Unamuno at this early stage, attacked Wilde as the apostle of decadence, echoing the condemnations of Max Nordau's *Degeneration*. Over the same period, their Latin American contemporary was developing his personal aesthetic under the influence of Wilde and Verlaine, whom Darío had also met in Paris. Not surprisingly, *The Picture of Dorian Gray* was the defining text. Darío cites both *Intentions* and *Dorian* on several occasions from 1893 to 1896. But most importantly, on 8 December 1900, he extolled the greatness of Wilde in a warm obituary: 'a man has just died, a true and great poet' (3:468). He recognizes that Wilde's legacy must rest not on his popular comedies but rather on 'his poetry and his tales [which] are worth the finest pearls' (472). He continues: 'the best of the work by this *poète maudit*, by this admirable outcast, are his poems in verse and in prose' (474). Darío recounts how the two spoke in a café on the Boulevard des Italiens (cf. Cabezas 148). In his autobiography, published in Barcelona in 1912, Darío adds significantly: 'and now, in England and everywhere, his glory is reestablished' (1:150). Thus, substantially before Wilde's adoption by Spanish readers at the time of World War I or by Russian modernists as soon as 1904, Darío, who would give *modernismo* its name, had embraced Oscar Wilde. It was also Darío who brought modernism's influence to Spain, and with it, a more flattering vision of Wilde. This early Latin admiration for Wilde, dating from the 1880s in Martí and the 1890s in Darío, would be extended by 1914 in Spanish translations by the Puerto Rican essayist and critic Miguel Guerra Mondragón.

Well before World War I and the publication of Spanish-language translations, Jorge Luis Borges (1899-1986) had also discovered Wilde, destined to become a lifelong companion in spirit. Borges, who admitted that he wrote in Spanish but was influenced by English writers, makes only passing reference to a Martí or a Darío (Guibert 83), but his salutes to Wilde are many, from his first publication to his last. This was a precocious child, more of a prodigy than Darío, even more outspoken in his youthful commitments than Martí, and above all particularly well travelled in the realms of gold, both literary and geographical. Like his predecessors in the cult of Wilde, Borges was decades ahead of his time in expressing his esteem. Born in the penultimate year of the last century, hence briefly also Wilde's contemporary, Jorge Luis Borges was of that Victorian generation for which Wilde was not acceptable. Martí had heard Wilde in New York; Darío had spoken with him, in thickly accented French, in *fin-de-siècle* Paris; Borges discovered him directly through his books, in Buenos Aires and in English. For the ten-year-old Georgie — as Borges, brought up bilingually in English and Spanish, was then called — Wilde became his author when his translation of a story by Wilde appeared in the Buenos Aires daily *El País* in 1909 (Bervellier 289). Of *The Happy Prince and Other Stories*, a collection hailed from Yeats to Updike, the most popular is said to be the maudlin tale of 'The Selfish Giant' (Green v). Borges's focus on the title story instead is revealing: in it a young statue achieves perfection through the supreme sacrifice of his eyes and is cared for until death by a devoted swallow. The timid Borges likely read this sad parable as emblematic of his own destiny since blindness had haunted his family as far back as his great-grandfather. The cruelly nearsighted Borges, set from his earliest years in his determination to be a writer, clearly foresaw that the martyrdom of blindness lay ahead for him as it had for his father, under whose name the story was published. Still more might be made of Georgie's attachment to this moving tale of an immobile statue: 'El principe feliz' was Borges's first published effort as well as Wilde's first appearance in Latin America. Their long-standing collaboration and Borges's continued commitment to making Wilde's stories available to a Spanish-speaking audience were confirmed almost sixty years

later in his preface to an Argentinian version of Wilde's
Cuentos.

As Georgie grew up into Borges, his interest gravitated
toward other works by Wilde, but the old passion never abated.
Willis Barnstone asked Borges what were the books he liked to
read when he was young (9). Borges's immediate reply was
those he still loved at that time, in 1980.[3] Until the April 1993
publication of the first volume of his *Oeuvres complètes* Borges
had authorized the reprinting of little of his pre-1926 prose,
which included not only his translation but his essays on *The
Ballad of Reading Gaol* in the review *Nosotros* (1921) and in
the collection *El tamaño de mi esperanza* (1926). Even though
these first attentions to Wilde were consigned to limbo, Borges's
interest in Wilde remained strong to the last, as ample
published testimony documents. Several later essays, readily
available and frequently translated, are devoted entirely to
Wilde. All attest a more comprehensive, more balanced, and
more mature appreciation, no doubt one reason Borges never
disowned these. Some forty years after translating Wilde,
Borges evidently felt the need to speak out on this writer too
readily dismissed or too categorically praised — by himself,
among others. In his essay 'About Oscar Wilde' Borges justifies
his personal preferences as he accounts for his 'reading and
rereading Wilde over the years' (80). Playing with the pivotal
terms and notions of *The Importance of Being Earnest*, Borges
insists that Wilde's language is 'simple' but that the pleasure
we derive from him is 'constant'. Yet, he teasingly maintains,
'Wilde's technical insignificance can be an argument in favour
of his intrinsic greatness' (80). Thus his judgements on Wilde
remain sweeping and provocative: Borges invokes 'the provable
and elementary fact that Wilde is almost always right'[4] or
insists that 'Wilde is among those fortunate writers who can do
without the approval of the critics and even, at times, without
the reader's approval' (81). These are assertions which are
eminently worthy of the wit that was Wilde, who is here
pastiched in new paradoxes by a Borges appreciative of those
of his model. In sum, Borges judges the paradoxer
paradoxically.

A short notice also appears in *An Introduction to
English Literature*: this is a selective, personalized history in

which Borges deals comprehensively, if schematically and severely, with Wilde's entire production. Not surprisingly, Borges the historian of literature does not praise uniformly all the works. *The Picture of Dorian Gray* he deems 'overburdened with epigrams and excessive preciosity' (57), but of course this judgement did not deter him from citing *Dorian* on many other occasions.[5] Mentioned only to be dismissed as 'decorative pieces' are poems like 'The Sphinx' and 'The Harlot's House', though these will be acclaimed again later. *The Ballad of Reading Gaol*, which had won full and flattering attention in earlier writings, is now characterized as 'pathetic'. Nor do the early plays fare much better: 'They suffer somewhat from sentimental excesses', writes Borges. Yet he praises as 'delightful' *La importancia de ser Severo* (cf. French *Constant*, Catalan *Fidel*, Portuguese *Prudente*, Italian *Franco*, Romanian *Onest*, German *Ernst*). For the purpose of these published lectures, Borges is naively professorial and deliberately tongue-in-cheek: he says *Earnest* is 'purely simple' (56). As we all know, precisely from *Earnest*, 'the truth is rarely pure, and never simple.' Thus Borges in characterizing *Earnest* as a 'delightful and purely simple game of absurdities' is himself playing the same amused game as Wilde before a new audience. What then remains of Wilde's *oeuvre* in Borges's short-title catalogue? Two categories dominate: Borges's first love, the parables for children, and his mature interest, the criticism for adults. The tales, the genre in which Borges excelled, remain the centrepiece to this appreciation, where they are singled out for praise in oral and written versions. And, concludes Borges, 'his aesthetic essays are admirable', echoing the impressionistic term of Darío. There are countless other references to Wilde,[6] but the cardinal points remain unchanged in Borges's salute to a fellow lover of paradoxes playing hide and seek behind the deceptive simplicity of their languages.

In *Atlas*, the last of Borges's books to be published in his lifetime, Wilde again receives the homage of an entire essay. In Paris that year for the last time, Borges made a pilgrimage to the little hotel called *l'Hôtel*, as anonymous in name as was the room in what had earlier been the *Hôtel d'Alsace* when Sebastian Melmoth died there, says Borges, 'almost anonymously'. Here, in the essay and at the hotel,

Borges comes to terms with Wilde and his legacy. He dismisses
'a certain famous ballad' — so famous that he is reluctant to
name it in this study in anonymity. Indeed, neither Wilde's
banished name nor his ominous alias appears in the title of the
essay, 'Note Dictated from a Hotel in the Quartier Latin'. *The
Ballad* is qualified as 'not the most admirable of his works' —
again the same 'admirable', but now in understatement. He
continues, 'I would say the same of his *The Picture of Dorian
Gray*, a vain and lavish rewriting of the [most] renowned [but
unnamed!] novel by Robert Louis Stevenson.' In this final essay,
on Wilde and Borges, the author asks, 'What is the final
savour left us by the works of Oscar Wilde? The mysterious
savour of bliss. We think of champagne [which Wilde drank
copiously in his last days], that other *fête*. We recall with joy
and gratitude *The Harlot's House, The Sphinx*, the aesthetic
dialogues, the essays, the fairy tales, the epigrams, the
lapidary bibliographic notes and the unending comedies that
provide us with a host of stupid characters who are quite
ingenious.' Borges concludes once and for all, as if intent to
capture the paradoxical nature of Wilde's fascination through
a shared taste for pastiche: 'A technical criticism of Wilde is
beyond me. To think of him is to think of an intimate friend, one
we have never seen but whose voice we know and every day
miss.' This then is the ultimate recognition: a paradox worthy
of Wilde, indeed inherited from Wilde's Cecily, who had said,
as Borges the Memorious unfailingly recalls: 'The absence of old
friends one can endure with equanimity. But even a momentary
separation from anyone to whom one has just been introduced is
almost unbearable.' Wilde, I never knew thee, Wilde I'll never
know, intimates Borges: for Wilde was the steady companion of
childhood, the old friend one can perhaps do without 'with
equanimity', but he is also the recent acquaintance, the ever-
new companion incompletely known, who haunts us all
inexorably until the last. In Paris and in old age, Borges at long
last, after seventy-five years of frequenting Wilde, has
identified his haunting genius and laid the old Canterville
ghost to rest in peace at last.

The fate of *Dorian Gray* is revealing here. Wilde's
greatest prose masterpiece, it was dismissed as poisonous by
Wilde's contemporaries and rejected as self-caricatural by

Borges who had no time or sight for the novel. The culmination
of Wilde's penetration and assimilation in Latin America came
when *Dorian* was championed by Brazilian novelist Clarice
Lispector (1924-77). For Lispector, as for the young Borges, as for
Reinaldo Arenas's young Celestino,[7] Wilde writes for a
youthful readership. Here as in Borges, it is the author and his
works who are remembered, not the man whom Martí had
admired and Darío had approached when others mocked or
shunned him. But the novelty in Lispector is that in promoting
Wilde to a tender audience she proposes not his children's
literature, as his collections of tales are sometimes classified,
but his most powerful work. *The Picture of Dorian Gray* is
offered to an adolescent readership, not as a tale of the
grotesque and the arabesque like the Poe stories Lispector also
proposed to Brazilian youth, but as a parable little different
from Wilde's fairy tales. For Lispector the fascination of
Dorian lies not in its model of aestheticism and decadence that
so frightened or incensed an earlier generation, but in its
graphic portrayal and satisfying resolution of moral issues
suitable for and now accessible to all. The most damning work of
the *poète maudit* has been validated, even endorsed for all
audiences. We know that Clarice was particularly attentive to
the import of children's readings: she also wrote for just that
perhaps specialized readership. Lispector also added a
preface to her adaptation, one of a handful to appear in Brazil
since the first translation of *Dorian* by João do Rio, who
completed his in London and published it with Garnier
posthumously in Paris and Rio in 1923. Fifty years later,
Lispector teaches the enduring value of Wilde's novel: 'for
there is truth in [these characters and concepts]. And truth is for
all time'(8). Undeniable too, beyond Clarice's long-standing
interest in writing for children as well as adults, is that on the
shelf of adaptations signed by her, spanning Swift, Fielding
and Walter Scott to Doris Lessing and Agatha Christie, from
Edgar Allan Poe to Jack London and Lillian Hellman, from
Roscicrucian mysteries to Chagall's wife's memoirs, to my
knowledge only *Dorian Gray* receives the honor of a preface
personally penned by Clarice to pay tribute to the text and the
author's relevance.[8]

Thus sixty-five years after a precocious boy called Georgie assured for Wilde's fairy tale a grownup audience in Buenos Aires, a mature woman promoted his adult fiction to a juvenile readership in Rio de Janeiro. In this way Wilde — his so-called juvenile fiction translated by Borges for adults, his adult writings adapted by Lispector for the young — was made available for expanded audiences across Latin America.[9] Each translation provoked some critical notice: 'El príncipe feliz' was adopted as a text for classroom study while *O retrato* was praised as an effective adaptation in the style of Lispector. Of this attention the showman in Wilde would certainly have approved. In 1909 as in 1974, a new generation was reading Oscar Wilde in Spanish and Portuguese. If at the beginning of the century, the fairy tales alone were fair game for one exceptional English-speaking nine-year-old Bonaerense, by 1974 *Dorian Gray* was judged appropriate in Portuguese for any and all Carioca twelve-year-olds. As Borges himself has insisted, every great book in the long run becomes children's literature (Barnstone 131).

In my remarks I have not sought to trace borrowings or influence, if any. Poe, Whitman and Faulkner have enjoyed an unrivaled influence in Latin America; Oscar Wilde, like his *Earnest*, remains unique, frustrating any attempts to trace the origins of his inspiration or to localize his influence at home or abroad (Lawler and Knott; Cobb). Instead I have undertaken to document some of the respect and a few of the repercussions in Wilde's fortunes in Latin America. That warm reception took place, as we have seen, in several stages: penetration in the 1880s thanks to Martí's articles: admiration in the *fin-de-siècle* years through Darío's supportive essays, obituary and memoirs; translation, visibility and respectability across the lifelong appreciations of Borges; and finally, at long last, but again ahead of other nations, assimilation within the library of world literature sanctioned and recommended for all audiences by Clarice Lispector.

NOTES

1   Davis has in passing addressed our subject (1973; 1977), aptly observing that 'la acogida que se le dio a Wilde en Hispanoamérica merece más investigación' (1975, 68). Botero's study is limited to translations of *The Ballad of Reading Gaol* in Colombia from 1929-1952. The so-called Peruvian Oscar Wilde, Abraham Valdelomar (1888-1919), important in the founding of Peruvian *criollismo*, is a minor figure (unlike Wilde) and the comparison seems ill-founded (Schwartz 2:47-48). Among other *wildianos* is his Brazilian translator, João do Rio, pseudonym of Paulo Barreto (1881-1921). Cf. also Mikhail, passim. Spanish and Portuguese texts are cited from available English versions (*con retoques*); other translations are mine.

2   Wilde by no means provides the first case of a European author perhaps admired more in Latin America than at home. Speaking of *Lamartineanas* (Rio, 1869), Paul Hazard writes: 'Est-il un seul pays, en Europe ou dans le monde entier, qui ait élevé à Lamartine, l'année même de sa mort, un monument plus noble et plus émouvant?' (121).

3   We might recall here by way of comparison that Borges's contemporary Nabokov as a child had discovered a parallel passion for Lewis Carroll, whose *Alice in Wonderland* he translated into Russian and eventually saw published as his own first literary exercise. But Nabokov, unlike his Humbert Humbert, soon forgot his first love; Borges, on the other hand, never rejected Wilde from among his mature tastes.

4   As cited by Borges's namesake, Anthony Burgess, Ellmann summarizes Wilde's charm for a modern audience in similar terms: 'so generous, so amusing, and so right' (Burgess xi).

5   In his participation in the discussion over *Lolita*, which the blind Borges could not read, he expanded the debate to related issues in the reception of *Dorian*. Ever fascinated with his own double, Borges also remembered Dorian in his study of the *Doppelgänger* theme in *The Book of Imaginary Beings* (52).

6   If not Borges's last word, then certainly a summary to his lifelong dialogue with Wilde came in an interview with confidante Esther Maria Vázquez: 'Oscar Wilde, who was not a great writer, left us better phrases than someone like Schopenhauer who was superior to him' (105). Perhaps for Borges as for Nabokov, to whom I have traced a preliminary parallel, and who insisted that ideas without words are worthless, Wilde's enduring importance rests on his paradoxes which stir readers like Borges and us to rethink the familiar but constraining points of reference around us (cf. Wellek 4:409). Borges devoted his lifework to questioning the limitations of time, space and identity, and in this he salutes a master in Wilde. As Borges notes in his famous essay on Kafka, 'every writer *creates* his own precursors'; among his own predecessors, Wilde finds a *place de choix*.

7   We note in passing the case of Cuban writer Reinaldo Arenas, who published his first novel, *Celestino antes del alba*, before

fleeing his homeland in 1980. The rest of his works appeared during his exile in Paris and New York, where he died in 1990. In his Cuban *roman à clé*, this *romancier maudit* cites three masters in epigraphs to the three chapters of his book. Lorca is expressly named there in the third epigraph but also in covert form in the dedication to the book: 'para Maricela Cordovez', i.e., 'para el marica cordobés' (Soto 352). The other two epigraphs are from Wilde's 'The Young King' and Borges's 'Insomnio', suggesting a rich intertextuality linking these three writers whom Arenas admired, even if they were not uniform in their appreciation of one another. Borges had mixed feelings toward Wilde; he evidently felt little esteem for Lorca, in whose premature death he revelled. There is no evidence that Lorca would have known Wilde or Borges. The active or latent homosexuality linking these three authors to the author and the protagonist of *Celestino* is the unspoken subject of the novel.

8   One Brazilian critic draws a parallel between Wilde's 'The Nightingale and the Rose' and Lispector's 'Bichos'(Hill in *Seleta* 26), on the transference of vital energy to a rose. When Lispector writes of 'the number of times we murder for love' (*Family Ties* 92) should we also hear an echo of *Reading Gaol*?

9   From 1909 to 1974, each transformation contains its part of publicity, its dram of deception. Borges's translation of 'The Happy Prince' seemed the work of the mature writer that was his father, Jorge Borges, under whose name it appeared; Lispector's publisher promises that his edition of *Dorian* is complete, when in reality it is radically shortened and simplified for a juvenile audience, though without being bowdlerized. Borges's translation was assumed to be the work of his father; Lispector's adaptation may not be her work. Of various Portuguese versions of English- and Yiddish-language authors whom Lispector introduced or reintroduced to a Brazilian audience, whether she indeed is responsible for the translations or simply submitted the work of an acquaintance under her more prestigious name is not clear. Borges acknowledged that his translations of Melville, Woolf and Faulkner were largely the work of his mother, in contrast to his personal commitment to Wilde. Such collaborative exercises evidently posed no problem for the two nominal translators, both impatient to see Wilde made available to a broader readership, adult or juvenile, Hispanic or Lusophone. And each in turn, sooner or later, like José Martí before them, contributed a personal preface attesting to a public commitment to the dissemination of Wilde's writings in Latin America.

REFERENCES

Ackroyd, P. *The Last Testament of Oscar Wilde*. London, Sphere, 1984.

Balderston, D. *The Literary Universe of Jorge Luis Borges*. Westport, Greenwood, 1986.

Barnstone, W. *Conversations avec J. L. Borges à l'occasion de son 80e anniversaire*. Trans. A. Laflaquière. Paris, Ramsay, 1984.

Bervellier, M. *Le cosmopolitisme de Jorge Luis Borges*. Paris, Didier, 1973.
Bodet, J. T. *Rubén Darío: abismo y cima*. Mexico, Fondo de cultura, 1966.
Borelli, O. *Clarice Lispector: Esboço para um possível retrato*. Rio, Nova Fronteira, 1981.
Borges, J. L. 'About Oscar Wilde'. *Other Inquisitions, 1937-1952*. Trans. R. L. C. Simms. NY, Simon and Schuster, 1954, pp. 79-81.
—. 'An Autobiographical Essay'. *The Aleph and Other Stories, 1933-1969*. Trans. N. T. di Giovanni. NY, Dutton, 1978, pp. 201-60.
—. 'La Balada de la cárcel de Reading'. *El tamaño de mi esperanza*. Buenos Aires, Proa, 1926, pp. 131-35.
—. 'El caso *Lolita*'. *Sur* 260 (Sept. - Oct. 1959), 49-50.
—. 'Note Dictated from a Hotel in the Quartier Latin'. *Atlas*. Trans. A. Kerrigan. NY, Dutton, 1985, pp. 68-69.
—. *Oeuvres complètes*, 1. Ed. J. P. Bernès. Paris, Gallimard, 1993.
—. 'Oscar Wilde y un poema'. *Nosotros* (Buenos Aires), 49 (April 1925), 444-46.
—. 'Prólogo'. Oscar Wilde, *Cuentos*. Trans. M. O. de Grant. Buenos Aires, Atlántida, 1966, p. 3.
—. (With M. Guerrero) *The Book of Imaginary Beings*. Trans. N. T. di Giovanni. London, Penguin, 1974.
—. (With M. E. Vázquez) *An Introduction to English Literature*. Trans. L. C. Keating and R. O. Evans. London, Robson, 1974.
Botero, E. 'Versiones colombianas de la "Balada de la cárcel de Reading"'. *Universidad Pontificia Bolivariana* 27, 95 (1964), 88-95.
Burgess, A. 'Introduction'. Oscar Wilde, *The Picture of Dorian Gray*. Ed. D. Crystal and D. Strange. London, Penguin, 1992.
Cabezas, J. A. *Rubén Darío, un poeta y una vida*. Buenos Aires, Espasa-Calpe, 1954.
Charrière, C.. 'Oscar Wilde: le martyr du paradoxe'. Review of *Oeuvres complètes*, Tome 1. *Le Figaro*, 18 December 1992, p. 8.
Cobb, C. W. 'José Asunción Silva and Oscar Wilde'. *Hispania* 45 (1962), 658-61.
Coletes Blanco, A. 'Oscar Wilde en España, 1902-1928'. *Cuadernos de filología inglesa* 1 (1985), 17-32.
Darío, R. *Obras completas*. Ed. M. Sammiguel Raimundez. Madrid, Aguado, 1950-55.
Davis, L. E. 'Guerra Mondragón como traductor de Oscar Wilde: interpretación de la estética moderna en Puerto Rico'. *Sin Nombre* 6, 2 (Oct. - Dec. 1975), 66-81.
—. 'Max Nordau, *Degeneración* y la decadencia de España'. *Cuadernos hispanoamericanos* 326-27 (1977), 1-17.
—. 'Oscar Wilde in Spain'. *Comparative Literature* 25 (1973), 136-52.
Dendle, B. J. 'Galdós, La Jeunesse, and Oscar Wilde: Enrique Gómez Carillo's Tribute to Galdós'. *Anales Galdosianos* 23 (1988), 133-36.
Ellmann, R.. *Oscar Wilde*. London, Penguin, 1987.
Fay, E. G. 'Rubén Darío in New York'. *MLN* 57, 8 (Dec. 1942), 641-48.
Fishburn, E. and P. Hughes. *A Dictionary of Borges*. London, Duckworth, 1990.
Fletcher, I. and J. Stokes. 'Oscar Wilde'. R. J. Finneran, ed. *Anglo-Irish Literature: A Review of Research*. NY, MLA, 1976, pp. 48-137.

Green, R. L. *Modern Fairy Stories*. London, Dent, 1955.
Guibert, R. 'Jorge Luis Borges'. *Seven Voices*. Trans. F. Partridge. NY, Knopf, 1973, pp. 75-117.
Harris, W. V. 'Oscar Wilde'. D. J. DeLaura, ed. *Victorian Prose: A Guide to Research*. NY, MLA, 1973, pp. 459-64.
Hazard, P. 'Traductions de Lamartine et de Victor Hugo au Brésil'. *Revue de littérature comparée* 11, 1 (1931), 117-26.
Lawler, D. L. and Charles E. Knott. 'The Context of Invention: Suggested Origins of *Dorian Gray*'. *Modern Philology* 73 (1976), 389-98.
Lida, R.. *Rubén Darío, modernismo*. Caracas, Monte Avila, 1984.
Lispector, C. *Family Ties*. Trans. Giovanni Pontiero. Austin, University of Texas, 1972.
—. 'Introdução'. Oscar Wilde, *O retrato de Dorian Gray*. Texto em português de Clarice Lispector. Rio de Janeiro, Ediouro, 1974.
—. *Seleta*. Ed. R. C. Gomes and A. G. Hill. Rio, Instituto Nacional do Livro, 1975.
Martí, J. *Obras completas*. Havana, Trópico, 1940, 1943. 28: 65-69. [Cited by Davis 1973, 139 and 1975, 68.]
—. 'Oscar Wilde'. *Ensayos sobre arte y literatura*. Havana, Letras Cubanas, 1979, pp. 65-74.
Mikhail, E. H. *Oscar Wilde: An Annotated Bibliography of Criticism*. London, MacMillan, 1978.
Moeller-Sally, B. F. 'Oscar Wilde and the Culture of Russian Modernism'. *Slavic and East European Journal* 34, 3 (Winter 1990), 459-72.
Monegal, E. R. *Jorge Luis Borges: A Literary Biography*. NY, Dutton, 1978.
Roditi, E. *Oscar Wilde*. Norfolk, New Directions, 1947.
Rollemberg, M.. 'As máscaras Literárias de Oscar Wilde'. *Caderno de leitura* 4 (Mar. - Apr. 1993), 3-4.
Rosenstein, R. 'Lispector's Children's Literature'. D. Marting, ed. *Clarice Lispector*. Westport, Greenwood, in press.
Schwartz, K. *A New History of Spanish American Fiction*. Coral Gables, University of Miami, 1971.
Soto, F. '*Celestino antes del alba*: escritura subversiva/sexualidad transgresiva'. *Revista iberoamericana* 57 (Jan. 1991), 345-53.
Vázquez, M. E. *Borges: Images, dialogues et souvenirs*. Trans. F. Maspero. Paris, Seuil, 1985.
Wellek, R. *A History of Modern Criticism, 1750-1950*. New Haven, Yale, 1965.
White, S. F. *La poesía de Nicaraqua y sus diálogos con Francia y los Estados Unidos*. Mexico, Limusa, 1992.
Wilde, Oscar. *Plays, Prose Writings and Poems*. Ed. I. Murray. London, Dent, 1975.
—. *O retrato de Dorian Gray*. Tradução de J. do Rio. Rio and Paris, Garnier, 1923; Rio, Imago, 1992.

REDISCOVERING THE IRISH WILDE

Neil Sammells

The mournful sexton of St Michan's Church in Dublin — famous for the mummified bodies in its vaults and for the dilapidated remains of Handel's organ — will tell the curious visitor that members of Oscar Wilde's family are buried in its tiny, crumpled graveyard. A search of the worn and shattered headstones is likely to prove fruitless, but the observant student of Wilde will not go away unrewarded. Inside the church he or she might spy a memorial tablet set upon the wall: to one Thomas Bunbury of Clontarf, who died on the fifteenth of December 1790, aged 61. The tablet tells us that it was placed there by his son, Hugh Mill Bunbury, in 1816 on a visit to Dublin, after an absence of twenty eight years. The coincidence is revealing, as is the younger Bunbury's somewhat cavalier attitude to his filial duties: when, in *The Importance of Being Earnest*, Algernon Moncrieff escapes from the regimen of respectability he does so on the pretext of visiting a permanent invalid friend who is not only fictional, he is also *Irish*. Bunbury is the absent Irish presence at the heart of the quintessential 'English' comedy of manners. 'Bunburying' to Wilde is not just a way of escaping the claims of duty, it is a covert and comic acknowledgement of his own doubleness of identity and of the Irishness without which he would have — as Algy might put it — a 'very tedious time of it'.

G. J. Renier notes in his 1933 half-crown biography that Wilde 'was not effeminate. He was powerful, robust, and Irish'. It is clear that Renier regards the charge of effeminacy as a serious one: he dismisses *The Picture of Dorian Gray* by noting that the novel merely 'gives one the sense of ease one experiences in the presence of a beautiful and empty-headed woman with whom one is not forced to live'. However, his insistence on Wilde's Irishness is double-edged. He can employ it to rescue Wilde from one accusation, but only by levelling another. Renier says of Wilde's sexual preferences that the homosexual temperament was present in him to a fairly marked degree, though not to such an extent that it prevented marriage and procreation; 'but' — and here, so to speak, is the rub — 'upon this temperament was superimposed a lack of self-control due to his nationality.'[1] Renier's maladroit manipulation of racial and cultural stereotypes is something Wilde would have found both menacing and amusing. In his essay 'Pen, Pencil and Poison', about the artist, forger and serial killer Thomas Griffiths Wainewright, Wilde exploits notions of 'Irishness' to his own ends. The piece is subtitled 'A Study in Green' and Wilde claims that a fondness for green — the national colour — denotes an artistic temperament in individuals and is said in nations to denote a laxity of morals.[2] Green, in other words, is the colour of the artist, the decadent, the subversive, the *Irish*.

This series of sliding identifications is crucial to Wilde and to our understanding of the importance to him of both his nationality and his nationalism. His penchant for the green carnation buttonhole is symptomatic: it is the badge of a homosexual coterie, a demonstration of the self-consciously modern and refined taste which prefers the artificial to the natural, and a declaration of national allegiance which refracts and politicises both. It is, in effect, a languidly insistent and coded declaration of *difference*. As Wilde said, on the banning of *Salome*: 'I am not English. I am Irish, which is quite another thing.'[3]

However, the nature of Wilde's Irishness sets the editors of *The Field Day Anthology of Irish Writing* (1991) at odds with themselves and with each other. In his introduction to the section dealing with drama from 1690 to 1800, Christopher Murray retreads what he says is something of a *cliché* and identifies a characteristic Irish wit which he describes as 'more subversive' than that of English writers; behind the mask of the laughing Irishman, he tells us, 'be it Farquhar or Goldsmith or Shaw or Wilde, lay the determined enemy of English falsity'. However, such subversive potential seems compromised; Murray also notes that 'from William Congreve to Oscar Wilde the profile of the expatriate Irish playwright is of the polished man of letters, as eager for social status in England as for literary fame. He wrote primarily to please the English arbiters of taste.' Murray makes Wilde's wit seem strangely anodyne and ornamental; political questions, Murray claims, 'hardly entered the picture at all before the arrival on the scene of W. B. Yeats'.[4] Murray's discussion is uneasy and self-contradictory; it seems more than a little coloured by Daniel Corkery's mechanically nationalistic analysis in *Synge and Anglo-Irish literature* (1931) and his condemnation of expatriate writers like Wilde 'who did not labour for their own people', preferring to write 'not for their brothers and co-mates in exile' but 'for their kinsfolk in England'.[5] Echoing Corkery's insistence on the importance of 'the land' to his construction of Irishness, Murray claims that Irish drama only became fully political — and by implication genuinely subversive — with the return of Yeats to Dublin and his founding of the Irish Literary Theatre in 1899.

Murray is not alone among the editors of the anthology in finding Wilde's work compromised by his English context. Seamus Deane says of his poetry that it is vulgar in its facility of feeling and rhythmic automatism; as in all of Wilde's work, Deane continues, 'the subversive, even radical critique of society that is implicit in what he has to say, finds no release within the linguistic conventions which he mocked but by which he remained imprisoned.'[6] John Wilson Foster's discussion of contemporary Irish fiction looks to its antecedents and compares the 'natural flight from provincialism to London of Shaw, Wilde and Moore' with the later 'more painful and thought-out exile of Joyce'.[7] The charge, though implicit, is clear, and is the same as Murray's: Wilde concedes too readily — if understandably — to English arbiters of taste in his pursuit of metropolitan success.

However, the comments of W. J. MacCormack and Declan Kiberd take a different tack. MacCormack claims of *The Canterville Ghost* that it is a parodic reworking of the gothic mode in Irish fiction which suggests that 'an invasion of manners is no less an invasion than the Norman conquest: Wilde is as much a political writer as Maria Edgeworth and, like her, he understands that style is a miniature politics'. Nevertheless, the possibility that the playful manner might obscure the subversive potential of the writing is hinted at. Wilde's politics, he concludes, 'were consistently, if not always evidently, radical'.[8] Wilde's radicalism is amplified by Declan Kiberd who insists that he 'was, to the end of his days, a militant republican'; indeed, Kiberd revises the analyses of some of his colleagues by seeing Wilde's expatriate status not as a compromise but as a confrontation. He and Shaw 'challenged, by personal behaviour as well as by artistic skill, the prevailing stereotypes of the Irish in Britain'. On the question, though, of Wilde's relationship with English arbiters of taste and, in particular, with the linguistic conventions which Deane thinks confounded Wilde, Kiberd is less decisive. He says that Wilde and Shaw 'tried, with much success, to liberate the enemy language from its historic freight of meaning for an Irish person'.[9] However, in an excerpt from a 1984 *Field Day* pamphlet which is itself anthologised, Kiberd sees this success as crucially qualified: 'the forces which neutralised the subversive paradoxes of Wilde and Shaw are no less potent in the 1980s than they were in the 1880s.'[10]

So, the compilers of the new canon shift uneasily in their attempts to account for the nature of Wilde's Irishness and for the effect it has upon his work. For Murray and Deane, in particular, Wilde's is a story of compromise, of metaphorical imprisonment in English literary convention anticipating literal incarceration in Reading Gaol. Kiberd's analysis is more stimulating in this respect; his is not a narrative of contamination, invoking an Irish essence which cannot survive its English environment. This is the key; the Irish Wilde is best understood not in essentialist terms nor best explained in the context of artistic and personal defeat. Wilde's Irishness is a function of *difference*; it is defined — not demeaned — by his English context. The Irish Wilde, at his best, expresses himself in a series of subversive literary strategies and a distinctive wit which are the response of a colonial subject to discourses which, as Terry Eagleton puts it, are 'on the side of Caesar'.[11]

It is George Bernard Shaw who recognises both the nature and the importance of Wilde's Irishness most clearly. In a sense, he is repaying a compliment from Wilde who had described *Widowers' Houses* as 'Op. 2 of the great Celtic School'.[12] (Needless to say, Op. 1 was one of his own plays:

Lady Windermere's Fan.) Shaw claims in an 1895 review of *An Ideal Husband* (according to Wilde, Op. 5 of the great Celtic School) that the 'subtle and pervading levity' of the play is an offensive tactic; counting Wilde as an ally in subversion, Shaw defines their Irishness in differential rather than essentialist terms. 'Ireland', he declares, 'is of all countries the most foreign to England.' He thus redefines England's colonial relationship with *John Bull's Other Island*: the arrogant assumption of assimilation is displaced by an insistence on foreignness, on 'otherness', on *difference*. In *An Ideal Husband*, Wilde's foreignness expresses itself in the exposure of insider-dealing and political hypocrisy in the imperial metropolis. (In *Lady Windermere's Fan* it is given surrogate voice in the antipodean 'cool' of Hopper, another colonial, who nonchalantly undercuts the aristocratic prejudices of the Duchess of Berwick; productions which insist on playing Hopper as simply a rather dim suitor to the 'little chatterbox', Lady Agatha, run the risk of finding that Wilde's joke is on them.) Significant also is the refusal of *An Ideal Husband* to observe distinctions between the serious and the frivolous, the central and the marginal: distinctions it is in the nature of discourse to defend and deploy. Shaw proclaims that to the Irishman 'there is nothing in the world quite so exquisitely comic as an Englishman's seriousness'.[13] By locating the epigram as the centre of Wilde's comedy, Shaw recognises that his strategies are both political and linguistic — and, of course, symptomatic of Wilde's Irishness. Shaw's emphasis on the implications of Wilde's 'playful' manner is a telling response to those like W. J. MacCormack who fear that the subversive potential of the work might be obscured by its comic surface.

In 'The Critic as Artist' Wilde describes language as the parent and not the child of thought. In the context of Wilde's Irishness, the remark sheds much light on his predicament as a colonial subject operating within the discourses of his imperial masters. Other Irish playwrights have solved the problem in their own way. Synge, for instance, successfully 'unenglishes' English, bending it to the rhythms and cadences of Irish, to express his mocking denial of authority in all forms.[14] Sean O'Casey's tactics are similar in his creation of dramatic dialogue which blends realism with a heightened, poetic fantasy. Wilde, on the other hand, 'outenglishes' English. His characters speak with an elegance and an almost extraterritorial precision which exploits English to its own destruction. Wilde's consciousness of his foreignness informs his parodic engagement with language; as an Anglo-Irishman he contrives to 'distance himself within' English, thus registering his paradoxical position in the colonial power-structure between England and Ireland. The political realities of his colonial situation give a practical urgency to Wilde's subversive strategies; English, the master-discourse, is exploited to the point where it describes only a void. 'Miss Fairfax', says Jack nervously in *The Importance of Being Earnest*, as his speech curls back around emptiness, 'ever since I met you I have admired you more than any girl... I have ever met since... I met you' (p. 329).

The subversive strategies of Wilde's 'playfulness' and wit can be seen, at an important level, as the breaking down of antithesis — a point made forcefully by Declan Kiberd.[15] *The Picture of Dorian Gray* is a complex but illuminating case. The novel can be read as a critique of naked hedonism in which Dorian pays a terrible price for his Faustian bargain. It can also, as its first reviews show, be read as nothing of the sort. When the novel was first published in volume-form, Wilde added a preface which seemed to identify as his the aesthetic creed with which Lord Henry corrupts Dorian. It is here that we find the famous claims that 'all art is quite useless' and that 'there is no such thing as a moral or an immoral book. Books are well-written, or badly written. That is all' (p. 7). In other words, the Paterese of the preface acts an 'amoral' corrective to the narrative which follows. However, in his public defence of the novel, Wilde can be seen having it both ways. In a crucial subversion of accepted categories he aestheticises the novel's moral content. He refuses to regard the ethical and the aesthetic as opposites in the manner described by Susan Sontag as symptomatic of Western thinking since Plato, which — she insists — distinguishes the two by only ever calling the aesthetic into question and never the ethical.[16] This refusal is behind the loaded phasing of a letter to the *Scots Observer* in August 1890: 'You ask me, sir, why I should have the ethical beauty of my story recognised. I answer, simply because it exists, because the thing is there.'[17] Here we have it: *ethical beauty*. The seemingly innocuous phrase is redolent of Wilde's refusal to rest easy in comfortable distinctions. Wilde's most common tactic in attacking binary oppositions — what Derrida might call 'violent hierarchies' — is to invert the established value-structure by elevating the aesthetic above the ethical. (Another spatial metaphor: the aesthetic margin displaces the ethical centre.) We can see this in individual jokes: we are told that Thomas Griffiths Wainewright's murders are less heinous than his influence on journalistic prose; in *The Importance of Being Earnest* Cecily is accustomed to offering Ernest's good taste as an excuse for his leading such a bad life. However, Wilde also goes one stage further and *deconstructs* antitheses by showing — as Declan Kiberd notes — that the qualities we might expect to find on one side of any given opposition are, in fact, equally present on the other. In the two most substantial essays in *Intentions*, this is clearly the case: 'The Critic as Artist' shows that criticism is actually more creative than artistic production; 'The Decay of Lying' asserts that art is more real than life (Where, asks Wilde, if not from the Impressionists, do we get those wonderful brown fogs that come creeping down our streets?). Wilde's playful subversion of conventional notions of gender is similarly constituted: Mrs Erlynne displaces masculine authority and control, remaining unflappably cool while the male 'dandy', Lord Darlington, loses himself in sentimental rhetoric; Salome displays traditionally 'male' sexual aggression in her advances to the virginal Iokanaan; in *The Importance of Being Earnest* Cecily and Gwendolen are the incarnations of appetite which, in Algy, exists only in the diminished form of a craving for muffins and cucumber sandwiches — the girls disarm their prospective partners with the invention and avidity of their pursuit. In *De Profundis* Wilde makes the telling comment that 'what the paradox was to me in the sphere of thought, perversity became to me in the sphere of passion' (p. 913). Although, G. J. Renier, for one, would not be very convinced by the argument that Wilde's 'feasting with panthers' is given a degree of intellectual interest as the corollary of his deconstruction of sexual and linguistic difference, there is no doubting the clarity of insight with which Wilde outlines his subversive enterprise.

In effect, Wilde's textual strategies display difference in order to deny it. The same is true of his adroit manipulation of his Irishness. Wilde is, to quote Owen Dudley Edwards, 'at once the metropolitan sophisticate and the loyal son of the Celtic periphery'.[18] As a member of the Anglo-Irish Ascendancy, Wilde is implicated in English domination, yet contemptuous of it, a contradiction enacted in his precise deployment, and disarming, of the language itself. Rediscovering the Irish Wilde is not a matter of excavation, of scraping away the accretions of Englishness to reveal a Celtic core: it is, rather, a matter of recognising alternative identities simultaneously maintained. Wilde's Irishness is not defeated by his Englishness — however uncomfortable this might make the anthologists. Instead, the Irish Wilde is defined both by and against the English Wilde.

NOTES

1   G. J. Renier, *Oscar Wilde* (London, Nelson, 1933), pp. 95-94.
        Wilde finds himself in somewhat mixed company in this series of
        'short biographies'. Other subjects are Cecil Rhodes, St Paul
        and Lenin. Renier does not attempt an answer to the Irish
        problem, but he does chance his arm on the sexual one: 'It is not
        by persecution but by science that the mass   production of
        homosexuals will be averted' (p. 96).
2   *Complete Works of Oscar Wilde* (London, Collins, 1966), p. 996.
        Following quotations relate to this source.
3   R. Ellmann, *Oscar Wilde* (London, Hamilton, 1988), p. 377.
4   S. Deane, ed., *The Field Day Anthology of Irish Writing* (Derry,
        Field Day, 1991), vol. I, pp. 506-7, 502, 507.
5   Ibid., vol. II, p. 1008.
6   Ibid., vol. II, p. 721.
7   Ibid., vol. III, p. 940.
8   Ibid., vol. II, p. 846.
9   Ibid., vol. II, pp. 373, 372.
10   Ibid., vol. II, p. 639.
11   T. Eagleton, *Saint Oscar* (Derry, Field Day, 1989), p. viii.
12   R. Hart-Davis ed., *Letters* (Oxford, Oxford University Press,
        1979), p. 112.
13   G. B. Shaw, *Saturday Review*, 12 Jan. 1895, pp. 44-5.
14   S. Deane, *A Short History of Irish Literature* (London,
        Hutchinson, 1986), pp. 149-54.
15   S. Deane, ed., *The Field Day Anthology*, vol. II, pp. 372-76.

16   S. Sontag, *Against Interpretation* (New York, Farrar, Strauss and Giroux, 1967), p. 23.
17   For a discussion of the critical reception of *The Picture of Dorian Gray*, and Wilde's defence of it in the press, see S. Mason, *Oscar Wilde: Art and Morality* (New York, Haskell House, 1971). The book was originally published in 1907.
18   O. Dudley Edwards, ed., *The Fireworks of Oscar Wilde* (London, Barrie & Jenkins, 1989), p. 30.

WILDE'S DARK ANGEL AND THE SPELL OF DECADENT CATHOLICISM

Ronald Schuchard

> Tempter, should I escape thy flame,
> Thou wilt have helped my soul from Death.
> Lionel Johnson, 'The Dark Angel'

Ever since Frank Harris assured us that 'no one will understand Oscar Wilde who for a moment loses sight of the fact that he was a pagan born', and Boris Brasol informed us that Wilde was a man 'whose fundamental craving in life was self-gratification', and Vincent O'Sullivan averred that Wilde was 'totally devoid of an interior life', his many biographers have been loathe to allow that his life and art were driven by any spiritual hunger.[1] Even Richard Ellmann declared that Wilde's interest in Roman Catholicism was but another 'forgery' of his personality, an 'attractive fiction' of his early career.[2] The encrusted portrait of Wilde as priest of paganism, apostle of aestheticism, host of homoeroticism and victim of Victorian culture has refused to accommodate the image of Wilde as spiritual voyager. The two locales of his Catholicism, at Oxford and on his deathbed, have long been submerged by a widespread scepticism that discourages any attempt to reconstruct his spiritual odyssey even as his works and accumulated evidence invite it. But if in the 1990s we are to rediscover Wilde, if we are to restore the soul to his aging portrait, we must admit his dark angel and follow their voyage on the malefic seas of decadent Catholicism.

Wilde was already torn by conflicting sensual and spiritual desires when he matriculated at Oxford in 1874, and he would be further torn by antithetical claims on his body and soul as he began to seek refuge from a frightening sensuality in Roman Catholicism. He was almost forgetful of the fact that his mother, a Protestant with Nationalist-Catholic leanings, saw to his instruction and conditional baptism as a Catholic when he was eight or nine years old,[3] but he was ever mindful of his Protestant father's determined resistance to the alarming affinity for Catholicism that Wilde had shown in his association with Jesuit priests at the Church of St Francis Xavier in Upper Gardiner Street, Dublin. Thus, during Wilde's first term at Oxford, where his father thought him free of such pernicious influences, there were many silent ironies: as Wilde read Pater's *Studies in the History of the Renaissance* (1873), his Catholic sense of sin and guilt was strongly intact; as he began the lavish decoration of his rooms at Magdalen, he found his closest friend in David Hunter Blair, who was preparing his own path to Rome; as he responded to his spiritual impulses, he began to brood upon the louring presence of 'the silent Sphinx', the first incarnation of the dark angel who would drive him to the Church through the *via negativa* of lust, sin and degradation.

David Hunter Blair, 'Dunskie', much of whose testimony has been excluded from the record (with the usual license that the word of clerics is not to be trusted in conversion matters), quickly sensed Wilde's dual nature, noticed that he liked to pose as a dilettante and idler while steathily engaged in voracious reading, and kept pressure on him to vent his spiritual life. Later in the year, at the end of Lent Term, Blair journeyed to Rome to be received into the Church, and when he returned to Oxford Wilde opened up to him: 'Oscar was greatly interested in the step I had taken [...] and shewed me what I had not known before, how deep, and I am sure genuine, was his own sympathy with Catholicism, and how much moved he was by my having taken the step which I did.'[4] Though Wilde told him that his father's 'grave displeasure' kept him from a similar course, and that at Trinity College he feared being 'cast off altogether' had he converted, Blair 'never had any doubt where his interest and his sympathy lay' (p. 126). During the next two years Wilde accompanied Blair to various Catholic services and functions at the new Jesuit Church of St Aloysius, including 'fascinating' sermons by Cardinal Manning. Blair introduced him to several priests, including a German Jesuit at the Catholic chapel in St Clements, 'Father H.', who also discerned the spiritual temperament under Wilde's jesting manner. 'Beneath the superficial veneer of vanity and foolish talk', he confided to Blair after many talks with Wilde, 'there is, I am convinced, something deeper and more sincere, including a genuine attraction towards Catholic belief and practice. But the time has not come' (p. 130).

There were other friends to keep that time away, particularly Lord Ronald Gower, a critic, writer, sculptor and well-known London aesthete who occasionally came up to see Wilde and his friend Frank Miles. Curiously, biographers have paid no attention to Gower's role in Wilde's Oxford life, except to quote with amusement his diary entry on their first meeting in June 1875, where he observed that Wilde was a 'pleasant cheery fellow, but with his long-haired head full of nonsense regarding the Church of Rome. His room is filled with photographs of the Pope and Cardinal Manning.'[5] Lord Gower, a veritable Lord Wotton nine years senior to Wilde, was wholly unsympathetic to Wilde's Catholic aspirations and willfully set himself up as a foil to the influence of Blair, whom he portrayed to Wilde as 'a dangerous proselytizer'. Blair believed that Gower's 'whole influence was exerted in the direction of keeping Oscar out of the Church. Whenever they met he would use the weapons of ridicule and sarcasm, at which he was fairly adept, to laugh his friend out of his Catholic proclivities. To Blair, Gower had become a greater blocking force than Sir William Wilde, who had died in April but continued to intimidate his son from the grave. 'I have always felt', Blair wrote in perspective, 'that Ronald Gower was one of the principal factors in deterring Oscar [...] from following at that time his natural bent towards Catholicism.'[6] As the tug-of-war between aestheticism and Catholicism ensued, Gower would gradually make it clear to Wilde that there would be no place for a pious papist in his London circles.

Undaunted by Gower, Blair redoubled his efforts to bring Wilde safely into the fold, even turning to the gaming rooms of Monte Carlo to secure his passage to the Vatican. In March 1877 Blair went to Rome with William Ward, another of their anti-Catholic friends, whom Wilde urged to let himself 'feel the awful fascination of the Church, its extreme beauty and sentiment'.[7] Wilde wrote to Ward that though he

was stuck in Oxford 'I may go over in the vac. I have dreams of
a visit to Newman, of the holy sacrament in a new Church, and
of a quiet and peace afterwards in my soul. I need not say,
though, that I shift with every breath of thought and am
weaker and more self-deceiving than ever'(L 31). Blair, who
must have been shown Wilde's letters, now pressed him to join
them in Rome. As he had missed opportunities to visit the
Holy City the previous two summers, Wilde was anxious to
come, but as he had recently joined his first London club, he had
to plead an empty purse. Not to be denied, Blair travelled to
Monte Carlo to stake £2 on the salvation of Wilde's soul,
coming away from the tables with £60 to cover Wilde's travel
expenses. Wilde sensed that he was on the threshold of a
momentous decision, writing to a friend before departure that
this was 'an era in my life, a crisis. I wish I could look into the
seeds of time and see what is coming' (L 34). What was coming
was a weakening rather than a surrender of will.

Wilde set out for Rome in the company of his old
Trinity tutor, Rev. John Pentland Mahaffy, a classical
Hellenist who had no sympathy for either Paterian
aestheticism or Roman Catholicism. They were scheduled to
part ways at Genoa, but by that point Mahaffy, determined to
redirect his former student toward Hellenistic scholarship,
had persuaded Wilde to forego Rome and accompany him to
Greece by way of Ravenna. Though Wilde was 'awfully
ashamed' (L 34), he found the proposal irresistible, and a
triumphant Mahaffy wrote rather gleefully to his wife that
Wilde had 'come round under the influence of the moment from
Popery to Paganism, but what his Jesuit friends will say, who
supplied the money to land him in Rome, it is not hard to guess.
I think it is a fair case of cheating the devil'.[8] To assuage his
shame and fulfill his obligation to Blair, Wilde returned by
way of Rome, where a patient Blair placed him under the
outreached hands of Pius IX for a blessing and prayer of
conversion. For his encouraging reward, Blair received from
Wilde that day the manuscript of the first of several
devotional poems.

Blair believed that Wilde's conversion was finally at
hand, but when Wilde returned to Oxford for the summer term,

Blair was dismayed to find him vacillating and full of lame excuses. Blair wrote in exasperation on 1 June 1877:

> It is useless to talk of your weakness and want of principle — truly a strange reason for turning your back on what alone will make you strong [...] and as for your want of faith and enthusiasm to believe that God, who has given you grace to see His truth, will not also keep you firm when you choose to embrace it — you *know* He has called you to be a child of the Church, but you are unwilling to give up a hundred and one little sins, it is sheer cowardice, nothing more. It is not even, with you, a question of choosing between two religions, the false and the true — no you must be a Catholic or nothing. Your choice is between God and the devil, neither more nor less. How *can* you hesitate?[9]

He closed angrily and with finality on the matter, saying that though he would continue to pray for Wilde he did not wish to see any more of his Roman sonnets. Blair later realized that a serious change had occurred: 'He had become Hellenized, somewhat Paganized, perhaps, by the appeal of Greece to his sensitive nature; and Rome had retired into the background.'[10] 'Poor Dunskie', Wilde wrote to Ward, after hearing that a Protestant 'cousin' (actually a bastard half-brother) had virtually cut him out of his will for being 'on the brink' of conversion, 'I know he looks on me as a renegade; still I have suffered very much for my Roman fever in mind and *pocket* and happiness' (*L* 45).

Something had indeed changed. Gower, Ward, Mahaffy and the ghost of Sir William Wilde may have cooled his Roman fever, and the refreshing Hellenic spirit hailed in his Newdigate Prize poem 'Ravenna' may have temporarily relieved his thoughts of a sorrowful and betrayed Christ in Gethsemane, but by April 1878 a lower fever allegedly invaded Wilde's mind and body, syphilis, possibly contracted from a prostitute named 'Old Jes' in Oxford.[11] He had written to Ward that 'I get so wretched and low and troubled that in some desperate mood I will seek the shelter of a Church which simply enthralls me by its fascination' (*L* 31).[12] In May 1878, after an unspecified illness that Ellmann believes to have been the secondary siege of syphilis, Wilde slipped off in that desperate mood to the Brompton Oratory in London to meet with Father Sebastian Bowden, to whom he was driven in 'aimlessness and misery' to confess not only his 'temporal misfortune' but his 'life's history and [...] soul's state'.[13] But Bowden, who may have conveyed a stonger sense of Victorian conformity than Catholic sanctity to Wilde, was to be as disappointed as Blair: on the appointed day for his reception into the Church, Wilde sent a bunch of altar lilies in his place.

What followed was not a spiritual apostasy, as his biographers would have it, but the beginning of a long spiritual sickness, and the new Hellenic spirit was but a plaster for an ailing Catholic consciousness. *Something,* whether syphilis or not, had so terribly darkened his mind that reparation through conversion seemed impossible ('O Lord, I am not worthy'). Wilde's retreat from orthodox Catholicism was not, as critics argue, merely the typical Oxford undergraduate's boredom with 'the Catholic question', anymore than it is explained by Dorian Gray's refusal, in face of his rumoured interest in the Catholic communion, to fall 'into the error of arresting his intellectual development by any formal acceptance of creed or system, or of mistaking, for a house in which to live, an inn that is but suitable for the sojourn of a night.'[14] Wilde, who had felt the Sphinx move upon him, was in any event overcome by a greater disease than syphilis, by an insidious sensual-spiritual affliction of the soul, the symptoms of which are evident in such places as his Oxford Commonplace Book, where he tries to accommodate Hellenism to Baudelaire's desperate cry,

> O Seigneur! donnez moi la force et le courage
> De contempler mon coeur et mon corps sans dégoût.[15]

and in 'Ravenna', in his sympathy with Dante's knowledge of the steep stairs of another's suffering and

> all the petty miseries which mar
> Man's nobler nature with the sense of wrong.[16]

Blair, now in Benedictine orders and unable to assist his guilt-ridden friend, placed a final stake on Wilde's soul: he gave to Ogilvie Fairlie, a papal Chamberlain who had dined with Blair and Wilde in Rome, a diamond ring, on condition that he deliver it to the Church of St Agostino upon news of Wilde's eventual conversion.

When Wilde came down to take his place among the aesthetes in London, he already feared that the price of drifting with every passion was the loss of a soul's inheritance, and thus he began to conceal every trace of his internal life with the superfices of aestheticism — wit and paradox, epigram and phrase — using his genius of verbal inversion to create an artifical temperament that would wholly mask his underlying sense of sin and suffering. And when he slipped out of the public eye to the brothels of London, New York and Paris, *le poète maudit* charted in his poems the spiritual slippage and dislocation that had begun to undermine the flamboyant *flâneur*. In his great Hellenic sigh of self-abandonment, 'Hélas!' (1881), written after Baudelaire's early poem ['Hélas!'], he laments the loss in 'the honey of romance' of that 'austere control' that once kept the now-marred 'secret' of the self in reach of God. [17]

Two years later, playing the dandy in Paris, Wilde had begun to explore the phantom psychology of sensual abandonment and spiritual terror in 'The Harlot's House', where the poet and his love envision a phantasmagoria of ghostly dancers, silhouetted skeletons and phantom lovers wheeling and whirling to the romantic strains of Strauss's 'The Heart of True Love'. The poet immediately warns his love of the terrible dance of death, but she hears only the enchanting violin and goes in to join them, leaving the poet with the blunt reality of his internal drama: 'Love passed into the house of lust'. At that horrific moment, with the poet's abandoned soul in the grip of death, the seductive tune turns 'false', the shadows of the *danse macabre* withdraw, and the very dawn hesitates before the frightful magnitude of the event, the eternal consequence for the soul.

At this same time, in Paris, he was driven at last to write 'The Sphinx', to confront in verse the 'loathsome mystery' first summoned to his Magdalen rooms by another phantom, 'a songless tongueless ghost of sin'. 'Hideous animal, get hence' he cries to the Sphinx,

> You wake in me each bestial sense, you make
> me what I would not be.
>
> You make my creed a barren sham, you wake
> foul dreams of sensual life,
> And Atys with his blood-stained knife were
> better than the thing I am.

He takes refuge from the Sphinx with his personal crucifix — the Good Friday crucifix of the twisted, tortured Christ, still dying on the cross, watching and weeping in vain with his 'pallid burden', unrisen and unvictorious — a crucifix symbolic not of faith, but of universal suffering and the hope of redemption, now Wilde's single secret defense against the 'poisonous melodies' of the Sphinx.[18] It was the first hint of a turn that Wilde's individualistic interest in Christ had taken — toward the doctrine of mystical substitution: suffering willingly in expiation of his own sins and vicariously for the sins of others. Wilde was already at the threshold of decadent Catholicism.

In 1884, allegedly free of syphilis, married and on his honeymoon, Wilde encountered Joris-Karl Huysmans's *A Rebours*, the sensational 'yellowbook' that would rival Pater's *The Renaissance* in Wilde's mind and whose hero, Des Esseintes, would become for Dorian a kind of prefiguring type of himself' (*DG* 142).[19] The primary influence of this book on Wilde's imagination has for a century escaped critics who habitually describe it, only to dismiss it, merely as 'the guidebook of decadence' which Wilde drew upon for his catalogue of aesthetic sensations in chapter eleven of *Dorian Gray*. But Wilde was less interested in the exquisite refinements and bizarre pleasures of Des Esseintes than he was in the strange spiritual malady of which they were symptoms.

For Wilde, as for Dorian, Huysmans's 'whole book seemed to him to contain the story of his own life, written before he had lived it' (*DG* 142). Schooled under the Jesuits, Des Esseintes gradually falls away in disillusionment from the petrified Catholicism of his adolescence into dreams of 'a refined Thebaid [...] in which he might take refuge from the incessant deluge of human stupidity'.[20] His bouts of splenetic boredom and his continuous oscillation between scepticism and faith lead him into erotic fantasies, sensual depravities and artificial sensations until his contempt of life develops into a horror of life and a paralysis of will. Gradually realizing that his perverted sensual desires are manifestations of subverted spiritual desires, he finds temporary solace in a Catholicism that is seasoned with 'a touch of magic' and 'a touch of sadism', a decadent Catholicism based on a subtly depraved and perverse type of mysticism' which could not be discussed with a priest lest he withdraw in 'sheer horror' (*AR* 215). Finally, in great weariness of body and spirit, Des Esseintes expresses his desire to repossess the mysteries and dogmas of the Church, but as his will fails him he can only make a despairing *hélas*-like cry: 'Lord, take pity on the Christian who doubts, on the unbeliever who would fain believe, on the galley-slave of life who puts out to sea alone, in the night, beneath a firmament no longer lit by the consoling beacon-fires of the ancient hope!' (*AR* 220).

What attracted Wilde to *A Rebours* was the drama of a soul similar to his own; indeed, Wilde's account of his own spiritual debauchery after leaving Oxford might well have been spoken by Des Esseintes:

> I let myself be lured into long spells of senseless and sensual ease. I amused myself with being a *flâneur*, a dandy, a man of fashion [...]. I became the spendthrift of my own genius, and to waste an eternal youth gave me a curious joy. Tired of being on the heights, I deliberately went to the depths in the search for new sensations. What the paradox was to me in the sphere of thought, perversity became to me in the sphere of passion. Desire, at the end, was a malady, or a madness, or both [...]. I was no longer the Captain of my Soul, and did not know it.
> (*L* 466)

Of equal interest to Wilde was Huysmans's characterization of the decadent spiritual phenomenon in 'a very special literature' (*AR* 149), that of the writers of the French Catholic revival — Baudelaire, Barbey d'Aurevilly, Verlaine and others — who portray the soul in feverish states of spiritual sickness and contagion. Savouring in religion the charms of sin and sacrilege, the delights of eroticism and sadism, the closeness of sinner and saint, these authors manifest in their works the whole sensual-spiritual spectrum of decadent Catholicism: heresy, blasphemy, satanism, occultism, various forms of Manicheism and extreme forms of doctrine. Huysmans, an apostle of Baudelaire, vividly describes the master's deliberate descent into 'the bottom of the inexhaustible mine', into 'those districts of the soul where the monstrous vegetations of the sick mind flourish':

> There, near the breeding ground of intellectual aberrations and diseases of the mind — the mystical tetanus, the burning fever of lust, the typhoids and yellow fevers of crime — he had found, hatching in the dismal forcing-house of *ennui*, the frightening climacteric of thoughts and emotions.
>
> He had laid bare the morbid psychology of the mind that has reached the October of its sensations, and had listed the symptoms of souls visited by sorrow, singled out by spleen [...]. (*AR* 146-7)

But the author who held the greatest fascination for Des Esseintes was Barbey d'Aurevilly, whose *Un Prêtre Marié* (1865) and *Les Diaboliques* (1874) were seen to be 'constantly tacking to and fro between those two channels of Catholic belief which eventually run into one: mysticism and sadism' (*AR* 160). The two novels explore the effects on the soul of a dichotomous belief in Christ and Satan, but it was the treatment of the latter in *Les Diaboliques* that gripped the attention of Huysmans's protagonist: 'this book, among all the works of contemporary apostolic literature, was the only one to reveal that state of mind, at once devout and impious, towards which nostalgic memories of Catholicism, stimulated by fits of neurosis, had often impelled Des Esseintes' (*AR* 164). He was especially intrigued by Barbey's exploration of 'that bastard child of Catholicism', sadism, which like heresy and blasphemy, cannot arise in the mind of an unbeliever; it presupposes a religion to be violated: 'it consists first and foremost in a sacrilegious manifestation, in a spiritual debauch, in a wholly idealistic, wholly Christian aberration' (*AR* 162). The powerful attraction of sadism to the sufferer lies in the flouting of Catholic precepts, or in observing them in reverse (*à rebours*), by committing, in order to offend Christ the more grievously, the sins that Christ most expressly proscribed —

profanation of the sacred and carnal debauch. After his homosexual seduction by Robert Ross in 1886, Wilde's vigorous sexual inversion would, as the decadents had described, further compound the religious inversion, leading ultimately to what Wilde would describe as 'absolute madness — the insanity of perverted sensual instinct' (*L* 411).

Wilde clearly found in Huysmans, Barbey and other pre-conversion decadents the syndrome of his own spiritual condition, and for the rest of his life he was to follow the spiritual progress of the French revivalists and to employ them as models for his own life. After revealing the influence of Huysmans at his trial, he specifically requested at Reading Gaol a copy of *En Route* (1895), in which Huysmans recounts the final stages of his conversion, and though Wilde told Ross he thought the book 'over-rated', he found the subject 'delightful' and the 'names of the mystical books' fascinating (*L* 520-2). And it is probable that, having discovered Barbey d'Aurevilly in *A Rebours* in 1884, Wilde also read Barbey d'Aurevilly's *Ce qui ne meurt pas* (1884), an early study of infinite pity, 'that unalienable pity which, when all sentiment and passion is mowed down in women's hearts, is of all their feelings — WHAT NEVER DIES!', and it still seems possible that Wilde translated the novel as *What Never Dies* in the months before his death.[21] Baudelaire, whose cry of spiritual despair and bodily disgust ('Ah! Seigneur!') was never far from the surface of Wilde's consciousness, would inspire not only the figure of Wainewright in 'Pen, Pencil and Poison', but his prose poems, which explore the inverted relations of the lustful and sinful to Christ and God. Even Wilde's deathbed conversion was to be the mirror image of Baudelaire's — in and out of consciousness, partly paralysed and speechless, the hand raised to the parish priest in acceptance of the last sacraments. And Verlaine, whom Wilde met in Paris in 1883, was also one of his spiritual travellers: 'We owe to [Christ] [...] Verlaine and Verlaine's poems' (*L* 482), he wrote, fully aware of the remarkable parallels in their separate journeys: shortly after his marriage Verlaine entered into a destructive relationship with the much younger Rimbaud, whom he shot and wounded, and after two years of imprisonment he was brought back to the Catholic faith of his childhood, recording his spiritual recovery in the poems of *Sagesse* (1881), only to fall back repeatedly into wretchedness and degradation. To Wilde, however, Verlaine's was one of 'the most perfect lives I have come across in my own experience', and in his own imprisonment he would describe Verlaine as 'the one Christian poet since Dante' (*L* 488).

Though Wilde was to convert his own religious inversions into the substance of his art, he kept his aesthetic mask marvellously intact, however bankrupt and destructive he now knew aestheticism, as a philosophy of life, to be. When Yeats met him in the late 1880s he was at the height of his powers as the framer of perfect sentences, still proclaiming Pater's *The Renaissance* as his 'golden book' (which many critics would later mistake for Dorian Gray's 'yellow book'), and telling Yeats of his efforts to create a Christian heresy for a story (*Aut* 130,136). At the same time, however, he had begun to intensify his study of the personality of Christ, who would become Wilde's model for the artist's life. 'Jesus was often in his thoughts and he always spoke of Him with admiration', observed a rather disbelieving Frank Harris. 'This was the deeper strain in Oscar Wilde's nature though he was always disinclined to show it. Habitually he lived in humorous talk, in the epithets and epigrams he struck out in the desire to please and astonish his hearers.'[22] But as he entered the great creative period of 1887-1891 the deeper strain had begun to govern his art, as Wilde, admitting having lived 'on honeycomb', later confessed:

> I had to pass on. The other half of the garden had its secrets for me also. Of course all this is foreshadowed and prefigured in my art [...] a great deal of it is hidden away in the note of Doom that like a purple thread runs through the gold cloth of *Dorian Gray*: [...] it is one of the refrains whose recurring *motifs* make *Salome* so like a piece of music and bind it together as a ballad; in the prose-poem of the man who from the bronze of the image of the 'Pleasure that liveth for a Moment' has to make the image of the 'Sorrow that abideth for Ever' it is incarnate. It could not have been otherwise.
> (*L* 475-6)

Wilde was now to cultivate in the mental gardens of his aesthetes their evil flowers of corruption and crime, lust and sin, letting his Catholic, tragic consciousness undermine the shallow roots of aesthetic philosophy, a philosophy based upon a romantic, self-redemptive view of life. To this effect Wilde drew in 'Pen, Pencil and Poison' (1889) the wondrous Wainewright, the aesthete *par excellence* whose entire personality was, the narrator fancies, created out of sin, and whose fancied personality was to attract the attention of T. S. Eliot.

Eliot was both a student and a teacher of Wilde's works, giving extension lectures on the aestheticism of Pater and Wilde and assigning his students to read *Intentions, The Importance of Being Earnest* and *The Ballad of Reading Gaol*.[23] He soon came to think that 'the best of Wilde' was in *Intentions* (1891),[24] and in his Clark Lectures of 1926 he focused on a single story in that volume, 'Pen, Pencil and Poison', to place Wilde among Baudelaire and other French writers who had become preoccupied, behind their satanic poses, with the problem of Good and Evil. The existence of a pose, he observes on the eve of his own conversion,

> implies the possibility of a reality to which the pose pretends. One of the constant by-products of this revival of morality is Satanism; but even Satanism — the cultivation of Evil — in any of its curious forms, in part of Baudelaire, in Barbey d'Aurevilly, in Huysmans, in Wilde's *Pen, Pencil and Poison* — is a derivative or an imitation of spiritual life.[25]

Eliot was not deceived by Wilde's satanic poses or blasphemous postures; he perceived that the peculiar currents of religious feeling that flow from Baudelaire in France and Newman in England proceed 'even in a degraded and popularised form to Oscar Wilde'.[26] To Eliot, satanism and blasphemy, rather than being signs of doubt, are signs of faith, and in his study of Baudelaire he dismissed these surface manifestations of rebellion in presenting him as 'a serious and Catholic Christian'. Though Eliot may have seen Wilde as a Baudelaire *manqué*, by placing him squarely in the Baudelaire-Barbey-Huysmans tradition of decadent Catholicism he presented him as a counter-romantic, as a proto-modernist, as yet another whose *ennui* may be explained as 'a true form of *acedia*, arising from the unsuccessful struggle towards the spiritual life'.[27]

Yeats, too, was aware of the destructive effects of a morbid spiritual emotion that wreaked its 'subtil violence' on Wilde and other members of his generation — Johnson, Dowson, Beardsley — all of whom were caught up in a Catholicism that 'deepened despair and multiplied temptation' (*Aut* 314). To Yeats, the 'terrible beauty' of Wilde's life 'was an attempt to escape from an emotion by its exaggeration' (*Aut* 287), and he quoted Johnson's 'The Dark Angel' as a prelude to one of the most important questions to be asked about Wilde and the 'doomed generation' of the nineties: 'Why are these strange souls born everywhere to-day? with hearts that Chistianity, as shaped by history, cannot satisfy' (*Aut* 315).

When Wilde invites us to pull the 'purple thread' of Doom in *Dorian Gray*, it is to expose the fear of damnation that underlies an excess of sensual pleasure, to colour the spiritual terror that accompanies Dorian's gradual recognition of the 'terrible reality' of the soul (*DG* 238). There are elements of Wilde in each of his personae, and though his readers have thought him to be Lord Wotton he declared that 'Basil Hallward is what I think I am' (*L* 352). It is Basil who possesses a conscience and who tells Harry, in presence of Dorian, of the 'terrible price' that an aesthete must pay for 'individualism' and 'beautiful sins': 'Oh!' exclaims Basil, when challenged on the ways one has to pay, 'I should fancy in remorse, in suffering, in [...] well, in the consciousness of degradation' (*DG* 90). And though Harry protests that such 'medieval emotions are out of date', he knows, as Dorian will learn, that a moral conscience is the bane of aestheticism.

Thus, the aspiring aesthete must eventually kill his conscience, and the narrator later intervenes to tell us what the psychologists say of Dorian's 'passion for sin' and the consequent paralysis of will: 'Choice is taken from them, and conscience is either killed, or, if it lives at all, lives but to give rebellion its fascination, and disobedience its charm [...]. Callous, concentrated on evil, with stained mind, and soul hungry for rebellion, Dorian hastened on' (*DG* 210). But if Dorian has killed Basil, he has yet to kill his portrait, which becomes for Dorian a 'monstrous soul-life' that torments him with its 'hideous warnings' (*DG* 247). Soon enough, the malignant psychology of sin metastasizes into the phantom psychology of damnation. 'I have no terror of Death', Dorian tells Harry in nervous exhaustion. 'It is the coming of Death that terrifies me. Its monstrous wings seem to wheel in the leaden air around me' (*DG* 225). But Wilde leaves Dorian *in extremis*, paralysed by his fear of spiritual terror, capable only of stabbing at the terrible, uncloseted reality of his soul, thereby killing himself. And Wilde leaves each reader to discover in Dorian Gray his own sins: 'What Dorian Gray's sins are no one knows', wrote Wilde. 'He who finds them has brought them' (*L* 266).

Wilde's devouring sin was lust, the speciality of his dark angel, and from the moment he encountered Salome as 'the symbolic incarnation of undying lust' (*AR* 66) in *A Rebours*, she became the figure in whom he would meditate the dark psychology of his sin. 'His "Salome" I say', mused Enrique Gomez Carrillo, the Spanish critic whom he met in Paris while composing the play, 'and I am in error; for there were ten, no, a hundred Salomes that he imagined, that he began, that he abandoned.'[28] He sought his Salome in poets and in painters and in the Gospels, Carrillo recalled, but Wilde found the biblical Salome 'dry and colourless; without lavishness, extravagance or sin. Above all, sin'. Wilde created his Salome fully under the spell of his French forerunners, writing his sadistic masterpiece in French to identify it with the decadent tradition which he consciously extended. He would frequently say to Carrillo, 'I am mad like des Esseintes', and Carrillo fully believed him, describing the similarity of their morbid quests and how Wilde would often recite to his friends Huysmans's famous description of Salome in Gustave Moreau's *The Apparition*.[29]

Wilde inevitably situated his symbolic drama in yet another harlot's house, Herodias's banquet hall, a veritable cauldron of unholy loves — homoerotic, promiscuous, incestuous, lustful. The characters gaze upon their objects of desire 'too much', Herod upon Salome with 'mole's eyes', while all about them are omens of retribution, and in the cistern below Iokanaan utters his terrifying prophecies of the coming of Christ, who is mocked and derided. At the beginning, only Iokanaan can hear 'the beating of the wings of the angel of death', but soon the wingbeats reach Herod, progressively terrifying him: 'Why do I hear this beating of the wings in the air?' he cries as Salome demands the head of Iokanaan. They are the same monstrous wings that terrify Dorian, but in *Salome* Wilde is intent to move beyond spiritual terror, to open the darkest recesses of the psychology of lust, to explore the spiritual sadism of Barbey d'Aurevilly. Salome's desire to seduce Iokanaan was brought on by what she calls a 'strange music', yet another poisonous melody that gradually maddens her as her love-hate advances are repelled. After the decapitation of Iokanaan, Salome is driven to bite the mouth of the severed head 'the way one bites a ripe fruit'. Hers is the supreme sensual-spiritual debauch. 'What shall I do now, Iokanaan?' she asks in her sadistic swoon, holding the love that lust has destroyed. 'Neither the rivers nor the great waters can extinguish my passion.' Her insatiable state at this moment, so beyond the sinful imagination that the lecherous Herod has her killed, recalls Eliot's description in 'Whispers of Immortality' of what Donne knew so well about

> the anguish of the marrow
> The ague of the skeleton;
> No contact possible to flesh
> Allayed the fever of the bone.

implying that raging carnal fevers are fuelled by an innate spiritual fever. But of the moderns who came to study Wilde, it was perhaps the blasphemous Joyce who most accurately felt the febrile brow of Salome. Joyce, who had himself fallen away from Catholicism, and who was himself allegedly haunted by the guilt and disgust of syphilis, observed of Wilde's art in 'Oscar Wilde: The Poet of *Salome*' (1909) that 'at its very base is the truth inherent in the soul of Catholicism: that man cannot reach the divine heart except through that sense of separation and loss called sin'.[30]

Lord Alfred Douglas was the dark angel's last great gift to Wilde. They were actually introduced in the spring of 1892 by Lionel Johnson, who subsequently directed his poem 'To the Destroyer of a Soul' at Wilde, or so Yeats believed, but it also serves as a prelude to 'The Dark Angel', which does such 'subtil violence' to the soul and through whom

                    the gracious Muses turn
        To Furies.

Johnson later broke with Wilde over his distasteful public homosexuality, and even Aubrey Beardsley remarked that Wilde and Bosie were 'really very dreadful people'.[31] Playing Rimbaud to Wilde's Verlaine, Bosie joined Wilde in the destructive and ruinous relationship that is fully recounted in *De Profundis*, where Wilde, placing himself in Dante's eighth circle between Gilles de Retz and Marquis de Sade (*L* 414), describes how he 'let myself be lured into the imperfect world of coarse uncompleted passions, of appetite without distinction, desire without limit, and formless greed' (*L* 463). And yet, for all that it calls Bosie to task, and for all the perversity to which Wilde admits, *De Profundis* moves beyond the hellish three-year affair and trials to become Wilde's purgatorial treatise on sin and suffering, sorrow and humility. Indeed, the ultimate aim of the letter was to teach Bosie, who had come to Wilde to learn the pleasures of life and art, 'something much more wonderful, the meaning of Sorrow, and its beauty' (*L* 511).

        Since the close of his Oxford days Wilde had been attracted to figures of vicarious suffering, especially Christ, and now in Reading Gaol he gave that doctrine primacy over all others in Catholic thought, as did Huysmans and many other authors of the revival.[32] 'There is still something to me almost incredible', he wrote, 'in the idea of a young Galilean peasant imagining that he could bear on his own shoulders the burden of the entire world [...] and not merely imagining this but actually achieving it, so that at the present moment all who come in contact with his personality, even though they may neither bow to his altar nor kneel before his priest, yet somehow find that the ugliness of their sins is taken away and the beauty of their sorrow revealed to them' (*L* 477). If the sinner could not accept Christ's visible Church, he might imitate Christ's true suffering by taking on the expiation of his own sins and those of the whole of mankind. 'Sorrow, then, and all that it teaches one, is my new world', he wrote, and as he presented Christ as the 'supreme individualist' and model for the artist, so he identified sorrow as 'the supreme emotion of which man is capable [...] at once the type and test of all great art' (L 472-3). Where he once pursued the art of pleasure, he would now pursue the art of suffering, taking Francis of Assisi as his patron saint. Ever the heretic in art and religion, Wilde went on to take the doctrine to its 'dangerous' aesthetic limits, asserting that Christ himself 'regarded sin and suffering as being in themselves beautiful, holy things, and modes of perfection [...]. That it is the true creed I don't doubt myself' (L 486-7).

In his heresy, and even in his avowed humility, Wilde was writing in his public voice, declaring himself to be a 'born antinomian' and a would-be founder of 'an order for those who cannot believe: the Confraternity of the Fatherless' (L 468), but if these were the last expressions of an aesthetic mask, there were also those of the decadent Catholic: 'There is not a single degradation of the body which I must not try and make into a spiritualising of the soul' (L 469). When Wilfrid Blunt asked Robert Ross if Wilde was sincere in *De Profundis,* he replied, 'as much as possible in a man of Oscar's artificial temperament. While he was writing he was probably sincere, but his style was always in his mind. It was difficult to be sure about him.' [33] Ross would never be sure about Wilde's religious impulses, though Wilde had already told him, prophetically, that 'Catholicism was the only religion to die in'.[34] Wilde still believed in self-realization, but not self-redemption.

It was not easy for Wilde to put off his mask and manner when he finally determined to bring his dark spiritual voyage to light on being released from Reading Gaol on 18 May 1897. The next day, in the company of More Adey and Stewart Headlam in London, his first act, like Durtal in *En Route,* was to send a letter to the Catholic Retreat House in Farm Street asking for a six-month stay. When the Jesuits replied that they could not accept him at his impulse of the moment, that it must be thought over for at least a year, 'he broke down and sobbed bitterly' (L 564).

The painful irony that Wilde's long-repressed desire to be received into the Church was seen as an 'impulse of the moment' was to follow him to his deathbed. So successfully had he created his 'artificial temperament' that even his closest friends could not entertain his desperate cries for faith. That night he crossed the channel to Dieppe, where he was met by

Ross and Reginald Turner. Soon after arrival he told Ross, himself a convert, of his desire to become a Catholic. 'I did not believe in his sincerity', he later confided in Blunt, 'and told him if he really meant it, to go to a priest, and I discouraged him from anything hasty in the matter [...]. I would willingly have helped him if I had thought him in earnest, but I did not fancy religion being made ridiculous by him.'[35] Turner must have asked him why the Catholic rather than the Anglican Church, for Wilde said to him, 'The Catholic Church is for saints and sinners alone. For respectable people the Anglican Church will do.'[36]

'I am going tomorrow on a pilgrimage', Wilde wrote to Ross from Berneval on 31 May, rather self-mockingly as he prepared to visit the chapel of Notre Dame de Liesse. 'It has probably been waiting for me all these purple years of pleasure, and now it comes to meet me with Liesse (Joy) as its message' (*L* 582). But Wilde was discouraged, and would remain so, by the resistance of Ross, More Adey and others to his conversion. 'I wish you were not so hard to poor heretics', he wrote to Ross from Berneval, 'and would admit that even for the sheep who has no shepherd there is a Stella Maris to guide it home. But you and More, especially More, treat me as a Dissenter. It is very painful, and quite unjust'(*L* 582-3). Wilde did seek out the local French priest and came close to being received there, but whether it was the priest, whom Wilde told of his heresies, or Wilde himself who hesitated, is unknown, but Wilde continued to chaff Ross for standing in the way of his salvation. 'I am not at all a moral man', said Ross in explanation, 'but I had my feeling on this point and so the matter remained between us.'[37]

Meanwhile, Wilde turned to *The Ballad of Reading Gaol*, writing to Laurence Housman that the poem is 'terribly realistic for me, and drawn from actual experience, a sort of denial of my own philosophy of art in many ways'.[38] In his portrayal of the extinguishing of human dignity in Reading Gaol, he is keen to suggest that there is one human drive that is inextinguishable even there:

> And all, but Lust, is turned to dust
> In Humanity's machine.

Once again the phantoms are aswarm, the 'forms of Fear', the 'shapes of Terror' the shadows of Dread, Doom and Horror all engaged 'in ghostly rout', in another *danse macabre*. But though the prisoners suffer at the hands of Degradation, Despair and Sorrow — the warders of the imprisoned self — the poet asserts that only in suffering is redemption possible:

> How else may man make straight his plan
> And cleanse his soul from Sin!
> How else but through a broken heart
> My Lord Christ enter in?

For the next two years Wilde carried his broken heart around Europe, kneeling 'like a real Roman', Ross observed, to priests in Rome and Naples and to the Pope in Rome, returning on Holy Thursday, twenty-three years after his interview with Pius IX, to be blessed by Leo XIII. Though he had, like Verlaine, fallen into drink and promiscuity once again, he kept his wit and decadent humour about him for such occasions: 'I was deeply impressed, and my walking-stick showed signs of budding; would have budded indeed, only at the door of the chapel it was taken from me by the Knave of Spades' (*L* 821). Nonetheless, as he wrote to More Adey, he returned to be blessed 'many times', but in his comic manner he seemed to assure Adey that he had not disappointed him by going over: 'My position is curious: I am not a Catholic: I am simply a violent Papist. No one could be more "black" than I am. I have given up bowing to the King. I need say no more' (*L* 825).

Wilde had come full circle to the threshold of Catholicism, passing through the *via negativa* and the *via dolorosa* but never into the Church. Three weeks before his death he granted an interview to the Paris Correspondent of the *Daily Chronicle*, muttering 'most savagely' that 'much of my moral obliquity is due to the fact that my father would not allow me to become a Catholic. The artistic side of the Church and the fragrance of its teaching would have cured my degeneracies. I intend to be received before long.'[39] If Wilde was somewhat unfair and insincere in placing the moral and historical burden of separation solely on his father, he was equally so in the implication that he would have been happy as an 'Art-Catholic'. Wilde, like the decadent French revivalists, wanted a 'hard' religion or none at all. Ross was particularly wary of placing before Wilde any priest who was not sufficiently prepared for 'a rather grave intellectual conflict', admitting that Wilde had become 'deeply read in Catholic philosophy of recent years' (*L* 859). But only in shame and disgrace could Wilde bring his unqualified Catholic yearnings into public view; only at death's door could he surrender his will.

The scepticism and disbelief that followed upon Wilde's deathbed conversion on 29 November 1900 continue among the many who cannot imagine that the Prince of Paradox could lapse into Catholicism. Ross, who fulfilled his standing promise to call a priest if Wilde's death became imminent, stated that though Wilde held up his hand in response to the priest's questions, 'he was never able to speak and we do not know whether he was altogether conscious.'[40] Ellmann, who could not bring himself to accept Wilde's surrender, privileged Ross's uncertainty about Wilde's consciousness to deflate the significance of the moment: 'The application of sacred oils to his hands and feet may have been a ritualized pardon for his omissions or commissions, or may have been like putting a green carnation in his buttonhole.'[41] But Father Cuthbert Dunne, the Irish-born priest who administered the last rites and visited Wilde on several occasions, was in each instance satisfied of Wilde's full consent. 'At these subsequent visits', wrote Dunne, 'he repeated the prayers with me again and each time received Absolution.'[42]

When news of Wilde's death arrived, William Ward wrote apprehensively to Hunter Blair: 'Pray tell me if you can', he wrote, 'whether poor Oscar was received into the Catholic Church before his death [...] I sincerely hope so; and I only wish that he had taken that step years ago; it might have saved him from much.'[43] When Blair confirmed that Father Dunne had received him into the Church, Ward expressed his heartfelt relief and 'deep satisfaction'. For his part, Blair called in his old debt, and within a fortnight Ogilvie Fairlie set out for Rome to deliver to St Agostino's Church the diamond ring that Blair had staked on Wilde's conversion in 1878.

Wilde's Oxford friends knew all along that his conversion was inevitable, but most of those who met him in the 'eighties and 'nineties were denied knowledge of his spiritual nightmare by the power of his personality and the genius of his mask. It was a perfect mask, and they testified to its beauty and perfection with certitude, denying the hints and guesses of a darker consciousness. But as we rediscover Wilde in the 1990s, we should deny no longer the fact that beneath the glittering *carnaval* of the Happy Prince of Aesthetes was the *danse macabre* of the decadent Catholic.

NOTES

1   F. Harris, *Oscar Wilde: His Life and Confessions* (New York, Covici, Friede, 1930), p. 36; B. Brasol, *Oscar Wilde, the man, the artist, the martyr* (1938; rpt. New York, Octagon Books, 1975), p. 47; V. O'Sullivan *Aspects of Wilde* (New York, Henry Holt, 1936), p. 212.
2   Oscar Wilde (New York, Knopf, 1988), p. 297.
3   Wilde was instructed and christened at St Kevin's Church, Glencree, by the Rev. Lawrence Charles Prideaux Fox, whose 1905 account is reprinted in S. Mason's *Bibliography of Oscar Wilde* (London, T.Werner Laurie, 1914), pp. 118-19.
4   D. H. Blair, *In Victorian Days* (London, Longmans, Green, 1939), p. 125.
5   *My Reminiscences* (London, Kegan Paul, 1895), p. 134.
6   *In Victorian Days*, pp. 132-3.
7   *The Letters of Oscar Wilde*, ed. R. Hart-Davis (London, Rupert Hart-Davis, 1962), p. 31; hereafter abbreviated *L* and cited parenthetically in the text.
8   Quoted by W. B. Stanford and R. B. McDowell in *Mahaffy* (London, Routlegde & Kegan Paul, 1971), p. 41; part of the letter, located in the Shane Leslie papers (TCD), is quoted differently by Ellmann, p. 70: 'The Jesuits had promised him a scholarship in Rome, but thank God, I was able to cheat the Devil of his due.'
9   A copy of the letter is in the Richard Ellmann Collection at the University of Tulsa. It is partly quoted by Ellmann in *Oscar Wilde*, p. 74, but the provenance is not noted.
10   *In Victorian Days*, p. 136.
11   This is the contested and probably unprovable thesis of Ellmann's *Oscar Wilde* (see p. 92), but he was not the first of Wilde's biographers to assert or advance it. That Ellmann wrestled extensively with the reliability and complexity of factual transmission before reaching his own conclusion is evident in his letter of 4 February 1981 to Rupert Hart-Davis (Tulsa): 'Did you discuss the matter with Vyvyan? The reason I ask is that among the Home Office papers is a letter from Sherard asking whether the medical records of Reading Prison

indicated that Wilde had syphilis. He says that Vyvyan
Holland told him Wilde did have it, and he wants to verify or
validate the idea. The records do not have anything on this
point [...]. You remember Brasol indicates he heard about it from
Sherard, and correspondence between Brasol and Sherard
indicates that Sherard didn't want to tell Brasol he had got it
from Vyvyan, so simply said he thought he had heard it in
America!

      I've been racking my brains trying to figure out why
Ross, who presumably informed Vyvyan as well as Ransome,
might have made up the idea that Wilde had syphilis, but
nothing seems to be sufficient cause. It seems to me possible that
Vyvyan had the information from his guardian Adrian Hope. Is
there any chance of finding out what Hope might have thought?
[...] Why Ross encouraged Ransome to introduce the matter,
gratuitously as you say, is mysterious. There was perhaps a
persistent rumour, the extent of which he overestimated, and he
may have preferred to lay it at rest by absolute candour [...].
Please forgive my returning to this matter. It's hard to discuss it
with anyone but you.

      Otho's [Constance's brother] letter confirms that
Wilde and Constance did not have sexual intercourse after
1886 [...]. Wilde couldn't have stopped sexual relations, given
her loving nature and their living in the same house, without
saying he had syphilis. (He obviously, and as Otho confirms,
never hinted that he had homosexuality!) He could have made it
up as a story, and for a while I thought that. But on the whole I
don't think he did make it up, do you?'

12   Ward later wrote in 'An Oxford Reminiscence' that Wilde's
letters to him 'show [...] that his final decision to find refuge in
the Roman Church was not the sudden clutch of the drowning
man at the plank in the shipwreck, but a return to a first love, a
love rejected, it is true, or at least rejected in the tragic process
of his self-realization, yet one that had haunted him from early
days with a persistent spell'. See V. Holland, *Son of Oscar
Wilde* (New York, Dutton, 1954), p. 219.
13   Quoted in Ellmann, *Oscar Wilde*, p. 93.
14   Oscar Wilde, *The Picture of Dorian Gray*, (Harmondsworth,
Penguin Books, 1972), p. 148; hereafter abbreviated *DG* and
cited parenthetically in the text.
15   *Oscar Wilde's Oxford Notebooks*, ed. P. Smith II and M. Helfand
(N.Y. & Oxford, Oxford University Press, 1989), p. 135.
16   Wilde alludes to *Paradiso* XVII, 58-60, when Caccicaguida tells
Dante that, slandered and in penury, he must go into exile in evil
company, and quotes the concluding lines of Baudelaire's 'Un
Voyage à Cythère'. In June 1875 Wilde had described to his
mother Giotto's fresco of Dante 'trudging up the steep *stairs* (*L*
9), and he alluded to the scene again for the opening lines of 'At
Verona' (1881). The two allusions had become crucial to his
image of himself as artist when he recalled them in *De Profundis*
(*L* 480): 'Those who have the artistic temperament go into exile
with Dante and learn how salt is the bread of others, and how
steep their stairs: they catch for a moment the serenity and calm

of Goethe, and yet know but too well why Baudelaire cried to
God:

> O Seigneur, donnez-moi la force et le courage
> De contempler mon corps et mon coeur sans dégoût.

17   See Baudelaire's untitled poem, 'Hélas! qui n'a gémi sur autrui,
sur soi-même?' (*Oeuvres complètes*, I (Paris, Editions Gallimard,
1975), p. 201), in which he describes his conflict between
earthly and heavenly love. Wilde told W.B. Yeats, who asked
permission to use one of his poems in an Irish anthology, that
'Hélas!' was his 'most characteristic poem' (*Autobiographies*
(London, Macmillan, 1955) p. 286; hereafter abbreviated *Aut*
and cited parenthetically in the text). The American critic
Percival Pollard was the first to perceive the veiled spiritual
temperament of the poem, writing in his introduction to
Recollections of Oscar Wilde (Boston and London, John W. Luce,
1906): 'One may conceive that in Wilde a perverse sense of
loyalty to art kept him from ever displaying the real depth
below his obvious insincerities [...] and the rumour of his
paradoxic brilliance was too secure and too amusing for him to
risk shattering it with glimpses of more serious depth. Yet who
can read his sonnet, "Hélas!" [...] without feeling that under the
glitter and the pose there was something else, something the gay
world of London knew nothing of?' (p. 19).

18   Boris Brasol observed astutely in his discussion of 'The
Sphinx': 'Still, here and there, against all these impious reveries
of an ill-directed mind, the eye suddenly catches the fading
silhouette of some religious vision — a strange antithesis
suggesting the thought that Wilde's soul, as in a schizophrenic
split, was divided into two distinct selves which dwelt there in
a state of constant combat, seeking to unite in some as yet
undivined synthesis.' But Brasol dismisses his perception of
Wilde's 'religious vision' under the weight of succeeding years:
'But as the years passed by, the content of his brilliant intellect
became increasingly polluted with sexual obsession of the
saddest kind, until the memory of God and Good vanished and
faded from his arid heart' (*Oscar Wilde*, p. 143).

19   In response to an inquiry about the 'yellowbook' in *Dorian
Gray*, Wilde wrote that 'it is partly suggested by Huysmans's *A
Rebours* [...]. It is a fantastic variation on Huysmans's over-
realistic study of the artistic temperament in our inartistic age'
(*L* 313).

20   *Against Nature (A Rebours)*, trans. R. Baldick (Harmondsworth,
Penguin Books, 1959), p. 22; hereafter abbreviated *AR* and
cited parenthetically in the text.

21   *What never Dies*, translated under Wilde's pseudonym,
Sebastian Melmoth, was published in Paris in 1902 with the
initials O.W. stamped on the cover. In his *Life of Oscar Wilde*
(1906), Sherard listed the translation as a spurious work (p.
460). Though it was included as volume 9 in the Uniform
Edition of *The Writings of Oscar Wilde* (London and New
York: A.R. Keller, 1907) and in subsequent American
collections, Robert Ross did not include it in his 14-volume
edition of *The Writings of Oscar Wilde* (1908). In a 1909 edition

of *Dorian Gray*, the Paris publisher Charles Carrington attached a note entitled 'Nota Bene' to an end-leaf stating that the publisher no longer offered the two translations of *The Satyricon of Petronius* and *What Never Dies* as the works of Sebastian Melmoth or Oscar Wilde (Mason, p. 350). Ellmann did not attempt to solve the problem, stating that though Wilde told Mrs Georgina Weldon that he would translate the novel, Robert Ross said he never did (*Oscar Wilde*, p. 561). In a circular of 12 April 1920 (Merlin Holland Collection), issued by Ross's solicitors shortly after his death to advise dealers of authorized and unauthorized editions of Wilde's works, it was pointed out that *The Priest and the Acolyte* and the two translations, *The Satyricon of Petronius* and *What Never Dies*, '(even when bearing his name on the title-page) were neither written, translated, nor edited by the late Mr. Oscar Wilde'. Though the authority of the statement is evidently based on Ross's knowledge of Wilde and on Christopher Millard's research into the printed editions of his works, the justification for the 'fact' of Wilde's non-authorship is less than conclusive: 'Any one with a slender knowledge of the French, Latin or English languages will be able to realize for himself that the Author of *Salome*, who was a Demy (scholar) of Magdalen College, Oxford and Greek Gold Medalist at Dublin, was incapable, even in his declining years, of the grammatical and grosser solecisms characterising these publications.'

22   F. Harris, *Oscar Wilde: His Life and Confessions*, pp. 96-7.
23   See my 'T.S. Eliot as an Extension Lecturer', *The Review of English Studies*, 25 (August 1974), pp. 293, 295.
24   'A Preface to Modern Literature: Being a Conspectus Chiefly of English Poetry, Addressed to an Intelligent and Inquiring Foreigner', *Vanity Fair*, 21 (November 1923), p. 44.
25   *The Varieties of Metaphysical Poetry*, ed. R. Schuchard (London, Faber & Faber, 1993), p. 209.
26   *Ibid*. p. 162.
27   *Selected Essays*, 3rd Enlarged Edition (London, Faber & Faber, 1986), p. 423.
28   'How Oscar Wilde Dreamed of Salome', in *Oscar Wilde: Interviews and Recollections*, I, ed. E. H. Mikhail (London, Macmillan, 1979) p. 194.
29   *Ibid*. p. 195. For Huysmans's description of Moreau's painting, see *AR* 67-8.
30   *The Critical Writings of James Joyce*, ed. E. Mason and R. Ellmann (Ithaca, NY, Cornell University Press, 1989), p. 205. Joyce's phrasing appears to derive from Yeats's *The Tables of the Law* (1897), which he had once set to memory: 'and in my misery it was revealed to me that man can only come to that Heart [of God] through the sense of separation from it which we call sin' (*Mythologies* (London, Macmillan, 1959), p. 305). For a compelling study of Joyce's conscious guilt over his syphilis, and the manifestation of that guilt in his works, see K. Ferris, *Mr. Germ's Choice: James Joyce and the Burden of Disease* (Lexington, Kentucky, University of Kentucky Press, 1994).

31   *Robert Ross Friend of Friends*, ed. M. Ross (London, Jonathan Cape, 1952), p. 29.
32   For the most comprehensive and probing study of the elements of decadent Catholicism in late-nineteenth-century France, including a chapter on 'Vicarious Suffering', see R. Griffiths, *The Reactionary Revolution: The Catholic Revival in French Literature 1870-1914* (New York, Frederick Ungar, 1965).
33   See W. S. Blunt, *My Diaries*, Part Two (London, Martin Secker, 1920), pp. 125-6.
34   Quoted in Ellmann, *Oscar Wilde*, p. 583.
35   Blunt, *My Diaries*, p. 126.
36   Quoted in Ellmann, *Oscar Wilde*, p. 583.
37   Blunt, *My Diaries*, p. 126.
38   *More Letters of Oscar Wilde*, ed. R. Hart-Davis (London, John Murray, 1985), p. 153.
39   Quoted in Rev. Edmund Burke, 'Oscar Wilde: The Final Scene', *London Magazine* (May 1961), p. 39.
40   Blunt, My Diaries, p. 126.
41   Ellmann, *Oscar Wilde*, p. 584.
42   Burke, 'Oscar Wilde: The Final Scene', p. 41.
43   Quoted in Blair, *In Victorian Days*, p. 141. Ward was later to offer his own analysis of Wilde's tragic struggle: 'Deliberately he had cultivated, as it seems to me, moods and feelings and appetites and states of thought so warring and so contradictory that at length the mould of sanity and self-control broke. He had made his mind a stage on which incongruous scenes continually shifted, across which strange characters [...] passed and repassed in a carnival of mad confusion [...]. He had turned his mind into a laboratory in which he might test his own experiences and he fell a victim to his own experiments.' Cf. V. Holland, *Son of Oscar Wilde*, p. 221.

WILL TO POWER, POETIC JUSTICE, AND MIMESIS IN *THE PICTURE OF DORIAN GRAY*

Theoharis Constantine Theoharis

A moral allegory of supra-moral aestheticism; a densely specific, verisimilar case study of an ostentatiously unrealistic event; Faust's turn as a shallow, impressionable, Frenchified, English dandy — these forced conjunctions, among others, make *The Picture of Dorian Gray* Oscar Wilde's supreme and most sustained venture into paradox. Inversion, slant reciprocity, and sundering reconciliations move the plot forward; meditations on art's transmission of eternity into time give the plot conceptual and emotional gravity. The classical and modernist thinking which Wilde includes in Dorian's story figure the artistic relation of time and eternity in many different and complex ways. One enigma in this relation — whether the boundary of eternity and time fixed by art is sealed or porous — frames the narrative and thought of this novel. The issue ambiguously renders Dorian Gray's protagonistic picture both surface and symbol of the modernist inheritance of classical norms for beauty and value. Classical and modern thought certainly dispute the boundary's nature and function separately — consider Plotinus versus Aristotle on the object and end of mimesis, and Baudelaire versus Flaubert. My case here is that Wilde makes his fictional inquiry into aesthetic ontology an argument with traditional as well as contemporary authority.

Late Victorian aestheticism tilted against ethical realism's control over art with the gossamer lance of useless, ecstatic beauty. Ethical realism's classical sponsor, of course, is Aristotle's *Poetics;* numerous bids are still in in the scholarly community for the philosophical sponsorship of modernist aestheticism. Within the constraints of brevity imposed by the occasion, I would like to suggest here that Nietzsche's visionary thinking about Dionysiac will to power plays throughout Dorian's double life, and allows Wilde to transform rather than erase ethical realism's claim on beauty. Read against Nietzsche's thought, the poetic justice which ends *The Picture of Dorian Gray* confutes both the conventional sanction and disapproval which have always attended didactic resolution of the formal tension which makes for beauty. Of the great artists, perhaps Wilde's Miss Prism states the conventional sanction of poetic justice most fluently. In the second act of *The Importance of Being Earnest*, describing her abandoned three volume novel to Cecily, that good, superannuated governess says: 'The good ended happily, and the bad unhappily. That is what Fiction means.'

Alas, that is not what reality means, hence the critical complaint that such resolution is failed imitation. In a Nietzschean sense, Reality is Fiction in *The Picture of Dorian Gray*, especially the reality of the soul's self-awareness. By shifting the soul's dynamic quality from life to the imitation of life and then back to life again, Wilde teases out the central, unresolved ambiguity in Aristotle's aesthetics — what ontological status does a copy, or more precisely, a transplanted form, have. By having a painting and its subject undergo reciprocal changes of fortune, Wilde also refines Nietzsche's solution of the Aristotelian ambiguity. Form, which Nietzsche reconceives as illusory Apollonian stasis, and as primordial Dionysiac ruin, the ultimately uncontainable force which form holds only to release — both govern mimesis in *The Picture of Dorian Gray*. Enacting both Nietzschean conceptions of form in his aesthetic fable, Wilde preserves the ethical realism which Aristotle derived from form's primacy, and which Nietzsche sought to eliminate, but does so on his own aesthetic terms. Exceeding Aristotle and Nietzsche in his imitation of the innocent pictured criminal, Wilde wickedly makes good on the misleadingly neutral postulation in the book's preface — 'Vice and virtue are to the artist materials for an art'. Prism might wince at this, but a good director would have her smile with hearty approval.

Wilde calls Dorian's soul the protagonist of this tale, and calls the tale a tragedy, often enough to provoke and reward careful attention to the various meanings of those terms.

Their colloquial meanings — 'soul' as an intensification of the loose notion of personality, and 'tragedy' as synonymous with extravagant, unlooked for suffering induced by personality — sufficiently govern the readings which any of the characters in the story, or their contemporaries, might have made of it. A necessary part of the pleasure of this, or any story, comes from reading it, as much as possible, from the colloquial perspective of its protagonists and contemporary audience. A superadded pleasure comes from taking the outside view of the tale, which in this case involves answering Wilde's arch appeals for learned understanding of technically philosophical and literary meanings, classical and modern, for the terms 'soul' and 'tragedy'. In part, Wilde invites such response by withholding it from his characters, or giving it to them flippantly. In part, philosophy and literary criticism are powerfully evoked by the meaning of 'soul' most flippantly omitted from the book. While conventionally arty religious feelings dart about the text, no theological values or meanings of the terms 'soul' or 'guilt' or 'innocence' appear. Dorian's contemplation of the beauty of priest's vestments provides a patina of ecclesiastical opulence, but no more. In Christianity's absence, the conceptual and formal values of this soul's tragedy — its critical significance — come largely from the modernist collision of Aristotle's thinking on the subject and Nietzsche's. A brief précis of these confluent theories should yield the kind of learned pleasure Wilde plays out for those doomed to exceed the comfort of colloquial response.

Aristotle's *Poetics* argues that tragedy shows the reason good actions by good people end badly. Presenting the most painful and apparently meaningless experience as pleasantly, nobly intelligible, tragedy makes the supreme claim for rational pursuit of life's value. Simultaneously arousing the strongest emotional claims of chaos, and submitting them to the intensely clarifying dominion of reason, tragedy enhances the native but perishable conviction that life has order. It does so, paradoxically, by gradually and completely reversing an agent's reasoned attempt to govern changing fortune. This reversal indicates that a disguised and superior order of cause has all along been embedded in and governing the agent's apparently reasonable project. Pursuit of that imperfect project at once makes and unmakes the protagonist, who, in the moment of reversal and recognition, discovers the inadequacy of his or her known aims and the implacable reality of the unknown aims he or she has witlessly but flawlessly advanced. Imitation of tragic action reconciles appearance and reality, it makes substantial the instability of natural and human circumstances by showing that they enact stable, lawful change. Aristotle calls the emergence of that lawful change, accomplished by the plot, and experienced by the audience as catharsis, the 'soul' of tragedy.

This is the crucial point of contact between Wilde's novel and Aristotle's aesthetic theory. To a great extent, Dorian's story enacts the *Poetics'* account of the soul as an organic and aesthetic principle of formal inversion in life, and art's representation of life. In art and life, the soul's inversion passes through convulsive metamorphoses to apocalyptic achievement of fixed identity. Aristote left at least one aspect of that final fixity ambiguous in his theory: namely, how much of the pleasure and pain of cathartic recognition is experienced by the agent and by the spectators of the tragic action, and how these experiences differ not only in their nature, but also in their effect on the agents and spectators of the tragic deed. Wilde spotlights that ambiguity in the climax of his tale, by having Dorian act as agent and spectator of the apocalyptic reversal which fixes the final, permanent identity of his pictured and organic soul. Poetic justice is a crude name for the ethical satisfaction and instruction cathartic revelation of reality's lawful change provides. When Aristotle, and numerous later critics, disparage poetic justice, they balk at implausible and structurally inorganic reversals. By making Dorian's cathartic reversal fabulously implausible, but classically organic — what tragic ending is more structurally coherent or just than the innocent criminal's remorseful self-appraisal — Wilde satisfies the colloquial, sentimental vindictiveness which Prism and her cheerfully philistinic ilk demand of art. At the same time he spins ethical realism, the approved resentfulness of fixing the villain, back into purely aesthetic restoration, into fixing the picture of ideal beauty.

The key element in this structural *sprezzatura*, of course, is the mimetic implausibility of Dorian's double-life as an aging picture and an ageless man. The implausibility governs the novel's plot, culminating in the inadvertently suicidal assault Dorian makes on his pictured soul, which survives apocalyptic death and regains its original beauty unscarred by the expiating, sacrificial piercing — a crucial detail as far as the rejection of Christianity in the book is concerned. Clearly, this implausibility departs most significantly from the pragmatic, ethical realism by which Aristotelian action makes reality's lawful changes intelligible. Despite the famous aestheticism of the novel, epitomized in the preface's final dictum 'All art is quite useless', Wilde works the implausible fortunes and power of Dorian's pictured ideal beauty into more than an anti-Aristotelian fable of art's inviolable self-grounding.

Dorian's beauty is the subject and agent of ambiguously moral and amoral influence. Indeed the tale's plot concerns nothing but that influence. The physical implausibility of an aging picture of a non-aging man, in addition to playfully reversing the compensatory Keatsian comfort that a thing of beauty is a joy forever, allows Wilde to speculate about occult scientific laws governing beauty's influence, especially over passion. The picture's implausible life makes the mystery of beauty an occasion for Wilde to speculate about four primary enigmas in European intellectual history that might be solved by this occult science: to speak ontologically, the relation of form and matter; to speak epistemologically, the relation of idea and fact; to speak aesthetically, the relation of form and content; and to speak psychologically, the relation of soul and body. The plot figures all these relations as power dynamics, as modes of cause, or to use Wilde's repeated term for creative order, 'influence'. Basil Hallward, Dorian Gray, and Lord Henry Wotton all variously experience and exert 'influence' over beauty's mystery, but only the painter and his subject have direct scientific, experimental knowledge of beauty's implausible power over nature.

Wotton regards beauty as the meeting place of the oppositions listed above, and speculates at the end of chapter four, as follows:

Soul and body, body and soul — how mysterious they were! There was animalism in the soul, and the body had its moments of spirituality. The senses could refine, and the intellect degrade. Who could say where the fleshy impulse ceased, or the physical impulse began? How shallow were the arbitrary definitions of ordinary psychologists ! And yet how difficult to decide between the claims of the various schools! Was the soul a shadow seated in the house of sin? Or was the body really in the soul, as Giordano Bruno thought? The separation of spirit from matter was a mystery, and the union of spirit with matter was a mystery also.

He began to wonder whether we could ever make psychology so absolute a science that each little spring of life would be revealed to us. As it was we always misunderstood ourselves, and rarely understood others. Experience was of no ethical value. It was merely the name men gave to their mistakes. Moralists had, as a rule, regarded it as a mode of warning, had claimed for it a certain ethical efficacy in the formation of character, had praised it as something that taught us what to follow and showed us what to avoid. But there was no motive power in experience. It was a little of an active cause as conscience itself. All that it really demonstrated was that our future would be the same as our past, and that the sin we had done once, and with loathing, we would do many times, and with joy.

It was clear to him that the experimental method was the only method by which one could arrive at any scientific analysis of the passions; and certainly Dorian Gray was a subject made to his hand, and seemed to promise rich and fruitful results.[1]

The primary passion Wotton wishes to understand is ecstatic apprehension of beauty, hence his fascination with Dorian's life. While Wotton's experimental connoisseurship never gets near the implausible wellspring of Dorian's beautiful life, his musing does present the elements for a conceptual, if not scientific, analysis of the mysteriously aesthetic and ethical life of his friend's picture. While the ethical pragmatism of mimesis vanishes under the ironically Pateresque dismissal of experience Wotton conducts, something more than Pater's *carpe momenti belli* is at work in the passage cited here. The convergence of so many oppositions in passion for beauty, especially the interpenetration of mind and body, together with the dismissal of acccumulated experience as substance or motive of life's springs in human consciousness invites a Neitzschean reading of the soul and tragedy in Dorian's story. Of the various contradictory assertions that do the work of arguments in Nietzstche's writing, one cluster bears directly on Wilde's modernist revision of the ethical realism Aristotle's *Poetics* bequeathed to Europe — Nietzsche's celebration of Dionysiac self-creation, the will to power's ceaseless internal generation of resistance and internal mastery of such resistance. That Wilde had some acquaintance with Nietzsche's thinking from his travels to Paris in the years before the composition of the novel has been cursorily indicated by critics.[2] In the brief time remaining, I want to show, in broad outline, how some ideas from Nietzsche spin irony through the Aristotelian poetic justice which ends Dorian's aesthetic passion.

   Nietzsche's first account of tragedy, *The Birth of Tragedy* (1872), retains the appearance/reality dichotomy from Aristotle's analysis of the genre, but reverses the ancient argument about formal representation of substantial reality. The formal coherence of tragic plot, in Nietzsche's case, becomes an Apollonian illusion of stasis which ethical and aesthetic consciousness ambiguously generates to summon and resist submission to the underlying Dionysian force of formless, dynamic chaos. In the catastrophic reversal, the tragic protagonist submits to this dynamic ruin, ecstatically, not with somber rational discovery of reality's changeless intelligible order. Later in Nieztzsche's career, in the great works of the 1880's, especially *Thus Spoke Zarathustra*, and *Beyond Good and Evil*, the dynamic interchange of static identity and purely aspiring power in consciousness, the building of ever more stately mansions in the soul, becomes the central action of life, a personal and cosmological command. In these later works, the appearance/reality dichotomy vanishes, and the apocalyptic command to Phoenix self-creation, living dangerously, becomes incessant play with no end asserted or conceived. Anti-moral, with a high premium on the mysterious intensity of opposites converging, with rapturous celebration of aesthetic order simultaneously suffered and exerted in consciousness, Nietzsche's modernist account of the tragic spirit of Dionysus has obvious affinities with the aestheticism of Pater, and Huysmans, which critics correctly cite as sources for Dorian's story.

Unlike the Aristotelian agent, the Nietzschean willer comes to be not by engaging the plausible, but by projectively asserting himself against and through the implausible. The impediments to such self-creation are various weaknesses of will, which the failing soul figures to itself as wrongs it has suffered, wrongs it can only right by anachronistic submission to morality and reason. These conventional guarantors of plausibility degenerate, in Nietzsche's thinking, into names for delusional, desperate, or exhausted vengeance against life's unanswered, unanswerable calls to power. The pragmatically ethical conscience implausibly imitated in Dorian's picture presents the enduring romance his conscience has carried out with the plausible world. In that romance, Dorian has debauched his joyous will to power by never detaching it from the traditional association of ideal beauty with virtue. Implausibly, given the power his beauty has to govern nature, Dorian has fallen short of his best self, from the Nietzschean as well as Aristotelian point of view. Thus the final implausible transfer of his exhausted soul's form from the slashed picture to the murdered man, and the corollary transfer of his original aesthetic will to power from the guilty creature back to the innocent image, fuse Miss Prism's idea of poetic justice and Nietzsche's ecstatic homage to the shape-shifting, vindicating spirit of Dionysus. Wilde's preface to the novel provides the best gloss for the double ending by which the story enacts and frustrates the conventional double resolution of poetic justice. Dorian succumbs to the rage of nineteenth century realism, Aristotle's progeny, and the rage of nineteenth century Romanticism, Nietzsche's forebear. He dies of seeing and not seeing his face in art's stylized glass.

NOTES

1   Oscar Wilde, *The Picture of Dorian Gray*, edited by P. Ackroyd (London, Penguin Books, 1985), pp. 83-84.
2   See F. N. Oppel's *Masks & Tragedy, Yeats & Nietzsche* (Charlottesville, University of Virginia Press, 1987), pp. 19-20, 57.

THE STORY-TELLER AT FAULT

Deirdre Toomey

When Yeats recalls Oscar Wilde in 'Four Years',[1] it is not as a writer (Wilde's books merely date the experiences recalled) nor as 'the lion of the season', but as a talker — 'an excellent talker'.[2] Speech, conversation, the oral takes precedence over writing. Yeats asserts this aggressively; 'only when [Wilde] spoke, or when his writing was the mirror of his speech, or in some simple, fairy tale, had he words enough to hold a subtle ear [...] his plays and dialogues have what merit they possess from being now an imitation, now a record of his talk.'[3] And later, in *The Tragic Generation*, he recalls the oral version of Wilde's story, 'The Doer of Good', which Wilde called, 'the best story in the world':

> Christ came from a white plain to a purple city, and as He passed through the first street He heard voices overhead, and saw a young man lying drunk upon a window-sill. 'Why do you waste your soul in drunkenness?' He said. 'Lord, I was a leper and You healed me, what else can I do?'. A little further through the town He saw a young man following a harlot, and said, 'Why do you dissolve your soul in debauchery?', and the young man answered, 'Lord I was blind and You healed me, what else can I do?'. At last, in the middle of the city He saw an old man crouching, weeping on the ground, and when He asked why he wept, the old man answered, 'Lord, I was dead, and you raised me into life, what else can I do but weep?'.

Yeats concludes with heroic disparagement 'Wilde published that story a little later, but spoiled it with the verbal decoration of his epoch, and I have to repeat it to myself as I first heard it, before I can see its terrible beauty'.[4] A year later, in 1923 when Yeats wrote an introduction to *The Happy Prince and other Fairy Tales* he expanded this stance:

405

[I]ndeed when I remember him with pleasure it is always the
talker I remember [...]. Behind his words was the whole power
of his intellect, but that intellect had given itself to pure
contemplation [...]. The further Wilde goes in his writings from
the *method of speech*[my italics] from improvisation, from
sympathy with some especial audience the less original he is, the
less accomplished.

Again Yeats recalled and praised 'The Doer of Good':

It has definiteness, the simplicity of great sculpture, it adds
something new to the imagination of the world, it suddenly
confronts the mind — as does all great art — with the
fundamental and the insoluble. It puts into almost as few as
possible words, a melancholy that comes upon a man at the
moment of triumph.[5]

Yeats when reading a story such as 'The Fisherman and
his Soul' tried to recreate it in its primary oral version —

I try to imagine it as it must have been when he spoke it, half
consciouly watching that he might not bore by a repeated effect
or unecessary description, some child or some little company fo
young painters or writers. Only when I so imagine it do I
discover that the incident of the young fisherman's
dissatisfaction with his mermaid mistress, upon hearing of a girl
dancing with bare feet was witty, charming and characteristic...
In the written story that incident is so lost in decorations that
we let it pass unoticed at a first reading, yet it is the crisis of the
tale. To enjoy it I must hear his voice once more, and listen once
more to that incomparable talker.[6]

Yeats's privileging of the oral over the written was not
the effect of hostility or envy — Yeats admired Wilde as a man
and was almost incapable of literary envy. Yeats's aesthetic
judgement is also a mark of an Irish cultural valuing of the oral
over the written. Wilde himself praised the young Yeats for
his story telling —'he made me tell him long Irish stories and
compared my art of story-telling to Homer's.'[7] Both writers
came from the most oral culture in Western Europe, a culture
which retained primary orality as well as oral/writing
diglossia well into the twentieth century. Yeats himself
manifested a productive tension between extreme endorsement
of oral culture (his concern with folk-lore, his gathering of oral
texts, his experiments with chaunting) and extreme concern

with the text elaborately realised in an object, the book. Wilde's tension between writing and talking was a hostile symbiosis: he told a journalist that there should be a more satisfactory way of 'conveying poetry to the mind' than by printing it,[8] and frankly told Gide that writing bored him.[9]

Many of Wilde's listeners did not have an Irish context into which to place his orality; but they still valued his oral tales over their written versions. André Gide (who said '*Dorian Gray*, at the very begining was a splendid story, how superior to *La Peau de Chagrin*. Alas, written down what a masterpiece manqué'[10]), Charles Ricketts, Gabrielle Enthoven, Aimée Lowther, Ernest La Jeunesse, Henri de Régnier, Jean Lorrain and many others have recorded Wilde's tales and over 80 have been collected by Guillot de Saix.[11] Vincent O'Sullivan, who recorded several tales, glossed Wilde's inability to write after 1897 thus:

> The impulse to write was never very strong in Wilde. The impulse to compose — yes. But that he satisfied by talking.

O'Sullivan also comments on the importance of 'immediate applause' for Wilde.[12] Certainly Wilde's late rejection of writing is tied to the difficulty of being published — although Leonard Smithers would have published anything Wilde wrote. Yet by contrast, if Yeats had been proscribed by all the publishers in the world, he would still have spent half the day writing — despite his authentic, demonstrable love of oral culture. Yeats isolates this difference in identifying Wilde as a 'man of action' whose 'half civilised' Irish blood could not tolerate the 'sedentary toil' of writing.[13]

Wilde lacked any strong sense of ownership in his oral tales — an identifying characteristic of oral cultures, in which the text belongs to the whole community. Thus in Ireland in the 1840s, when Peter O'Leary heard the great Munster folk tale *Séadna*, the tale was the property of the whole community, although told by Peig Labhrais and memorised by the young O'Leary, who published it from memory 50 years later.[14] When the adolescent W.B. Maxwell, Mary Braddon's son, confessed to Wilde that he had published a tale of Wilde's which he had heard at his mother's house, Wilde responded aimiably, 'stealing my story was the act of a gentleman, but not telling me you had stolen it was to ignore the claims of friendship'. Wilde merely asked him not to appropriate another tale — the tale 'I told you about a man and a picture' — that is the oral version of *Dorian Gray*.[15] Wilde was equally mild in his response to Aimée Lowther's announcement that she was about to publish his fine oral tale 'The Poet'.[16] Once Wilde was dead any pretence of restraint in this area ceased. Guillot de Saix has noted much French appropriation of Wilde's tales. Frank Harris published a plodding version of 'The Miracle of the Stigmata'[17] a tale which was also obviously of use to George Moore in *The Brook Kerith*; Arthur Symons's tale 'Esther Kahn' is a plagiary with naturalistic colouring of Wilde's oral tale, 'The Actress'.[18] A more unexpected plagiarist is found in Evelyn Waugh, who had evidently heard Wilde's oral tale 'Aunt Jane's Ball' at second hand, possibly in Ireland: Waugh published an embarrassingly inferior plagiary 'Bella Fleace gave a Party' as late as 1932.[19]

Oral texts and oral culture are always contextualised and responsive to a particular audience: oral poets for example 'rhapsodise' differently to a different audience; the audience's reaction is part of the tale — the so called 'sounding-board' effect.[20] The beholder's or listener's share in an oral culture is of comprehensive constructive significance; it directs the tale. What is not accepted is not the text. The context in which the tale is told will also alter the text; thus when — say — on Christmas Eve, 1899, in the Calisaya Bar, Paris, surrounded by the usual suspects (Jean de Mitty, Ernest La Jeunesse, Robert Sherard), Wilde told 'The Miracle of the Stigmata', it would have been in a version which *responded* to this time and context.[21] Yeats points to the way in which Wilde would adjust the telling of a story in progress to the impatience of children or the unsophisticated. Vincent O'Sullivan discussing what he terms 'the machinery of [Wilde's] talk' emphasises Wilde's 'extraordinary tact in choosing subjects which would suits his listeners and in judging his effects... he did not try to enforce his moods; he gave the impression of adapting himself to the moods of others.'[22] La Jeunesse, who spent much time in the Calisaya Bar with Wilde, gives a gripping account of the *process* of oral story telling:

> Slowly, word for word, he would invent in his feverish
> stumbling agony of art, curious fleeting parables [...]. He wasted
> himself entirely in words [...] the chaos of hope of words and
> laughter, the mad sequence of half completed sentences with
> which this poet plunged, proving to himself his till
> unextinguished fancy [...]. He attempted his stories all over
> again. It is like nothing save the bitter, blinding brilliance of a
> super-human firework.[23]

The struggle which La Jeunesse represents here is not so much
that of composition, but of 'stitching and unstitching', of
adjustment of a tale to a particular audience, a particular
context.

In oral cultures, words are not *things*, dead, 'out there'
on a flat surface, as they are to literates living in a
chirographic-typographic culture. In Walter Ong's account, to
pre-literates living in *verbomotor* cultures, words are events.

> The fact that oral people commonly and in all likelihood
> universally consider words to have magical potency is clearly
> tied in at least unconsciously, with their sense of the words as
> necessarily spoken, sounded and hence power driven [...] in a
> primary oral culture, where the word has its existence only in
> sound [...] the phenomenology of sound enters deeply into human
> beings' feeling for existence as processed by the spoken word.
> For the way in which the word is experienced is always
> momentous in psychic life.[24]

Ong's account of the magical, penetrative, internalised
experience of the spoken word is perfectly realised in chapter
two of *The Picture of Dorian Gray* — a work which began as an
oral tale.

> Words! Mere words! How terrible they were! How clear and
> vivid and cruel! One could not escape from them. And yet what
> a subtle magic was in them! They seemed to be able to give a
> plastic form to formless things [...]. Mere words! Was there
> anything so real as words?[25]

Dorian's will is penetrated and corrupted by the magical
spoken word: the fatal book — so over-emphasised in analysis
of this novel — is a subsidiary matter in the catastrophe.

Gesture, and the somatic element are vital in oral cultures and related to the physicality of the story-telling mode. Ong points to the totality of the oral experience:

> The oral word [...] never exists in a simply verbal context as a written word does. Spoken words are always part of a total existential situation, which always engages the body. Bodily activity beyond mere vocalisation is not adventitious or contrived in oral communication, but is natural and even inevitable.[26]

Eric Havelock in analysing Greek oral poetry has suggested an erotic element in this somatic component, shared by artist and audience.[27] And Havelock's position on oral composition is anticipated by Wilde in 'The Critic as Artist':

> The great poet is always a seer, seeing less with the eyes of the body than with the eyes of the mind [...] a true singer also, building his song out of music, repeating each line over and over again to himself [...] chanting in darkness.[28]

Charles Ricketts remembered Wilde's tendency to pause upon certain key words in a tale. There 'would even be a slight movement of the hand as if to arrest their sound' and Wilde's subtle but expressive use of gesture and mimesis —

> a chance word, even an interruption, might conjure up a prose poem [...]. The poet we divine in his early verse, remained ever present and spontaneous in his speech. There was besides, the cadenced and varied intonation, pausing on a word, a sentence, as a violinist accents and phrases his music. Wilde possessed and used all vocabularies, slang alone excepted — even that of the Victorian Philistines and moralists, ever his accusers. One also heard the beloved voices of the men he admired in his youth [...] Ruskin [...] Tennyson [...] Rossetti [...] Swinburne [...]. I would not describe this gift as mimicry, it was hardly more than a variation in intonation or a movement of the eyes.[29]

Other characteristics of orality — the agonistic structure found in 'The Decay of Lying' and 'The Critic as Artist', the lack of a hierarchy between text and interpretation (a profound element in Wilde's aesthetic) can be identified in his written *oeuvre*. Wilde's love of the aphorism (and his elevation of aphorism above narrative in *The Picture of Dorian Gray*) is also typical of the oral mode.[30] 'The Decay of Lying' endorses that very aspect of oral culture which, according to Havelock, Plato attacked in *The Republic*.[31]

Another area in which oral culture differs absolutely from literate culture is in its attitude to cliché, stereotype and plagiary. These cardinal sins of literacy are cardinal virtues of orality. Originality in an oral culture consists not in inventing an absolutely new story but in stitching together the familiar in a manner suitable to a particular audience, or by introducing new elements into an old story. The persistent charge against Wilde of plagiary would seem oxymoronic in an oral culture. Wilde's tendency to start from the very familiar or traditional in his oral tales — something already given and known, the Bible, Fairy Tales, is again fully characteristic of orality. A remarkable defense of Wilde's type of artist is given by Ernest La Jeunesse:

> When a thaumaturg — and I choose the words purposely, one that Wilde respected highly — undertakes to fool the public he has the right to choose his material where he finds it; one does not expect of him moral and social lessons, but inventions, tricks, words a touch of heaven and a touch of hell, and what not else; he must be Proteus and Prometheus, must be able to transform all things and himself; he must be confessor, prophet and magician; he must dissect the world with the exactness of a doctrinarian and create it all anew the moment after, by the light of his poetic fancy; he must produce formulas and paradoxes, and even barbaric puns with nothing save their antiquity to save them.
>
> For this price — a well paid one — he can find distraction after the manner of the gods or the fallen angels and seek for himself excitements and deceptions, since he has advanced, and eventually crossed the borders of ordinary human emotions and sensations.[32]

Wilde's major cycle of Biblical tales exemplifies this characteristic of the oral in its dependence on traditional material known to all his listeners. Some tales are endearingly slight, such as the version of 'The Woman Taken in Adultery' which represents her indignant husband's position — he casts the first stone.[33] Others are expressive of Wilde's profoundest conceptions and beliefs — specifically his identification of Christ with the figure of the Artist. Christ is the type of the perfectly realised personality 'entirely and absolutely

himself', the very basis of whose nature was 'the same as that
of the nature of the artist [...] Christ's place is indeed with the
poets'.[34] Jean Lorrain recalled an oral tale which extends the
Raising of Lazarus, noting that the first half of the tale is no
more than an elegant reaction of John 11: after Lazarus has been
raised from the dead, the 'variante du poète' begins.

> Et Lazare marcha. Tous s'en furent alors en criant au miracle.
> Mais Lazare, ressuscité, demeure triste. Au lieu de tomber aux
> pieds de Jésus, il restait à l'écart, avec un air de reproche. Et
> Jésus s'approcha demanda tendrement:
>   – Toi qui reviens de chez les morts, ne me diras-tu rien,
> Lazare?
> Et Lazare lui dit:
>   – Pourquoi m'as-tu menti, pourquoi mens-tu encore en
> leur parlant du ciel, de la gloire de Dieu? Il n'y a rien Rabbi,
> rien par delà la mort, et celui qui est mort est bien mort, je le sais,
> moi qui m'en reviens de là-bas.
> Et Jésus un doigt sur la bouche avec un regard implorant vers
> Lazare, lui répondit:
>   – Je le sais. Ne leur dis pas.[35]

Another Biblical story told to Yeats is recalled by him in
epitome.

> One day [Wilde] began, 'I have been inventing a Christian
> heresy', and he told a detailed story, in the style of some early
> Father, of how Christ recovered after the Crucifixion, and
> escaping from the tomb, lived on for many years, the one man on
> earth who knew the falsehood of Christianity. Once Saint Paul
> visited his town and he alone in the Carpenter's quarter did not
> go to hear him preach. Henceforth the other carpenters noticed
> that, for some unknown reason, he kept his hands covered.[36]

A full version of the tale, entitled 'The Miracle of the
Stigmata' was collected by Guillot de Saix, who gives the
context of its telling, of its specified setting, 35 A.D. in the
Jewish quarter in Rome and presents a variant ending to Yeats's
version. After Christ's death his fellow-carpenters discover
the nail marks in his hands and feet and declare this to be a
great miracle. To Coulson Kernahan, his editor at Ward, Lock
& Co., Wilde talked very seriously about his obsession with
the figure of Christ (Kernahan was deeply religious):

Shall I tell you what is my greatest ambition — even more than an ambition — the dream of my life? Not to be remembered hereafter as an artist, poet, thinker or playwright, but as the man who reclothed the sublimest conception the world has ever known [...] with new and burning words, with new and illuminating symbols, with new and divine vision, free from the accretions of cant which the centuries have gathered around it. I should therefore be giving the world back again the greatest gift ever given to mankind since Christ Himself gave it.

Wilde is arguing — as he so often did — for a new Evangel, a heterodox fifth Gospel. He told Kernahan part of a story of the return of Christ, 'The Useless Resurrection', but was interrupted at the crisis and never returned to finish[37] this, his most ambitious and most ideologically and aesthically charged of the tales of Christ. It was later collected and printed in full by Guillot de Saix.

Un jour, un terrassier arabe au service d'un entrepreneur de fouilles qui ne recherchait que des monnaies anciennes, heurta de son pic par hasard, au flanc de la montagne du Calvaire, la pierre d'un tombeau. Et s'étant fait aider par ses camarades pour soulever la lourde dalle, il découvrit au creux de l'étroit sépulcre creusé dans un roc, un mort encore enveloppé dans son linceul intact.

L'entrepreneur de fouilles fit transporter cette macabre découverte dans un musée où les savants à lunettes se penchant sur elle avec soin démaillotèrent le défunt de ses bandelettes et découvrirent avec stupéfaction un corps momifié, portant évidentes, encore ourlées d'un sang desséché, noirâtre et craquelant, des plaies aux poignets, aux pieds et au flanc. C'était bien là, sans nul doute, le corps même de celui qui avait été crucifié sous Ponce-Pilate.

Ainsi des générations avaient été illusionnées comme le furent les saintes femmes et les premiers disciples, illusionnés également ceux-là qui avaient cru pouvoir établir avec certitude l'emplacement du sépulcre appartenant à Joseph d'Arimathie et construire sur cet emplacement un sanctuaire où les genoux des fidèles étaient venus user les pierres.

Les journaux s'emparèrent de l'événement, le Pape fut chassé du Vatican dont on fit une sorte de temple de la Vérité Scientifique où l'on exposa sous verre à la curiosité publique le cadavre par qui le mensonge séculaire avait été assassiné. Et de ce fait, la foi chrétienne, basée sur le dogme de la Résurrection subit une éclipse passagère.

Mais, le dimanche de Pâques suivant, un triste dimanche sans cloche, au premier pâle rayon de soleil qui vint le toucher assez tard dans la matinée, le corps inerte reprit vie, brisa les vitres de son cercueil transparent et, devant les visiteurs et les gardiens prosternés, traversant d'un essor glorieux la Voûte Vaticane, disparut à leurs yeux. Une nouvelle religion dut naître et se répandre, ayant d'autres apôtres, d'autres martyrs aussi. De-ci, de-là, le Christ apparut à d'autres pélerins pour se justifier aux hommes et fonder un culte de beauté sur des bases nouvelles. Il prêcha que, si l'on suivait sa doctrine, il n'y aurait plus ni riches, ni pauvres, ni luttes de classes, ni guerres, mais seulement, dans la grande unité des races divisées, des hommes s'aimant les uns et les autres devant l'éphémère et constant miracle de la vie. Il affirma qu'il était revenu pour abolir les souffrances de ceux-là qui sont légions et dont la demeure est parmi les tombes, tous les opprimés, les enfants des usines, les voleurs, les vagabonds des grands chemins, les gens en prison, les proscrits, bref de tous ceux qui sont muets sous le glaive de l'oppresseur, et dont le silence est entendu par Dieu seul.[38] Il dit à chacun: 'Sois toi-même. Ta perfection est en toi.'[39] Mais sans doute était-il venu trop tard dans un monde trop vieux.

A cette révélation suprême par une bouche de lumière, des savants donnèrent des explications rationnellement scientifiques. Jésus renonça pour toujours à reparaître aux yeux des hommes, et tout retomba dans l'apathie des jours sans croyance et sans joie.[40]

In all these tales, Christ is the type of the Artist, a thaumaturge and a perfectly realised personality but doomed to rejection and to a failure which is central, not extraneous to his power. In 'The Useless Resurrection' the themes of both 'The Critic as Artist' and 'The Soul of Man under Socialism' are dramatised. It is a tale in which Wilde's Joachimism can be detected; the Christ who returns is a Third Age Christ, Christ as the Holy Spirit, a Divine Being who preaches with a mouth of light not flesh. His gospel, 'Be thyself', the gospel of 'The Soul ol Man Under Socialism', is a Third Status gospel, a gospel of the Age of the Spirit.[41] But it fails, and 'The Useless Resurrection' has the same trajectory as Yeats's occult tales, 'Rosa Alchemica', 'The Tables of the Law' and 'The Adoration of the Magi', ending in greyness, apathy, despair.[42]

One of Wilde's most popular oral tales, 'The Poet' survives in many accounts — told sometimes as a trifle to amuse a journalist, at other times as a serious highly worked exposition of the nature of imagination and its relation to experience. Gide gives a crude *résumé* of this tale in his memoirs of Wilde, omitting a crucial episode.[43] Equally reduced *résumés* are given by Coulson Kernahan, Henri de Régnier and Jean-Joseph Renaud. Full versions are given by

Gabrielle Enthoven, Aimée Lowther and Charles Ricketts. Ricketts, who heard this tale c. 1889, published it in 1932, in a version which is probably very close to the most refined oral text — Ricketts acknowledges having heard it many times:

> Now a certain man was greatly beloved by the people of his village, for, when they gathered round him at dusk and questioned him, he would relate many strange things he had seen. He would say, 'I beheld three mermaids by the sea who combed their green hair with a golden comb.' And when they besought him to tell more, he answered: 'By a hollow rock I spied a centaur; and, when his eyes met mine, he turned slowly to depart, gazing on me sadly over his shoulder.' And when they asked eagerly, 'Tell us, what else have you seen?', he told them: 'In a little copse a young faun played upon a flute to the dwellers in the woods who danced to his piping.' One day when he had left the village as was his wont, three mermaids rose from the waves who combed their green hair with a comb of gold, a centaur peeped at him behind a hollow rock, and later, as he passed a little copse, he beheld a faun who played on a pipe to the dwellers in the wood.
>
> That night, when the people of the village gathered at dusk, saying, 'Tell us, what have you seen to-day?' he answered them sadly: 'To-day I have seen nothing.'[44]

This tale and in particular the motif of the centaur slowly turning his head obsessed Ricketts, who was puzzled by Gide's omission of this detail. 'Strangely enough Gide omits the episode of the centaur, yet this detail has remained vivid in my memory, for Wilde, by an almost imperceptible turn of the head, when speaking, conjured up the movement of the receding creature.'[45] And in 1923, when Oscar Wilde came through on the astral plane[46] to the famous Dublin medium, Hester Dowden — he discussed *inter alia* his dislike of *Ulysses*, which he had been absorbing in the ether —Ricketts wrote to Hester Dowden, asking her to cross examine Wilde's ghost as to the correct version of 'The Poet' and the detail of the centaur's head.[47] This fine motif of the centaur's twisted head, expressed by the story teller's movement is perhaps an unconscious absorption of Wilde's own experience at the Olympia excavations in April 1877 —Wilde was always to claim that he had been present when the great statue of Apollo was discovered. The west pediment of the Temple of Zeus at Olympia is a magnificent centauromachy and perhaps a memory of the twisted head of the centaur Eurytion is preserved in this tale — and in the story teller's movement while telling it.[48]

Yeats alone of Wilde's friends had the Irish Nationalist context in which to place a valuing of the spoken over the written, and to understand the larger cultural and political implications of such a stance. In *Autobiographies* Yeats recalls J. F. Taylor's speech defending the Irish language at Trinity — which Yeats called the greatest *extempore* speech ever made. Taylor had responded to arguments which insisted on the marginality and poverty of Irish language and culture with a speech which ended with a vision of Moses defying Pharaoh: 'I see a man at the edge of the crowd; he is standing listening there, but he will not obey' [...] had he obeyed he would never have come down the mountain carrying in his hands the Tables of the Law in the language of the outlaw.'[49] To concern yourself with folk culture and 'the language of the outlaw' was in Ireland to be radically nationalist. As late as 1899, it was being argued by Robert Atkinson of Trinity that modern Irish was merely a 'patois' not an authentic language, and that Irish folk tales were disgusting and worthless: 'so low! I do not want to know about the vulgar exploits of a dirty wretch who never washed his feet [...] that he never washed his feet and had an interview with the Pope, and married the Princess So-and-so' was his response to 'Guleesh na Guss Dhu' from Douglas Hyde's *Beside the Fire*.[50] When folk tale collectors such as Sir William Wilde or Douglas Hyde took down the tales of pre-literate peasants in the West, they were engaging in something more than an anthropological or literary exercise; they were making a statement of cultural and political Nationalism.

Oscar Wilde can be associated with those Protestant Nationalists — Sir William Wilde, Lady Wilde, Douglas Hyde, Lady Gregory, Yeats, Synge — who, by linking themselves to a despised, indigenous, pre-literate culture, with folk tales and folk parables, re-identified with Ireland,[51] with 'the unwritten tradition which binds the unlettered [...] to the beginning of time and the foundation of the world'.[52] Wilde himself drew on tales collected in the West by his father and published by his mother — Lady Wilde's 'The Priest's Soul' became an after dinner tale for him in Paris [53] — and some of the images of Irish folk tales affected his sensibility. Wilde's description of his experiences with rough trade as being like 'feasting with panthers' seems to have more than an accidental link with Lady Wilde's 'A Wolf Story', an uncanny homoerotic version of the Grateful Beast motif; a young farmer seeking strayed animals is benighted in a hut with a ferocious old couple. Two wolves walk in and transform themselves into dark handsome but sinister young men with glittering eyes; one shows much affection for the farmer and protects him, thanking him for having once removed a thorn from his side.[54]

Yeats thought that 'all art should be a Centaur, finding in the popular lore its back and strong legs'[55] and Wilde's 'The Poet' — the classicised tale which obsessed Ricketts enough to badger Wilde's ghost as to its essential elements — is rooted in Irish folk culture. It is an inversion of a celebrated Irish Folk Tale 'The Story-teller at Fault', first published by Griffin in *Tales of a Jury Room*, and collected in many oral versions.[56] The motif seems unique to Ireland. A king's story teller finds himself at a loss for a new tale. His wife points to an old grey ragged beggar man who has suddenly appeared on their land; the story-teller gambles with the beggar, loses horse, hounds, land and wife, and eventually gambles himself away; the beggar then tranforms the story-teller into a hare and the story-teller's own hounds chase him, while his wife watches. Transformed back the story-teller by an extraordinary narrative manoeuvre becomes the assumed observer of the beggar's magical antics at the court of a neighbouring Lord. Here the beggar plays a variety of tricks including that of producing a silken rope from a bag, throwing a hare and a red-eared hound up it and sending a young woman and a young man after the animals. The beggar then returns to the Court of the story-teller's Lord and reassembles story-teller and wife on their own land — pulling them out of narrative space to do so — and reveals himself to be *Aengus Og*. The story-teller then has only to tell the King of his own magical adventures that day and he has a never ending, never failing tale.

As so often in his oral tales, Wilde respects the morphology of the original tale but inverts the 'moral'; the 'fault' ends his tale, rather than is its occasion. So 'The Poet', this richly classicised tale with its *l'Art pour l'Art* aesthetic

418 *Rediscovering Oscar Wilde*

and its centaur from the Olympia Pediment is an Irish folk tale
inverted, a product of the dying oral culture to which Wilde
was tied by what Yeats called 'his half-civilized blood', the
culture of those who listened to spoken tales, undivided by
book culture — 'friend by friend, lover by lover'.[57]

NOTES

1   *Autobiographies* (London, Macmillan, 1955, pp. 130-9).
2   See *Uncollected Prose by W.B. Yeats*, Vol I, ed. J. P. Frayne
     (London, Macmillan, 1970), p. 354.
3   *Autobiographies*, p. 135.
4   *Autobiographies*, p. 286.
5   W. B. Yeats *Prefaces and Introductions: Uncollected Prefaces and
     Introductions*(CEW VI), ed. by W. H. O'Donnell (London,
     Macmillan, 1988), pp. 147-150. The version given here differs
     slightly from that given in *Autobiographies*. The italics are mine.
6   *Ibid.*, p. 149.
7   *Autobiographies*, p. 135.
8   See P. W. H. Almy, 'New Views of Mr Oscar Wilde', *The
     Theatre*, March 1894.
9   A. Gide, *Oscar Wilde* (London, William Kimber, 1951), p. 29.
10   A. Gide, *Oscar Wilde*, p. 29.
11   In *Les Songes merveilleux du Dormeur éveillé / Le Chant du
     Cygne* / contes parlés d'Oscar Wilde (Paris, Mercure de
     France, 1942).
12   *Aspects of Wilde* (London, Constable, 1936), pp. 34, 75.
13   *Autobiographies*, p. 138.
14   O'Leary serialised the tale in the *Gaelic Journal* 1894-1897.
15   *Time Gathered: Autobiography* (London, Hutchinson, 1931),
     p. 97.
16   See R. Hart-Davis (ed.) *Letters* (London, Rupert Hart-Davis,
     1962), p. 809.
17   In *Unpath'd Waters* (London, John Lane, 1913).
18   First published in *The Smart Set* in October 1902, and collected
     in *Spiritual Adventures* (London, Constable, 1905).
19   *Harper's Bazaar*, March 1933, collected in *Work Suspended and
     Other Stories* (London, Chapman and Hall, 1949).
20   For an excellent survey of Orality Theory see W. J. Ong *Orality
     and Literacy* (London, Routledge, 1991). See also E. Havelock,
     The Muse Learns to Write (New Haven, Yale University Press,
     1986).
21   *Le Chant du Cygne*, pp. 124-7.
22   *Aspects of Wilde* , pp. 41, 37.
23   *Recollections of Oscar Wilde*, ed. P. Pollard (Boston & London, J.
     W. Luce & Co., 1906) pp. 71, 83.
24   *Orality and Literacy*, pp. 32-33, 72.
25   *The Picture of Dorian Gray*, ed. I. Murray (London, Oxford,
     New York, Oxford University Press, 1974), p. 19.
26   *Orality and Literacy*, pp. 67-8.

27   '[D]esire has her dwelling near the muses.' See *Preface to Plato* (Oxford, Blackwell, 1963), pp. 124-5.

28   *The Artist as Critic*, ed R. Ellmann (London, W. H. Allen, 1970), p. 351.

29   *Oscar Wilde Recollections* by J.-P. Raymond & C. Ricketts (London, Nonessuch, 1932), pp. 13-4.

30   'The rounded sentence began its career in the [...] days of oral communication, when information depended on word of mouth and retention of doctrine depended on the memory', E. Havelock, *The Liberal Temper in Greek Politics* (New Haven, Yale University Press, 1957), p. 126. Wilde was doubly sensitive to orality in that not only did he come from an oral culture, but in studying classics for more than seven years, he would have been aware of the interface between orality and literacy at the time of Plato.

31   See Havelock, *Preface to Plato, passim.*

32   La Jeunesse, *Recollections of Oscar Wilde,* ed. P. Pollard (Boston & London, J.W. Luce & Co., 1906) pp. 70-1.

33   *Le Chant du Cygne,* p. 98.

34   See *De Profundis,* Letters, p. 477.

35   *Le Chant du Cygne,* p. 287. I give this tale and a subsequent tale in French as undoubtedly these versions were given in French by Wilde.

36   *Autobiographies,* p. 137.

37   Needless to say Kernahan used what he had heard as the basis of a novel, *The Man of No Sorrows* (London, Cassell and Company, 1911). This work also uses the *topos* of 'The Doer of Good'.

38   This passage closely resembles one in *De Profundis:* 'the sufferings of those whose name is legion and whose dwelling is among the tombs, oppressed nationalities, factory children, thieves, people in prison, outcasts, those who are dumb under oppression and whose silence is heard only of God' (Letters p. 477). However, it seems likely that the oral version came first.

39   See 'The Soul of Man under Socialism'; '*Know thyself* was written over the portal of the antique world. Over the portal of the new world, *Be thyself* shall be written. And the message of Christ to man was simply *Be Thyself*. That is the secret of Christ' ('The Artist as Critic', p. 263).

40   *Le Chant du Cygne,* pp. 170-2. This is clearly Wilde's French rather than that of a native speaker; certain usages are literary and obsolete, viz. 'Illusionnées'.

41   For which see M. Reeves and W. Gould *Joachim of Fiore and the Myth of the Eternal Evangel in the Nineteenth Century* (Oxford, Clarendon, 1987), pp. 180-84.

42   See *The Secret Rose, Stories by W. B. Yeats: A Variorum Edition,* ed. W. Gould, P. L. Marcus and M. Sidnell (London, Macmillan, 1992), pp. 125-73.

43   A. Gide, *Memoirs,* pp. 18-19.

44   See *Oscar Wilde Recollections,* pp. 18-9.

45   Ricketts, *Oscar Wilde Recollections,* p. 16.

46   H. T. Smith (ed.), *Psychic Messages from Oscar Wilde* (London, T. Werner Laurie, 1924).

47   ALS Ricketts to T.S. Moore December 1923 (*B.L. Add MS* 61719). Needless to say Ricketts got little satisfaction from Hester Dowden on this matter.
48   Even if Wilde had not seen the centaurs while at Olympia, he would undoubtedly have consulted E. Curtius, F. Adler et al., *Die Ausgrabungen zu Olympia* (Berlin, 1875-81, 5 v.). Plate XXIV of Vol. 3 shows Deïdameia and the Centaur Eurytion from the West Pediment.
49   *Autobiographies*, pp. 96-7. The speech was given to the Law Students' Debating Society on October 24, 1901. It is also quoted in *Ulysses*, Ch. 7 ('Aeolus').
50   Atkinson, Professor of Celtic Languages at Trinity, was giving evidence very hostile to modern Irish and to folk culture, which he thought 'abominable', before the Commission on Intermediate Education (Ireland) on 22 February 1899 (reported in the Daily Express, Dublin, 23 February 1899).
51   Wilde was a Nationalist. He always insisted on his Irish status, and was very proud when his son, Cyril, announced that he was a Home Ruler. Vincent O'Sullivan confused Wilde's anti-Boer position and his admiration for Queen Victoria with a Unionist stance. Shaw was also anti-Boer — and none would doubt his radicalism. Arthur Griffith, the founder of *Sinn Fein*, was at this time in favour of a dual Monarchy and for an Independent Ireland to have some part in the British Empire.
52   W.B. Yeats, What is 'Popular Poetry'?, *Essays and Introductions* (London, Macmillan 1961), p. 6.
53   G. de Saix (ed.) *Contes et Propos d'Oscar Wilde* (Paris, Arthème Fayard, 1949) p. 9.
54   *Ancient Legends, Mystic Charms and Superstitions of Ireland*, (London, Ward and Downey, 1887) I, pp. 31-35.
55   *Autobiographies*, p. 191.
56   See S. Ó'Suilleabháin, *The Types of the Irish Folk Tale* (Helsinki, F.F. Communications No. 188, 1963), type 2421b.
57   'All the old writers [...] wrote to be spoken or to be sung, and in a later age to be read aloud to hearers [...] who gave nothing up of life to listen, but sat, the day's work over, friend by friend, lover by lover' (*Samhain*, 1906 in *Explorations*, sel. Mrs W.B. Yeats [London, Macmillan, 1962; New York, Macmillan, 1963], p. 221). See also 'Speaking to the Psaltery' and 'The Return of Ulysses' (Essays and Introductions, pp. 14, 199).

WILDE'S READING OF
CLEMENS ALEXANDRINUS

Emmanuel Vernadakis

> The more disciples he had, the sadder the Master of wisdom, who possessed the perfect knowledge of God, became. Thus he questioned his soul:
> - Why is that I am full of sorrow and fear [...]?
> And the soul replied:
> - God filled thee with the perfect knowledge of Himself, and thou hast given this knowlegde away to others. The pearl of great price thou hast divided, and the vesture without seam thou hast parted asunder. He who giveth away wisdom robbeth himself. He is as one who giveth his treasure to a robber. Is not God wiser than thou art? Who art thou to give away the secret that God hath told thee?[1]

According to 'The Teacher of Wisdom', from which this brief extract is taken, knowledge cannot or ought not to be given away. This esoteric view of knowledge which is neither shared nor taught means that in Wilde philosophical and religious learning is concealed rather than flaunted. It is hard to believe why Wilde should have wanted to conceal it, it seems so out of character. Indeed, certain passages of his critical work would lead one to suspect that his knowledge is too pretentiously aired for it to be anything but superficial. However, Wilde was the great-grandson of an archdeacon as well as a vicar; both his uncles on his father's side were priests; he was a pupil in a Protestant school and was constantly tempted by Catholicism. In addition he studied Greek civilization and philosophy in Dublin and then at Oxford with sufficient interest to make the Journey to Greece. His family and cultural background therefore leave no doubt as to the mark left on him by Greek philosophy and Christian religion. The purpose of this paper is to show how they are exploited in his work.

To this end, I propose an approach to Wilde through one of his key sources, Clemens of Alexandria. Authors choose their own ancestry, and if Wilde chose Clemens, we have the starting point of Wilde's problematic on the relationship between philosophy and religion, which are skillfully combined in the gnostic's work. I therefore assume that Wilde refers to his chosen ancestor's point of view in order to form his own, which I shall attempt to elucidate through a tale, 'The Happy Prince', and a poem in prose, 'The Teacher of Wisdom'. My aim is to emphasize the philosophical and religious qualities of Wilde's work.

*   *   *

Wilde never mentions the name of Clemens of Alexandria. In the absence of a first-hand document,[2] the proof that he had read Clemens's work can only be established indirectly.

In November 1891, he informed everyone who was of any literary importance in Paris — except Mallarmé — of his plan to write a *Salomé* in French. He was talking about it at length before he had even started writing it. Enrico Gomez Carrillo, a young Guatemalan diplomat who was at the time fascinated by Wilde,[3] seems to have distilled the 'pure ideas' of the play in his novel *The Gospel of Love*.[4] This work deals with the same themes, uses the same devices, refers to the same events, embraces the same vision of things, shares the same sources as Wilde's French play to the extent that through the novel's Byzantine feasts we see Salome rise out of her author's imagination and dance before the Parisian symbolist crowd. For example, *The Song of Songs* is quoted in *Salome*[5] as we know. Gomez Carrillo also discourses on the initial incest as it occurs in *The Song of Songs*. He continues with the verse from *Ecclesiastes*. 'Never smile at your daughter' which, in *Salome*, triggers and justifies the advice given by the sensible Herodias to her fickle husband: 'You must not look at her [Salome]. You are always looking at her.' Then, 'the flame of this mad mixture of family ardour and perverse ecstasy', leads Gomez Carrillo 'to the tragic evening of the tetrarch's feast, to Salome's lips', where finally, 'it burns out'.[6] What could be a coincidence in one work cannot be a coincidence in two. Hence,

The Gospel of Love should be considered as entirely dependent on *Salome*, and as such, a precious source of information as regards its component material.

From incest to homosexuality, Gomez Carrillo composes an apologia to sinful love and mentions 'the words of Jesus to Salome':

> Eat of every plant except for those which are bitter.[7]

He refers to the apocryphal *Gospel According to the Egyptians*, composed of 'logia' (words of Jesus) addressed to someone named Salome:

> Salome [says]: 'I have done well, then, in not bearing children [...].' The Lord answers and says: 'Every plant eat thou, but that which hath bitterness, eat not.'[8]

Did Wilde know this apocryphon? Given the connection between *Salome* and *The Gospel of Love*, it would be most surprising if he did not. This indirect proof becomes more concrete when we find the same words in 'The Fisherman and his Soul', written before *Salome*, in which the Soul repeats them to the fisherman:

> What is the trouble of thine about the things of sin? Is that which is pleasant to eat not made for the eater? Is there poison in that which is sweet to drink?[9]

This time we are fortunate for the *Gospel According to the Egyptians* was discovered in its entirety in 1972.[10] In the 19th century it was only known through fragments quoted in Clemens of Alexandria's *Stromateis*.[11] Therefore, Wilde must have read the Alexandrine gnostic's work before meeting Gomez Carrillo.

Wilde may have come to appreciate Clemens's thinking through one of his Parisian friends, for neo-Platonism was in vogue at the time in symbolist circles. Pierre Louÿs for example, to whom *Salome* was dedicated, possessed a 1614 edition of Clemens's complete works.[12] Oscar's relationship with the Alexandrine, however, predates his friendship with

Pierre Louÿs or Gomez Carrillo, and goes deeper and is more long-lasting.

*   *   *

In 1888, Wilde published 'The Happy Prince', in which the characters are a statue and a swallow. The statue is gilded with leaves of gold, has two sapphires for eyes, a large ruby on the sword-hilt and a heart made of lead. It appears to be in part inspired from this passage of Clemens's *Exhortation of the Gentiles*:

> A sculptor [...] was working on a statue of Osiris. He was provided with leaves of gold [...] and lead [...] all sorts of precious stones which were found in Egypt, fragments of sapphires, hematites, emeralds and topazes.[13]

Moreover, Egypt, where Clemens pronounces his *Exhortation*, is the swallow's homeland. In this work, Clemens calls the Pagans to cease venerating statues which have no feelings:

> Swallows foul images without respecting either Aesculapius or Minerva. You can learn from these birds how true it is that [...] images have no feelings.[14]

It is clear that Wilde had read Clemens before 1888, as he wrote 'The Happy Prince' as a counter example to the *Exhortation of the Gentiles*: the swallow in this tale respects the images to the point of dying for love of the statue of the Happy Prince. We can learn from this bird how true it is that statues have more feelings than men.

'The Happy Prince' takes the opposite view to Clemens: the *Exhortation of the Gentiles* exhorts the Gentiles to embrace Christianity; through an implicit 'Exhortation of the Christians' Wilde appears to attempt the opposite in his tale: to exhort Christians to embrace the religion of the Gentiles. Was Verlaine right?[15] Was Wilde a 'true pagan'?

This pagan alignment is nevertheless couched in a Christian morality. Stripped of its riches, which are distributed to the poor with the help of the swallow, the statue becomes worthless in the eyes of men. So they melt it down to make another. But fire, which, according to Clemens has consumed many images and in so doing has proved they are perishable, cannot destroy the statue's heart, which broke for love of the swallow. It is thrown on a dust-heap beside the dead swallow. An angel which is looking for the town's two most precious objects takes the swallow and the heart back to God:

> 'You have rightly chosen,' said God, 'for in my Garden of Paradise this little bird shall sing for evermore, and in my city of gold the Happy Prince shall praise me.'[16]

Symbol *par excellence* of the paganism which venerated it, the statue is resuscitated in heaven. God accepts what is imperishable in it — its heart of lead — while restoring the perishable gold of its coating by placing it in his city of gold. This is derived from the wholly orthodox concept that after the Last Judgement the imperishable soul will recover its body and flesh. Yet, in restoring to life not a man but a symbol, God integrates what is imperishable in the statue into His kingdom; in other words, he integrates the eternal truth of paganism into Paradise.

A similar issue appears in 'The Fisherman and his Soul', the tale which also refers to Clemens. The strict priest, who at the outset curses the Sea-folk and all pagan creatures, ends up by recognizing and blessing them: 'All the things in God's world he blessed.'[17] In both cases, Wilde proceeds to widen one system by integrating another into it, even though it is to all probability radically different. While the systems he uses here are religious, the process stems from a philosophical attitude of harmonizing opposites, which recurs throughout his work.

This attitude is manifest in the very conception of *Salome*, for which, once again, he draws on Clemens's work.[18] In it he creates an alliance between Salome, who represents the claims of the flesh, and Iokanaan, who reflects the aspirations of the mind. Impossible in reality, the reconciling of opposites can only be achieved in the realms of idealism. Thus, Wilde's utopia *The Soul of Man Under Socialism*, presents an ideal society based on the reconciliation between two notions as diametrically opposed as socialism and individualism.

This reconciliation of opposites results in philosophy and religion being inextricably linked in Wilde's work, just as they are in Clemens's, but in a different way. Both consider that the two concepts belong to two schools of thought which appear to be opposites: philosophy belongs to the Greek world, religion — Christianity — stems from Hebrew thinking. Clemens sets out to prove that there is a continuity of thought between Greek philosophy and Christianity which is comparable to the continuity between Christianity and the Prophets of Israel. Because philosophers are searching for truth, Christianity satisfies them by providing an answer: there is no other truth than God. In other words, the conflict is factitious, and it suffices to believe in God for the oppositon between Hellenism and Hebraism, or between philosophy and religion, to disappear.

Wilde does not share this vision, which is rooted in deep religious faith. In 'The Happy Prince', he integrates philosophy into religion, Hellenism into Hebraism, not through their continuity but through their conflict. He joins them together as by establishing a symbolic relationship between their opposite poles. The two opposite parts form one entity which each could evoke separately. This is where his conception differs from that of Clemens, who, nevertheless, provides the starting point for this — sophistry (?).

Thus, by means of philosophy, the blatantly Victorian morality of 'The Happy Prince' traverses paganism to attain a more discreet Christian truth: that of the 'Good Samaritan', the parable which translates the idea of 'Love thy neighbour as thyself' into 'Love thine enemy'. Wilde's tale — or is it also a parable? — turns God Himself into a Good Samaritan who welcomes His enemy into His kingdom where He restores his lost riches to him. Similarly, by means of Christian morality, his tale reveals a philosophy of criticism which is capable of reconciling not only Clemens but also Plato with art.

According to Plato, the 'idea', which is perceived mentally and not through one's senses, constitutes the only truth of which reality casts a mere shadow. Reality, the shadow of truth, deceives us. As for art, which reflects reality, it deceives

us twice over, as it is only the shadow of a shadow. To discover
the truth of an object, such as the statue of the Prince for
example, we can only trust the 'idea' which thereby becomes
the intellectual equivalent to form.[19] Wilde imagines his
statue with a brilliant coating, corresponding to the power of
art, which deceives us about its reality. The heart of lead, a
black and vulgar material, is precisely the reality which art
prevents us from seeing. Our perception of art and the reality of
the Prince are but shadows which deceive us about his truth,
his form in the domain of the intellect. The form here is no
other but the idea of love, which is sufficiently true to break
the satue's heart of lead.

Criticism should be built on Platonic form: one must
perceive the truth, the idea of a work without being deceived
by its shadow or the shadow of its shadow. But given that
Wilde is an artist himself, and —

> The artist is always looking for [...] the mode of existence in
> which [...] the outward is expressive of the inward; [...] in which
> form reveals, [...].[20]

he uses the idea to justify its shadow.

In the eyes of the supreme judge and artist, it is the
broken heart which justifies the dazzle of the statue.
Therefore, for any appreciation we must proceed from the
Platonic form to the shadow, or in other words, from the
interior to the exterior, from content to form. This procedure is
not practicable, if like Clemens we engage only reason:

> It is true that art has great power. But it is not great enough to
> deceive those who are driven by reason.[21]

According to Wilde, art deceives for as long as reason is
dissociated from love. Hence, his Happy Prince is happy only
by name, and men, guided by reason and blind to the love which
makes him suffer for them, are taken in. A broken object, made
of vulgar material and which will not melt down is necessarily
thrown out — what else can be done with it? God, for His part,
is not taken in, for in order to undertake appreciation from the
interior to the exterior, from truth to appearance, He conforms
to the morality of the Good Samaritan, which as we have seen,

prevents Him from hating His enemy. God the Father thereby conforms to the teaching of God the Son, whose fundamental principle is one of love.[22]

Thanks to the principle of the Son (Christianity) the religion of the Father (Hebraism) and that of men (paganism) are thereby bound up in one and the same system, which includes their contradiction in its unity. With its Christian predominance, this is certainly not religious in the sense that monotheistic religions attach to the term, for, contrary to them, it excludes nothing except exclusion itself.

The concept of criticism in Wilde reveals a system where comprehension of opposites by means of love becomes the indispensable condition of the intimate communion of man with the principle of the being. We therefore pass from philosophy and religion to the domain of mysticism.

*   *   *

According to Clemens, a mystic gnostic, knowledge is acquired through love and leads man to God-truth. He writes:

> This man was ignorant, he asked; after asking he found the master; after finding him, he believed; after believing he hoped; after being led from hope to love, he likened himself to the beloved object, by attempting to become the same as the object of his love.[23]

In *De Profundis*, Wilde follows suit when he says that 'it was only through love that one could approach either the heart of the leper or the feet of God'.[24] However, is he talking about the same love? In Clemens, the role of the master is to lead the ignorant man to belief. Love only appears afterwards and grows between the man and the truth which he believed in. It is a matter of direct love between man and God where the master merely plays the role of initiator. Transported by hope, the initiated tries to liken himself to God by means of love. In 'The Teacher of Wisdom' (the beginning of which we already know) Wilde develops a different vision.

The Master of Wisdom, saddened to have lost the greater part of his perfect knowledge of God, subsequently becomes a hermit. One can assume that the principle which unifies him with God is the one Clemens describes which leads man to assimilate himself into and resemble the object of his love. Assimilation and resemblance here are perfect, for in order to obey the Soul's recommendations: 'Is not God wiser than thou art? Who art thou to give away the secret that God hath told thee?',[25] the Hermit becomes as wise as God and no longer gives his secret away to men. This state, which, in Wilde is akin to Clemens's view of love, lasts until the Hermit gives away his perfect knowledge of God to a robber in order to save him:

> And when the Hermit had given away his knowledge of God, he fell upon the ground and wept, and a great darkness hid from him the city and the young Robber, so that he saw them no more. And as he lay there weeping he was aware of the One who was standing beside him [...]. And He raised the Hermit up, and said to him: 'Before this time thou hadst the perfect knowledge of God. Now thou shalt have the perfect love of God.'[26]

It is not the knowledge of God but the love of man which reveals the love of God. This is what Wilde's Hermit discovers in sacrificing precisely what Clemens's ignorant man — the Robber in the poem in prose — strives to attain. Love, which in Clemens is the means, becomes the end in Wilde. Sacrificed to love for man, the love of God-knowledge leads to God-love; in other words, the sacrifice of love in the name of love reveals a higher love:

> For each man kills the thing he loves,
> Yet each man does not die.[27]

Whether or not Clemens is the origin of the Master of Wisdom and the other characters who teach divine knowledge in Wilde's work, he is certainly one of Wilde's main sources. As such, he has enabled us to establish that Wilde's work, whose mystical content justifies the sophist form, reaches philosophical and religious depth through the unity of comprehended opposites. The trigger of this mechanism, identical to its driving force and the principle it pursues, is love, which engenders its own betrayal. Through death it gains a new dimension, which is greater but nevertheless open to sacrifice.

Wilde does not share the same views as Clemens. But the work of the latter certainly stimulated positively the imagination of the former. If he never mentions Clemens, it is because the influence of the Alexandrine is profound and genuine, and in Wilde the profound and genuine are neither flaunted nor taught, but are to be detected and discerned.

NOTES

1   Oscar Wilde, *Poems and Essays*, Collins, London, 1956, p. 176.
2   Written in haste, the catalogue of the public sale of Oscar Wilde's library (24 April 1895), which would have been a precious source of information, contains practically no details on the more than one thousand eight hundred volumes it contained. Here is an extract :
>   A Japanese book on fishes, coloured plates, O.W.'s *Salomé* bound in silk, 3 Nos of *The Spirit Lamp*, *Japanese Tales*, and large paper copies of O.W.'s Poems etc., some presentation copies (20).

   A.N.L. Munby (publisher), *Sale Catalogues of Libraries of Eminent Persons*, vol. 1, London, 1971. See also catalogues: Forster, *Mrs Wilde*, London, 1 August 1900, and *Vivian Holland*, London, 20-21 April 1953.
3   For the Wilde/Gomez Carrillo relationship, see R. Ellmann, *Oscar Wilde*, London, 1987; Chapter 13, pp. 322-4.
4   E. Gomez Carrillo, *The Gospel of Love (L'Evangile de l'Amour)* translated from Spanish into French by P. Lebesque, Paris, Bibliothèque Charpentier, 1923.
5   See among others, F. Brass, 'Oscar Wilde *Salomé*:Eine Kritische Quellenstudie', Bern-Leipzig, Robert Noske, 1913.
6   Op. cit., pp. 144-5.
7   Op. cit., p. 140.
8   M. de Genoude (translator-publisher), *Les pères de l'église*, Paris, 1893; vol. 5, Clément d'Alexandrie, *Stromates*, Book III, chapter 9, p. 255.
9   Oscar Wilde, *Complete Shorter Fiction*, Oxford University Press, Oxford, New York, 1990, p. 231.
10 By Professor Puech.
11 'A series of passages from Clemens of Alexandria are our chief source of knowledge.' R.-J. Montague, *The Gospel According to the Egyptians*, in *The Apocryphal Gospels, Acts, Epistles and Apocalypses*, Oxford, Clarendon Press, 1924, p. 10.
12 D. Hensei, *Clementis Alexandrini opera graece et latine quae extant*; Parisiorum typis regis; Lutetiae. In *Catalogue de la vente publique de la bibliothèque de Pierre Louÿs*, Hôtel Drouot, 4-9 April 1927, article 505, p. 11.
13 Clemens of Alexandria, *Discours de Clément d'Alexandrie pour exhorter les Païens à embrasser la Religion Chrétienne*, translated into French by C. Guillaume de Luyne, Paris, 1684,

p. 112. It is perhaps in this same text, and not in Lucien (Cf. R. Merle, *Oscar Wilde*, Paris, 1984, p. 175) that Wilde also found the argument of his poem 'Charmides', published in 1881. The sacrilege of the poem between the hero and the statue of Athena could have occured in his mind by the association of the two following passages:

> Les Athéniens [...] dans le dessein de lui [i. e. Alcibiades] faire épouser Minerve, firent les préparatifs des noces. Il méprisa la Déesse et refusa d'épouser une statue. Il mena Lamia, sa bonne amie dans la Citadelle, la mit dans le lit de Minerve et fit voir à cette vieille fille toutes les postures d'une jeune débauchée. (p. 137)
>
> On dit qu'une jeune fille fut amoureuse d'une image, et qu'un jeune homme le fut aussi d'une autre qui estoit dans l'isle de Cnidos. L'excellence de l'art leur avait imposé. Car jamais une personne de bon sens n'auroit embrassé une statue. Jamais elle ne se seroit enfermée avec un corps mort dans un tombeau et jamais n'aurait aimé un démon ou une pierre. (p. 147)

14   *Ibid.*, p. 130.
15   R. Ellmann, *Op. cit.*, p. 322.
16   *Op. cit.*, p. 103.
17   *Ibid.*, p. 236.
18   Concerning the way in which Wilde uses *Stromateis* in his play see my Ph. D. thesis, *Le Prétexte de Salomé*, Université Paris 7; December 1988.
19   A.S. Reber, *Dictionnary of Psychology*, Penguin Books, London, 1983, p. 340 (definition of the Platonic idea).
20   *De Profundis*, in Oscar Wilde, *Poems and Essays*, Collins, London and Glasgow, 1956, p. 193.
21   *Exhortation of the Gentiles, Op. cit.*, p. 154.
22   In *De Profundis*, Wilde expresses his point of view on Christ's recommendation 'Forgive thine enemies'. He maintains that it is pronounced not through love of one's enemy but through love of self, hence making us understand that there is no difference between our own life and the life of others. Wilde here justifies a feeling — love of one's enemy — which, outside faith, is unjustifiable. Love of self filters love of others to give it a rational substance which subsequently develops into compassion.
23   *Stromateis, Op. cit.*, Book V, Chapter 3, p. 299.
24   'It was only through love that one could approach either the heart of the leper or the feet of God.' *Op. cit.*, p. 200.
25   See note 1.
26   Oscar Wilde, *Poems and Essays, Op. cit.*, 'The Teacher of Wisdom', p. 178.
27   *Ibid.*, The Ballad of Reading Gaol, p. 153.

JOHN MELMOTH AND DORIAN GRAY: THE TWO-FACED MIRROR

Marie-Noëlle Zeender

Apart from Dracula, the two most scandalous figures of the Irish fantastic literature of the nineteenth century are perhaps John Melmoth and Dorian Gray. It is quite significant that Wilde should have adopted the assumed name of Sebastian Melmoth during his exile abroad. It was a useful mask which concealed his real identity, but it was also a form of homage paid to his most famous ancestor, Charles Robert Maturin. Indeed, the author of *Melmoth the Wanderer* was Oscar Wilde's great-uncle, and he earned his living as a minister of the Anglican Church. In spite of this, he was a kind of dandy and like his grand-nephew, he could be 'the gayest of the gay, passionately fond of society'.[1] Through the mysterious alchemy of genetics, his eccentricities might very well have been transmitted to Wilde, not to mention part of his inspiration.

One might think at first sight that Melmoth, the romantic satanic hero and Dorian, the *fin de siècle* dandy don't have much in common. A closer study of the two novels could prove the contrary, and that the influence of Maturin on Wilde's only novel is far from being insignificant.

To sum up briefly, each story is about a man who sells his soul to gain some power that makes him superior to the rest of mankind. Melmoth thus prolongs his life considerably; as for Dorian, he retains his good looks and his youth. In both cases the hero is introduced to the reader indirectly, by means of a portrait which is more like a magic mirror than just a painted effigy. At one point of the story, each painting is hidden from other people's eyes, because it conceals such a terrible secret that it has to be destroyed. But if *Melmoth the Wanderer* begins with the destruction of a picture, *The Picture of Dorian Gray* ends with the destruction of one. The symmetry is all the

more disconcerting as, at the beginning, Dorian is physically
speaking exactly the opposite of what Melmoth is. Indeed, he
is represented as 'a young man of extraordinary personal
beauty',[2] whereas the Wanderer, who is middle-aged, has
nothing particularly 'remarkable' apart from his eyes which
reflect his damnation even on the canvas. The magic attraction
they exert on young John is particularly revealing:

> [...] the eyes [...] were such as one feels they wish they had never
> seen [...]. They gleamed with demon light.[3]

In fact, the infernal glare of the Wanderer is quite
comparable to Dorian's gaze when Basil Hallward discovers
what his masterpiece has become after a while.' This is the
face of a satyr [...]. It has the eyes of a devil',[4] he exclaims
horrified. However justified his surprise may be, he should
have kept in mind the mysterious effect produced on him by the
boy when he met him for the first time. As he confesses to Lord
Wotton:

> When our eyes met, I felt that I was growing pale [...]. I knew
> that I had come face to face with someone whose mere
> personality was so fascinating that, if I allowed it to do so, it
> would absorb my whole nature, my whole soul, my very art
> itself.[5]

In other words, the artist was actually captivated by the
sitter's vampire eyes before making his portrait. When he
writes his name in vermilion letters — the very colour of blood
— to sign his masterpiece, we can't help thinking of a
mysterious pact. The strange absorption which took place then,
indicates that Dorian's eyes are just as destructive as
Melmoth's gaze of Medusa. In spite of their beauty — or rather
because of it — they fascinate, they devour, they paralyse the
prey. Basil is not their only victim, Lord Henry succumbs too, as
for Sybil Vane, when Dorian ruthlessly rejects her, his gaze
seems to annihilate her before she commits suicide:

> She crouched on the floor [...] and Dorian Gray, with his
> beautiful eyes, looked down at her.[6]

In this respect, what Lacan defines as the 'scopic relation',[7] is at the core of the novel. It is obvious that sight is Dorian's most developed sense as well as his curse. Whenever he 'gives the eye', if we may say so, it entails tragic consequences, even on himself. Indeed, he has a very close relationship with his own mirror-portrait in which he 'sees himself seeing himself' with delight, but also with other pictures. This is particularly manifest in chapter XI, when he is described strolling along the picture-gallery of his ancestors. Then, he seems incapable of making the difference between reality and representation.[8] He lives in the realm of anamorphoses, of aberrations or 'depraved perspectives',[9] which condition all his conceptions as well as his behaviour.

Such phenomena are common in the Gothic tradition. The picture of Melmoth is seemingly invested with a monstrous and autonomous life, and it even gives the impression that inanimate things can watch the living. As young Melmoth is reading the manuscript in his uncle's closet, he has the unbearable feeling of being spied upon and sees 'the picture gazing at him from the canvas'.[10] To some extent, the very gaze of the portrait urges him to destroy it at once, but its impact is so powerful that even after having torn the canvas to pieces and burnt it completely, he is haunted by the presence of the Wanderer. It is true that unlike Dorian, Melmoth can survive the destruction of his effigy, he is independent of it. Dorian does not share this characteristic, not only are his acts strongly influenced by the painted image, but his life is entirely governed by it. He is thus totally manipulated before murdering Basil Hallward:

> Dorian Gray glanced at the picture, and suddenly an uncontrollable feeling of hatred for Basil Hallward came over him, as though it had been suggested to him by the image on the canvas [...].[11]

The same manipulation occurs at the end of the book, and the victim this time is Dorian himself, who has forgotten the invisible umbilical cord linking him to his portrait. In this case, Lacan's definition of Holbein's painting *The Ambassadors*: 'This picture is simply what any picture is, a trap for the gaze', perfectly suits Wilde's novel. As we have seen, Dorian's gaze traps the artist first, then the cynical Lord Wotton afterwards and finally himself. All the characters are the victims of this aberration and as a consequence, they live under the spell of misleading illusions. This is why the whole world soon becomes a stage for Dorian, a theatre where he finds a real contentment in being an actor and a spectator of his own life, always in search of new sensations. To satisfy them, he indulges in the dangerous game of the multiplication of personality — a modern transposition of Melmoth's power of ubiquity — most symbolic of his schizoid tendencies, and actually enjoys this status of surrogate being. His hedonistic conceptions, transmitted to him by Lord Henry, lead him to develop a growing curiosity about life from a purely artistic point of view. So that, if he is a real Narcissus, there are also in him strong Faustian aspirations. A little like Melmoth, he becomes initiated into various arts, which, although they are not directly related to witchcraft or the supernatural proper are nonetheless strange, all the more so since they are solitary and secret occupations. Among these, the careful observation, day after day, of his corrupted portrait is a form of occult learning of some forbidden knowledge. The morbid fascination it exerts on him is a source of exquisite pleasure, at least at the beginning :

> He would examine with minute care, and sometimes with a monstrous and terrible delight, the hideous lines that seared the wrinkling forehead, or crawled around the heavy sensual mouth [...].[13]

At this stage, he is the exultant voyeur of his own horrible spiritual decay. He could then make his the motto of the parricide monk leading Monçada through the bowels of the Inquisition, *'Emotions are my events'*.[14] The comparison is far from being fortuitous because Dorian is also a kind of parricide, since he killed the artist who gave him life and substance. Furthermore, he really finds his pleasure in the sadistic contemplation of horror and degradation, as his fascination for Nero and Caligula or the great criminals of the Renaissance shows. Like the monstrous monk, he is an *'amateur in suffering'*.[15]

Melmoth, who enjoys haunting the darkest recesses to watch other people's torments before offering his pact, is of a similar nature. He actually revels in teaching the pure Immalee to suffer and showing her a *speculum mundi* in which men are presented through the distorting perspective of his magic telescope. He claims that he is 'commissioned to trample on and bruise every flower in the natural and moral world — hyacinths, hearts, and bagatelles of that kind'[16] and as a matter of fact, Dorian acts exactly in the same way. All his *conquêtes* are as many flowers that he has ruthlessly crushed. Sybil Vane and all the other women that he meets are described as roses, violets, lilies or white narcissi when he is in love with them, then once he has seduced them, they are reduced to nothing. All his love affairs, even with men, have tragic consequences. Basil accuses him of being responsible for the suicide of a boy in the Guards and asks him why his friendship is 'so fatal to young men'.[17]

If the Wanderer is presented as the embodiment of evil, the tempter who claims that his 'was the great angelic sin — pride and intellectual glorying!',[18] Dorian and even Lord Henry can also be understood as such. Isobel Murray does not fail to underline that 'in Basil's garden Lord Henry acts the part of the serpent in Eden'.[19] The scene may be compared with Maturin's *Tale of the Indians* in which Melmoth is constantly referred to as 'the serpent' striving to corrupt Eve. What is still more striking is that Immalee, who is totally ignorant of what the difference between sexes may be, lives as a perfectly happy little Narcissus on her wild isle. She tells the stranger that she has a wonderful companion whom she describes in the following way:

> My friend lives under the water, but its colours are so bright! It kisses me too, but its lips are very cold; and when I kiss it, it seems to dance, and its beauty is all broken into a thousand faces, that come smiling at me like little stars.[20]

Immalee is in a state of innocence that recalls Chateaubriand's *Atala* for instance, she has no sense of what evil can be. Dorian is far less ingenuous about his own narcissistic image essentially because it is revealed to him by Lord Henry in fact. Before the 'temptation scene' indeed, the boy has no real notion of his own beauty. Once poisoned by Harry's hedonistic theories, Dorian falls in love with his visual representation, and then infects in his turn all those he approaches. 'They say that you corrupt every one with whom you become intimate',[21] Basil tells him reproachfully, and it proves to be true.

Although Dorian has a very different purpose, his power of seduction is much more harmful than Melmoth's. They both charm and torment their preys but at this game, he is far superior as far as evil matters are concerned, to the poor Wanderer who never manages to obtain satisfaction and is doomed to fail from the start. Everything shows that Melmoth's quest is hopeless and that he is predestined from the start to eternal damnation. In this respect the Preface to *Melmoth the Wanderer* written by Maturin, whose Calvinistic leanings are well-known, is quite explicit. Indeed, to justify his romance he said that he drew his inspiration from one of his sermons, itself inspired by Mark 8.36, in which he asked — and answered — the following question:

> Is there any one of us who would, at this moment, accept all that man could bestow, or earth afford, to resign the hope of his salvation? — No, there is not one — not such a fool on earth, were the enemy of mankind to traverse it with the offer.[22]

Most unexpectedly, at the end of *The Picture of Dorian Gray*, Lord Henry partly echoes similar considerations when he casually asks Dorian whose mood is particularly sombre, 'By the way Dorian [...] what does it profit a man if he gain the whole world and lose — how does the quotation run? — "his own soul"?'[23] The only difference is that Harry claims that he does not believe in the soul of man, which he considers as pure superstition. 'No: we have given up our belief in the soul',[24] he tells Dorian who does not dare to answer simply because he has seen the horrid reality of its existence reflected on the canvas of his picture.

* * *

There is in fact some inescapable determinism, a terrible sense of doom in the story of Dorian. Everything shows that he only gets what he deserves after selling his soul to a mysterious and unidentified god. His is not 'the great angelic sin' certainly, but what could be called the great narcissistic sin, self love, which amounts to the sin of pride in fact. In other words, if Melmoth has offended God Almighty, Dorian has offended some jealous pagan god, and is bitterly punished for it. Basil's curious considerations in the first chapter then take on their full meaning:

> Your rank and wealth, Harry; my brains [...] my art, whatever it may be worth; Dorian Gray's good looks — we shall all suffer for what the gods have given us, suffer terribly.[25]

The punishment inflicted on Dorian is violent death, with all the most horrible visible attributes of mortality which have been suddenly accelerated. Dorian then shares this with the Wanderer who at the end of his adventures reveals the most extreme signs of decrepitude: 'His hairs were white as snow, his mouth had fallen in, the muscles of his face were relaxed and withered.'[26] Dorian's lot is not any better, his body lies 'withered, wrinkled, and loathsome of visage'[27] at the foot of his wonderful portrait which has resumed its former appearance and mocks him contemptuously.

* * *

When his book was condemned for immorality, Oscar Wilde's reaction was to retort that 'Dorian Gray was too moral' and that it showed that 'all excess as all renunciation, brings its own punishment'.[28] This is true to a large extent, and from a purely moral point of view, Dorian proves to be exactly as foolish as Melmoth. In spite of this, the two characters remain fascinating because they embody what Wilde defined under different circumstances as 'the seduction of sin'.[29] There is something Byronic in both of them, especially in their refusal of human limits. Melmoth even manages to arouse in the reader a form of sympathy, perhaps because of his relationship with Immalee/Isidora. However monstrous their union may be, we feel here and there, in the few tears he sheds, that the Wanderer suffers terribly from not being allowed to love. Even his final repentance and his death are particularly moving. Such is not the case as far as Dorian is concerned, he never fully attracts our sympathy even when he tries to be good because he is too self-centered. In fact, he belongs to the world of abstractions; he is a living masterpiece, but he is also 'a face without a heart',[30] as he lucidly realises at the end. He can be compared to a two-faced mirror which, like a kind of Janus, would reflect the most exceptional beauty on one face, and the most revolting ugliness on the other.

We have seen in this short survey that Wilde's indebtedness to Maturin is real, but on the whole it remains superficial because the message is different. *Melmoth* is a profoundly religious work, *Dorian Gray* is not. Yet, the two novels have subversive undertones. As Douglas Grant wrote, 'Maturin is a brilliant psychologist of the perverse',[31] as for Wilde he is an 'aesthete' of the perverse. His preface is clear in this respect, it is an assertion of the superiority of aesthetics over ethics and a thinly veiled criticism of the Victorian society. By stating that 'it is the spectator, and not life, that art really mirrors',[32] Wilde implied that the reader too was two-faced, just like Dorian Gray, the most 'admirable emblem' of duplicity 'in the native land of the hypocrite'.[33]

NOTES

1   R. E. Lougy, *Charles Robert Maturin*, Lewisburg, Bucknell University Press, 1975, p. 15.
2   *Complete Works of Oscar Wilde*, with an Introduction by V. Holland, London and Glasgow, Collins, 1976, p. 18.
3   C. R. Maturin, *Melmoth the Wanderer, A Tale*, London, Oxford University Press, 1968, pp. 17-18.
4   Op. cit., p. 122.
5   Ibid., p. 21.
6   Ibid., p. 76.
7   J. Lacan, *The Four Fundamental Concepts of Psycho-analysis*, Edited by J.-A. Miller, Translated by A. Sheridan, Penguin Books, 1991, p. 83.

8   Cf. Op. cit., pp. 112-113, Dorian's mother's picture is described
        in such terms that her eyes seem intensely alive, 'The carnations
        of the painting had withered, but the eyes were still wonderful
        in their depth and brilliancy of colour. They seemed to follow
        him wherever he went.'

9   Cf. J. Baltrusaitis, *Aberrations, les perspectives dépravées, Essai
        sur la Légende des Formes,* Paris, Flammarion, 1983.

10   Op. cit., p. 59.
11   Op. cit., p. 122.
12   Op. cit., p. 89.
13   Op. cit., p. 10.
14   Op. cit., p. 204.
15   Ibid., p. 207.
16   Ibid., p. 346.
17   Op. cit., p. 117.
18   Ibid., p. 499.
19   *The Picture of Dorian Gray,* Edited with an Introduction by I.
        Murray, London, Oxford University Press, 1974, p. XIII.
20   Op. cit., p. 284.
21   Op. cit., p. 118.
22   Op. cit., Preface.
23   Op. cit., p. 161.
24   Ibid., p. 162.
25   Ibid., p. 19.
26   Op. cit., p. 540.
27   Op. cit., p. 167.
28   Quoted by Ellmann, *Oscar Wilde,* Penguin, 1988, p. 303.
29   Ibid., p. 530
30   Op. cit., p. 161.
31   Op. cit., p. X.
32   Op. cit., p. 17.
33   Ibid., p. 118.

NOTES ON CONTRIBUTORS

ANTONIO BALLESTEROS GONZÁLEZ is Professor of English Literature in Universidad Autónoma of Madrid, and was previously Professor of English and American Studies at the Universidad Complutense of Madrid and the Universidad of Castilla-La Mancha. He has published numerous articles on different literary topics, covering the Literary Fantastic, Beckett, Joyce, Sterne, and the Renaissance. His main work so far is *Narciso: mito y dualidad conceptual en la literatura inglesa victoriana* (1993, forthcoming), which deals with the myth of Narcissus and the motif of the double.

MARIANO BASELGA is Associate Professor of English at the Universidad Autónoma of Madrid. He previously taught at the University of Castilla-La Mancha. He graduated in English Philology at the Complutense University of Madrid and is now at the University of Salamanca. He has published different articles on English Syntax, English Literature, and has recently translated into Spanish Virginia Woolf's *Mrs Dalloway*.

PIA BRÎNZEU is Associate Professor of English Literature at the University of Timisoara (Romania). She has written a book on the contemporary British and Romanian novel — *The Glass Armour* — as well as a series of articles on Renaissance literature, narratology and semiotics. She is editor-in-chief of *Caiete de semiotica* (Timisoara).

EDWARD BURNS is Senior Lecturer in the Department of English in the University of Liverpool. His publications include *The Chester Mystery Plays: Modern Staging Text*, and *Restoration Comedy: Crises of Identity and Desire* (both 1987) and *Character: Acting and Being on the Pre-Modern Stage* (1990). He has directed and designed plays and operas in Liverpool and elsewhere. These include Beckett's *Happy Days*,

Ben Jonson's *Bartholomew Fair* and the 'Miracles' section of the *Chester Mystery Plays* at Chester Cathedral. He is currently working on an Arden edition of Shakespeare's *First Part of Henry the Sixth*.

RICHARD ALLEN CAVE is Professor of Drama and Theatre Arts at Royal Holloway in the University of London. His publications include *A Study of the Novels of George Moore, Terence Gray and the Festival Theatre Cambridge, New British Drama in Performance on the London Stage: 1970-1985, 'The White Devil' and 'The Duchess of Malfi', Ben Jonson, Charles Ricketts' Stage Designs*, and a biography of the painter and scenic designer Robert Gregory. He has directed the whole canon of Yeats's plays, which he has edited for Penguin Books. Professor Cave is currently editing Wilde's plays also for Penguin Books.

DAVIS COAKLEY is a consultant physician and Director of the Mercer's Institute for Research on Ageing at St James's Hospital, Dublin. He is Professor of Geriatric Medicine at Trinity College Dublin and is currently Dean of the Faculty of Health Sciences of the university. He has written and edited several books on different aspects of medical science, the history of medicine and Irish literature. He is Chairman of the Trinity Oscar Wilde Society and he is currently completing a book entitled *Oscar Wilde — The Importance of Being Irish*.

JEAN M. ELLIS D'ALESSANDRO is a researcher in English Language and Literature at the University of Florence. She was language correspondent for the Italian language journal *Le Lingue del Mondo*, and has published articles on English writers such as Shakespeare, D. H. Lawrence, and Yeats. She has written a book on Oscar Wilde, *Hues of Mutability* (1983), and published the manuscript poems of Anne, the Countess of Winchilsea (1991), together with a book of critical research into her poetry. She is currently working on a series of essays concerning writers and their use of rhetoric.

MASOLINO D'AMICO is Professor of English Literature at the University of Rome. Books: *Scena e parola in Shakespeare*

(1974), *Dieci secoli di teatro inglese* (1981), *Hemingway* (1988), and *Byron: Vita attraverso le lettere* (1990). Since 1989 he is Drama Critic for *La Stampa*. He has translated and adapted for the Italian stage some 25 English plays, and has edited the works of Swift and E. M. Forster, the poems of Burns and Rochester. He has translated Bellow, Burgess, Greene, Virginia Woolf. His interest in Wilde dates from the days he was at Trinity College, Dublin, and his M. Litt. thesis on 'Wilde's Aesthetic Ideas' (1964). Since then he wrote *Oscar Wilde: il critico e le sue maschere* (1973), and he edited Wilde's works for Mondadori, Wilde's poems for Newton Compton and Wilde's letters for Einaudi.

LAWRENCE DANSON is Professor of English at Princeton University. He has written articles and books on Shakespeare and Renaissance drama (*Tragic Alphabet*, 1974, *The Harmonies of The Merchant of Venice*, 1978) and on the *fin-de-siècle* (*Max Beerbohm and the Act of Writing*, 1989). His edition of *Intentions* and 'The Portrait of Mr W. H.' will appear in the Oxford English Texts *Complete Works of Oscar Wilde*. Recent articles include 'Oscar Wilde, W. H., and the Unspoken Name of Love' (1991), 'Gazing at *Hamlet*' (1992), 'The Catastrophe is a Nuptial: The Space of Masculine Desire' (1993), and 'Wilde in Arden, or the Masks of Truth'.

DENIS DONOGHUE is one of the most outstanding literary critics of the English-speaking world. He was born in Tullow, County Carlow in Ireland and received his higher education at University College Dublin and Cambridge University. He was a Lecturer in Dublin, Cambridge, Pennsylvania, and New York. At present, he holds the Henry James Chair of English at New York University. His books include *The Third Voice, Connoisseurs of Chaos, The Ordinary Universe, The Sovereign Ghost, Ferocious Alphabets, The Arts without Mystery, Warrenpoint, Being Modern Together,* and *The Pure Good of Theory*. Three volumes of his selected essays have been published: *We Irish, Reading America,* and *England, Their England*. Since late January 1991, he has also been an advisor to the Princess Grace Irish Library.

JOSEPH DONOHUE is Professor of English at the University of Massachusetts at Amherst, where he has taught dramatic literature since 1971. He has taught also at Princeton University, the University of Pittsburgh, Columbia University, and the University of Freiburg. He is the editor of the semi-annual journal *Nineteenth Century Theatre*, general editor of *The London Stage 1800-1900*, and is the author of *Dramatic Character in the English Romantic Age* (1970), *Theatre in the Age of Kean* (1975), and a number of other essays on English drama from the late eighteenth to the early twentieth centuries. He is currently preparing a volume of plays for the *Oxford English Texts* edition in progress of the *Complete Works of Oscar Wilde* and is at work on a critical book on Wilde and the theatre.

IRENE EYNAT-CONFINO is Senior Lecturer in the Department of Theatre Arts at Tel-Aviv University. She is the author of *Beyond the Mask: Gordon Craig, Movement, and the Actor* (1987), and has published numerous articles on Adolphe Appia, Gordon Craig, Oscar Wilde, and movement and space perception in theatre. She is also the translator of Maeterlinck's plays into Hebrew. She is now working on the meaning of fantastic elements in modern Western theatre.

MICHAEL PATRICK GILLESPIE is a Professor of English at Marquette University, Milwaukee. His books include *Inverted Volumes Improperly Arranged* (1983), *A Catalogue of James Joyce's Trieste Library* (1986), *Reading the Book of Himself* (1989), and *Oscar Wilde* (1990). He is currently completing a reader response analysis of Wilde's canon and a book length study of *The Picture of Dorian Gray*.

ROBERT GORDON joined Goldsmiths' College, University of London as Senior Lecturer in 1990, having previously been Senior Lecturer in Drama at Royal Holloway College. He is author of *Red Earth*, a play about women's experiences of apartheid (1985) and *Waterloo Road*. In 1989 he devised and directed *The Decay of Lying*, which explored the relationship between the life and work of Oscar Wilde. Publications include articles on Orton, Rattigan, Wycherley, Simon Gray and Pinter.

His book on Tom Stoppard was published in the Macmillan *Text and Performance* Series in 1991. He has been Visiting Lecturer at Duke University, Colby College, the State University of New York and the University of the Witwatersrand.

WARWICK GOULD is British Academy Research Reader in English Literature at Royal Holloway and Bedford New College, University of London. He is author of *Joachim of Fiore and the Myth of the Eternal Evangel in the Nineteenth Century*, and co-editor of *The Secret Rose, Stories by W. B. Yeats: A Variorum Edition* (1992). He is currently working on two volumes in the Macmillan *Collected Edition of the Works of W. B. Yeats, Mythologies and Early Essays*. He is also preparing *The Collected Letters of W. B. Yeats Volume II* (1896-1900).

MERLIN HOLLAND, son of Vyvyan Holland and grandson of Oscar Wilde, writes, lectures and broadcasts regularly on all aspects of Wilde's life and works. For twenty-five years he has been in the unique position, through having to administer the few remaining copyrights in Wilde's writings (mostly letters and unpublished fragmentary manuscripts), of being in close touch with the latest academic research while presenting his grandfather to a wider general audience. He has recently introduced a 'Collected Wilde' for the Folio Society and the reset and enlarged 1994 Collins *Complete Works of Oscar Wilde*. For both editions he selected some of the best of Wilde's journalism to show an unfamiliar and neglected side of Wilde — the hard-working professional writer. He is also the wine-correspondent of British magazine — *The Oldie*. After Wilde's conviction, his wife, Constance, and their sons were forced to change their name to Holland after being refused accommodation at a Swiss hotel. The family has never reverted to the name Wilde.

JOEL H. KAPLAN is Professor of English and Drama at the University of British Columbia. A frequent contributor to theatre and drama publications, he is co-author of *Theatre and Fashion* (1994) and co-editor of *The Edwardian Theatre* (forthcoming). He is preparing Oscar Wilde's society plays for the Oxford English Texts Edition, editing a special 'Oscar Wilde' number of *Modern Drama*, and co-authoring *Wilde on Stage*. In 1989 his Canadian performance troupe, the Adelphi Screamers, produced Wilde's *Florentine Tragedy*.

PATRICIA KELLOGG-DENNIS is Professor of English Literature at Rider College, Lawrenceville, New Jersey. She earned her PhD at New York University in Comparative Literature specialising in the myth of Salome in Symbolist literature and art. She has had one play produced and has published several poems.

MELISSA KNOX is an Assistant Professor of English at St Peter's College, Jersey City, New Jersey. Her book, *Oscar Wilde: 'A Long and Lovely Suicide'*, a psychobiographic study, will be published by Yale University Press in 1994. Her articles on Thomas De Quincey and on Henry James have appeared in *The Psychoanalytic Review*, *American Imago*, and *Psychoanalytic Quarterly*. She is working on a psychobiography of Anais Nin.

DONALD LAWLER is Professor of English at East Carolina University, Greenville, North Carolina. He is editor of the award-winning *Victorians Institute Journal*. Professor Lawler has published widely in nineteenth- and twentieth-century English and American literature. He has co-edited the Magill Surveys of Science Fiction and Fantasy (5 volumes each), *Approaches to Science Fiction*, *Vonnegut in America*, the Norton Critical Edition of Oscar Wilde's *The Picture of Dorian Gray*, and *A Study of the Revisions of* The Picture of Dorian Gray. He is currently preparing a study of Oscar Wilde.

JERUSHA McCORMACK is a Lecturer in the Department of English at University College, Dublin, where she teaches modern English and American literature. In the context of Wilde studies, she is best known for her two books on John Gray, a 'decadent' poet of the 'nineties said to be the 'original of Dorian': a full-length biography (*John Gray: Poet, Dandy and*

Priest), and an edition of his Selected Prose. She is currently working on a book about Wilde and Ireland.

BART MOORE-GILBERT is lecturer in English at Goldsmiths' College, University of London. He is the author of *Kipling and 'Orientalism'* (1986) and has edited *Literature and Imperialism* (1984), *Cultural Revolution? The Challenge of the Arts in the 1960s* (1992) and *The Arts in the 1970s: Cultural Closure?* (1993). He is the author of articles on Wilde, Kipling and the post-war English novel and is currently working on a Reader in Post-colonial theory and a book on representations of India 1757-1990.

ISOBEL MURRAY is a Senior Lecturer at the University of Aberdeen. Her published work is divided between editions of Wilde and articles about him, and articles and editions dealing with modern Scottish fiction. These last include two edited volumes of Naomi Mitchison and others by J. MacDougall Hay and Robin Jenkins, and she published *Ten Modern Scottish Novels* with Bob Tait in 1984. She is one of the jury of the Saltire Society Scottish Book of the Year award. The chief Wilde editions are the Oxford English Novels *Picture of Dorian Gray* (1974), the *Complete Shorter Fiction* (1979), the Oxford Authors *Oscar Wilde* (1989), and *The Soul of Man and Prison Writings* (1990).

SYLVIA OSTERMANN is Assistant Professor of English at the University of Jena. Her doctoral dissertation was devoted to C. P. Snow. She is now conducting post-doctoral research on her habilitation on Doris Lessing. Her publications include essays on Doris Lessing, Mary Shelley, Peter Shaffer and Oscar Wilde.

NORMAN PAGE is Emeritus Professor of Modern English Literature, University of Nottingham, and Emeritus Professor of English, University of Alberta. His publications include *The Language of Jane Austen* (1972), *Speech in the English Novel* (1973), *Thomas Hardy* (1977), *A. E. Housman: A Critical Biography* (1983), *E. M. Forster* (1987), and *An Oscar Wilde Chronology* (1991). His most recent book is *Tennyson: An*

Illustrated Life (1992), and he is currently working on a study of Auden and Isherwood's Berlin period.

KERRY POWELL is professor of English at Miami University, Oxford, Ohio, where he is director of graduate studies. He is the author of *Oscar Wilde and the Theatre of the 1890s* (Cambridge University Press, 1990), and has written on Wilde for *Philological Quarterly, Modern Drama, Nineteenth Century Theatre, Victorian Newsletter, Papers on Language & Literature,* and other journals. He is currently writing a book on women and Victorian theatre that is scheduled for publication in 1996.

MARÍA PILAR PULIDO took her degree in English Philology in the University of Zaragoza (Spain). She is at present engaged in writing a doctoral dissertation on Lady Wilde 'Speranza' in the Université Lumière of Lyon II. Her area of research covers the period from the rise of *The Nation* newspaper to the fall of Parnell.

PETER RABY is a senior lecturer at Homerton College, Cambridge, where he is Head of the Drama Department. He previously spent three years at the Shakespeare Festival Theatre, Stratford, Ontario, as dramaturge. He has published two biographies, *Fair Ophelia: Harriet Smithson Berlioz* (1982) and *Samuel Butler* (1991), and a critical study, *Oscar Wilde* (1988). He has also written adaptations for the stage, including *The Government Inspector*, and stage and television versions of *The Three Musketeers*. His most recent publication is an edition of Samuel Butler's *The Way of All Flesh* (1993), and he is currently working on an edition of Wilde's plays.

GERD ROHMANN is Professor of English at the University of Kassel (Germany). He previously taught at the University of Marburg where he wrote his doctoral thesis on *Aldous Huxley und die französische Literatur*. He studied American, Anglo-Irish, and French Literature at the Universities of Marburg, London, and the Sorbonne. His main publications are devoted to Bernard Shaw (1978), Laurence Sterne (1980), and Samuel Beckett (1988). He also published articles on Metaphysical

Poetry, Defoe, Jane Austen, Dickens, Poe, James Joyce, Virginia Woolf, and Frank O'Connor.

ROY ROSENSTEIN is Professor of Comparative Literature at the American University of Paris. He also taught at City University of New York, University of Rochester, and University of Oregon. He held a Fullbright senior lecturership to Brazil in 1992, and is currently visiting professor at the University of Paris IV (Sorbonne). He co-edited *The Poetry of Cercamon and Jaufre Rudel* (1983) and *Etienne Durand: Poésies Complètes* (1990) and has contributed to *Dictionary of the Middle Ages* (1982-89), *Le Sonnet à la Renaissance* (1988), *Clarice Lispector* (in press), *Handbook to the Troubadours* (in press), and other collective volumes.

NEIL SAMMELLS is Principal Lecturer and Head of English at Bath College of Higher Education, having taught previously at the University of Newcastle-upon-Tyne, and is a member of the Executive Committee of the British Association for Irish Studies. He is the author of *Tom Stoppard: the Artist as Critic* (1988) and co-editor, with Paul Hyland, of two collections of essays: *Irish Writing: Exile and Subversion* (1991) and *Writing and Censorship in Britain* (1992). He is the founder and co-editor (also with Paul Hyland) of the journal *Irish Studies Review* and General Editor of the Longman series, *Crosscurrents*. He is currently preparing a new collection for publication: *Writing and America*.

C. GEORGE SANDULESCU holds degrees from the Universities of Bucharest, Leeds, and Essex. His interests are equally divided between twentieth century fiction — with special emphasis on Joyce and Beckett — and present-day theories of language, with particular emphasis on the analysis of literary discourse. He is currently Director of the Princess Grace Irish Library of the Principality of Monaco, and General Editor of the publications issued by this Library. Greek by origin, he is a fluent speaker of several languages. This linguistic background makes him feel a particular attraction for Joyce's own list of Forty Languages. His publications include *The Joycean Monologue* (1979), *Language for Special Purposes*

(1973), *The Language of the Devil* (1986), and the co-edited *Assessing the 1984 'Ulysses'* (1986).

RONALD SCHUCHARD, Professor of English at Emory University, has recently edited T. S. Eliot's Clark and Turnbull lectures, *The Varieties of Metaphysical Poetry* (Faber and Faber, 1993), and is co-editor of volumes III (in press) and IV of *The Collected Letters of W. B. Yeats*. As chair of the Richard Ellmann Lectures in Modern Literature, he has edited the first two volumes in the series, Seamus Heaney's *The Place of Writing* (1989), and Denis Donoghue's *Being Modern Together* (1991).

THEOHARIS CONSTANTINE THEOHARIS is Associate Professor of Literature at Massachusetts Institute of Technology, and Senior Editor of *The Boston Book Review*. He is the author of *Joyce's Ulysses: An Anatomy of the Soul*, and *The Loss of Action in Modern Tragedy: Aristotle, Nietzsche, Ibsen*. He has lectured widely in the United States and Europe.

DEIRDRE TOOMEY is a co-editor of *The Collected Letters of W. B. Yeats*, Volume II, 1896-1900 (Clarendon Press, forthcoming), of Early Essays in the new *Macmillan Collected Edition of the Works of W. B. Yeats*. She is assistant editor of *The Complete Graphic Works of William Blake*, ed. David Bindman (1978), research editor of *Yeats Annual*, and editor of *Yeats and Women*: Yeats Annual No 9 (London: Macmillan, 1991).

EMMANUEL VERNADAKIS is a lecturer in the Department of English at the University of Angers (France). He studied French and English literature at the University of Paris VII-Jussieu. He has published several articles both in French and Greek, including 'Love, Death and Truth in Oscar Wilde's *Salome*' (1989), 'Oscar Wilde, Tennessee Williams: their Courtesans and the Accomplishment of the Act' (1993), 'A Quest for Unity: the Patterns of Sin, Suffering and Harmony in Nineteenth Century European Literature' (1993).

MARIE-NOËLLE ZEENDER is a Senior Lecturer in the English Department at the University of Nice (France), and is specialized in the Irish Gothic tradition. Her doctoral dissertation was entitled *Le Miroir dans les Oeuvres de Maturin, Le Fanu, Wilde et Stoker*. She has published articles on the Irish fantastic, e. g. Le Fanu and Swedenborg (1980), and L'Irlande Romantique et Fantastique dans *The Snake's Pass* (1993). She is now working on an annotated bibliography of Irish Gothic and fantastic literature, from the origins to 1914.

APPENDIX
The Conference Programme: 28-31 May 1993

FRIDAY 28

14.30-15.45	Registration.
16.00-16.45	FORMAL OPENING:
	H.S.H. Prince Albert of Monaco,
	H.E. John H.F. Campbell,
	C. George Sandulescu.
16.45-18.00	Merlin Holland: 'Plagiarist or Pioneer?'.
18.30-20.00	Welcoming Cocktail Party given by H.E.
	and Mrs Jean-Michel Dasque, Consul Général
	de France in Monaco.

SATURDAY 29

9.30-11.00	Paper Session One: Neil Sammells, Deirdre Toomey, María Pilar Pulido, Davis Coakley.
11.00-11.30	Intermission
11.30-13.00	Paper Session Two: Robert Gordon, Warwick Gould, Jerusha McCormack, Joel H. Kaplan.
15.00-16.30	Paper Session Three: Bart Moore-Gilbert, Roy Rosenstein, Lawrence Danson.
16.30-17.00	Intermission
17.00-19.00	Paper Session Four: Antonio Ballesteros González, Sylvia Ostermann, Marie-Noëlle Zeender, Isobel Murray.

SUNDAY 30

9.00-11.00   Paper Session Five: Jean Ellis D'Alessandro,
              Masolino D'Amico, Kerry Powell.
11.00-11.30   Intermission.
11.30-13.00   Paper Session Six: Theoharis Constantine
              Theoharis, Pia Brînzeu, Michael Patrick
              Gillespie.

15.00-16.30   Paper Session Seven: Edward Burns, Melissa
              Knox, Patricia Kellogg-Dennis, Irène Eynat-
              Confino.
16.30-17.00   Intermission.
17.00-18.30   Paper Session Eight: Joseph Donohue, Richard
              Allen Cave, Peter Raby.

21.00-23.00   One-Man Show by Alan Stanford of Dublin.

MONDAY 31

9.30-11.00   Paper Session Nine: Emmanuel Vernadakis,
              Donald Lawler, Norman Page.
11.00-11.30   Intermission.
11.30-13.00   Denis Donoghue: 'The Oxford of Pater,
              Hopkins, and Wilde'.

15.00-16.30   Paper Session Ten: Ronald Schuchard, Mariano
              Baselga, Joseph Bristow.
16.30-17.00   Intermission.
17.00-19.00   Paper Session Eleven: Gerd Rohmann, Jacques
              de Langlade, Scott Wilson.
19.00-19.30   Closing addresses:
              Merlin Holland,
              C. George Sandulescu.

INDEX